WITHDRAWN

Anthology of Western Reserve Literature

D1227271

WITHDRAWN

Anthology of *Western Reserve Literature*

EDITED BY

David R. Anderson

&

Gladys Haddad

The Kent State University Press

KENT, OHIO, AND LONDON, ENGLAND

DEC 0 1 1992

LIBRARY

810.8097713
Ar 86

© 1992 by The Kent State University Press, Kent, Ohio 44242
All rights reserved
Library of Congress Catalog Card Number 92-4313
ISBN 0-87338-461-X
Manufactured in the United States of America

Due to the length of permissions acknowledgments, a continuation
of the copyright page appears on pages 307–309

Library of Congress Cataloging-in-Publication Data
Anthology of Western Reserve literature / edited by David R. Anderson
and Gladys Haddad.
p.   cm.
Includes bibliographical references.
ISBN 0-87338-461-X
1. American literature—Ohio—Western Reserve. 2. Western Reserve
(Ohio)—Literary collections.   I. Anderson, David, R. (David
Rollin), 1942–   . II. Haddad, Gladys.
PS571.O3A85 1992
810.8'097713—dc20   92-4313

British Library Cataloging-in-Publication data are available.

Contents

Fiction

Poetry

PART 2 THE TWENTIETH CENTURY
Nonfiction Perspectives: Memoirs and Reminiscences

Fiction

Poetry

Acknowledgments

Compiling an anthology of regional literature can be a risky business. Avoiding becoming trapped by provincial jingoism that celebrates any scrap of writing simply because it is local can be as dangerous as focusing only on the big names that are instantly recognized but are not necessarily representative of the variety of a region's writing. Many people who love the Western Reserve and its singular qualities have helped us to avoid these pitfalls.

This anthology of Western Reserve literature had its genesis more than a decade ago with a grant to Hiram College from the National Endowment for the Humanities for the teaching of regionalism in the humanities. John Strassburger, now Dean of Knox College in Galesburg, Illinois, steered a careful course as director of Hiram's Center for Regional Studies between the Scylla of parochial indulgence in local lore for its own sake and the Charybdis of overlooking significant material simply because it is local. The late Michael Starr of the Hiram College Department of History was a persuasive advocate of regional literature before English faculties could be convinced of its aesthetic and pedagogical value. We are indebted to them both.

The reprinting of A. G. Riddle's *The Portrait,* a bicentennial project of the Mantua Historical Society in 1976, made it possible for David Anderson to incorporate a Western Reserve novel in a nineteenth-century American literature course and to begin evaluating the place of regional literature in the canon. Gladys Haddad's publication with Harry Lupold of *Ohio's Western Reserve: A Regional Reader* (1988) confirmed the need for a complementary volume that would illustrate the range of literary expression in northeastern Ohio.

Many people have contributed to the search for materials to include in the anthology. Adrienne Jones, chair of the Black Studies department at Oberlin College, directed us to important sources of African-American culture. Judah Rubinstein advised us of the rich history of

Jewish literature in Cleveland. John Grabowski, curator of manuscripts; Nancy Schwartz, Jewish archives; Bari Stith, research associate, all of the Library of the Western Reserve Historical Society, assisted in locating important materials, published and unpublished, in that treasure house for Western Reserve research. Grace Butcher made her d.a. levy collection available, which includes not only the poetry but also other valuable material on this intriguing moment in Cleveland poetry history. John Shaw suggested and generously shared letters from the James A. and Lucretia R. Garfield correspondence which he is editing for the University of Michigan Press. Sandra Parker, Carol Donley, David Fratus, Hale Chatfield, and Charles McKinley, members of the Hiram College Department of English, were supportive at all stages of the book and have themselves tried out some of the selections in their classes. Joanne Sawyer, archivist of the Hiram College Archives, was helpful in providing early correspondence. Lisa Johnson, humanities reference librarian of the Hiram College Library, maintained a sense of humor through the most complicated bibliographic questions. Lilith Kunkel, Bill Austin, Rosanne Factor, and Mary Lou Selander of the interlibrary loan service of the Hiram College Library were able to locate and retrieve obscure editions of regional materials from virtually everywhere through the electronic marvel of OCLC. Thomas Huntington Hubbard provided access to the Colbert Huntington Greer Collection. Joseph M. Erdelac was gracious in allowing us to use William Sommers's watercolor *Sunday Morning Apples*. We thank all of these people for the felicities to be found in these pages, while at the same time we excuse them for any of the errors of omission or commission that are ours.

The regional poetry collection of the Special Collections of the Kent State University Library was a rich source particularly for twentieth-century poetry.

We are, of course, not the first people who were ever interested in the literature of northeastern Ohio and the Western Reserve. In preparing the anthology we have used the following scholarly works and are indebted to the groundwork these writers provided us: William Coyle, ed., *Ohio Authors and Their Books 1795–1950;* William Ganson Rose, *Cleveland: The Growth of a City;* Nina Gibans and James Shelley, "Literature," in *The Encyclopedia of Cleveland History;* and Edward Ifkovic, "The Ethnic Imagination: Cleveland's Immigrant Writers," in *The Birth of Modern Cleveland 1865–1930.*

Edward J. Smerek, former Dean of Hiram College, and the Summer Research Grant Committee provided a stipend that supported a summer's work on the project, and the Vencl/Carr Faculty Assistantship Fund of Hiram College supported Michael Grzesiak, a student assistant for the project in the spring of 1989. The American Association of State and Local History, through funds made available to them by the National Endowment for the Humanities and the Ohio Historical Society with Lake Erie College and Hiram College, provided assistance for travel, duplication of materials, and a student assistant. Sylvia Yankey, Hiram College vice president for development, was diligent in securing funding to underwrite the expense of permissions; we are especially grateful for the financial assistance of Frederick W. Martin and Cecelia Herman.

Joanna Hildebrand, a copy editor at The Kent State University Press, was thorough in editing our manuscript; she made important and useful suggestions. We wish to thank Kelly Umbaugh who did the word processing. To Sigrid Anderson go the kudos for overseeing last minute details and supervising the production of the manuscript from sometimes recalcitrant floppy disks when teaching duties called David to England at that crucial juncture. She also helped decipher the German handwriting of the Alsbacher Document. *Danke, Sisi, vielmals.*

David R. Anderson
Hiram College

Gladys Haddad
Case Western Reserve University
Western Reserve Historical Society

Anthology of Western Reserve Literature

Introduction

Northeastern Ohio—specifically the Western Reserve of Connecticut—was settled at a time when American cultural identity was approaching a crisis. After twenty-five years as a nation, and little more than fifteen as a constitutional republic, America in 1800 was being pressed to define what its culture was to consist of and how that culture would define the nation. Americans felt the need to separate themselves from Britain's cultural sphere at the same time that they required unifying characteristics for themselves in a relatively new land. Fiercely held regional loyalties were not abandoned with the adoption of the new Constitution, nor would they be restrained to the satisfaction of many during the rest of the nineteenth century. Cultural attitudes branded the language and literature of a people so far from the mother country as provincial, often unworthy of serious consideration by people who assumed that literature in English rightfully belonged to an island many thousands of miles to the east. Philip Freneau so despaired of the possibility of an American literary culture in the eighteenth century that he wondered, "What use for poetry where men have no idea of its efficacy and influence over the human mind."[1]

The establishment of the Northwest Territory through the Ordinance of 1787 provided in many ways an unprecedented opportunity for the fledgling United States. Here would be the first settlement that was entirely new, and here it might be possible to create a uniquely American civilization. Ironically, the place names that dot the landscape seem to contradict this: Athens, Sparta, Medina, Mecca, Mesopotamia, Rome, Paris, Lisbon, Berlin. But in fact these names reflect an optimism that in this place a new civilization might arise that would be equal to that of the old world and would fulfill entirely the promise of past civilizations in new and unique ways. In his "Essay on

---

1. Philip Freneau quoted in Lewis Leary, *That Rascal Freneau* (New Brunswick, NJ: Rutgers UP, 1941) 340.

American Scenery" (1836), the Hudson River painter Thomas Cole re-marked that "American associations are not so much of the past as of the future. Seated on a pleasant knoll, look down into the bosom of that secluded valley. . . . You see no ruined tower to tell of outrage—no gorgeous temple to tell of ostentation; but freedom's offspring—peace, security, and happiness dwell there, the spirits of the scene."[2]

Just as American writers generally had to confront prejudice against the literature and culture of a new nation, writers who were separated by geography and mentality from the East were specifically called on to justify their work. As much as the new West provided the impetus for an American literature, there was always the danger that such a lit-erature would be too narrow in focus and too reflective of a limited kind of life. What could there be in a local scene that would interest people who lived outside that locale? Ralph Waldo Emerson and Nathaniel Hawthorne, as much as any two nineteenth-century writers, provided a rationale for the literature of the local and commonplace that could at the same time be useful as a way to unite regions in ways uniquely American, rather than dividing them through sectional hos-tility. In "The American Scholar" (1837) Emerson threw out his fa-mous gauntlet: "I ask not for the great, the remote, the romantic, what is doing in Italy or Arabia; what is Greek art, or Provencal minstrelsy; I embrace the common, I explore and sit at the feet of the familiar, the low." Hawthorne confessed several years later, in *The Scarlet Letter,* his classic work which focuses on a specific site in Puritan New England, that "the page of life that was spread before me seemed dull and com-monplace only because I had not fathomed its deeper import."[3]

As the nation expanded following ratification of the Constitution, regions were established that were distinct from the original thirteen colonies. To what extent would these new settlements be dependent on the original settlements or take new direction for their culture? And should that new culture differ dramatically from the old, would it be acceptable? The Western Reserve of Connecticut, explored and sur-veyed by the Connecticut Land Company in the waning years of the eighteenth century, retained a specific New England identity through-out much of the nineteenth century. There was a homogeneity in the original eight (later twelve) counties of northeastern Ohio that was scarcely true for the rest of the nation. The settlers, as census records and innumerable epitaphs in country and city graveyards attest, were

2. Thomas Cole, "Essay on American Scenery," *The American Monthly Magazine* Jan-uary 1836: 11–12.
3. Ralph Waldo Emerson, "The American Scholar," *The Complete Works of Ralph Waldo Emerson,* vol. 1, ed. Edward W. Emerson (Cambridge, MA: Riverside, 1903) 111; Nathaniel Hawthorne, "The Custom House," *The Scarlet Letter,* The Centenary Edition of the Works of Nathaniel Hawthorne, vol. 1 (Columbus: Ohio State UP, 1962) 37.

for the most part New Englanders who saw their mission into the wilderness in a manner not unlike their Puritan forebears. Even after the admission of the State of Ohio to the Union in 1803, the Western Reserve kept its special character in community organization, religion, education, and architecture. Many of its early educational institutions took its name, most of them actually doing so after the Reserve had passed out of existence as a legal entity. Even though there are few geographical characteristics to distinguish the Reserve from its neighboring counties, the spiritual heritage of the population brought set boundaries that were reflected in the ways people identified themselves.

Even near the end of the twentieth century, long since the hegemony of New England over the Reserve, the term "Western Reserve" is used with astonishing frequency, identifying everything from a telephone company to a pizza shop, from a major university to a hardware store. (Check any telephone directory in northeastern Ohio under "Western Reserve" for a startling list of services that have seemingly little to do with the Connecticut Land Company.) This naming suggests that the boundaries of the Reserve, though perhaps not entirely certain in the minds of the modern inhabitants of its three and one half million acres, still have a hold over our desire to identify with a particular historical and cultural place rather than the generic "American" intellectual landscape.

There are many reasons why some regional Americans come to cherish the local and the immediate over the national, which are linked to the expression of home love. Louise Erdrich, a regional writer of the upper Midwest, has suggested that

> through the close study of a place, its people and character, its crops, products, paranoias, dialects and failures, we come closer to our own reality. It is difficult to impose a story and a plot on a place. But truly knowing a place provides the link between details and meaning. Location, whether it is to abandon it or draw it sharply, is where we start.[4]

Perhaps the Western Reserve's most famous son, James A. Garfield, most succinctly stated the underlying rationale for looking at a region's literature—particularly the literature of our own region—in a letter addressed to A. G. Riddle, the author of *Bart Ridgeley* and *The Portrait*, nineteenth-century novels set on the Reserve: "It was no small risk you made, when you undertook to localize a story, away from the great centers of fashion and activity. But you have shown that life is a life—with all its deep tragedies of childhood and youth, whether in Parkman

4. Louise Erdrich, "Where I Ought To Be: A Writer's Sense of Place," *New York Times Book Review* 28 July 1985: 2.

or on the field of Waterloo."[5] We turn, then, to the literature of our own region for many reasons: pride in place; curiosity to find what others have learned and perceived about what we know and experience; and a need to come to a better understanding of ourselves and how the insights of literature can help us explain the tacit and puzzling in our existence.

The editors of this anthology have used a broad definition of regional literature in choosing examples to represent the artistic achievement of the Western Reserve. The works included were written by people who were either born or lived in the Western Reserve or whose works reflect an interest in the region even though they may not have lived here for any great length of time. Where possible, pieces have been selected to reflect a particular aspect of northeastern Ohio, whether landscape, demography, or a historic event as reflected in literature.

The literature of the Western Reserve presents a unique voice in regional writing and local color, which in the United States have been long associated with rural and agrarian experience. The Reserve, however, moved from its beginnings as the prime example of the pastoral charm of a transplanted New England to the preeminent American urban industrial and financial center of the late nineteenth century, dominated by Cleveland and the industrial satellites of Akron and Youngstown. As a result, writers who were interested in our region created a certain dissonance in the regional tradition by exploiting not only the nostalgic charm of the passing rural landscape, but also the immigrant, working class, industrial landscape of the southern shore of Lake Erie.

Like all regionalists, the writers of the Western Reserve of Ohio were exploring the essential American-ness of their particular surroundings. One of the unique qualities of the writers in this anthology is their desire to explore urban Cleveland, as well as the countryside, as an integral part of their definition of a uniquely American literature.

Besides the extent to which the actual Western Reserve is reflected in literature, the appraisal of a selection's literary merit has been coupled with the intention to evaluate and to illustrate ways that less-well-known regional literature reflects the persistence of national literary trends. At the same time, this anthology displays the multiculturalism which is a salient characteristic of northeastern Ohio; the literature re-

5. A letter from James A. Garfield to A. G. Riddle, Washington, DC, 15 March 1873, *The Riddle Papers in the Western Reserve Historical Society Library and a few of the Letters therein* (Privately published, n.d.) 5, A. G. Riddle Collection, Hiram College Archives, Hiram, OH.

flects the ethnic, racial, class, religious, and gender diversity particularly associated with the writing of the region.

The writing of the Western Reserve has also been marked by a variety of literary genres. In addition to poetry and fiction, writers on the Reserve have expressed themselves through letters, narratives, sermons, and hymns, all of which reflect their fascination with written expression as a mode of artistic communication. The range of writers and the types of writing they produced are truly remarkable; with pen in hand, early settlers on the Reserve expressed their joys and their sorrows in myriad ways. Much of the writing reflects the education and the background of native New England, and for a truthful picture of the Reserve, it is important to present a wide range of writers, from the sophisticated to the naive. Even the simplest letter writers of the early nineteenth century had a clearly posited reading audience; that their letters have survived to our time attests to the staying power of their prose and the effect it had on the recipients of the letters and their descendants.

This anthology is divided into the nineteenth and twentieth centuries; this is a practical division, since each half covers approximately the same span of time. There is also a perceptible change in literary interests from the nineteenth to the twentieth century, which is true not just on the Reserve but in literary history in general. Readers in the nineteenth century were interested in *belles lettres,* imaginative and artistic forms such as poetry, drama, and fiction, but there was a strong tradition of instructive and uplifting literature as well. Letters and narratives provided an important nonfictional outlet for the literary aspirations of people who had neither the inclination nor the aesthetic need for more traditional types of literature. Similarly in the twentieth century, many writers have turned to personal narrative—autobiography primarily—for the expression of literary inspiration.

The nineteenth-century section of the anthology begins with nonfiction literary forms of that century. The time span from the letters of the Huntingtons to the correspondence of Edward Rowland Sill reflects enormous changes taking place in life-style and literary taste. The conventions of nineteenth-century letter writing, learned from exercise books in New England schools, are of interest to later readers for their artistry as much as for the personal news that the letters contain. Many readers will also see the ways in which the contents of these letters reflect the social and cultural context of the Reserve in the nineteenth century. Collections of correspondence have been passed down from pioneer families whose husbands and fathers were active in politics in the state or national capital. The yearning of children for their absent fathers and the reluctance of wives to be left for long periods of time are recurrent motifs of the early letters, suggesting by the frequency of occurrence that the letters follow a kind of formula—whether conscious or unconscious it would be hard to say—that belongs to nineteenth-century familial correspondence.

Stemming from his conviction that the symbolic nature of these expressions preserved a unique experience, James Garfield, in a speech at Burton in 1873, called on families of pioneers to save their letters, diaries, and journals for future generations:

> There are townships on this Western Reserve which are more thoroughly New England in character and spirit than most of the towns of New England to-day. Cut off as they were from the metropolitan life that had gradually been moulding and changing the spirit of New England, they preserved here in the wilderness the characteristics of New England as it was when they left it at the beginning of the century. This has given to the people of the Western Reserve those strongly marked qualities which have always distinguished them.[6]

The letters were indeed saved, and they become sacred talismans for many a family's identity. These artifacts of family and community life are important to modern readers not simply as curiosities, but because they touch on the basic values of our lives and the ways in which all people connect across time. The prescient eloquence of Joseph Badger's letter to his children, for instance, teaches the virtue of tolerance toward the Indian, a concept that was to be important for all people in the Reserve as the nineteenth century progressively greeted ever larger numbers of varied peoples who had to be integrated into the communal life of the region. The Alsbacher Document is another tangible celebration of the intangible threads that bind community members to their religious and cultural heritage and to each other over a long period of time. Written to a specific German Jewish community that was emigrating to America, this letter is an important literary expression of the heritage of mutual respect and admiration for *all* peoples in northeastern Ohio.

Stylistically, the letters are important literary documents for several reasons: the orthography of the earliest letters, preserved as originally written, reveals both the educational levels of the writers as well as certain characteristics of nineteenth-century speech on the Reserve. The importance of standardized phrases to writers like Nabby Hitchcock—a country woman—and Hannah Huntington—a sophisticated city woman—are important in tracing the development of modes of expression. The letters of Samuel Huntington and James A. Garfield are

6. James A. Garfield, "The Northwest Territory," *The Works of James Abram Garfield*, ed. Burke A. Hinsdale (Boston: Osgood, 1883) 88.

important not only as the relics of prominent figures in American life but for the frankness and elegant articulation which they reveal. Furthermore, the conscious literariness of E. R. Sill's letter to a young woman in California is particularly striking when placed beside the naive expression of Amasa Clark; yet both writers are united, at opposite ends of the nineteenth century, by topographical description that revels in the beauties of the Ohio landscape. Each of these correspondents responded to an aspect of northeastern Ohio thought to be singular in its beauty and attraction.

Just as letters provide insight into nineteenth-century life on the Reserve, personal narratives of the Reserve are also documents of early life in the region. Although many of them have been discounted for lack of historical accuracy, they had literary importance for their writers and retain dramatic impact today. Elisha Whittlesey's account of the execution of a local Indian has near mythic quality as it reveals the elemental struggle of white settlers to take possession of the land. Modern readers may, in fact, squirm at the biases in the account, but the narrative is an important successor to similar writings from New England, as well as a precursor to later nineteenth-century accounts of the far West. Hair-breadth escapes and primal scenes of evil and divine retribution indicate the ways in which nineteenth-century narrators pictured their own roles as the storytellers. A more sympathetic view of the native American is to be found in Hudson and Emma Rood Tuttle's retelling of a local story, "The Legend of Minehonto." It preserves a small part of the native American experience which has had more prominence in place names than in any actual collective remembrance in northeastern Ohio.

Because of space constraints it was not possible to include them, but mention must be made of Henry Howe's accounts of early Ohio, published as *Historical Collections of Ohio* in 1847, as well as the various county histories published in the 1870s, which have long been read skeptically by historians. As literature, however, they have served as the source for many twentieth-century novelists, from Conrad Richter in his Ohio trilogy *The Awakening Land* (1940–50) to Scott Sanders's *Wilderness Plots* (1983) and Hugh Nissenson's account of the War of 1812 in *The Tree of Life* (1985). Howe is a great storyteller, and his contribution to the Reserve's portrait remains important.

In contrast to Howe's anecdotal history, the more personal narratives of Julia Foote and Salmon Brown alert the modern reader to the central role played by the Reserve in the fight for abolition. The strength of New England roots, evident in the strict morality of the early Reserve, is reflected in the uncompromising prose of these two figures. The memorial to John Brown by his son Salmon is clearly a transcript of oral memories and retains the charm of the colloquial speech of the villages and towns of the area. Joseph Joel's account in the *Jewish Messenger* (1866) of a Passover Seder celebrated on the battlefields of the Civil War by soldiers from Cleveland presents an unexpected juxtaposition of intensely held religious and secular values, particularly for modern observers who assume that the Western Reserve experience was exclusively a Protestant one.

Newspapers and journals played a significant role in encouraging literary efforts in the new settlement. The earliest published essays— from the Reserve's first newspaper, the Trumbull County *Trump of Fame* (1812–16), or Cleveland's earliest magazine, the *Mothers' and Young Ladies Guide* (1837–40)—suggest how the rhetorical restrictions of the eighteenth-century periodical essay were subtly transformed by the frontier experience: formal in language and structure, such writing was often tempered by the realities of living in fledgling communities. Other early Reserve newspapers were the *Hudson Western Intelligencer* (1827–30), the *Hudson Observer and Telegraph* (1830–33) and the *Ravenna Star* (1832–33).

Again, restraints of length dictated against including it in this anthology, but the literature of religious conflict and fervor is integral to understanding Western Reserve life in the 1800s. Sermons and speeches, often very long, had a role in nineteenth-century literary life that was very different from our modern age. Sermons and speeches were written, heard, and studied with an ardency not unlike the attention given today to the "media." There are many different styles of religious rhetoric in these writings, indicating the range of expression available to the adherents of the region's sects. Utopian vision was one of the shapes such fervor took, and the story of religious and utopian impulses is found in manifold forms throughout the century. The Mormons and the Shakers produced an interesting body of visionary writing. The divine revelations of Joseph Smith (1805–44), received while he was living in Kirtland and Hiram in the 1830s, were delivered in language derived for the most part from the cadences of the 1611 Authorized Version of the Bible. The seventeenth-century style of Smith's language lent validity to his visions because archaic formulation holds such sway over religious utterance in English. Members of the North Union community of Shakers in Cleveland, on the other hand, fell into trance-like states and recorded spirit messages whose originality of language reminds the reader of the visionary writings of William Blake or Emanuel Swedenborg.

More conventionally derived from the great homiletics of Puritan New England are the sermons of Charles Grandison Finney (1792–1875), Oberlin's scion of an unbroken preaching tradition reaching back to Jonathan Edwards and Cotton Mather. Thoroughly organized, logically structured, spiced with irony and humor, Finney's sermons earned him the reputation of one of the most important preachers in nineteenth-century America. Oberlin was the source of some of the most inspired rhetoric on the Reserve, also producing many examples of antislavery sentiment. Elsewhere in the Reserve, in Akron in 1851, the plea of Sojourner Truth's, "Ar'n't I a Woman?" gained international admiration for its unvarnished eloquence directed at the types of prejudice mitigating the rights of women of all races.

The stern New England tradition of the Reserve did not exclude other traditional literary forms. Fiction written in and about the Reserve reflects the tastes and trends of the Victorian era. Here, again, the diversity of writers and the variety of matters that involved them remains of interest to the modern reader. All of the major issues that were discussed and analyzed in Ohio find expression in the work of regional fictionalists. Not at all provincial in style or subject matter, their stories and novels are refreshing and direct; many of the characters and actions sketched in these pieces have a mildly ironic touch, as though the writers themselves were conscious of the unfair treatment they might expect at the hands of Eastern critics.

Albert Gallatin Riddle, prolific local writer from Newbury, paints in his novels a fictional portrait of early life on the Reserve. He was especially interested in the religious turmoil in rural counties, and particularly vivid are his own first-hand experiences with the Mormons and the Campbellites as seen through his fictionalized characters. Likewise, Albion Tourgée and John Hay (erstwhile secretary to Abraham Lincoln) left behind authentic portrayals of Western Reserve people and events at midcentury.

The humor of Artemus Ward and the character sketch from the *Atlantic Monthly* by Edward Rowland Sill reflect a national readership for journalism originating in the Reserve that is paralleled by William Dean Howells's important national position as a writer and critic in establishing nineteenth-century literary taste. Howells represents a proud tradition of journalism in the Western Reserve. His reminiscence of his printer father, "The Country Printer," originally printed in *Scribner's*, is not only a fine representation of the genre of the journalistic essay, but it also provides insight into the life of a working journalist in nineteenth-century Jefferson. Howells's view of the inhabitants of the village where he lived tells a great deal about the intellectual climate, even in the rural reaches of the Reserve, that encouraged literature:

We found these transplanted Yankees cold and blunt in their manners; but we did not undervalue their virtues. They formed in that day a leaven of right thinking and feeling which was to leaven the whole lump

of the otherwise proslavery or indifferent State; and I suppose that outside of the antislavery circles of Boston, there was nowhere in the country a population so resolute and so intelligent in its political opinions.
They were very radical in every way, and hospitable to novelty of all
kinds.[7]

From his beginnings on the Reserve, Howells became the preeminent American literary critic of the nineteenth century as well as one of
the century's most important novelists. He was a vocal advocate of literary realism and promoted many regional writers (not only of Ohio)
to their places of national prominence. An excerpt from Howells's *The
Coast of Bohemia* appears at first haughty in its rejection of provincial
culture in his hometown of Jefferson. Later in the same novel, however,
the arrogant narrator has his comeuppance when he falls in love with
the Ohio artist whose work he found so lacking in refinement in the
early pages of the novel. Likewise, Sarah Bolton's story skewers the
pretensions of Cleveland literary society, though not without well-
deserved jabs at the vapidity of the Eastern literary establishment.

Perhaps the most original voices in nineteenth-century fiction in
northeast Ohio are to be found in Constance Fenimore Woolson,
Charles Chesnutt, and Martha Wolfenstein. Each examined a difficult
segment of life in northeastern Ohio with honesty and disarming
frankness and addressed a social issue truthfully, though local color
writers are sometimes accused of overlooking problems. They form an
interesting trio; the descendant of a distinguished American literary
family, an African-American, and the daughter of Jewish immigrants
together represent the intellectual rigor that marked the Reserve
throughout its first century.

Western Reserve writers also heeded the muse of poetry, and their
productions are as varied as their voices. In the same issues of the Reserve's first newspaper, the *Trump of Fame,* that were breathlessly reporting news from the Battle of Lake Erie, a young couple from
Aurora was engaging in a rather public, albeit poetic, courtship. Or, as
was customary in newspapers of the day, were the poems reprinted
from the Philadelphia *Aurora,* and the coincidence of the name with one
of Portage County's earliest settlements a windfall for the *Trump?*
Their love lyrics—planted perhaps as a hoax by the editors to increase
readership—are squarely in the passé, by 1812, tradition of eighteenth-
century satire, witty, pointed, and charming products of frontier life.

The other poets of the Reserve produced solid nineteenth-century
verse that utilized the traditional forms and subject matter of English
romantic verse. The poets paid strict attention to precedent; the Reserve produced no Walt Whitman or Emily Dickinson to challenge the

7. William Dean Howells, "The Country Printer," *Scribner's* 13 (May 1893): 548.

norms. Nevertheless, Reserve poets were listened to and read throughout the country; for example, Edward Rowland Sill was widely read
and compared with Tennyson, and Edmund Vance Cooke commanded
wide respect as the dean of Cleveland poets. Cooke's career bridges the
fin-de-siècle, so he is represented in both sections of the anthology,
first with a backward-looking view to the hero of the Battle of Lake
Erie in the War of 1812 and in the twentieth century with a populist
political poem celebrating Cleveland's great hero, Mayor Tom L.
Johnson.

The poetry of hymnology also had a respectable place in Western
Reserve literature. Jessie Brown Pounds of Hiram and Cleveland wrote
a hymn with the traditional theology and imagery of the late nineteenth century. "Beautiful Isle" was a favorite of President William
McKinley and was sung at his funeral in 1901. The Shaker musical tradition in Cleveland bore fruit of a very different kind. Musically revolutionary, the hymns of Jeremiah Ingalls, among others, reflect a
visionary insight into the relationship of music and mystical language
and predate by nearly three-quarters of a century attempts by Gertrude
Stein and her circle in Paris in the 1920s to fuse music and poetry in
magical and transcendental ways. The Reserve's canal and lake cultures
also produced a body of folk song whose music and poetry were collected and preserved by projects in the twentieth century. Collectors in
the 1930s found throughout Ohio the traditional tunes and ballads that
are heard throughout the English-speaking world, but they had been
adapted to sailors' and boatmen's lives on the Great Lakes and in the
Ohio River Valley.

Nineteenth-century writers on the Reserve were the progeny of
New England. The literary forms they chose, the rhetorical models
they followed, and the issues that were close to them reflect concerns
they shared with their Eastern counterparts. Many critics observe a
changed literary taste and emphasis on certain literary forms during
the World War I era (some place the change in the years just before
1900); traditional forms that marked the early history of settlement
and development on the Reserve were replaced by more obviously "artistic" forms of writing. Much of this had to do with changes that
took place in the publishing industry and with the reading public,
which turned increasingly toward diversion and entertainment in its
literary interests.

Twentieth-century writers present evidence of the ways in which the
Western Reserve reflects changes in the whole country. After the Civil
War, much of the potential of the Western Reserve was realized, and
northeastern Ohio became an industrial and economic giant as the
frontier moved westward. Whereas the line of settlement through the
1840s had still marked the Reserve as "the West," after the Civil War

the Mississippi became the boundary in the imagination of most Americans. The original close link with New England that had given the counties of northeastern Ohio their distinctive character seemed all but broken, forgotten in the mass migration from other sections of the country as well as by large numbers of Europeans who made up a new industrial work force.

The founding of the Western Reserve Historical Society in 1867 marks the end of the Reserve as a region whose identity was self-evident. It was paramount to representatives of the original families that the source of the region's identity be preserved through conscious effort, because there no longer existed a shared definition of the area. Pluralism, not only in Ohio but in all of American society, posed a distinct threat to the "Old Faith" in a cultural homogeneity. A pluralistic society—as well as a pluralistic culture—makes it much harder to distinguish a particular region by its peculiarities. It might be said that as the Western Reserve served as a microcosm of New England in the nineteenth century, in the twentieth it has become a microcosm for the nation in all its variety. In the products of the northeastern Ohio writers of this century may be read the literary history of the United States.

In the twentieth century, reminiscence and autobiography have replaced the letter, diary, and narrative for conveying the details of everyday life to a reading public. The business of nostalgia and advice is a major one in our time; artists and prominent figures are interested in presenting their thoughts in a more refined and completed form than the *in situ* writing of nineteenth-century personalities. The record calls out for a more permanent form than the handwritten tomes of the grandparents. Clarence Darrow, for instance, fondly remembers in his memoirs and in his novel *Farmington* (1904) a time of uncomplicated, rural Western Reserve bliss that contrasts sharply with the pungent memories of urban African-American Cleveland set down by Jane Edna Hunter and Langston Hughes. Ruth McKenney's observations of the passions surrounding an Akron strike, *Industrial Valley* (1939), belong to the genre of Depression-era writings dealing with the gritty daily lives in the industrial workplace. Kenneth Patchen's very personal memory of his family in the industrial Mahoning Valley between Warren and Youngstown brings home the emotional cost of working-class life.

Although the immediacy of vernacular spelling and turns of phrase which lend charm to earlier personal narratives are not characteristic of most modern narratives (the exception being the extraordinary, faithful reproduction of dialect in the reminiscences of Sara Brooks), readers will find in these various recollections an interesting and rounded version of life in twentieth-century northeastern Ohio.

The fiction selections present no unity of techniques or form that might mark them distinctly of this region, but the writers have used northeastern Ohio in two interesting ways. There is, first, a substantial body of fiction—not represented in the anthology because of its length—that capitalizes on the historic past of the Reserve, attempting to recapture for the modern reader what life was like at the time of the early exploration of the Reserve and the War of 1812 (a particular favorite). At least one twentieth-century writer, Marguerite Allis, never lived in northeastern Ohio, but her long-term interest in Connecticut, about which she wrote many historical novels, led her to continue the Connecticut story to New Connecticut. Mary Schumann, of Youngstown, wrote several novels fictionalizing life in the Old Northwest, including *My Blood and My Treasure* (1941), a novel about Oliver Hazard Perry, and *Strife Before Dawn* (1939), which retells the tale of "Brady's Leap," an event of the War of 1812 familiar to residents of the Kent area in Portage County.

Second, literary realism influenced the major early twentieth-century writers of the Reserve. With its emphasis on the truthful portrayal of even mundane aspects of life, realism was a suitable vehicle for the nostalgia for the immediate past, for a simpler time uncomplicated by the tensions of modern American life, represented in part by the evocative work of Walter Havighurst. Constance Fenimore Woolson's realistic tales in the second half of the nineteenth century already pointed in the direction of a gentle, yet authentic view of the Reserve. Although she may be only tentatively called the "mother" of regional realism (William Dean Howells would, perhaps, more validly claim paternity), the example of her writing is an important factor for defining a regional impulse unique to the Reserve. J. William Terry's short story "Step-Sisters" continues the gentle realism of Woolson and Howells even while dealing with subject matter that might well have offended their genteel sensibilities.

Other fiction deals honestly with the modern urban settings of Cleveland, Akron, or Youngstown; the reader finds realistic portrayals of the seamier side of a region teeming with immigrant life and no longer an agrarian outpost of New England Calvinist values. Chester Himes describes a crime- and police-ridden Cleveland that the Puritan founders would have been loathe to acknowledge. Herbert Gold's nonfiction memoir *My Last Two Thousand Years* as well as his fiction, particularly the novels about his Russian-Jewish upbringing on Cleveland's West Side (*Fathers* [1966] and *Family* [1981]), are convincing evidence of the Western Reserve's maturation as a source of urban art forms. Urban tragedy, embodied in the catastrophic Cleveland natural gas explosion in 1944, forms the basis for Don Robertson's *The Greatest Thing Since Sliced Bread* (1965).

The myriad immigrant groups that populate twentieth-century northeastern Ohio appear in many fictional guises: Frank Mlakar in *He, the Father* (1950), Jo Sinclair, and Raymond De Capite all suggest in

their characters not so much an Ohio melting pot as a rich bouilla-
baisse of European settlers and their descendants for the delectation of
reading gourmands. It is amusing to speculate how Amasa Clark or
Samuel Huntington might have reacted to the various fictional adventures of Slovenians, Russian Jews and assimilated Jews, or Italians, all
of whom are the legitimate inheritors of the early dreams of New England in Ohio.

All of the twentieth-century fiction writers included in this anthology are interested in the portrayal of character more than in the topography of the region. Their fiction suggests ways in which the
region has fostered a brand of individualism that is often perceived by
other regions as characteristically Midwestern. Sherwood Anderson,
who grew up in Clyde, just outside the western edge of the Reserve, is
widely acknowledged as the founder of a whole new school of American writing about the Midwest. Anderson's own experiences as a
young man in Cleveland, after fleeing the confines of Clyde, influenced
a lifetime of work that portrayed the deleterious effects of small-town
Midwestern life on the psyche. Similar to Anderson's young heroes,
Elsinore, a young woman in Dawn Powell's *Dance Night* (1930), escapes the hypocrisy of small-town life for the bright lights and glitter of
Cleveland, albeit by streetcar. The young man pumping gas in James
McConkey's short story "The Medina Road" is also derived in many
ways from the Anderson prototype of the small-town innocent on the
verge of self-discovery; the reader, though, is not told whether his ten-
tative epiphany will have long-term significance.

There is a notable feistiness in the men and women who people the
fiction of the area, a willingness to persevere in the face of all kinds of
forces that would deter lesser beings. Women writers in northeastern
Ohio, particularly, have created a wealth of individuals who will not
soon be forgotten, from Mary Schumann's Captain Brady to the crusty
matriarch of Joan Chase's *During the Reign of the Queen of Persia* (1983),
a novel of rural Ohio in the fifties and early sixties, and Rita Dove's
very contemporary bag lady on the streets of downtown Cleveland.
Alix Kates Shulman's Cleveland teenager became the vanguard of a
generation of American women; Toni Morrison's black heroine in the
1973 novel *Sula,* set in Lorain in the early years of this century, em-
bodies beauty, independence, and integrity in ways that Sojourner
Truth or Julia Foote might have reeled at but would have applauded.
The characters created by northeastern Ohio women writers are not
just interesting in the local context; they have been recognized nationally for their vigor and authenticity.

Twentieth-century poetry of this region also reflects the variety that
is a part of the literary history and taste of the entire nation. There is
no "school" of Western Reserve poetry; there have been, though, im-

portant local centers, academic as well as popular, that have had a major impact on encouraging the writing and publishing of poetry. The literary circle—including Hart Crane—that gathered around William Sommer in the twenties and thirties at Brandywine; the Poetry Center started at Fenn College and continued at Cleveland State University; the Poets League; Bits Press; and publications such as *Hiram Poetry Review, Free Lance,* and *Gamut,* to name just a few, have all had significant impact on poetry writing in northeastern Ohio.

Indications of the importance of the poetry of a region are the awards it attracts: Richard Howard, Mary Oliver, and Rita Dove have all been Pulitzer Prize winners; Langston Hughes won the Spingarn Prize; Robert Wallace received the William Rose Benet Prize of the Poetry Society of America; Richard Howard merited the American Book Award; Howard, Robert Wallace, Mary Oliver, and Alberta Turner have all been awarded the Cleveland Arts Prize. Guggenheim fellowships have also been awarded to a stellar group, beginning in 1931 with Hart Crane to be followed by Langston Hughes, Kenneth Patchen, Richard Howard, Mary Oliver, and Rita Dove. This is but a sampling of the recognition given to poets whose roots have found sustenance in the soil of the northeast corner of Ohio.

Beginning with Langston Hughes, a number of area poets examined the African-American poetic experience in their work. Hughes, Russell Atkins, James Kilgore, and Rita Dove subtly integrate qualities of mainstream modern American poetry into their singular experiences in Cleveland and Akron. At the same time, other regional poets explored the more recent connections of the area to its New England forebears. Vachel Lindsay, an Illinois poet, was a student at Hiram College at the turn of the century. He acknowledged, toward the end of his life, the strong influence the landscape and people of the Reserve had on his work, which fused local materials with a mystic vision of a great, united continent. Inspired to some extent by the vigor of Lindsay's exploitation of vernacular materials, Hart Crane triumphantly fused in *The Bridge* (1930) regional materials—such as the millrace in Garrettsville—with both the Brooklyn Bridge and a metaphysical structure that accommodated the vastness of the American physical and spiritual landscape. Richard Howard's moving tribute to Crane, "Decades," suggests that the Western Reserve is the birthplace of modern American poetry because it was Crane's home (and, incidentally, his own).

Poets as different from each other as Jake Falstaff and Mary Oliver have turned to historic materials of early Ohio for their inspiration. Even d. a. levy, in poetry filled both with satiric humor and anger, acknowledges the historic roots of Cleveland at the same time that he forges a brash language and form that is congruent with his role of local poetic guru in the hip sixties.

The reader recognizes in the poetry of Kenneth Patchen, Grace Butcher, Hale Chatfield, David Citino, and many others the familiar topography of both urban and rural northeast Ohio. The landscape lacks the drama of the Far West or the ocean and the cities are missing some of the sparkle of the "great" urban centers, but worthy of consideration is these poets' ability to suggest the unique qualities of the Western Reserve experience and to transform them into art.

One identifying characteristic of the literature of this region is its avoidance of extremes. There is a moderation in the writing of the Reserve that has, for the most part, eschewed the fashionable experiments of the avant-garde, though that is not to say that there have not been writers who were at the vanguard. The selections in this anthology indicate how many nationally known writers are associated with the Western Reserve, and at the same time shows that the primary position of these writers has been at the center of literary fashion, rather than at the edges.

All selections in the anthology have been reprinted as they are found in the sources (except that salutations and signatures in letters have been uniformly placed for easier identification and readability). The editors have avoided changing spelling or presentation so that the reader will have a direct experience of all the works, particularly handwritten documents printed here for the first time whose idiosyncracies reflect the diction and style of the periods. The anthology is not exhaustive; space constraints forbade the reprinting of longer works or works not easily extracted from the context of a longer work, so many writers of the Western Reserve could not be included or are represented with only a very small sample of their work. The reader is encouraged to let this anthology serve as an initiation into the literature of the Reserve and to consult the lists for each century of other works by writers who are represented as well as those who are not. Just as importantly, the anthology should serve to whet the reader's appetite for the literature of all American regions, particularly those regions which are now overlooked. William Coyle's *Ohio Authors and Their Books 1796–1950* (now nearly thirty years old and ready for an update) and the *Ohioana Quarterly* of the Martha Kinney Cooper Ohioana Library Association are good places to start. David van Tassel and John Grabowski's *The Encyclopedia of Cleveland History* is another excellent place to find out about writers specifically associated with Cleveland.[8] Local librar-

8. William Coyle, *Ohio Authors and Their Books 1796–1950* (Cleveland: World, 1962); David van Tassel and John Grabowski, *The Encyclopedia of Cleveland History* (Bloomington: Indiana UP, 1987). Other helpful guides for exploring Western Reserve literature are William Ganson Rose, *Cleveland: The Growth of a City* (1950; Kent, OH: Kent State UP, 1991), and Thomas F. Campbell and Edward M. Miggins, eds., *The Birth of*

ies and their reference librarians are invaluable resources for finding additional works by the authors we have selected, as well as other regional examples.

Modern Cleveland 1865–1930 (Cleveland: Western Reserve Historical Society, 1988). John J. Murray, ed., *The Heritage of the Middle West* (Norman: U of Oklahoma P, 1958) is also useful on the general topic of regionalism in literature. A general work on various aspects of Western Reserve history is Harry F. Lupold and Gladys Haddad, eds., *Ohio's Western Reserve: A Regional Reader* (Kent, OH: Kent State UP, 1988).

PART ONE

The Nineteenth Century

LIBRARY

LIBRARY

Nonfiction Literary Perspectives

LETTERS AND NARRATIVES

Letters to and from a New Land

Hannah (1770–1818) and Samuel (1765–1817) Huntington, transplanted New Englanders, settled in 1801 on the Western Reserve at Cleveland on the banks of the Cuyahoga River. Samuel pursued a political career that required frequent and long absences from home; but his ambition eventually earned Ohio statehood and him the governorship (1808–10). With the help of two servants and a female companion, Hannah managed the family's home and farm, which was far from any close neighbors, and raised six children, five sons and one daughter. In this wilderness outpost the Huntingtons struggled against harsh elements and ever-present disease. Their letters illustrate epistolary styles common to late eighteenth-century writers. Samuel's formal rhetoric contrasts sharply with Hannah's less-structured, more direct prose.

Cleveland 25 April, 1804

My dearest best of treasures
    where are you I am almost distracted I have looked this last projected time out & I am bewildered—you mentioned that you have been indisposed I am fearful that you have represented it too light, by the last account I have heard it was suppos' that the assembly would rise the 15 since that you have had time if you were well to come home but you are sick & the best of friends cannot administer consolation equal to her who wishes to share all your trouble—we too are sick & distress'd it will not relieve your anxiety one moment to inform you of any thing but what can I do I cannot see you & I must write—I kept the fever & ague till I was put to bed our child was suppos'd to be the victim of it—for 4 hours there was every exertion to preserve it without any effect—it was buried the 27th of March I was as comfortable as I usually have been here to fore except 3 of the hardest fits that I ever had

after that I gain'd strength as fast as might be expected till the ague return'd upon me i have had my 3 fit today—Margaret has it badly martha not so bad but still she is sick I am unable as yet to attend to much out doors but as much as could be accomplished by Margaret has been done—

I would not my dear husband spend another such winter as this for—what—I know not, is honour a compensation for your absence—and the many troubles & vexations that I have experienced in the two journeys that you have been, I love my children. I love my family—but what is that children family & the whole world without you is barren & joyless—they may say I am weak foolish even a worshipper of flesh & blood what care I, it is my glory & happiness that I feel as I do—let your station in life be ever so exalted little will it gratify me if it must be purchased at so high a price as our separation—I do not wish to have you sink into oblivion & be tied to my apron strings far very far from it—I want the emoluments of your offices to be such as to enable us to live in a different state of society—but I have wrote til I can hardly see the paper and I shall tell you all this before you will have this letter but it has been a consolation to write to pour out my soul to join the partner of all my blessing would to heaven that I could pour them into your bosom at this moment—adieu thine till death

HANNAH HUNTINGTON

April 30

my dear husband what am I to think this month is out & you are not return'd & I have nothing from you conjecture is lost in itself—I feel as though I was quite out of the reach of any communication of a public nature adieu

thine most fervently H HUNTINGTON

Washington (Kentucky) October 8th 1805

My dear Hannah,

Since my last letter to you I have been in better health and now as well as common at this season. Not a word has yet reached me from you or any part of the family since I left home—you may judge of the cause of some anxiety therefore when you reflect that sickness and accidents might happen of which I might be ignorant and that hope, strong as it is, would not always be sufficient to cheer me. If I could be sure that Mr. Ruggles was keeping school & our children were making daily improvements I should be less uneasy, if he is not I trust that what spare time you have will be dedicated to their instruction—especially to reading & spelling—I shall come home by the way of Pittsburgh & bring Frank along & keep him at school at home if there is any this winter—your friends and acquaintances at Marietta are well & make many inquiries after you—Mrs. Tysmmer met her husband at Marietta and has rode with us ever since on her way home. I wish you were as good a horsewoman as she. nothing would then be wanting but the *will* to have you come as far as Marietta next [word missing] I calculate this letter to reach you soon enough to have your answer at Chilicothe the middle of November. I wish you to inform me whether Ruggles keeps school or expects to do it the coming winter—whether the family are & have been well & everything else that you think proper—as it will probably be the first news I shall get from you it will give me much satisfaction to have your particulars & to relieve the anxiety I might otherwise experience until I get home—with all the civilities & attentions I receive abroad my heart is constantly beating for *home* & the greatest source of weariness I know is the thought of a long time intervening before I shall be again in the bosom of my family—what transient pleasure I receive is derived from the belief that you expect me with the same impatience & from a comparison of the situation of others among whom I visit with our own, which, I can spare you gives me no reason to covet an exchange if their society is better as to neighborhood, I cannot think it is by their own fair idea—I shall write you again from Cincinnati. that will reach you too late to give an answer—in the mean time give my love to Margaret & the children & believe me to be with affection as ever, your husband

SAM HUNTINGTON

Nabby (1784–1867) and Peter (1791–1854) Hitchcock, newlywed in 1806, emigrated from Cheshire, Connecticut, to Burton and were among the first to settle the township. Peter entered public life as a state legislator and jurist and later became a judge in the Supreme Court of Ohio; then from 1817 to 1819 he was his district's representative to the U.S. Congress. Nabby bore ten children while living in Burton, five sons and five daughters. The Federal-style Hitchcock home was moved to the Century Village in Burton, where it may still be visited. Nabby and Peter's letters indicate the ways in which marriage was sustained in spite of long separation and disparate educational backgrounds.

Burton December 11 1817

My Dear Husband

Once more I am permitted to take my pen in hand to write to one that is ever in my mind and being seperated from that one causes me a great many painful ours but when I think of your situation being sepperated from companion and children to I ought to be contented with my situation but I cannot hardly bare the thought of our sepperation for four or five months what that time will bring about we cannot tell but whatever we are to meet with may not it be for the good of our souls I have a request to make to you that is that you would agree to set apart a time for secret prayer at ten o clock in the evening and I will endeavor to set apart the same time for that purpose I want you to let me no in your letter after receiving this perhaps you will say that it will do no good for me to pray but I intreat of you to try it and see only think how much you and all the rulers needs the assistance of the Lord to direct them to make such laws and rules as shall be for the good of men and for the glory of God

Friday evening

I had intended to have written more but have ben hindered this day and evening it is now between ten and eleven o clock and I am quite fatigued I shall write agin soon I hope that you will write often and inform me of your situation if agreeable or not so of your health and also of your spiritual welfare if you feel concerned about your soul which is of the greates importance to you if you could but no the anxiety that I have for your soul I should be glad neither in words nor with pen can I express my feelings uppon that subject I have this day had a quarter of Beefe of Beard he asks five dolars a hundred without the Tallow it is very good beefe we are all well as can be expected the family all wishes to be remembered to you yesterday Laurance was standing at the door he see too jentlemen riding by he say to mar if one of them was Par I would ask him to come in and stay till to morrow I remain your affectionate wife

NABBY HITCHCOCK

Washington Dec. 31. 1817

Dear Wife.

On yesterday with heart felt satisfaction I received your letter of the 11th. Instant and had intended to have devoted more time to answer it than what I shall now be enabled to do. But this is the less to be regretted as I intend writing often, so much so that you may hear from me as it were from day to day. To hear that you were all in comfortable health was a relief to my mind which it very much wanted and how should our hearts be drawn forth with gratitude to the supreme disposer of events for the blessing. The wishes you express for the welfare of my soul are such as I had reason to expect and how much would it be to my benefit did I but profess the same anxiety. But may we not hope that the prediction of the apostle may be fulfilled that the unbelieving husband may be converted by the believing wife. Not that I would be willing to admit that I am an unbeliever in the common acceptation of the term, but still I do claim to proffess the belief of the sincere and humble Christian. Your proposal on the subject of prayer I will endeavor to comply with so far as circumstances will permit. I need not inform you how much pleasure it would afford me to see the children as well as yourself. I have no doubt but you will take every possible care of them nor but that I shall be frequently called to their remembrance I remain in the enjoyment of health.

Yours most affectionately
P. HITCHCOCK

In 1832 Amasa Clark (1794–1855), a Baptist minister from Westfield, Connecticut, emigrated to Hiram, in Portage County, where he settled and farmed. The correspondence of Clark and his wife Aurilla (1794–1854) records his enthusiasm and her reluctance for a move to the Western Reserve. Their eventual settlement in Hiram is chronicled in letters, journals, and diaries, now preserved in the archives of the Hiram College Library. Amasa Clark's two letters published here were written (along with others) on one large sheet of paper; presumably he wrote rough drafts before posting them to New England. Aurilla Clark's letter is found alone with a Westfield postmark.

Palmyra June 20th 1832

I am now with Elder James McKelvy You can hardly imagine their plainness simplicity and Open hospitality. Nor can you imagine the beauty and luxuriousness of his fields. His pasture is like mowing and the green rank wheat and rye are delightful to the eye.—(As they would say,) I would like you had some of the good wheat It is healthy here probably as anywhere.—And the land yields about as much again as where we had lived. A man may verry easily possess himself of a good farm.
Notwithstanding Mr. Harts feelings he acknowledges the country is very healthy and land is twice as good and twice as cheap here as where he came from.—If he had an improved farm he would be unwilling to return. People that move from this place frequently return.—But don't you believe a word I say.—Think that it is a thinly settled dark barren gloomy place and when you come here perhaps you will not find it quite so bad as your imagination has painted. Flax is beautiful and I think abundant.

Mantua July 13th 1832

I have succeeded beyond my expectation in obtaining a place. And therfore can write sooner than I expected. I have bought 60 acres of land in Hiram Portage County for one hundred and eighty dollars to be paid one year from next September.—about one mile ½ from a neighborhood And joins a mill seat lot where it is expected a mill will soon be built and if it is there will soon be a large village.—Our house will be one mile from the Cuyahoga river and two miles north of the center of Hiram Standing in the road you can see the center of the town. The place is new but you will have many nabours 1 house is now built

opposit were ours will probable be I will give you a plan of the Farm.
The Brook runs most gently to the east and the land descends a little
both sides towards it. In the brook is 4 to 6 acres of the richest land.
there is no waste land as it is all good. The cold spring is as cold I think
as I ever tasted. The other large spring which is two or three rods on
Capt. Youngs land can, by carry it in logs a very few rods be brought
into the washroom and barn yard.—
—yesterday I went into the place with four of the brethren to where I
would begin to clean.—We kneeled down and sought the blessing of
God. Then cut over about an acre on the brook of such land as probably I have not been accustomed to labor on. The water in the springs
is soft and good. In the brook there is iron. The towns of Mantua and
Hiram are said to be amongst the most healthy in Ohio. I have been in
this state more than a month visiting and preaching in many towns and
there has been no funerals in my travels I have seen two or three
slightly sick with fever. The rash is among the children in some places.
We must not love the world nor be worldly minded. I feel it my duty
if the Lord will to provide for us a comfortable home. I enjoy my mind
more than usually well and have done for some time past. Give my
best regards to friends. Your letter will come to me in 7 or 8 eight days
after you put it in the office let me receive it about the 12th of next
month. I purpose to come home in the winter and start for Ohio the
1st of may. I intend to get in two acres of grass and a litle wheat the
faul. Like Mary you could say My soul doth magnify the Lord and my
spirit hath rejoiced in God my Saviour.

Yours
AMAS CLARK to
Aurilla Clark

Westfield [Massachusetts] July the 30 1832
Allmost two months and a half have passed away since I have seen you
and how many more will i know knot some think you have no idea of
returning home untill spring if you have not i wish you to let me know
in your next letter not put me off two or three months longer in every
letter mr. Sacket would be verry glad to take this place in september
and buy the hay and crops that are on the ground i was verry sorry to
hear you had bought a place you have not forgotten i trust what i have
said to you about it I sold the smallest pig the fore part of this month
it weighed 58 pounds they are onely 4ct per pound the colt has done
well this summer i was advised to take the mare from mr. otises by a
number of our friends and i thought she would do as well away as there
and i have her at home now Marilla says she will keep her some of the
time and others will for the youse [use] of her it caused me some trouble while she was theire. I will let you know when you return the rea-

son why i took her away if we live to see that time i did not write about it in the other i thought i would not trouble you about it if you were coming home as soon as you thought you should Marilla and i went to Bro Lelands last friday and found them well except Almira she was able to be about Mother came home with us she expects to stay one week. from theire we went to mr Dickinsons and i talked with him about the cow he thinks it best to dry her off and mr. Gridley thinks so she is in good order but does not give but a verry little milk i told them to do as they thought best mr Dickinson will take her next fall. from mr Dickinson we came to Westfield their we met a funeral p[r]osession. it was a child of mr Lays it was the second he had lost within a fortnight with the measels and before we got home we met another mourning family it was mr James Lewises returning from the grave they had buried their youngest child it was drowned in a tub of water. they have the measels at mr Allens and i am a fraid our children will have it i kept them away from their but their children came here i told them they must not i should not feel so about it if it did not go so hard with them in town their has a number died with that disorder were you here i should feel better about it mr Parsonses Tavern mr Roots and mr Jessups Stores were burnt on the night of the 28 June mr Parsons keeps a boarding house he takes my butter but no more. the people in Westfield are verry much alarmed about the Cholery it is in Hartford and all about they expect it will soon be in town. I herd it was in york State and in Ohio if it is i wish you to let me know in your next if you come home next fall or winter you will have time to sell the things but i fear you do not mean to. Nancy says mother have you wrote to have Father come home well you must ask little Amasa if he wanst to see Father he says yes. Marilla sends her respexcts to you and says you are a good comforter she does not think David will go on to Ohio if he does she hopes you will move on togeather. I do not know but you will think so much of your new farm in Ohio that you will forget that you have a family in Westfield i do not know when to look for another letter i hope you will write soon Marys health is good and has work enough. we have had preaching every saboth but three. Elder Willson preaches next saboth. i expect to go with butter tomorrow i have had no chance to send it since you left home i have not received any monny since you went away except for calf and butter eggs twice i want you to write when you will come home Adieu for the preasant Amasa Clark

AURILLA CLARK

Pioneer preacher Joseph Badger (1757–1846) came to the Western Reserve in 1800. In his ministry he organized churches, reached scattered settlements, and preached to the Indians, urging temperance and giving instruction on improving their land

and building schools. From Gustavus, in Trumbull County, where, in 1825, he organized his last church, he addressed his children in a letter which is included in *A Memoir of Reverend Joseph Badger; Containing an Autobiography and Selections from His Private Journal and Correspondence* (1851). The formality of Badger's prose reads more like a public document than personal correspondence.

Gustavus, January 28th, 1833.

Dear Children:

Having heard nothing directly from you for a considerable time, I observed to your mother this morning, that I would write again. You have remembrance in our prayers daily, that grace, mercy and peace, through our Lord, the Redeemer, may abide with you, and all the dear missionary family. What will be the result of the cruel oppression and removal of the Indian tribes from their ancient homes, we have yet to learn. That there is awful guilt and responsibility resting on the head of governmental departments, I have no doubt: notwithstanding the all-wise God, can in his own way bring good out of the evil, and light out of the gross darkness. Your statement in the Telegraph indicated that the mission would be removed in the spring, or be broken up. By the last Herald, we learn, that the flourishing mission among the Choctaws, is to be relinquished, by their removal. It is pleasant to learn that the Lord has not forsaken them in their new settlement. The persecution of the church in the 16th century brought the Pilgrims to America. It may be that the persecution of the Indians, and the churches springing up among them, will be the means of planting them in circumstances, eventually to promote both their civil and religious improvement. May it please the Lord so to order their inheritance. Let the infidel rage, and the people imagine vain things; the Lord reigneth, let the church abide under the court of his strong arm; and no evil can befall them. His governing providence constitutes walls and bulwarks for the defence of his people, that defy the legions that pour forth from the gates of hell.

Our circumstances are as comfortable as we ought to expect or wish for. We are not able to keep up with the grandeur, or as it is called by the softer name, affluence, prevalent even among professing christians.

If I was able to do more for the cause of our Lord among the heathen, I think it would be desirable. But my day of laboring and doing, is fast drawing to a close. It has become difficult for me on the change of air, from a cold, to a soft relaxing atmosphere, to speak at all in public, so as to be distinctly heard. The first Sabbath in this month was our communion, it being remarkably warm the week before; my lungs were so enfeebled, that it was with difficulty that I could perform the services, besides having a sermon read by one of the deacons. For a few

Sabbaths, since the air has become more dense and cold, I have continued to preach; but I expect at the opening of the spring, it will be my duty to relinquish my stated labors in the ministry. I have notified the people that it will be necessary for them to look up some one to supply my place. My health and strength otherwise than the failure of voice is uncommonly good for a man of my years, seventy-six the twenty eighth day of next month.

Your affectionate father,
JOSEPH BADGER

To the same.

The Alsbacher Document: An Ethical Testament originated on May 5, 1839, when a party of nineteen Bavarian Jews departed their village of Unsleben destined for America. They formed the first Jewish community in Cleveland and founded the congregation Anshe Chesed (Fairmount Temple). As a parting gesture, Lazarus Kohn, the village teacher, gave Moses Alsbacher, the leader of the party, a letter signed by 233 townsfolk. The following is a translation of the original German letter without its Hebrew blessing and Yiddish translation.

My dear friends Moses and Yetta Alsbacher:

I give you by way of saying goodby a list of names of the people of your faith with the dearest wish that you may present these names to your future heirs, yes, even to your great-grandchildren, of which may you have many, under the best family relationship and under pleasant economic circumstances. I further wish and hope that the Almighty, who reigns over the ocean as well as over dry land, to whom thunder and storms must pay heed, shall give you good angels as travel companions, so that you, my dear friends, may arrive undisturbed and healthy in body and soul at the place of your destiny, in the land of freedom.

But I must also, as a friend, ask a favor of you.

Friends! You are traveling to a land of freedom where the opportunity will be presented to live without compulsory religious education.

Resist and withstand this tempting freedom and do not turn away from the religion of our fathers. Do not throw away your holy religion for quickly lost earthly pleasures, because your religion brings you consolation and quiet in this life and it will bring you happiness for certain in the other life.

Don't tear yourself away from the laws in which your fathers and mothers searched for assurance and found it.

The promise to remain good Jews may never and should never be broken during the trip, nor in your homelife, nor when you go to sleep, nor when you rise again, nor in the raising of your children.

And now, my dear friends, have a pleasant trip and forgive me for these honest words to which the undersigned will forever remain true.

Your friend
LAZARUS KOHN
Teacher

Unsleben near Neustadt on the Saale
in Lower Franconia
in the Kingdom of Bavaria
the 5th of May 1839.

James A. Garfield (1831–1881) and Lucretia Rudolph (1832–1918) were classmates at the Geauga Seminary and Western Reserve Eclectic Institute (later, Hiram College) and married in 1858. In 1862, while serving in the Civil War, James was elected to represent Ohio's Nineteenth Congressional District in Washington, D.C. He was returned eight times, until his 1880 election to the presidency. When the Garfields' first-born, Eliza, called "Trot," became ill suddenly at age three, James was called back to Hiram. After the child's death, James resumed legislative duties in Washington, and he and Lucretia shared their grief through correspondence. Victorian sentiment strongly impressed itself on the language of this nineteenth-century Western Reserve couple.

Hiram, December 6, 1863.

My Dear Precious Husband:

I have just come from kneeling beside the bed where our little one breathed out her life. I have asked of Our Father a more perfect resignation of spirit to this great sorrow which has fallen upon our lives so heavily, and I hope that He has given it to me—to us both. I hope, dear Jamie, that you are trying to look up, through tears though it be, to our Savior's face and from His words of comfort gathering peace to your soul, and a larger strength to do well the work of life. These words have been much in my heart today: "The Father chasteneth whom He loveth," and the thought has come to me that not only has He honored us in giving us to keep a while a little nature so pure and noble but that he also loves us so well that He will make surer our clinging to Him by taking our cherished one to Himself, that where our treasure is, there may our hearts be also. These have been, Oh, such sad strange days that I fear there have been in my heart questionings and doubts which were almost wrong; but I hope God is lifting my spirit out from the shadow and that I am gaining a hold on a larger truer life, and I trust it is so with you, my dear one. Surely we can be thankful for this at least that we have come to be so much nearer and dearer to each other, that our love has been made so perfect through this great suffering. I feel that we need each other now as we have never before, and that we can the most truly live when near each other. Still I submit to whatever seems best and will try patiently and faithfully "to labor and to wait." My dear Jamie, you do not know the large place you won in my heart by your gentle care and attention when at home. It surprised me and made me love you so tenderly to see you taking care of our little girl, and watching beside her so gently; and so much dearer is our home now for the notice and care you took of it. I have almost feared that your heart was so saddened by the loss of our darling that you would dread to return here, and that our home would have little attraction for you now; but I hope it is not so. To me it is now a holy place, and I want it to be so to you. I do not feel like writing more now; but we will write to each other very often and live very near each other. I did not write yesterday as I promised since a letter would not go until tomorrow. With the enclosed letters were several sent to others directed to your care, two to Capt Farrar, one to Capt Swaim, one to William M. Conn, and one to A. H. Bodman. If you can tell me where to direct them, I will remail them. That you may be blessed and kept good and noble and true is the prayer of your loving trusting little wife, Crete.

P.S. I have concluded to make a separate package of your letters.
P.S. Commencing with the 13th verse of 1st Thessalonians, 4th Chpt, read through to the close of the Epistle. I find there much to comfort and strengthen my heart.

Crete.

Washington, Dec. 13, 1863

My Precious Crete:

Your dear noble letter of the 8th inst. came to me yesterday. It was balm to my heart, and it made me feel more than ever before how noble and true you are. Pray for me, dearest, that my heart may, like yours, become more resigned and see the hand of our good Father in this great sorrow. It is a lovely day, after a cold and cheerless morning of storm. I ought to be cheerful and happy as are the sun and the sky, and though your brave words have made me calmer and stronger, I still struggle with my grief and think [of] our precious darling with such a yearning agony of heart-break that at times it seems as though I could not endure it. I have read twice over this morning the passage you told me of from Thessalonians. It is touchingly tender and hopeful. I would that my heart could rest upon it as I when a child rested in my mother's words. I pray that my faith may grow stronger. I try to be hopeful but Tennyson speaks for me when he says:

> "Yet in these ears till hearing dies,
> One set slow bell will ever toll
> The passing of the sweetest soul
> That ever looked with human eyes."

How her image and little nature has grown upon me since she is gone. "Death has made His darkness beautiful with her." You must read "In Memoriam." It really seems as if it were written for us. Only a change of gender is needed to make it seem direct and real. I hope you have gotten my letters by this time. They have all been very hurried, but I know you will appreciate something of the amount of my work and will forgive my meagerness in what I write. Really, Dearest, I wish you would think whether you cannot manage to come back with me after the Holidays, if I return home then as I now hope to. It really does not seem as though I could stay here all this lonely winter. We will talk of it when I come. Do not fear that I will not love our home. It is more sacred to me than ever. I did for a little while think I could not live in it any more, but I think differently now. Tell me about the little boy. Is he well? How is your own health now? I hope you are being very careful and getting strong again. I sent you a draft the other day: did it reach you? Give my love to Mother and all the family. I am still stopping at the corner of N.Y. Avenue and 13th St. and logging away at the letters.

With all my heart, I am ever, Your own JAMES.

Edward Rowland Sill (1841–87) moved as a child from Connecticut to Cleveland and was educated at Western Reserve College. A graduate of Yale, he first taught in Cuyahoga Falls, and from 1875 to 1883 he held the chair in English at the University of California at Berkeley. He retired to spend his last years in Cuyahoga Falls to write and correspond with former students such as Miss E. B. The following letter to her appears in *The Prose of Edward Rowland Sill: With an Introduction Comprising Some Familiar Letters,* published after his sudden death following surgery at age 45.

To E. B.
[Cuyahoga Falls, Ohio,]
May 12, 1884.

Dear Miss B.—You recollect old Geo. Herbert after a season of dumps congratulates himself that once more he doth "relish versing"— So there are faint symptoms that now that the apple-trees are at last in blossom I may relish writing to my friends. Alack, I have not so many to whom I *ever* write, or from whom I am ever written to (I no longer teach the English language) that I need wait so long to write at least a brief scratch. Yet you know one will delay a long time, thinking that by and by he will be *just* in the mood and tense. The truth is I desire to hear from you. Otherwise there are hardly enough apple-trees out to move me, even this May morning. Is it any wonder people talk about the weather? For what is there that plays the deuce with us like that. I confess I am completely under it half the time—and more than half under, the balance. Rejoice, O young woman, in thy Berkeley! Why don't you come on and visit Connecticut? and stop here on the way! It's very pretty now, I assure you. Treacherous, a little, but full of greenery and blossoms. In New England no doubt it is still prettier. In the past week the sky—even in Ohio—has been summer blue. You remember what that is, between big round pearly white clouds? But for six months previously it was a dome of lead, or dirty white. Now and then, of a rare day, the color of a black and blue spot on a boy's knee. Once or twice in a month, when the sun tried to shine, the hue of a very poor skim milk. The gods economizing, no doubt, and taking that mild drink in place of nectar—or slopping it around feeding their cats—or the Skye terriers. If I recollect aright you have midsummer in May, there. Hot forenoons and bootiful fog in the evening? I would like to help you dig your garden. We have now apple, pear, and cherry trees in blossom, yellow currant, white and purple lilacs, flowering cherry: pansies, tulips, lily of the valley, and genuine solid green turf sprinkled with gold buttons of dandelions. The air is full of fragrance. The robins, bluebirds, wrens, and orioles are building wonderful nests all over the place. Three red and black game bantams are parading on the lawn, and seven baby bantams about as big as the end of my thumb are skittering around under the laylocs.

Are you all well, and good as ever? My love to all of both your houses. Don't wait long before writing.

Yours,
E. R. SILL

What the Land Was Like
PROSE ACCOUNTS

Elisha Whittlesey (1783–1863), a lawyer from Connecticut, moved to Canfield in 1807 and was appointed prosecuting attorney for the entire Reserve (1807–23). On leave from that position, he served during the War of 1812 as an officer under General William Henry Harrison. Whittlesey was in Cleveland to observe the first execution in the Western Reserve, that of an Indian named John O'Mic. Colonel Charles Whittlesey's (no relation) *Early History of Cleveland, Ohio* (1867) includes Seth Doan's recollection of the crime to set the stage for Elisha Whittlesey's first-person account. Whittelsey's writing captures the gathering intensity which culminated in O'Mic's death as well as a dramatic summer storm.

Statement of Seth Doan, 1841

"Omic was a fine looking young Indian, about twenty-one, and was hung upon the Public Square in this city, in the north-west corner, near where the old Court House and jail were then being erected. He was convicted of the murder of two trappers, Buel and Gibbs, while they were asleep, the night, near Sandusky city, for their traps and furs. Two other Indians, one older, the other a boy of fifteen were concerned with him, the older being taken near Carrying river, in the Maumee swamp, seized a musket from one part of the party who arrested him, and putting the muzzle under his chin, pulled the trigger with his foot and shot himself dead. The boy was considered as forced into participation by the others and was suffered to escape, and lived to be the ring-leader of two others, in the murder of John Wood and George Bishop, west of Carrying river in 1816, for which they were all executed in Huron county. The family of the murdered John Wood, are now, (1841) resident in this city. The skeleton of Omic is in possession of Dr. Isaac Town, of Hudson, Portage county."

Execution of O'Mic, June 24th, 1812.
BY THE HON. E. WHITTLESEY

I was present at the execution, and as distinctly recollect the facts I shall narrate, as I did the night of the day they occurred. I was not at the trial, but understood that Peter Hitchcock was assigned as counsel for the accused. The custody of the prisoner was assigned to Lorenzo Carter (there being no jail) because he was a man of uncommon energy, and because he had more influence over the Indians than any other man in the west, or at least in Cuyahoga county. Mr. Carter's house was on the high ground near the bank, to the right of the road that descended the hill to the ferry across the river and to the left of the street that leads to where the Light House now stands. The prisoner was confined in a chamber of Mr. Carter's house. Strong irons were above his ancles, with which was connected a staple that was driven into a joist that supported the floor, so that the prisoner could not go to any window. Probably I should have said with more accuracy, that a chain was attached to the fetters, and a staple was attached to the other end, which was driven into the joint, &c. After his conviction, O'Mic told Mr. Carter and Sheriff Baldwin, (who was from Danbury,) that he would let the pale faces see how an Indian could die; that they need not tie his arms, but when the time came he would jump off from the gallows.

Before Mr. Carter's house, in the direction of Superior street, was an open space somewhat extensive, and covered with grass. The religious exercises were held there. Several clergymen were present, and I think the sermon was delivered by the Rev. Mr. Darrow, of Vienna, Trumbull county. The military were commanded by Major Jones, a fine looking officer in full uniform, but he was in the condition that Captain McGuffy, of Coitsville, said he was when he was commanded to perform an evolution by his company and could not do it. His explanation was, "I know Baron Steuben perfectly well, but I cannot commit him to practice."

O'Mic sat on his coffin in a wagon painted for the occasion. He was a fine looking young Indian, and watched everything that occurred with much anxiety. The gallows was erected on the Public Square in front of where the old Court House was erected. After the religious services were over, Major Jones endeavored to form a hollow square, so that the prisoner should be guarded on all sides. He rode backwards and forwards with drawn sword, epaulets, and scabbard flying, but he did not know what order to give. The wagon with O'Mic moved ahead and stopped; but as the Sheriff doubted whether he was to be aided by the military, he proceeded onward. Major Jones finally took the suggestion of some one, who told him to ride to the head of the line, and double it round until the front and rear of the line met. Arriving at the gallows, Mr. Carter, the Sheriff and O'Mic ascended to the platform by a ladder. The arms of the prisoner were loosely pinioned. A rope was around his neck with a loop in the end. Another was let down through a hole in the top piece, on which was a hook to attach to the rope around the neck. The rope with the hook was brought over to one of the posts, and fastened to it near the ground.

After some little time Mr. Carter came down, leaving O'Mic and Sheriff Baldwin on the platform. As the Sheriff drew down the cap, O'Mic was the most terrified being, rational or irrational, I ever saw, and seizing the cap with his right hand, which he could reach by bending his head and inclining his neck in that direction, he stepped to one of the posts and put his arm around it. The Sheriff approached him to loose his hold, and for a moment it was doubtful whether O'Mic would not throw him to the ground. Mr. Carter ascended to the platform and a negotiation in regular diplomatic style was had. It was in the native tongue, as I understood at the time. Mr. Carter appealed to O'Mic to display his courage, narrating what he had said about showing pale faces how an Indian could die, but it had no effect. Finally O'Mic made a proposition, that if Mr. Carter would give him half a pint of whisky he would consent to die. The whisky was soon on hand, in a large glass tumbler, real old Monongahela, for which an old settler would almost be willing to be hung, if he could now obtain the like. The glass was given to O'Mic and he drank the whisky, in as little time as he could have turned it out of the glass. Mr. Carter again came down, and the Sheriff again drew down the cap and the same scene was re-enacted, O'Mic expressing the same terror. Mr. Carter again ascended to the platform, and O'Mic gave him the honor of an Indian, in pledge that he would not longer resist the sentence of the court, if he should have another half pint of whisky. Mr. Carter, representing the people of Ohio and the dignity of the laws, thought the terms were reasonable, and the whisky was forthcoming on short order. The tumbler was not given to O'Mic, but it was held to his mouth, and as he sucked the whisky out, Sheriff Baldwin drew the rope that pinioned his arms more tight, and the rope was drawn down to prevent the prisoner from going to the post, and to prevent him from pulling off his cap. The platform was immediately cleared of all but O'Mic, who run the ends of his fingers on his right hand, between the rope and his neck. The rope that held up one end of the platform was cut, and the body swung in a straight line towards the lake, as far as the rope permitted and returned, and after swinging forth and backward several times, and the weight being about to be suspended perpendicular under the center of the top of the gallows, the body turned in a circle and finally rested still.

At that time a terrific storm appeared and came up from the north north-west with great rapidity, to avoid which, and it being doubtful whether the neck was broken, and to accomplish so necessary part of a hanging, the rope was drawn down with the design of raising the body, so that, by a sudden relaxing of the rope, the body would fall several feet, and thereby dislocate the neck beyond any doubt, but when the body fell, the rope broke as readily as a tow string and fell upon the ground. The coffin and grave were near the gallows and the body was picked up, put into the coffin, and the coffin immediately put into the grave. The storm was heavy and all scampered but O'Mic.

The report was, at the time, that the surgeons at dusk raised the body, and when it lay on the dissecting table, it was easier to restore life than to prevent it.   ELISHA WHITTLESEY

Emma Rood (1837–1916) and Hudson (1836–1911) Tuttle, both born and bred on the Reserve, married in 1857 and settled on a Berlin Heights farm. Together they lectured on spiritualism, gave dramatic readings, and collaborated on and published many books, which he claimed he wrote while in a "semi-trance." "The Legend of Minehonto" is told in their *Stories from Beyond the Borderland*. This is very likely the earliest, if not the sole, nineteenth-century account of the pre-European inhabitants of the Western Reserve.

The Legend of Minehonto

There is a creek in Berlin, Ohio, bearing the not very euphonious name of "Old Woman Creek," with which is connected a thrilling incident of Indian life. This little stream empties into Lake Erie, three miles east of Huron river, and for a few miles resembles a canal more than a stream, as it flows through a broad valley, often marshy, with fields of

corn, and interspersed with wide acres of rush and flag. The stream
suddenly narrows and divides into two branches, one bending to the
west side of the township, and the other passing around the lovely village of Berlin Heights, breaking through the sandstone and shale in a
deep gorge, which is one of the picturesque portions of the vicinity.
Some of these scenes deserve to be copied by a master. Especially is the
view of the Parmenter Bridge, with the bluff, studded with evergreens,
clinging to the grey rocks, and the glimpse of the winding stream below worthy of attention.

Where the two streams unite, flowing parallel for a considerable distance, the valleys are deep, and thus a high ridge is formed, still
clothed with the original forest. This point, or promontory, was, in the
days of Indian supremacy, the site of a large village. Its natural defenses
were unequalled in all this region of country, and when the banks were
still further protected by palisades, and watched by vigilant sentinels,
the place was impregnable against the rude attacks of predatory bands.

The red man was not the first to discover the great natural advan-
tages of the position. The old Mound Builders, that mystic race, whose
origin or fate none can tell, had occupied it, and thrown up stronger
defenses than the Indians could execute. When that ancient race forti-
fied the point, the lake stood at a higher level, and the broad valley was
a shallow bay, into which this ridge projected. Their defenses were designed more for protection against invaders by water than by land, as
fleets of canvas could sail up the bay from the lake. These Mound
Builders understood the art of military engineering, and a mile below
this point, where the stream makes a wide bend, they erected another
fortification. This is on lands owned by Mr. Benschoter, and about half
of the works, overgrown with trees, are still plainly visible. At the foot
of the somewhat steep bank undoubtedly was a wharf, and directly opposite there was another similar fortification, so that between the three
works the bay was guarded and the interior protected from invasion.

The red man was a child in comparison with that old race. He set up
his rude line of palisades, and compensated for his want of skill by his
wariness and cat-like vigilance.

This village, called in their tongue Wabuck or tomorrow, was the
scene of the wild tragedy which gave the river its name it now bears.
To the Indians it was known as Minehonto, and it is to be regretted that
it lost its sweet sounding name.

In 1753, a daring Frenchman by the name of John Flamaron, nobly
born and moving in the most aristocratic circles of Paris, disgusted
with life, came to the new world. From Montreal, then a trading post,
he pushed his course westward. Ascending the St. Lawrence, he
coasted along Lake Ontario, carried his frail bark around Niagara Falls
and by the Rapids, and after several months entered the mouth of the

Huron river, drew his canoe on shore, and resolved to pass the night. Soon afterwards a party of Indians, who had been fishing in the lake, came to him. He understood their language, found them friendly in their intentions, and accepted their invitation to go with them to their village of Wabuck.

Here, having nothing else to do, he remained, hunting and fishing with the Indians, and engaging in their athletic sports. He became a great favorite, especially of the daughter of one of the leading chiefs, Wintasta by name, who was considered far and wide the most beautiful. Flamaron was not insensible to the graces of this forest child, and, had it not been for an untoward accident, he might have been adopted by the tribe, and their mutual love sanctioned by the chief.

Of course, the preference of Wintasta for the white intruder, when it became pronounced, awoke the jealously of other claimants, and they were many. Among them were three brothers, the eldest of whom, Ogontz by name, considered her as rightfully his, by the promise of her father. His rage was like the wild beast, but he cunningly suppressed it, vowing vengeance.

At the time of the great autumn hunt, as a preparation to the yearly feast of thanksgiving to the Great Spirit, a rivalry existed among the hunters as to who should bring in the most game. Flamaron took active part, as was his custom. The sun was low in the West as he bent his weary way homeward with his load of game, for his gun was a better weapon than the bow or arrow with which the Indians were provided, he was startled by the bounding of a fine deer across his path, and instantly elevating his gun, he shot it dead. While reloading his gun Ogontz appeared, coming in the opposite direction. Wrath was in his countenance and gesture.

"Bah, white face," he cried, "you rob me of Wintasta; no rob me of my deer!"

"I have no intention of taking your deer," replied Flamaron; "I did not know you were in pursuit."

"Coward, coward, liar! I don't want the deer; I want you!" He raised his bow, but Flamaron, with the rapid motion of a panther, sighted his rifle and fired.

There was a sharp report, and Ogontz, pierced through the heart, with a look of intense malignant hate on his countenance—expired without a groan.

Flamaron related the plain story to the assembled tribe. The chiefs acquitted him, but the two brothers of Ogontz demanded his blood as the price of their brother. From this there was no appeal of the rude justice of the red man.

Flamaron was bound to a tree, and the oldest of the brothers became his executioner. Wintasta, distracted with grief, tore herself from the arms of her mother and rushed to her lover. She threw herself on his bosom just in time to receive the fatal arrow, which passing onward pierced the hearts of both.

With lamentations the father buried Wintasta and her lover side by side, on the very point of the ridge, and an ash marked their resting place. Probably nothing remains of their earthly bodies; but love and trust like theirs will bloom in immortal verdure on the happy hunting grounds of the great spirit. After all was over, the soil pressed down, and the fire kindled and extinguished over the grave, the mother crept away, down to the bank of the stream, and threw herself therein. Not until the next day was her body recovered.

Not many years after this tragedy the white settlers began to occupy this section of the state, and, hearing the story of the drowning of Wintasta's mother, and not readily pronouncing the Indian name, they called the stream "Old Woman."

All have perished. The red man, the wild beasts, the forest wild, and now the quiet fields, under the taming hand of culture, replace, with dull prose, the poetry of the olden time.

Julia A. J. Foote (1823–1900), born in Schenectady, New York, was the daughter of former slaves who had purchased their freedom. She experienced Christian conversion at age fifteen, and married and moved to Boston at age eighteen where she joined the African Methodist Episcopal Zion Church and later received the call to a preaching career. Refused access to the pulpit in Boston, she held evangelistic meetings in her home and accepted invitations to preach in Philadelphia and New York. Her itinerant evangelism took her throughout New England, the Middle Atlantic states, Canada, Ohio, and, in 1851, Cleveland. This account of a Cleveland African-American community is preserved in *A Brand Plucked from the Fire: An Autobiographical Sketch* (1879).

My Cleveland Home—Later Labors

In June, 1851, we went to Canada, where we were kindly received. We labored in different churches with great success. We found many living Christians there—some holding high the light of full salvation, and others willing to be cleansed. After spending a few weeks there, we crossed to Buffalo, but did not make any stay there at that time.

The places visited during that year are too numerous to mention here. Suffice it to say, the great Head of the Church went before us, clearing the way and giving us unmistakable evidence of his presence in every battle. Hallelujah!

We returned to Columbus to fill an appointment which was awaiting us. After this, we made arrangements to go to Cleveland. One of the brethren engaged our passage and paid the fare, but we were not permitted to leave until four days afterward. At that time a colored person was not allowed to ride in the stage if any white passenger objected to it. There were objections made for three mornings, but, on the fourth, the stage called for us, and we had safe journey to Cleveland. We expected to make a visit only, as in other cities; but the All-Father intended otherwise, and, more than twenty years ago, Cleveland became my home. After settling down, we still continued to visit neighboring cities and labor for Christ.

It was about this time that I became afflicted with the throat difficulty, of which I shall speak later. Beloved, the dear Lord only knows how sorely I was tried and tempted over this affliction.

St. James speaks of temptations as being common to the most holy of men, and also as a matter of joy and rejoicing to such as are exercised thereby, if so be they are not overcome by them [James 1:2–4, 12–15]. I think all temptation has a tendency to sin, but all temptation is not sin. There is a diversity of temptations, and a diversity of causes from which temptations proceed. Some come immediately from our corrupt nature, and are in themselves sinful. Others arise from the infirmity of our nature, and these every Christian has to contend with so long as he sojourns in a tabernacle of clay. There are also temptations which come directly from the enemy of souls. These our blessed Lord severely labored under, and so do the majority of his children. "Blessed is the man that endureth temptation"!

During the years that I rested from my labors and tried to recover my health, God permitted me to pass through the furnace of trial, heated seven times hotter than usual. Had not the three-one God been with me, I surely must have gone beneath the waves. God permits afflictions and persecutions to come upon his chosen people to answer various ends. Sometimes for the trial of their faith, and the exercise of their patience and resignation to his will, and sometimes to draw them off from all human dependence, and to teach them to trust in Him alone. Sometimes he suffers the wicked to go a great way, and the ungodly to triumph over us, that he may prove our steadfastness and make manifest his power in upholding us. Thus it was with me. I had trusted too much in human wisdom, and God suffered all these things to come upon me. He upheld me by his grace, freeing me from all care or concern about my health or what man could do. He taught me to sit patiently, and wait to hear my Shepherd's voice; for I was resolved to follow no stranger, however plausibly he might plead.

I shall praise God through all eternity for sending me to Cleveland, even though I have been called to suffer.

In 1856, Sister Johnson, who had been my companion during all these years of travel, left me for her heavenly home. She bore her short illness without a murmur, resting on Jesus. As she had lived, so she died, in the full assurance of faith, happy and collected to the last, maintaining her standing in the way of holiness without swerving either to the right or the left. Glory to the blood that keeps us!

My now sainted mother, who was then in feeble health, lived with me in Cleveland for a few years. As the time for her departure drew near, she very much desired to visit her two daughters—one in Albany, the other in Boston. I feared she was not able to endure the journey, but her desire was so strong, and her confidence in God so great that he would spare her to see her girls again, that I finally consented that she should undertake the journey. I put her in charge of friends who were going east, and she reached my sister's house in safety. She had been with them but a few weeks, when she bade them a long farewell and passed peacefully to heaven. I shall see her again where parting is unknown.

The glorious wave of holiness, which has been rolling through Ohio during the past few years, has swept every hindrance out of my way, and sent me to sea once more with chart and compass.

> "The Bible is my chart; it is a chart and compass too,
> Whose needle points forever true."

When I drop anchor again, it will be in heaven's broad bay.

Glory to Jesus for putting into my hand that precious, living light, *"The Christian Harvester."* May it and its self-sacrificing editor live many years, reflecting holy light as they go.

If any one arise from the perusal of this book, scoffing at the word of truth which he has read, I charge him to prepare to answer for the profanation at the peril of his soul.

Joseph A. Joel (d. 1906) emigrated to this country from England when he was a boy. At the outbreak of the Civil War he enlisted in the 23rd Ohio Regiment with his companions William McKinley and Rutherford B. Hayes. In an article published in the *Jewish Messenger,* March 30, 1866, Joel recounted how Jewish soldiers commemorated the Seder in the wilds of West Virginia in 1862.

Passover in Camp
A REMINISCENCE OF THE WAR

The approaching feast of Passover, reminds me of an incident which, transpired in 1862, and which as an index of the times, no doubt, will prove interesting to a number of your readers. In the commencement of the war of 1861, I enlisted from Cleveland, Ohio, in the Union cause to sustain intact the Government of the United States, and became attached to the 23rd Regiment, one of the first sent from the "Buckeye State." Our destination was West Virginia—a portion of the wildest and most mountainous region of that State, well adapted for the guerrillas who infested that part, and caused such trouble to our pickets all through the war. After an arduous march of several hundred miles through Clarksburgh, Weston, Sommerville, and several other places of less note, which have become famous during the war, we encountered on the 10th of September, 1861, at Carnifax Ferry, the forces under the rebel Gen. Floyd. After this, we were ordered to take up our position at the foot of Sewell Mountain, and we remained there until we marched to the village of Fayette, to take it, and to establish there our Winter-quarters, having again routed Gen. Floyd and his forces. While lying there, our camp duties were not of an arduous character, and being apprised of the approaching Feast of Passover, twenty of my comrades and co-religionists belonging to the Regiment, united in a request to our commanding officer for relief from duty, in order that we might keep the holydays, which he readily acceded to. The first point was gained, and, as the Paymaster had lately visited the Regiment, he had left us plenty of greenbacks. Our next business was to find some suitable person to proceed to Cincinnati, Ohio, to buy us *Matzos*.[1] Our sutler being a co-religionist, and going home to that city, readily undertook to send them. We were anxiously awaiting to receive our מַצּוֹת[2] and about the middle of the morning of עֶרֶב פֶּסַח[3] a supply train arrived in camp, and to our delight seven barrels of *Matzos*. On opening them, we were surprised and pleased to find that our thoughtful sutler had enclosed two Hagodahs[4] and prayer-books. We were now able to keep the סֵדֶר[5] nights, if we could only obtain the other requisites for that occasion. We had a consultation and decided to send parties to forage in the country while a party stayed to build a log hut for the services. About the middle of the afternoon the foragers arrived, having been quite successful. We obtained two kegs of cider, a lamb, several chickens and some eggs. Horse-radish or parsley we could not obtain, but in lieu we found a weed, whose bitterness, I apprehend, exceeded anything our forefathers "enjoyed." We were still in a great quandary; we were like the man who drew the elephant in the lottery. We had the lamb, but did not know what part was to represent it at the table; but Yankee ingenuity prevailed, and it was decided to cook the whole and put it on the table, then we could dine off it, and be sure we had the right part. The necessaries for the *choroutzes*[6] we

1. Unleavened bread eaten during Passover.
2. *Mazzot,* or matzos.
3. *Ereb Pesah,* the day before Passover.
4. The ritual for the seder on the eve of Passover.
5. *Seder,* the home service on the first two nights of Passover.
6. *Haroset,* imitation clay made from a mixture of ground almonds, apples, and wine, symbolic of the mortar that Israelites in Egypt used in making bricks for the pharoah.

could not obtain, so we got a brick which, rather hard to digest, reminded us, by looking at it, for what purpose it was intended.

At dark we had all prepared, and were ready to commence the service. There being no *Chasan*[7] present, I was selected to read the services, which I commenced by asking the blessing of the Almighty on the food before us, and to preserve our lives from danger. The ceremonies were passing off very nicely, until we arrived at the part where the bitter herb was to be taken. We all had a large portion of the herb ready to eat at the moment I said the blessing; each eat his portion, when horrors! what a scene ensued in our little congregation, it is impossible for my pen to describe. The herb was very bitter and very fiery like Cayenne pepper, and excited our thirst to such a degree, that we forgot the law authorizing us to drink only four cups, and the consequence was we drank up all the cider. Those that drank the more freely became excited, and one thought he was Moses, another Aaron, and one had the audacity to call himself a Pharaoh. The consequence was a skirmish, with nobody hurt, only Moses, Aaron, and Pharaoh, had to be carried to the camp, and there left in the arms of Morpheus. This slight incident did not take away our appetite, and, after doing justice to our lamb, chickens and eggs, we resumed the second portion of the service without anything occurring worthy of note.

There, in the wild woods of West Virginia, away from home and friends, we consecrated and offered up to the ever-loving God of Israel our prayers and sacrifice. I doubt whether the spirits of our forefathers, had they been looking down on us, standing there with our arms by our side ready for an attack, faithful to our God and our cause, would have imagined themselves amongst mortals, enacting this commemoration of the scene that transpired in Egypt.

Since then a number of my comrades have fallen in battle in defending the flag, they volunteered to protect with their lives. I have myself received a number of wounds all but mortal, but there is no occasion in my life that gives me more pleasure and satisfaction then when I remember the celebration of Passover of 1862.

J. A. JOEL

7. *Hazzan,* cantor or reader of the service.

Salmon Brown (1836–1919) was one of John Brown's twenty children. He worked for abolition with his father in the Kansas Territory, but he was not with him at Harpers Ferry. Aged and infirm, and the last surviving son of John Brown, Salmon, in a reminiscent mood, spoke of the adolescence of his father and of his own childhood spent absorbing the values of a pioneer Western Reserve society. His daughter, Agnes Brown-Evans, who cared for Brown in his old age, recorded

his comments and compiled them for publication. The reminiscence was first published in the *The Outlook* on January 25, 1913.

My Father, John Brown
BY SALMON BROWN,
THE ONLY SURVIVOR OF TWENTY CHILDREN

Perhaps the most striking characteristic of my father, as his children
knew him, was his faith in God, his faith in his family, and his sense of
equity. For whatever else may be said of John Brown, he was true to his
God as he knew his duty, he was strongly devoted to the interests of his
family, and he never wronged a man where the interests of justice—as
he saw the situation—did not demand it of him. He was stern when
need be, but sympathetic and just always.

My memory goes back to the days long before the war, when slavery was not considered such a National sin as it was about the time
Lincoln came on the scene. My early recollections of my father have to
do with his hatred of slavery, his hatred for everything that would take
from one man a single right and give to his fellow even a petty advantage. He was just in his conception of the rights of men, and could
never understand why others were determined to reap where they had
not sown, to profit unjustly by the efforts of others.

My early recollections go back clearly to the old home at Hudson,
Ohio, where I was born, October 2, 1836. Our home was an old-
fashioned house, with a great rock nearly covering half an acre of land
and nearly as high as the house. A spring bubbled out of the side of
the rock, forming a basin and then running off in a "creek," as we
called it. I have clear recollections of being chased by Aunt Martha
and my sister Ruth all over the big rock in an effort to make me eat
butter on my bread. Like my father, I have always disliked butter; why,
I do not know.

In a large living-room was a fireplace ten feet long, with huge and-
irons and a crane and hooks to hang kettles upon. We boys would cut
logs two and three feet through for the fireplace, and at night, in winter, two great back-logs were covered with ashes to hold fire. Father
would sit in front of a lively fire and take up us children one, two, or
three at a time, and sing until bedtime. We all loved to hear him sing
as well as to talk of the conditions in the country, over which he
seemed worried. A favorite song with father and us children was
"Blow Ye the Trumpet, Blow."

We lived in an old whitewashed log house at Richfield, Ohio, with
a mill-pond and creek dam, with mud-turtles, which we boys would
fatten and eat. The turtles would jerk for twenty-four hours after being
cooked, it seemed to us. At Richfield three children died—three in less

than three weeks—a calamity from which father never fully recovered. Two years later another, a year old, was burned to death. Of the three that died at Richfield, Charles was very swift and strong, his legs and arms straight as broomsticks, of sandy complexion, quiet as a cat, but brave as a tiger. Peter was very stout, darker, the best-looking member of the family.

Father had fine Saxony sheep at Richfield. Later in his career, at Akron, while running sheep with Simon Perkins, he took first prize at the first World's Fair ever held (at London, England) in competition with all countries, exhibiting one hundred fleeces of Saxony lambs.

Father was a strict observer of the Sabbath. Sunday evenings he would gather the family and hired help together, and have the Ten Commandments and the Catechism repeated. Sometimes he would preach a regular sermon to us. Besides we had prayers morning and night of every day, with Bible reading, all standing during prayer, father himself leaning on a chair upreared on the forward legs, the old-fashioned Presbyterian way. He was greatly concerned over the spiritual welfare of us boys, whose beliefs were more or less reactionary. He constantly expostulated when with us, and in letters when away. His expressed hope was "that ye sin not, that you form no foolish attachments, that you be not a companion of fools."

Father had great confidence in us children. He never said "Don't tell," but simply trusted to our not telling. Before a child of seven or eight he would calmly discuss plans he would not have breathed before older persons.

Father was five feet ten inches in height, slightly stoop-shouldered after middle life, with eyes sky blue, hair dark brown till tinged with gray, nose hawked and thin, skin florid, spare but muscular in build. His form and features attracted the attention of strangers quickly. He always dressed in snuff-colored broadcloth for good clothes, and was always neat. He wore boots, as was the custom of those days, and wore white shirts with a plait on each side of the bosom. Usually he walked with his hands clasped behind him, often with his eyes on the ground, as if in deep thought. So far as I know he was never sick a day, and never missed a meal on account of his own illness. This was also true of his father.

Blood has always been thick in the Brown family. Family ties were firm, and the tendency has been strong to "stick together." I first noticed this family trait in my father's case when he would go to grandfather's bed—after he became old—and tuck the covers about him as a mother would do with her children.

Our old home was a model of orderliness, and quiet always prevailed when father was about. The meals were served leisurely, but with due order and silence. The long table where twelve children, the largest number ever living at any time (1843), sat down with keen appetites was a model of the time.

A favorite dish with us children was corn-meal mush cooked the whole afternoon long in a huge iron caldron, and served with rich milk or cream. It left a crust a half-inch thick in the caldron, and tasted, so I affirm to this day, like no other mush ever made. The table was always neatly set, never without a white tablecloth; the food was coarse, hearty farmers' food, always in abundance, and always well served. Frugality was observed from a moral standpoint; but, one and all, we were a well-fed, well-clad lot. Considerable hardship was entailed when father left to engage in the Kansas warfare; but real poverty never obtruded itself till his death.

There were no drones in the Brown hive. Little toddlers unable to help were at least not allowed to hinder; as soon as they had achieved a show of stable control of their uncertain little legs the world of work opened to them. There was no pampering, little petting. The boys could turn a steak or brown a loaf as well as their mother.

Despite his relentless sternness, and underlying it, cropping through in his later years, when paternalism of necessity gave way to comradeship, there ran in John Brown's nature a strain of intense tenderness. Suffering in himself he bore without a murmur; but every fiber of his being was wrung by the suffering of others. It brought out the woman in him, the John Brown little known to history, who sat around the great open fireplace at night with his children in his arms and sang them to sleep; who rose on the coldest night and paced the floor with a collicky child, while his wife, worn by child-bearing and child-rearing, lay in bed asleep; and who was ever the nurse in sickness, watchful, tireless, tender, allowing no one to lift the burden of the night watch from him. During a protracted illness of my mother he hovered over her night and day, sleeping for a fortnight only at intervals in his chair, unrelieved of his clothes, afraid to go to bed lest he oversleep.

His kindness toward dumb animals was proverbial. He was like the Israelite of old, sheltering the ninety-and-nine, but refusing shelter for himself till the straying hundredth was safely folded. A chilled and dying lamb was a spectacle upon which he would spend his energies till it either died or stood solidly upon its crooked legs. Even the Monday's wash, soaking in the tubs, was once put aside in order to thaw in the warm, soapy water the numbing death chill from a little straggler's bones.

Family worship was as inexorably a matter of habit as eating or sleeping. The burden of father's soul was the souls of his children, and he strove with them without ceasing. The day's work was ushered in and out with Scripture and prayer. Provided each with a Bible, we read in rotation, father leading with several verses from the large family Bible; mother following with several more from an old Bible bound in sheepskin which father himself had tanned; then on through the long line of children. During prayers all stood, father leaning against the back of a chair upreared on its forward legs, dead to the world and to the pranks of his unregenerate boys, who slyly prodded each other with pins and trampled upon each other's toes to relieve the tension. The week was opened by a Sunday service.

Our long trip from New York to Kansas brought many unusual experiences to the large family. Father outfitted well for the trip, which was beset with unforeseen hardships. But no one questioned the wisdom of the undertaking or feared the result.

At Brunswick, Missouri, we crossed the Missouri River. Near Independence was a slave pen, built like a chicken coop, only stronger and higher. Inside the pen was the auction block. This slave-selling stirred father to the depths of his soul. As he waited for the ferry he saw slaves handcuffed for the journey down the river to New Orleans. Cholera at that time was fearfully epidemic, people dying by hundreds on the boats. Jason's boy, four years old, contracted the disease and died there. The following spring father had the child's body removed to Kansas, thinking Jason would feel better to have the boy's body off Missouri soil.

On the first trip to Kansas father traded dogs with an old Quaker. The Quaker's dog was a ratter, which father wanted as a watch-dog. The trade was made on Sunday, but father would not exchange dogs till Monday.

One day an old Missourian came up to our wagon. "Whar you going?" he asked.

"To Osawatomie."

"Whar you from?"

"New York."

"You'll never live to get thar," informed the Missourian.

"We are prepared not to die alone," answered father quietly, and the man slouched off.

Father was a man of intense earnestness in all things that interested him. Events which changed the course of his life occurred unexpectedly and even strangely. While he was living in Pennsylvania it was the custom for every farmer to have a barrel of whisky in the house. It was also the custom to have "bees" and barn-raisings. A tavern-keeper was to have a barn-raising, and father was to be there. The tavern-keeper needed more liquor and sent to Meadville by father, then scarcely in middle life, for a three-gallon jug. The liquor cost twenty-five cents a gallon. On the road from Meadville father became thirsty and began taking "nips" from the jug. He was accustomed to drinking from his own barrel, and did not think the practice wrong. On the way to the barn-raising father realized that liquor was getting hold of him, and he became alarmed. He afterward spoke of the occurrence frequently. He reasoned that if liquor would lead him to drink from another man's jug it was surely gaining control over him—a thing he could not allow. Coming to a large rock by the roadway, he smashed the jug upon it, vowing that he would not be responsible for his neighbor's drinking at the barn-raising, where accidents might happen. He paid for the liquor, and when he reached home rolled his whisky barrel into the back yard and smashed it to pieces with an ax. No liquor was allowed about the house afterwards.

Father was strongly fixed in most of his habits. He worked with the same earnestness year after year; he ate regularly, and went to bed and arose at the same hours, whenever it was possible. It was always difficult for him to fit himself to circumstances; he wanted conditions to change for him—and he usually brought about the things he most desired. His persistence was as strongly developed as was his firmness. With it all the large family of boys usually held firmly to the idea that father was right; that his foresight was unusual.

Until the Harper's Ferry "trip" was planned father had never found reaction in the spirits of his boys. Wherever he had led we were glad to follow—and every one of us had the courage of his convictions. Whatever else may be said of the Brown family, I feel that no one will charge us with lacking in bravery at the time when the shadows lowered and there was that dreadful feeling that a great mistake had been made. When death—and the gallows—enters a family it is a time that tries men's souls.

It may have been fear that led me to revolt against the proposed trip to Virginia, which father urged us boys to join him in. I thought the matter over and concluded that I would not go, that for the first time I could not go side by side with father. He urged and reasoned, and regretted my determination to stay at home, perhaps as he had never regretted the act of any of his children. But I felt that the trip was a mistake, that it was not the wise thing to do, and stayed at home. The slaughter at Harper's Ferry showed me clearly that father had miscalculated somewhere; I had no fears of death as the result of the effort against slavery. We never learned just how father accounted for his being trapped as he was.

Father never did anything that he thought was not worth doing well. As a boy he learned the lessons of thoroughness from his father, a tanner who lived in Ohio. Before father was fifteen years of age he learned something of tanning skins and determined to learn the trade of a tanner. He had not told his father of his intentions, but one day a currying-knife would not take an edge until father put it on the stone.

In trying the knife father began graining a skin, and it was discovered that he had mastered much of the detail of the trade. Soon afterwards he was charged with a large part of the management of the tannery.

At eighteen the religious nature of father had developed until he determined to go to a New England college and study for the ministry. After a period of hard study he gave up the effort on account of inflammation of the eyes which had fastened itself upon him. At twenty he married and removed to Pennsylvania, where he took up wild land and built a tannery near Meadville. The land was covered with a heavy growth of hemlock, maple, and beech, and the task of clearing it was heartbreaking. The tannery was built of stone, and remains to this day. A great tan-bark yard—several acres of refuse—was soon developed, and here the first children had their playground. Every influence of the surroundings was rugged at least.

While father operated the tannery successfully and engaged in the sheep business with profit, his spirit was constantly struggling with the problems of the National life. He established at Springfield, Massachusetts, the first wool commission house in the United States, and operated it at a profit to himself and to wool-growers. When the Fugitive Slave Law was passed, he quickly made his warehouse a "station" on the "underground railway," sacrificing business and profit to principle. His blooded sheep industry was also sacrificed on the altar of freedom for the black man. Father may have been a fanatic, but he had some intensely practical and homely ideas which were lost sight of when his acts tended to throw the Nation into sectional strife and warfare. The country saw him as a reckless adventurer; his family knew him as a just and generous man.

Following the dark days at Harper's Ferry, the suffering of mother and the family was intense. Despised bitterly by all who sympathized with slavery and considered as the victims of a righteous wrath by many of the North, our family was long buffeted from pillar to post. Efforts to forget were fruitless. The passing years did not heal the horrible wounds made by the country father had tried so hard to help to a plane of higher living.

With nearly all my brothers and sisters gone to their reward, many of them before the Nation realized the importance of father's work, with more than half a century intervening since the tragedy at Harper's Ferry, during which time public judgment has calmed and changed materially, I feel that no apology is needed on behalf of John Brown, husband and father kind and true, however much some may still doubt the saneness of his work for the abolition of that horrible National curse, slavery.

Fiction

Albert Gallatin Riddle (1816–1902) was brought as an infant from Massachusetts to Newbury. He attended Western Reserve College and became a lawyer and prosecuting attorney in Chardon and then in Cleveland. In 1861 he was elected to Congress for one term, representing Cuyahoga, Lake, and Geauga counties. After moving to Washington, D.C., his literary interests gradually surpassed his legal activities and in 1873 completely absorbed him with the publication of his autobiographical novel *Bart Ridgeley: A Story of Northern Ohio.* Riddle's fiction was based on his Western Reserve background. "The Great Preacher," a chapter from *The Portrait* (1874), recounts the visit to Aurora of Alexander Campbell, an important ecumenical religious reformer.

The Great Preacher

An event of the season was the visit of Alexander Campbell to Northern Ohio, to counsel, comfort, consolidate, and confirm the churches upon the Reserve. Not wholly had they recovered from the secession of Rigdon; and, although the strong-headed Ryder soon recovered from his momentary tripping, the churches had languished, and minor differences in dogma had sprung up,—notably in reference to the many-sided and eminently practical doctrines of the true nature and office of the Holy Spirit. Mr. Campbell had never been upon the Reserve, although his venerable father had ministered much in that field. He had formed the purpose of this mission two years before, and his coming had long been anxiously looked and longed for among the disciples. Not only among them did the announcement of his coming produce a sensation. He was the most distinguished and formidable controversialist of his time.

He had already won the gratitude of Christians by the battle royal which he had fought for the general cause of inspired Christianity, with the powers of the common adversary, led by that amiable and wrong-headed philanthropist Robert Owen; he was the champion of Protestantism against the scarlet-robed woman of doubtful reputation; and, later still, he had laid lance in rest for the comforting dogma of endless

perdition. So that, Coeur de Lion as he was, of schism, in the Baptist
Church, and general heresy against creed and man-usage, the granite
basis of his theology retained the genuine imprint of the most essential
Calvinistic dogma.

Late in June, after the second corn hoeing, when the meadow grass
was maturing over the ripened strawberries, and ere the turning of the
grain, long after the calves had been weaned, and the sheep sheared,
whose fleeces in soft, white rolls were running into threads through the
rosy-tipped fingers of spinning-girls, and a lull had fallen upon the se-
verer work of the farmer, the greater preacher came.

It had rained the night before; and that Sunday morning was one of
marvellous fragrance and freshness, when Deacon Carman, mounted
on his favorite bay mare, Kate, and accompanied by Fred, on the snip-
nosed chestnut colt, rode out to the great meeting in the woods, near
the centre of Aurora. It was to be a primitive gathering, in a grand old
beech and maple forest, of all the faithful, of the inquiring and curious,
of the adjacent parts of Portage, Geauga, and Cuyahoga Counties, then
as populous as now. To and across the State road, west, and then
south-westerly, the ride was nearly ten miles to the point of meeting.
They started alone, passed footmen and heavy wagons, and joined
other horsemen, till, as they neared the place, they were lost in a general procession, that broke up and gathered about the stand. The
woods were full of horses and carriages, and the hundreds already there
were rapidly swelled to many thousands; all of one race,—the Yankee;
all of one calling, or nearly,—the farmer; hardy, shrewd, sunburned,
cool, thoughtful, and intelligent. The disciples were, from the first,
emancipated from the Puritan slavery of the Sabbath; and, although
grave, thoughtful, and serious, as they were on this Sunday morning,
it was from the gravity and seriousness of the occasion, and little from
the day itself,—an assemblage that Paul would have been glad to
preach to.

At the hour of eleven, Mr. Campbell and his party took their places
on the stand; and after a short, simple, preliminary service, conducted
by another, he came forward to the front. He was then about forty
years old, above the average height, of singular dignity of form, and
simple grace of manner. His was a splendid head, borne well back,
with a bold, strong forehead, from which his fine hair was turned back;
a strong, full, expressive eye, aquiline nose, fine mouth, and prominent
chin. He was a perfect master of himself, a perfect master of his theme,
and, from the moment he stood in its presence, a perfect master of his
immense audience.

At a glance he took the measure and level of the average mind before
him—a Scotchman's estimate of the Yankee—and began at that level;
and as he rose from it, he took the assembled host with him. In nothing

was he like Rigdon; calm, clear, strong, logical, yet perfectly simple. Men felt themselves lifted and carried, and wondered at the ease and apparent want of effort with which it was done.

Nothing could be more transparent than his statement of his subject; nothing franker than his admissions of its difficulties; nothing more direct than his enumeration of the means he must employ, and the conclusions he must reach. With great intellectual resources, and great acquisitions, athlete and gladiator as he was, he was a logician by instinct and habit of mind, and took a pleasure in magnifying, to their utmost, the difficulties of his positions, so that when the latter were finally maintained, the mind was satisfied with the result. His language was copious, his style nervous, and the characteristic of his mind was direct, manly, sustained vigor; and under its play he evolved a warmth which kindled to the fervor of sustained eloquence, and which, in the judgment of many, is the only true eloquence. After nearly two hours, his natural and logical conclusion was the old pentecostal mandate of Simon Peter, and a strong, earnest, manly and tender call of men to obedience. There was no appeal to passion, no effort at pathos, no figures or rhetoric, but a warm, kindling, heated, glowing, manly argument, silencing the will, captivating the judgment, and satisfying the reason; and the cold, shrewd, thinking, calculating Yankee liked it.

As the preacher closed, and stood for a response, no answering movement came from any part of the crowd. Men were running it over, and thinking. Unhesitatingly the orator stepped down from the platform, upon the ground, and moving forward in the little open space, began in a more fervid and impassioned strain. He caught the mind at the highest point of its attainment, and grasping it, shook it with a half indignation at its calculating hesitation, and carrying it with a mighty sweep to a still higher level, seemed to pour around it a diviner and more radiant light; then, with a little tremor in his voice, he implored it to hesitate no longer. When he closed, low murmurs broke and ran through the awed crowd; men and women from all parts of the vast assemblage, with streaming eyes, came forward; young men, who had climbed into the small trees from curiosity, came down from conviction, and went forward to baptism; and the brothers and sisters set up a glad hymn, sang with tremulous voices, clasping hands, amid happy tears.

Thus, in that far-off time, in the maple woods, under the June sun, the gospel was preached and received.

Fred, who had tied the horses in the woods, and placed the saddles between the spreading roots of an old elm, near the stand, in such a way as to form a convenient and elevated seat, sat or stood upon them, and never took his eyes from the face of the speaker during the delivery of his masterly oration. Much of it was within the easy grasp of his comprehension; as a whole, it was beyond it, and the labor was too sustained for his boyish mind to follow. Nevertheless, the impression upon his imagination was very great, and the wish of standing in the midst of an immense concourse, as on the present occasion, its centre and dominant soul and mind, and of pouring out upon it an oversweeping tide of irresistible speech, argument, logic and metaphor, and of seeing men move and bow before it, as now he saw men about him, took, for the time, complete mastery of him, and gave rise to dreams that ever after haunted him. After the service, he went with Mr. Carman to the house of one of the disciples, where they had dinner, and rode home in the cool of the sweet June night.

Charles Farrar Browne (1834–67) was a twenty-three-year-old New Englander when in 1857 he took a job on the news desk of the *Cleveland Plain Dealer*. A bon vivant and natural raconteur, he presented the city news in whimsical terms, employing a burlesque manner when writing of public affairs that ranged from prize fights and races to spiritual meetings and public gatherings. Adopting the pseudonym "Artemus Ward" in 1858, he introduced Cleveland to his imaginary "Show bizness," sardonic observations conveyed by the calculated misspellings of bumpkin persona. In 1860 he left the *Plain Dealer* to join the staff of *Vanity Fair*, where he gained an international reputation. Browne died of tuberculosis at age thirty-two. His publications are collected in four volumes of *The Complete Works of Artemus Ward*. Like many nineteenth-century humorists (Mark Twain, perhaps the most familiar), Ward cultivated dialect stories as a sure bet for audience laughter.

Oberlin

About two years ago, I arrove in Oberlin, Ohio. Oberlin is whare the celebrated college is. In fack, Oberlin *is* the college, everything else in that air vicinity resolvin around excloosivly for the benefit of that institution. It is a very good college, too, & a grate many wurthy yung men go there annooally to git intelleck into 'em. But its my onbiassed 'pinion that they go it rather too strong on Ethiopians at Oberlin. But that's nun of my bizness. I'm into the Show bizniss. Yit as a faithful historan I must menshun the fack that on rainy dase white people can't find their way threw the streets without the gas is lit, there bein such a numerosity of cullerd pussons in the town.

As I was sayin, I arroved at Oberlin, and called on Perfesser Peck for the purpuss of skewerin Kolonial Hall to exhibit my wax works and beests of Pray into. Kolonial Hall is in the college and is used by the stujents to speak peaces and read essays into.

Sez Perfesser Peck, "Mister Ward, I don't know 'bout this bizniss. What are your sentiments?"

Sez I, "I hain't got any."

"Good God!" cried the Perfesser, "did I understan you to say you hav no sentiments?"

"Nary a sentiment!" sez I.

"Mister Ward, don't your blud bile at the thawt that three million and a half of your culled brethren air a clankin their chains in the South?"

Sez I, "not a bile! Let 'em clank!"

He was about to continner his flowry speech when I put a stopper on him. Sez I, "Perfesser Peck, A. Ward is my name & Ameriky is my nashun; I'm allers the same, tho' humble is my station, and I've bin in the show bizniss goin on 22 years. The pint is, can I hav your Hall by payin a fair price? You air full of sentiments. That's your lay, while I'm a exhibiter of startlin curiosities. What d'ye say?"

"Mister Ward, you air endowed with a hily practical mind, and while I deeply regret that you air devoid of sentiments I'll let you have the hall provided your exhibition is of a moral & elevatin nater."

Sez I, "Tain't nothin shorter."

So I opened in Kolonial Hall, which was crowded every nite with stujents, &c. Perfesser Finny gazed for hours at my Kangaroo, but when that sagashus but onprincipled little cuss set up one of his onarthly yellins and I proceeded to hosswhip him, the Perfesser objected. "Suffer not your angry pashuns to rise up at the poor annimil's little excentrissities," said the Perfesser.

"Do you call such conduck as *those* a little excentrissity?" I axed.

"I do," sed he; sayin which he walked up to the cage and sez he, "let's try moral swashun upon the poor creeter." So he put his hand upon the Kangeroo's hed and sed, "poor little feller—poor little feller—your master is very crooil, isn't he, my untootered frend," when the Kangaroo, with a terrific yell, grabd the Perfesser by the hand and cum very near chawin it orf. It was amoozin to see the Perfesser jump up and scream with pane. Sez I, "that's one of the poor little feller's excentrissities!"

Sez he, "Mister Ward, that's a dangerous quadruped. He's totally depraved. I will retire and do my lasserated hand up in a rag, and meanwhile I request you to meat out summery and severe punishment to the vishus beest." I hosswhipt the little cuss for upwards 15 minutes. Guess I licked sum of his excentrissity out of him.

Oberlin is a grate plase. The College opens with a prayer and then the New York Tribune is read. A kolleckshun is then taken up to buy overkoats with red horn buttons onto them for the indignant cullered people of Kanady. I have to contribit librally two the glowrius work, as they kawl it hear. I'm kompelled by the Fackulty to reserve front seets in my show for the cullered peple. At the Boardin House the cullered peple sit at the first table. What they leeve is maid into hash for the white peple. As I don't like the idee of eatin my vittles with Ethiopians, I sit at the seckind table, and the konsequence is I've devowered so much hash that my inards is in a hily mixt up condishun. Fish bones have maid their appearance all over my boddy and pertater peelins air a springin up through my hair. Howsever I don't mind it. I'm gittin along well in a pecunery pint of view. The College has konfired upon me the honery title of T. K., of which I'm suffishuntly prowd.

William Dean Howells (1837–1920), son of an Ohio frontier journalist, grew up in Hamilton. At age twelve his formal education ended; his work in his father's print shop had the most significant impact on his future career. "The printing office was mainly my school," said Howells. Dubbed "Dean of American Letters" by his contemporaries, Howells was the dominant figure in American letters from 1890 to 1920; he was one of the United States' most productive and versatile writers of short stories, poetry, novels, drama, travelogues, criticism, and personal reminiscences. A realist, he portrayed familiar life and relied on personal memory and reflection, as in *The Coast of Bohemia* (1893), a recollection of an Ohio county fair. The "Pymantoning" of this selection is obviously derived from Pymatuning Lake on the Pennsylvania border of Ashtabula County, where Howells lived from age fifteen.

The Coast of Bohemia.

I.

The forty-sixth annual fair of the Pymantoning County Agricultural Society was in its second day. The trotting-matches had begun, and the vast majority of the visitors had abandoned the other features of the exhibition for this supreme attraction. They clustered four or five deep along the half-mile of railing that enclosed the track, and sat sweltering in the hot September sun, on the benching of the grand-stand that flanked a stretch of the course. Boys selling lemonade and peanuts, and other boys with the score of the races, made their way up and down the seats with shrill cries; now and then there was a shriek of girls' laughter from a group of young people calling to some other group, or struggling for a programme caught back and forth; the young fellows shouted to each other jokes that were lost in mid-air; but, for the most part, the crowd was a very silent one, grimly intent upon the rival sulkies as they flashed by and lost themselves in the clouds that thickened over the distances of the long, dusty loop. Here and there some one gave a shout as a horse broke, or settled down to his work under the gutteral snarl of his driver; at times the whole throng burst into impartial applause as a horse gained or lost a length; but the quick throb of the hoofs on the velvety earth and the whir of the flying wheels were the sounds that chiefly made themselves heard.

The spectacle had the importance which multitude gives, and Ludlow found in it the effects which he hoped to get again in his impression. He saw the deep purples which he looked to see with eyes trained by the French masters of his school to find them, and the indigo blues, the intense greens, the rainbow oranges and scarlets; and he knew just how he should give them. In the light of that vast afternoon sky, cloudless, crystalline in its clearness, no brilliancy of rendering could be too bold.

If he had the courage of his convictions, this purely American event could be reported on his canvas with all its native character; and yet it could be made to appeal to the enlightened eye with the charm of a French subject, and impressionism could be fully justified of its follower in Pymantoning as well as in Paris. That golden dust along the track; the level tops of the buggies drawn up within its ellipse, and the groups scattered about in gypsy gayety on the grass there; the dark blur of men behind the barrier; the women, with their bright hats and parasols, massed flower-like,—all made him long to express them in lines and dots and breadths of pure color. He had caught the vital effect of the whole, and he meant to interpret it so that its truth should be felt by all who had received the light of the new faith in painting, who believed in the prismatic colors as in the ten commandments, and who hoped to be saved by tone-contrasts. For the others, Ludlow was at that day too fanatical an impressionist to care. He owed a duty to France no less than to America, and he wished to fulfill it in a picture which should at once testify to the excellence of the French method and the American material. At twenty-two, one is often much more secure and final in one's conclusions than one is afterwards.

He was vexed that a lingering doubt of the subject had kept him from bringing a canvas with him at once, and recording his precious first glimpses of it. But he meant to come to the trotting-match the next day again, and then he hoped to get back to his primal impression of the scene, now so vivid in his mind. He made his way down the benches, and out of the enclosure of the track. He drew a deep breath, full of the sweet smell of the bruised grass, forsaken now by nearly all the feet that had trodden it. A few old farmers, who had failed to get places along the railing and had not cared to pay for seats on the stand, were loitering about, followed by their baffled and disappointed wives. The men occasionally stopped at the cattle-pens, but it was less to look at the bulls and boars and rams which had taken the premiums, and wore cards or ribbons certifying the fact, than to escape a consciousness of their partners, harassingly taciturn or voluble in their reproach. A number of these embittered women brokenly fringed the piazza of the fair-house, and Ludlow made his way toward them with due sympathy for their poor little tragedy, so intelligible to him through the memories of his own country-bred youth. He followed with his pity those who sulked away through the deserted aisles of the building, and nursed their grievance among the prize fruits and vegetables, and the fruits and vegetables that had not taken the prizes. They were more censorious than they would have been perhaps if they had not been defeated themselves; he heard them dispute the wisdom of most of the awards as the shoutings and clappings from the race-track penetrated the lonely hall. They creaked wearily up and down in their new shoes or best shoes, and he knew how they wished themselves at home and in bed, and wondered why they had ever been such fools as to come, anyway. Occasionally, one of their husbands lagged in, as if in search of his wife, but kept a safe distance, after seeing her, or hung about with a group of other husbands, who could not be put to shame or suffering as they might if they had appeared singly.

II.

Ludlow believed that if the right fellow ever came to the work, he could get as much pathos out of our farm folks as Millet got out of his Barbizon peasants. But the fact was that he was not the fellow; he wanted to paint beauty not pathos; and he thought, so far as he thought ethically about it, that the Americans needed to be shown the festive and joyous aspects of their common life. To discover and to represent these was his pleasure as an artist, and his duty as a citizen. He suspected, though, that the trotting-match was the only fact of the Pymantoning County Fair that could be persuaded to lend itself to his purpose. Certainly, there was nothing in the fair-house, with those poor, dreary old people straggling through it, to gladden an artistic conception. Agricultural implements do not group effectively, or pose singly with much picturesqueness; tall stalks of corn, mammoth squashes, huge apples and potatoes want the beauty and quality that belong to them out of doors, when they are gathered into the sections of a county fair-house; piles of melons fail of their poetry on a wooden floor, and heaps of grapes cannot assert themselves in a very bacchanal profusion against the ignominy of being spread upon long tables and ticketed with the names of their varieties and exhibitors.

Ludlow glanced at them, to right and left, as he walked through the long, barnlike building, and took in with other glances the inadequate decorations of the graceless interior. His roving eye caught the lettering over the lateral archways, and with a sort of contemptuous compassion he turned into the Fine Arts Department.

The fine arts were mostly represented by photographs and crazy quilts; but there were also tambourines and round brass plaques painted with flowers, and little satin banners painted with birds or autumn leaves, and gilt rolling-pins with vines. There were medley-pictures contrived of photographs cut out and grouped together in novel and unexpected relations; and there were set about divers patterns and pretences in keramics, as the decoration of earthen pots and jars was called. Besides these were sketches in oil and charcoal, which Ludlow found worse than the more primitive things, with their second-hand *chic* picked up in a tenth-rate school. He began to ask himself whether people tasteless enough to produce these inanities and imagine them artistic, could form even the subjects of art; he began to have doubts of his impression of the trotting-match, its value, its possibility of importance. The senseless ugliness of the things really hurt him: his worship of beauty was a sort of religion, and their badness was a sort of blasphemy. He could not laugh at them; he wished he could; and his first impulse was to turn and escape from the Fine Arts Department, and keep what little faith in the artistic future of the country he had been able to get together during his long sojourn out of it. Since his return he had made sure of the feeling for color and form with which his country-women dressed themselves. There was no mistake about that; even here, in the rustic heart of the continent he had seen costumes which had touch and distinction; and it could not be that the instinct which they sprang from should go for nothing in the arts supposed higher than mantua-making and millinery. The village girls whom he saw so prettily gowned and picturesquely hatted on the benches out there by the race-course, could it have been they who committed these atrocities? Or did these come up from yet deeper depths of the country, where the vague, shallow talk about art going on for the past decade was having its first crude effect? Ludlow was exasperated as well as pained, for he knew that the pretty frocks and hats expressed a love of dressing prettily, which was honest and genuine enough, while the unhappy effects about him could spring only from a hollow vanity far lower than a woman's wish to be charming. It was not an innate impulse which produced them, but a sham ambition, implanted from without, and artificially stimulated by the false and fleeting mood of the time. They must really hamper the growth of aesthetic knowledge among people who were not destitute of the instinct.

He exaggerated the importance of the fact with the sensitiveness of a man to whom aesthetic cultivation was all-important. It appeared to him a far greater evil than it was; it was odious to him, like a vice; it was almost a crime. He spent a very miserable time in the Fine Arts Department of the Pymantoning County Agricultural Fair; and in a kind of horrible fascination he began to review the collection in detail, to guess its causes in severalty and to philosophize its lamentable consequences.

Albion Tourgée (1838–1906), jurist, diplomat, and author, was born in Williamsfield, Ashtabula County, and survived the Civil War to gain renown as a Reconstruction novelist. *Figs and Thistles: A Romance of the Western Reserve,* set in the North during the Civil War, is an autobiographical account of Tourgée's battle experiences. This is a thinly disguised portrait of Ashtabula and its encounter with progress, symbolized by the coming of the railroad.

From Love to Larceny

"Have you heard the news?" was the first word of greeting he heard as he drove his boat beside the little pier from which he had set forth. "No," with a sort of wonder, which he had never felt before, that there could be anything new in or about the vicinage of Rexville. "What is it?"

"The Bank of Aychitula was robbed last night!"

"Indeed!" with a throb of pleasure at his heart, instead of pain and horror. Here was the World coming to his very doors. Robbed! The forceful, the unusual, was at his hand. It was like the trumpet-call to the soldier dreaming of glory, or the welcome shout, "The sea! The sea!" to the stragglers of Xenophen's dispirited host.

He could learn no particulars. Robbed! That was all. How? How much? By whom? Not a word in answer to these questions. It was nothing to him. He had no deposits there nor in any other bank, he said to himself, as he grimly wondered at the burning desire he felt to know all about the crime. Every bank in the country might be robbed of every cent in its coffers and Markham Churr suffer no loss. Nevertheless, he could not rest until he knew all that could be learned of the occurrence. Aychitula was but five miles away. He was not in the least tired, though he had thought that he was, a moment before. If he were, the wind was rising and was easterly. Occasion joined with inclination, and in five minutes he was dashing over the rollicking waves towards Aychitula, a knight in search of his first dragon!

Aychitula was one of those small towns, common in the lake region of the Middle States, which shows by laminae, as it were, the successive stages of its growth. A social Agassiz, regarding it attentively, might trace its development with an ease and certainty equal to that with which the naturalist declares the era of a pre-Adamite fossil.

It was called a "lake town," but, in reality, the town itself was about two miles from the shore, as the crow flies, and a good half-mile further from the harbor which bore its name. The harbor, at the mouth of the stream upon the banks of which the town was built, had been a place of considerable importance before the native wildness of the present site had been impaired. Long before Perry had made the beautiful sheet of water famous as the scene of one of the most memorable exploits of naval warfare, this little port was a trading-station and a landing-place for the hardy pioneers of the Reserve who were seeking new fortunes in the inexhaustible fields of "the 'Hios," as Ohio was then generally called.

With the influx of settlers which followed the close of the war of 1812, Aychitula had become a place of no mean importance. So that the National Government was duly petitioned for an appropriation to build a wharf and lighthouse, and to deepen the channel on the bar. This was accordingly done, and the harbor constituted a port of entry, known and described in the return of the engineer as, "Aychitula Harbor, at the mouth of the Aychitula Creek, from Buffalo, west by south, ———— miles. Steady pier-light, on east side of inlet at 26 feet elevation from low-water level in channel. Bearing from bar inlet, S.S.W. Water on bar, 7 feet 8 inches. Harbor difficult when wind is westerly or northwesterly.

The worthy citizen who undertook to build the wharf and lighthouse and deepen the bar, under direction of the engineer in charge, was so fortunate as to be upon good terms with that officer, as it becomes a contractor to be with the agent of his paymaster. In consequence whereof, he soon found himself able to erect, on his own account, a store and warehouse upon the pier and soon thereafter his possessions were flanked by a low-browed tavern—its porch towards the landing, but its kitchen, stable, and dormitories stretched away back upon piles and piers, among which the restless waves splashed and fretted in a ceaseless turmoil. Before the channel on the bar had been deepened the two feet which his contract required for a width of three hundred feet, the contractor had become the owner of a little fleet of schooners, the first of which, with strange suggestiveness, was named after his friend, the engineer. In these days of corruption and clamor, such an event, when coupled with the noticeable prosperity of Squire Neal, would have been heralded from Maine to California—or, if we would give the compasses the widest stretch, from Florida to Alaska. But such was not the case at that time, both because Maine and Florida were only inchoate existences, and California undreamed of by even the wildest speculators, but also because in those days honorable and high-minded men held office and discharged their duties with integrity and zeal. Nevertheless, certain shipmasters who were accustomed to take their vessels out and in at at the new port of Aychitula were heard to declare that they had never been able to find the three hundred feet of channel at the bar which had been deepened to nine feet, as per contract, as the officer in charge had certified to have been done upon the vouchers by which Squire Neal drew his pay for work and labor performed. Yet, of course, the channel must have been deepened, as he declared, for he was a Major of Engineers, and certainly knew his duty.

Oddly enough, the new channel manifested a strange perversity. The Aychitula hitherto had been a very staid and well-behaved stream under all circumstances. Too large to be properly called a creek, it evidently felt all the dignity of a river, and governed itself in accordance with its ambition. From its mouth to its source in the big swamp, a hundred miles away—if we follow its curves and doublings (not more than a third of that upon the surveyor's map who had run the township lines and laid them off into sections and quarter-sections)—it did not approach the turbulence and forgetfulness of a fall. Now and then its dark, quiet surface was broken by a ripple, at the lower edge of which the bass and suckers lay in wait of any prey the dark waters might bring to them; but even this was rare. Its progress could not have been more decorous had it been the funeral march of that wonderful past attested by its rugged second bank, shelving over a hundred feet or more, and the wide bottom-meadows which had once been its bed. It took no note of time, but resolutely turned aside from all temptation to assume a swifter rate. Even the early and the later rains could not force it from its propriety. It grew turbid with wrath at the bare attempt to accelerate its current, but maintained its dignity, and simply spread itself calmly over the bottom lands and went on with added volume but an equal pace.

As was observed, this staid stream at once developed a peculiar perversity when its mouth became a port of entry, and its *fauces* were lined with wharves, and stores and taverns sprung up on its banks. The amount of *debris* which it carried down, and the persistency with which it dammed up its own outlet, were simply amazing to one who reflected on its irreproachable antecedents. It was said that its name was an Indian one, signifying "black water," and that it had, in consequence, partaken of the aboriginal spirit, and spurned the bonds and badges of civilization. Be that as it may, year after year, for many years, the Major certified, upon his official honor, that in his opinion the channel of the perverse stream needed opening and deepening in the interests of the "Lake Trade" and the numerous and rapidly increasing population dependent upon this port for communication with the outer world. Strangely enough, too, all the other lake ports were afflicted with a like infirmity. And, year after year, the representatives of the people in Congress assembled appropriated greater or less sums for their relief. And, year by year, Squire Neal was the contractor; and year, by year, he prospered, and was always on good terms with the engineer.

In those days the town of Aychitula was at the port; and a busy town it was, at which centered all the trade and travel of a vast back-country of rare fertility, settled by pioneers of unprecedented thrift and industry.

But time brought a change. Along the high sandy ridges which follow the undulations of the shore of the lake, from the St. Clair to its outlet, came, after a while, the weekly stage. The lake ceased to be the sole highway of travel, and along the parallel ridges grew up rival towns at little distances from the shore. Had the steamboat come a few years earlier, the chain of lake towns in Ohio, Pennsylvania and New York would have been upon the bluffs overlooking the ports, instead of being, as now, at points where the roads from the interior to the harbors intersect the stage-route from the East. The products from the interior, as well as their supplies, were hauled over the thoroughfare known as the "State Roads," which stretched to the southward, from the various ports. This was the course of freights and merchandise, but the ganglia of trade—the centers of life, such as life was in those slow days—were where the roads to the ports crossed the main stage-route from the Great East, the Mecca from which the elders had made hegira and to which the juniors would make pilgrimage.

At length the railroad came, upsetting all that had gone before, spurning alike the town upon the ridge, and the one at the harbor, and establishing at its depot, which was usually about midway between the two, yet a third point, to which both freight and travel flowed. Some of these once thriving towns the iron horse has utterly destroyed, as that which was at the port of Aychitula; and left others, like Rexville, petrified, as it were, by the first shriek of the locomotive. But those which stood upon the old highways to their various ports still kept their prominence and received fresh impetus from this new means of communication.

Each of these developments was peculiar to itself, and the buildings of the towns show at once the eras to which they severally belong.

As Markham Churr neared the wharf in the old harbor of Aychitula, through whose rotting piles the waves beat at will, he saw before him all that was left of the first era: vast wooden buildings, which had been massive in their day, now worn and decayed, chafed by the restless waves and still more restless winds; long stores and warehouses, whose piers had sunk away, and in which the storms had piled the sand as high as the rude teamsters from the southward had piled up the grain-sacks in the olden times. All was ruin and decay. The harbor, which might have withstood the stage-coach, had succumbed to the railroad. Squire Neal—well, the harbor had stood by him, and he by the harbor, until, like it, he had yielded to decay.

As Markham walked towards the town, he met with the relics of the second era—that of the stage-coach. On each side of the creek there was a town. That on the west appropriated the name Aychitula, while the other was more usually known as the "East Village." Wandering through this, Markham saw vast stables and sheds going to decay only less rapidly than the warehouses of the harbor. These were the caravansaries built to accommodate the hundreds of horses that stage travel made necessary; while the East Village itself was built to accommodate the travelers whom the stage-coach brought. Low, rambling taverns of almost limitless capacity, with one or two stores; great wooden houses, ornate with intricately-fretted cornices; and now and then a glaring-fronted, damp-walled brick, with its black metal knocker—one of the palaces of the stage-coach aristocracy. The broad streets were grass-grown and untrodden save along the sandy wagon-track.

He crossed the old wooden bridge, with its warning notice to the Jehus of the stage, which stared out in plain black letters from the weather-worn board, and came into the railroad station of Aychitula: from the past into the present. Here all was life and thrift. The paved sidewalks and busy throngs of the town contrasted strangely with the deserted harbor and the lonely streets he had just left.

In an hour he had noted, in close juxtaposition, the three stages of development which characterized the three generations that have lived and labored upon the Western Reserve.

John Hay (1838–1905), diplomat, statesman, historian, poet, and author, was a re-luctant resident of Cleveland after his marriage to Clara Louise Stone, daughter of wealthy Cleveland industrialist Amasa Stone, who built a home for them next to his own on Euclid Avenue. Hay, thought to be dissatisfied with the city's pro-vincial, pretentious, artificial society by some commentators, has been portrayed recently as content with his life in Cleveland. *The Bread-Winners* had its origins in the threatened violence of a Cleveland railroad strike that aroused fears of labor leaders. Published anonymously in 1884, Hay never acknowledged the book's authorship.

A Holiday Not in the Calendar

The next morning while Farnham was at breakfast he received a note from Mr. Temple in these words:

"Strikes will begin to-day, but will not be general. There will be no disturbance, I think. They don't seem very gritty."

After breakfast he walked down to the City Hall. On every street corner he saw little groups of men in rather listless conversation. He met an acquaintance crossing the street.

"Have you heard the news?" The man's face was flushed with plea-sure at having something to tell. "The firemen and stokers have all struck, and run their engines into the round-house at Riverley, five miles out. There won't be a train leave or come in for the present."

"Is that all?"

"No, that ain't a start. The Model Oil men have struck, and are all over the North End, shutting up the other shops. They say there won't be a lick of work done in town the rest of the week."

"Except what Satan finds for idle hands," Farnham suggested, and hastened his steps a little to the municipal buildings.

He found the chief of police in his office, suffering from nervousness and a sense of importance. He began by reminding him of the occur-rence of the week before in the wood. The chief waited with an absent expression for the story to end, and then said, "My dear sir, I cannot pay any attention to such little matters with anarchy threatening our city. I must protect life and property, sir—life and property."

"Very well," rejoined Farnham, "I am informed that life and property are threatened in my own neighborhood. Can you detail a few policemen to patrol Algonquin Avenue, in case of a serious disturbance?"

"I can't tell you, my dear sir; I will do the best I can by all sections. Why, man," he cried, in a voice which suddenly grew a shrill falsetto in his agitation, "I tell you I haven't a policeman for every ten miles of street in this town. I can't spare but two for my own house!"

Farnham saw the case was hopeless, and went to the office of the mayor. That official had assumed an attitude expressive of dignified and dauntless energy. He sat in a chair tilted back on its hind feet; the boots of the municipal authority were on a desk covered with official papers; a long cigar adorned his eloquent lips; a beaver hat shaded his eyes.

He did not change his attitude as Farnham entered. He probably thought it could not be changed for the better.

"Good-morning, Mr. Quinlin."

"Good-morning, sirr, to you." This salutation was uttered through teeth shut as tightly as the integrity of the cigar would permit.

"There is a great deal of talk of possible disturbance to-night, in case the strikes extend. My own neighborhood, I am told, has been directly threatened. I called to ask whether, in case of trouble, I could rely on any assistance from the city authorities, or whether we must all look out for ourselves."

The mayor placed his thumbs in the arm-holes of his waistcoat, and threw his head back so that he could stare at Farnham from below his hat brim. He then said, in a measured voice, as if addressing an assembly: "Sirrr! I would have you to know that the working-men of Buffland are not thieves and robbers. In this struggle with capital they have my profound sympathy. I expect their conduct to be that of perrfect gentlemen. I, at least, will give no orders which may tend to array one class of citizens against another. That is my answer, sirr; I hope it does not disappoint you."

"Not in the least," said Farnham, putting on his hat. "It is precisely what I should have expected of you."

"Thank you, sirr. Call again, sirr."

As Farnham disappeared, the chief magistrate of the city tilted his hat to one side, shut an eye with profoundly humorous significance, and said to the two or three loungers who had been enjoying the scene:

"That is the sort of T-rail I am. That young gentleman voted agin me, on the ground I wasn't high-toned enough."

Farnham walked rapidly to the office of the evening newspaper. He found a man in the counting-room, catching flies and trimming their wings with a large pair of office shears. He said, "Can you put an advertisement for me in your afternoon editions?"

The man laid down his shears, but held on to his fly, and looked at his watch.

"Have you got it ready?"

"No, but I will not be a minute about it."

"Be lively! You haven't got but a minute."

He picked up his scissors and resumed his surgery, while Farnham wrote his advertisement. The man took it, and threw it into a tin box, blew a whistle, and the box disappeared through a hole in the ceiling. A few minutes later the boys were crying the paper in the streets. The advertisement was in these words:

"Veterans, Attention! All able-bodied veterans of the Army of the Potomac, and especially of the Third Army Corps, are requested to meet at seven this evening, at No. ———— Public Square."

From the newspaper office Farnham went to a gunsmith's. The dealer was a German and a good sportsman, whom Farnham knew very well, having often shot with him in the marshes west of the city. His name was Leopold Grosshammer. There were two or three men in the place when Farnham entered. He waited until they were gone, and then said:

"Bolty, have you two dozen repeating rifles?"

"Ja wohl! Aber, Herr Gott, was machen Sie denn damit?"

"I don't know why I shouldn't tell you. They think there may be a riot in town, and they tell me at the City Hall that everybody must look out for himself. I am going to try to get up a little company of old soldiers for patrol duty."

"All right, mine captain, and I will be the first freiwilliger. But I don't dink you wants rifles. Revolvers and clubs—like the pleecemen— dat's de dicket."

"Have you got them?"

"Oh, yes, and the belts thereto. I got der gondract to furnish 'em to de city."

"Then you will send them, wrapped in bundles, to my office in the Square, and come yourself there at seven."

"Freilich," said Leopold, his white teeth glistening through his yellow beard at the prospect of service.

Farnham spent an hour or two visiting the proprietors of the large establishments affected by the strikes. He found, as a rule, great annoyance and exasperation, but no panic. Mr. Temple said, "The poor ———— fools! I felt sorry for them. They came up here to me this morning,—their committee, they called it,—and told me they hated it, but it was orders! 'Orders from where?' I asked. 'From the chiefs of sections,' they said; and that was all I could get out of them. Some of the best fellows in the works were on the committee. They put 'em there on purpose. The sneaks and lawyers hung back."

"What will they do if the strike should last?" asked Farnham.

"They will be supported for awhile by the other mills. Our men are the only ones that have struck so far. They were told off to make the move, just as they march out a certain regiment to charge a battery. If we give in, then another gang will strike."

"Do you expect to give in?"

"Between us, we want nothing better than ten days' rest. We want to repair our furnaces, and we haven't a ———— thing to do. What I told you this morning holds good. There won't be any riot. The whole thing is solemn fooling so far."

The next man Farnham saw was in a far less placid frame of mind. It was Jimmy Nelson, the largest grocer in the city. He had a cargo of perishable groceries at the station, and the freight hands would not let them be delivered. "I talked to the rascals," he said. "I asked them what they had against *me;* that they was injuring Trade!" a deity of which Mr. Nelson always spoke with profound respect. "They laughed in my face, sir. They said, "That's just our racket. We want to squeeze you respectable merchants till you get mad and hang a railroad president or two!" Yes, sir; they said that to me, and five thousand dollars of my stuff rotting in the depot."

"Why don't you go to the mayor?" asked Farnham, though he could not suppress a smile as he said it.

"Yes, I like that!" screamed Jimmy. "You are laughing at me. I suppose the whole town has heard of it. Well, it's a fact. I went and asked that infernal scoundrel what he was going to do. He said his function was to keep the peace, and there wasn't a word in the statutes about North Carliny water-melons. If I live till he gets out of office, I'll lick him."

"Oh, I think you won't do that, Jimmy."

"You think I won't!" said Nelson, absolutely incandescent with the story of his wrongs. "I'll swear by Matthew, Mark, Luke, and John, that I will thrash the hide off him next spring—if I don't forget it."

Farnham went home, mounted his horse, and rode about the city to see what progress the strike was making. There was little disorder visible on the surface of things. The "sections" had evidently not ordered a general cessation of labor; and yet there were curious signs of demoralization, as if the spirit of work was partially disintegrating and giving way to something not precisely lawless, but rather listless. For instance, a crowd of workmen were engaged industriously and, to all appearance, contentedly upon a large school-building in construction. A group of men, not half their number, approached them and ordered them to leave off work. The builders looked at each other and then at their exhorters in a confused fashion for a moment, and ended by obeying the summons in a sullen and indifferent manner. They took off their aprons, went to the hydrant and washed their hands, then put on their coats and went home in silence and shamefacedness, amid the angry remonstrances of the master-builder. A little farther on Farnham saw what seemed like a burlesque of the last performance. Several men were at work in a hole in the street; the tops of their heads were just visible above the surface. A half-grown, ruffianly boy, with a boot-black's box slung over his shoulder, came up and shouted, "You ———— ———— rats, come out of that, or we'll knock the scalps off'n you." The men, without even looking to see the source of the summons, threw down their tools and got out of the hole. The boy had run away; they looked about for a moment, as if bewildered, and then one of them, a gray-headed Irishmen, said, "Well, we'd better be a lavin' off, if the rest is," and they all went away.

In this fashion it came about that by nightfall all the squares and public places were thronged with an idle and expectant crowd, not actively mischievous or threatening, but affording a vast mass of inflammable material in case the fire should start in any quarter. They gathered everywhere in dense groups, exchanging rumors and surmises, in which fact and fiction were fantastically mingled.

"The rolling-mills all close to-morrow," said a sallow and hollow-eyed tailor. "That'll let loose twenty thousand men on the town,—big, brawny fellows. I'm glad my wife is in Clairfield."

"All you know about it! Clairfield is twice as bad off as here. The machine shops has all struck there, and the men went through the armory this afternoon. They're camped all along Delaware street, every man with a pair of revolvers and a musket."

"You don't say so!" said the schneider, turning a shade more sallow. "I'd better telegraph my wife to come home."

"I wouldn't hurry," was the impassive response.

"You don't know where we'll be to-morrow. They have been drilling all day at Riverley, three thousand of 'em. They'll come in to-morrow, mebe, and hang all the railroad presidents. That may make trouble."

Through these loitering and talking crowds Farnham made his way in the evening to the office which he kept, on the public square of the town, for the transaction of the affairs of his estate. He had given directions to his clerk to be there, and when he arrived found that some half-dozen men had already assembled in answer to his advertisement. Some of them he knew; one, Nathan Kendall, a powerful young man, originally from the north of Maine, now a machinist in Buffland, had been at one time his orderly in the army. Bolty Grosshammer was there, and in a very short time some twenty men were in the room. Farnham briefly explained to them his intention. "I want you," he said, "to enlist for a few days' service under my orders. I cannot tell whether there will be any work to do or not; but it is likely we shall have a few nights of patrol at least. You will get ten dollars apiece anyhow, and ordinary day's wages besides. If any of you get hurt, I will try to have you taken care of."

All but two agreed to the proposition. These two said "they had families and could not risk their skins. When they saw the advertisement they had thought it was something about pensions, or the county treasurer's office. They thought soldiers ought to have the first chance at good offices." They then grumblingly withdrew.

Farnham kept his men for an hour longer, arranging some details of organization, and then dismissed them for twenty-four hours, feeling assured that there would be no disturbance of public tranquillity that night. "I will meet you here to morrow evening," he said, "and you can get your pistols and sticks and your final orders."

The men went out one by one, Bolty and Kendall waiting for a while after they had gone and going out on the sidewalk with Farnham. They had instinctively appointed themselves a sort of bodyguard to their old commander, and intended to keep him in sight until he got home. As they reached the door, they saw a scuffle going on upon the sidewalk. A well-dressed man was being beaten and kicked by a few rough fellows, and the crowd was looking on with silent interest. Farnham sprang forward and seized one of the assailants by the collar; Bolty pulled away another. The man who had been cuffed turned to Kendall, who was standing by to help where help was needed, and cried, "Take me away somewhere; they will have my life;" an appeal which only excited the jeers of the crowd.

"Kendall, take him into my office," said Farnham, which was done in an instant, Farnham and Bolty following. A rush was made,—not very vicious, however,—and the three men got safely inside with their prize, and bolted the door. A few kicks and blows shook the door, but there was no movement to break it down; and the rescued man, when he found himself in safety, walked up to a mirror there was in the room and looked earnestly at his face. It was a little bruised and bloody, and dirty with mud, but not seriously injured.

He turned to his rescuers with an air more of condescension than gratitude. "Gentlemen, I owe you my thanks, although I should have got the better of those scoundrels in a moment. Can you assist me in identifying them?"

"Oh! it is Mayor Quinlin, I believe," said Farnham, recognizing that functionary more by his voice than by his rumpled visage. "No, I do not know who they were. What was the occasion of this assault?"

"A most cowardly and infamous outrage, sir," said the Mayor. "I was walking along the sidewalk to me home, and I came upon this gang of ruffians at your door. Impatient at being delayed,—for me time is much occupied,—I rebuked them for being in me way. One of them turned to me and insolently inquired, 'Do you own this street, or have you just got a lien on it?' which unendurable insult was greeted with a loud laugh from the other ruffians. I called them by some properly severe name, and raised me cane to force a passage,—and the rest you know. Now, gentlemen, is there anything I can do?"

Farnham did not scruple to strike while the iron was hot. He said: "Yes, there is one thing your Honor may do, not so much for us as for the cause of order and good government, violated to-night in your own person. Knowing the insufficiency of the means at your disposal, a few of us propose to raise a subsidiary night-patrol for the protection of life and property during the present excitement. We would like you to give it your official sanction."

"Do I understand it will be without expense to my—to the city government?" Mr. Quinlin was anxious to make a show of economy in his annual message.

"Entirely," Farnham assured him.

"It is done, sir. Come to-morrow morning and get what papers you want. The sperrit of disorder must be met and put down with a bold and defiant hand. Now, gentlemen, if there is a back door to this establishment, I will use it to make me way home."

Farnham showed him the rear entrance, and saw him walking homeward up the quiet street; and, coming back, found Bolty and Kendall writhing with merriment.

"Well, that beats all," said Kendall. "I guess I'll write home like the fellow did from Iowa to his daddy, 'Come out here quick. Mighty mean men gits office in this country.' "

"Yes," assented Bolty. "Dot burgermeister ish better as a circus mit a drick mule."

"Don't speak disrespectfully of dignitaries," said Farnham. "It's a bad habit in soldiers."

When they went out on the sidewalk the crowd had dispersed. Farnham bade his recruits good night and went up the avenue. They waited until he was a hundred yards away, and then, without a word to each other, followed him at that distance till they saw him enter his own gate.

Constance Fenimore Woolson (1840–94), great-niece of author James Fenimore Cooper, grew up in Cleveland. A regionalist and local colorist, she took a psychological approach to character development in her novels and short stories, such as "Wilhelmina," published first in the *Atlantic Monthly* in 1875 and collected in *Castle Nowhere: Lake Country Sketches* (1875). After 1879 she lived permanently in Europe where she was a contemporary of Henry James, who was a key influence on her work. The narrator of this story, a Cleveland grande dame vacationing in the country, is forced to confront her sentimentalized view of the pastoral life.

Wilhelmina

"And so, Mina, you will not marry the baker?"

"No; I waits for Gustav."

"How long is it since you have seen him?"

"Three year; it was a three-year regi-ment."

"Then he will soon be home?"

"I not know," answered the girl, with a wistful look in her dark eyes, as if asking information from the superior being who sat in the skiff, a being from the outside world where newspapers, the modern Tree of Knowledge, were not forbidden.

"Perhaps he will reenlist, and stay three years longer," I said.

"Ah, lady,—six year! It breaks the heart," answered Wilhelmina.

She was the gardener's daughter, a member of the community of German Separatists who live secluded in one of Ohio's rich valleys, separated by their own broad acres and orchard-covered hills from the busy world outside; down the valley flows the tranquil Tuscarawas on its way to the Muskingum, its slow tide rolling through the fertile bottom-lands between stone dykes, and utilized to the utmost extent of carefulness by the thrifty brothers, now working a saw-mill on the bank, now sending a tributary to the flour-mill across the canal, and now branching off in a sparkling race across the valley to turn wheels for two or three factories, watering the great grass-meadow on the way. We were floating on this river in a skiff named by myself Der Fliegende Hollander, much to the slow wonder of the Zoarites, who did not understand how a Dutchman could, nor why he should, fly. Wilhelmina sat before me, her oars idly trailing in the water. She showed a Nubian head above her white kerchief: large-lidded soft brown eyes, heavy braids of dark hair, a creamy skin with purple tints in the lips and brown shadows under the eyes, and a far-off dreamy expression which even the steady, monotonous toil of community life had not been able to efface. She wore the blue dress and white kerchief of the society, the quaint little calico bonnet lying beside her: she was a small maiden; her slender form swayed in the stiff, short-waisted gown, her feet slipped about in the broad shoes, and her hands, roughened and browned with garden-work, were yet narrow and graceful. From the first we felt sure she was grafted, and not a shoot from the community stalk. But we could learn nothing of her origin; the Zoarites are not communicative; they fill each day with twelve good hours of labor, and look neither forward nor back. "She is a daughter," said

the old gardener in answer to our questions. "Adopted?" I suggested;
but he vouchsafed no answer. I liked the little daughter's dreamy face,
but she was pale and undeveloped, like a Southern flower, growing in
Northern soil; the rosy-cheeked, flaxen-haired Rosines, Salomes, and
Dorotys, with their broad shoulders and ponderous tread, thought this
brown changeling ugly, and pitied her in their slow, good-natured way.

"It breaks the heart," said Wilhelmina again, softly, as if to herself.

I repented me of my thoughtlessness.

"In any case he can come back for a few days," I hastened to say.
"What regiment was it?"

"The One Hundred and Seventh, lady."

I had a Cleveland paper in my basket, and taking it out I glanced
over the war-news column, carelessly, as one who does not expect to
find what he seeks. But chance, for once, was with us, and gave this
item: "The One Hundred and Seventh Regiment, O. V. I. [Ohio Volunteer Infantry], is expected home next week. The men will be paid off
at Camp Chase."

"Ah!" said Wilhelmina, catching her breath with a half sob under
her tightly-drawn kerchief, "ah, mein Gustav!"

"Yes, you will soon see him," I answered, bending forward to take
the rough little hand in mine; for I was a romantic wife, and my heart
went out to all lovers. But the girl did not notice my words or my
touch; silently she sat, absorbed in her own emotion, her eyes fixed on
the hill-tops far away, as though she saw the regiment marching home
through the blue June sky.

I took the oars and rowed up as far as the island, letting the skiff float
back with the current. Other boats were out, filled with fresh-faced
boys in their high-crowned hats, long-waisted, wide-flapped vests of
calico, and funny little swallow-tailed coats with buttons up under the
shoulder-blades; they appeared unaccountably long in front and short
behind, these young Zoar brethren. On the vine-covered dyke were
groups of mothers and grave little children, and up in the hill-orchards
were moving figures, young and old; the whole village was abroad in
the lovely afternoon, according to their Sunday custom, which gave
the morning to chorals and a long sermon in the little church, and the
afternoon to nature, even old Christian, the pastor, taking his impos-
ing white fur hat and tasseled cane for a walk through the community
fields, with the remark, "Thus is cheered the heart of man, and his
countenance refreshed."

As the sun sank in the warm western sky, homeward came the villagers from the river, the orchards, and the meadows, men, women,
and children, a hardy, simple-minded band, whose fathers, for religion's sake, had taken the long journey from Wurtemberg across

the ocean to this distant valley, and made it a garden of rest in the wilderness. We, too, landed, and walked up the apple-tree lane towards the hotel.

"The cows come," said Wilhelmina as we heard a distant tinkling; "I must go." But still she lingered. "Der regi-ment, it must come soon, you say?" she asked in a low voice, as though she wanted to hear the good news again and again.

"They will be paid off next week; they cannot be later than ten days from now."

"Ten day! Ah, mein Gustav," murmured the little maiden; she turned away and tied on her stiff bonnet, furtively wiping off a tear with her prim handkerchief folded in a square.

"Why, my child." I said, following her and stooping to look in her face, "what is this?"

"It is nothing; it is for glad,—for very glad," said Wilhelmina. Away she ran as the first solemn cow came into view, heading the long procession meandering slowly towards the stalls. They knew nothing of haste, these dignified community cows; from stall to pasture, from pasture to stall, in a plethora of comfort, this was their life. The silver-haired shepherd came last with his staff and scrip, and the nervous shepherd-dog ran hither and thither in the hope of finding some cow to bark at; but the comfortable cows moved on in orderly ranks, and he was obliged to dart off on a tangent every now and then, and bark at nothing, to relieve his feelings. Reaching the paved courtyard each cow walked into her own stall, and the milking began. All the girls took part in this work, sitting on little stools and singing together as the milk frothed up in the tin pails; the pails were emptied into tubs, and when the tubs were full the girls bore them on their heads to the dairy, where the milk was poured into a huge strainer, a constant procession of girls with tubs above and the old milk-mother ladling out as fast as she could below. With the bee-hives near by, it was a realization of the Scriptural phrase, "A land flowing with milk and honey."

The next morning, after breakfast, I strolled up the still street, leaving the Wirthshaus with its pointed roof behind me. On the right were some ancient cottages built of crossed timbers filled in with plaster; sun-dials hung on the walls, and each house had its piazza, where, when the work of the day was over, the families assembled, often singing folk-songs to the music of their home-made flutes and pipes. On the left stood the residence of the first pastor, the reverend man who had led these sheep to their refuge in the wilds of the New World. It was a wide-spreading brick mansion, with a broadside of white-curtained windows, an inclosed glass porch, iron railings, and gilded eaves; a building so stately among the surrounding cottages that it had gained from outsiders the name of the King's Palace, although the good man whose grave remains unmarked in the quiet God's Acre, according to the Separatist custom, was a father to his people, not a king.

Beyond the palace began the community garden, a large square in the centre of the village filled with flowers and fruit, adorned with arbors and cedar-trees clipped in the form of birds, and enriched with an old-style greenhouse whose sliding glasses were viewed with admiration by the visitors of thirty years ago, who sent their choice plants thither from far and near to be tended through the long, cold lake-country winters. The garden, the cedars, and the greenhouse were all antiquated, but to me none the less charming. The spring that gushed up in one corner, the old-fashioned flowers in their box-bordered beds, larkspur, lady slippers, bachelor's buttons, peonies, aromatic pinks, and all varieties of roses, the arbors with red honeysuckle overhead and tan bark under foot, were all delightful; and I knew, also, that I should find the gardener's daughter at her never-ending task of weeding. This time it was the strawberry bed. "I have come to sit in your pleasant garden, Mina," I said, taking a seat on a shaded bench near the bending figure.

"So?" said Wilhelmina in a long-drawn interrogation, glancing up shyly with a smile. She was a child of the sun, this little maiden, and while her blonde companions wore always their bonnets or broad-brimmed hats over their precise caps, Wilhelmina, as now, constantly discarded these coverings and sat in the sun basking like a bird of the tropics. In truth, it did not redden her; she was one of those whose coloring comes not from without, but within.

"Do you like this work, Mina?"

"Oh—so. Good as any."

"Do you like work?"

"Folks must work." This was said gravely, as part of the community creed.

"Wouldn't you like to go with me to the city?"

"No; I's better here."

"But you can see the great world, Mina. You need not work, I will take care of you. You shall have pretty dresses; wouldn't you like that?" I asked, curious to discover the secret of the Separatist indifference to everything outside.

"Nein," answered the little maiden tranquilly; "nein, fraulein. Ich bin zufrieden" [no, ma'am, I'm content].

Those three words were the key. "I am contented." So were they taught from childhood, and—I was about to say—they knew no better; but, after all, is there anything better to know?

We talked on, for Mina understood English, although many of her mates could chatter only in their Wurtemberg dialect, whose provincialisms confused my carefully learned German; I was grounded in

Goethe, well-read in Schiller, and struggling with Jean Paul, who, for-
tunately, is "der Einzige," the only; another such would destroy life. At
length a bell sounded, and forthwith work was laid aside in the fields,
the workshops, and the houses, while all partook of a light repast, one
of the five meals with which the long summer day of toil is broken.
Flagons of beer had the men afield, with bread and cheese; the women
took bread and apple-butter. But Mina did not care for the thick slice
which the thrifty housemother had provided; she had not the steady,
unfanciful appetite of the community which eats the same food day after day, as the cow eats its grass, desiring no change.

"And the gardener really wishes you to marry Jacob?" I said as she
sat on the grass near me, enjoying the rest.

"Yes. Jacob is good,—always the same."

"And Gustav?"

"Ah, mein Gustav! Lady, *he* is young, tall,—so tall as tree; he run,
he sing, his eyes like veilchen [violets] there, his hair like gold. If I see
him not soon, lady, I die! The year so long,—so long they are. Three
year without Gustav!" The brown eyes grew dim, and out came the
square-folded handkerchief, of colored calico for weekdays.

"But it will not be long now, Mina."

"Yes; I hope."

"He writes to you, I suppose?"

"No. Gustav knows not to write, he not like school. But he speak
through the other boys, Ernst the verliebte of Rosine, and Peter of
Doroty."

"The Zoar soldiers were all young men?"

"Yes; all verliebte [sweethearts]. Some are not; they have gone to the
Next Country" (died).

"Killed in battle?"

"Yes; on the berge that looks,—what you call, I not know"—

"Lookout Mountain?"

"Yes."

"Were the boys volunteers?" I asked, remembering the community
theory of non-resistance.

"Oh yes; they volunteer, Gustav the first. *They* not drafted," said
Wilhelmina, proudly. For these two words, so prominent during the
war, had penetrated even into this quiet valley.

"But did the trustees approve?"

"Apperouve?"

"I mean, did they like it?"

"Ah! they like it not. They talk, they preach in church, they say
'No.' Zoar must give soldiers? So. Then they take money and pay for
der substitute; but the boys, they must not go."

"But they went, in spite of the trustees?"

"Yes; Gustav first. They go in night, they walk in woods, over the hills to Brownville, where is der recruiter. The morning come, they gone!"

"They have been away three years, you say? They have seen the world in that time," I remarked half to myself, as I thought of the strange mind-opening and knowledge-gaining of those years to youths brought up in the strict seclusion of the community.

"Yes; Gustav have seen the wide world," answered Wilhelmina with pride.

"But will they be content to step back into the dull routine of Zoar life?" I thought; and a doubt came that made me scan more closely the face of the girl at my side. To me it was attractive because of its possibilities; I was always fancying some excitement that would bring the color to the cheeks and full lips, and light up the heavy-lidded eyes with soft brilliancy. But would this Gustav see these might-be beauties? And how far would the singularly ugly costume offend eyes grown accustomed to fanciful finery and gay colors?

"You fully expect to marry Gustav?" I asked.

"We are verlobt [engaged]," answered Mina, not without a little air of dignity.

"Yes, I know. But that was long ago."

"Verlobt once, verlobt always," said the little maiden confidently.

"But why, then, does the gardener speak of Jacob, if you are engaged to this Gustav?"

"Oh, fader he like the old, and Jacob is old, thirty year! His wife is gone to the Next Country. Jacob is a brother, too; he write his name in the book. But Gustav he not do so; he is free."

"You mean that the baker has signed the articles, and is a member of the community?"

"Yes; but the baker is old, very old; thirty year! Gustav not twenty and three yet; he come home, then he sign."

"And have you signed these articles, Wilhelmina?"

"Yes; all the womens signs."

"What does the paper say?"

"Da ich Unterzeichneter [that I undersigned . . .],"—began the girl.

"I cannot understand that. Tell me in English."

"Well; you wants to join the Zoar Community of Separatists; you writes your name and says, 'Give me house, victual, and clothes for my work and I join; and I never fernerer Forderung an besagte Gesellschaft machen kann, oder will.' "

"Will never make further demand upon said society," I repeated, translating slowly.

"Yes; that is it."

"But who takes charge of all the money?"

"The trustees."

"Don't they give you any?"

"No; for what? It's no good," answered Wilhelmina.

I knew that all the necessaries of life were dealt out to the members of the community according to their need, and, as they never went outside of their valley, they could scarcely have spent money even if they had possessed it. But, nevertheless, it was startling in this nineteenth century to come upon a sincere belief in the worthlessness of the green-tinted paper we cherish so fondly. "Gustav will have learned its value," I thought, as Mina, having finished the strawberry bed, started away towards the dairy to assist in the butter-making.

I strolled on up the little hill, past the picturesque bakery, where through the open window I caught a glimpse of the "old, very old Jacob," a serious young man of thirty, drawing out his large loaves of bread from the brick oven with a long-handled rake. It was ginger-bread day also, and a spicy odor met me at the window; so I put in my head and asked for a piece, receiving a card about a foot square, laid on fresh grape leaves.

"But I cannot eat all this," I said, breaking off a corner.

"Oh, dat's noding," answered Jacob, beginning to knead fresh dough in a long white trough, the village supply for the next day.

"I have been sitting with Wilhelmina," I remarked, as I leaned on the casement, impelled by a desire to see the effect of the name.

"So?" said Jacob, interrogatively.

"Yes; she is a sweet girl."

"So?" (doubtfully).

"Don't you think so, Jacob?"

"Ye-es. So-so. A leetle black," answered this impassive lover.

"But you wish to marry her?"

"Oh ye-es. She is young and strong; her fader say she good to work. I have children five; I must have some one in the house."

"Oh, Jacob! Is that the way to talk?" I exclaimed.

"Warum nicht [Why not]?" replied the baker, pausing in his kneading, and regarding me with wide-open, candid eyes.

"Why not, indeed?" I thought, as I turned away from the window. "He is at least honest, and no doubt in his way he would be a kind husband to little Mina. But what a way!"

I walked on up the street, passing the pleasant house where all the infirm old women of the community were lodged together, carefully tended by appointed nurses. The aged sisters were out on the piazza sunning themselves, like so many old cats. They were bent with hard, out-door labor, for they belonged to the early days when the wild for-

est covered the fields now so rich, and only a few log-cabins stood on
the site of the tidy cottages and gardens of the present village. Some of
them had taken the long journey on foot from Philadelphia westward,
four hundred and fifty miles, in the depths of winter. Well might they
rest from their labors and sit in the sunshine, poor old souls!

A few days later, my friendly newspaper mentioned the arrival of
the German regiment at Camp Chase. "They will probably be paid off
in a day or two," I thought, "and another day may bring them here."
Eager to be the first to tell the good news to my little favorite, I hastened up to the garden, and found her engaged, as usual, in weeding.

"Mina," I said, "I have something to tell you. The regiment is at
Camp Chase; you will see Gustav soon, perhaps this week."

And there, before my eyes, the transformation I had often fancied
took place; the color rushed to the brown surface, the cheeks and lips
glowed in vivid red, and the heavy eyes opened wide and shone like
stars, with a brilliancy that astonished and even disturbed me. The
statue had a soul at last; the beauty dormant had awakened. But for the
fire of that soul would this expected Pygmalion suffice? Would the real
prince fill his place in the long-cherished dreams of this beauty of the
wood?

The girl had risen as I spoke, and now she stood erect, trembling
with excitement, her hands clasped on her breast, breathing quickly
and heavily as though an overweight of joy was pressing down her
heart; her eyes were fixed upon my face, but she saw me not. Strange
was her gaze, like the gaze of one walking in sleep. Her sloping shoulders seemed to expand and chafe against the stiff gown as though they
would burst their bonds; the blood glowed in her face and throat, and
her lips quivered, not as though tears were coming, but from the full-
ness of unuttered speech. Her emotion resembled the intensest fire of
fever, and yet it seemed natural; like noon in the tropics when the gorgeous flowers flame in the white, shadowless heat. Thus stood
Wilhelmina, looking up into the sky with eyes that challenged the sun.

"Come here, child," I said; "come here and sit by me. We will talk
about it."

But she neither saw nor heard me. I drew her down on the bench at
my side; she yielded unconsciously; her slender form throbbed, and
pulses were beating under my hands wherever I touched her. "Mina!"
I said again. But she did not answer. Like an unfolding rose, she revealed her hidden, beautiful heart, as though a spirit had breathed upon
the bud; silenced in the presence of this great love, I ceased speaking,
and left her to herself. After a time single words fell from her lips, broken utterances of happiness. I was as nothing; she was absorbed in the
One. "Gustav! mein Gustav!" It was like the bird's note, oft repeated,

ever the same. So isolated, so intense was her joy that, as often happens, my mind took refuge in the opposite extreme of commonplace, and I found myself wondering whether she would be able to eat boiled beef and cabbage for dinner, or fill the soft-soap barrel for the laundry women, later in the day.

All the morning I sat under the trees with Wilhelmina, who had forgotten her life-long tasks as completely as though they had never existed. I hated to leave her to the leather-colored wife of the old gardener, and lingered until the sharp voice came out from the distant house-door, calling, "*Veel*-helminy," as the twelve o'clock bell summoned the community to dinner. But as Mina rose and swept back the heavy braids that had fallen from the little ivory stick which confined them, I saw that she was armed *cap-a-pie* in that full happiness from which all weapons glance off harmless.

All the rest of the day she was like a thing possessed. I followed her to the hill-pasture, whither she had gone to mind the cows, and found her coiled up on the grass in the blaze of the afternoon sun, like a little salamander. She was lost in day-dreams, and the decorous cows had a holiday for once in their sober lives, wandering beyond bounds at will, and even tasting the dissipations of the marsh, standing unheeded in the bog up to their sleek knees. Wilhelmina had not many words to give me; her English vocabulary was limited; she had never read a line of romance nor a verse of poetry. The nearest approach to either was the community hymn-book, containing the Separatist hymns, of which the following lines are a specimen:—

> "Ruhe ist das beste Gut
> Dasz man haben kann:"

> "Rest is the best good
> That man can have,"—

and which embody the religious doctrine of the Zoar Brethren, although they think, apparently, that the labor of twelve hours each day is necessary to its enjoyment. The "Ruhe," however, refers more especially to their quiet seclusion away from the turmoil of the wicked world outside.

The second morning after this it was evident that an unusual excitement was abroad in the phlegmatic village. All the daily duties were fulfilled as usual at the Wirthshaus: Pauline went up to the bakery with her board, and returned with her load of bread and bretzels balanced on her head; Jacobina served our coffee with her slow precision; and the broad-shouldered, young-faced Lydia patted and puffed up our mountain-high feather-beds with due care. The men went afield at the blast of the horn, the work-shops were full and the mills running. But, nevertheless, all was not the same; the air seemed full of mystery: there were whisperings when two met, furtive signals, and an inward excitement glowing in the faces of men, women, and children, hitherto placid as their own sheep. "They have heard the news," I said, after watching the tailor's Gretchen and the blacksmith's Barbara stop to exchange a whisper behind the wood-house. Later in the day we learned that several letters from the absent soldier-boys had been received that morning, announcing their arrival on the evening train. The news had flown from one end of the village to the other, and although the well-drilled hands were all at work, hearts were stirring with the greatest excitement of a lifetime, since there was hardly a house where there was not one expected. Each large house often held a number of families, stowed away in little sets of chambers, with one dining-room in common.

Several times during the day we saw the three trustees conferring apart with anxious faces. The war had been a sore trouble to them, owing to their conscientious scruples against rendering military service. They had hoped to remain non-combatants. But the country was on fire with patriotism, and nothing less than a *bona fide* Separatist in United States uniform would quiet the surrounding towns, long jealous of the wealth of this foreign community, misunderstanding its tenets, and glowing with that zeal against "sympathizers" which kept star-spangled banners flying over every suspected house.

"Hang out the flag!" was their cry, and they demanded that Zoar should hang out its soldiers, giving them to understand that if not voluntarily hung out, they would soon be involuntarily hung up! A draft was ordered, and then the young men of the society, who had long chafed against their bonds, broke loose, volunteered, and marched away, principles or no principles, trustees or no trustees. These bold hearts once gone, the village sank into quietude again. Their letters, however, were a source of anxiety, coming as they did from the vain outside world; and the old postmaster, autocrat though he was, hardly dared to suppress them. But he said, shaking his head, that they "had fallen upon troublous times," and handed each dangerous envelope out with a groan. But the soldiers were not skilled penmen; their letters, few and far between, at length stopped entirely. Time passed, and the very existence of the runaways had become a far-off problem to the wise men of the community, absorbed in their slow calculations and cautious agriculture, when now, suddenly, it forced itself upon them face to face, and they were required to solve it in the twinkling of an eye. The bold hearts were coming back, full of knowledge of the outside world; almost every house would hold one, and the bands of law and order would be broken. Before this prospect the trustees quailed. Twenty years before they would have forbidden the entrance of these unruly sons within their borders; but now they dared not, since even into Zoar had penetrated the knowledge that America was a free country. The younger generation were not as their fathers were; objections had been openly made to the cut of the Sunday coats, and the girls had spoken together of ribbons!

The shadows of twilight seemed very long in falling that night, but at last there was no further excuse for delaying the evening bell, and home came the laborers to their evening meal. There was no moon, a soft mist obscured the stars, and the night was darkened with the excess of richness which rose from the ripening valley-fields and fat bottom-lands along the river. The community store opposite the Wirthshaus was closed early in the evening, the houses of the trustees were dark, and indeed the village was almost unlighted, as if to hide its own excitement. The entire population was abroad in the night, and one by one the men and boys stole away down the station road, a lovely, winding track on the hill-side, following the river on its way down the valley to the little station on the grass-grown railroad, a branch from the main track. As ten o'clock came, the women and girls, grown bold with excitement, gathered in the open space in front of the Wirthshaus, where the lights from the windows illumined their faces. There I saw the broad-shouldered Lydia, Rosine, Doroty, and all the rest, in their Sunday clothes, flushed, laughing, and chattering; but no Wilhelmina.

"Where can she be?" I said.

If she was there, the larger girls concealed her with their buxom breadth; I looked for the slender little maiden in vain.

"Shu!" cried the girls, "de bugle!"

Far down the station road we heard the bugle and saw the glimmering of lights among the trees. On it came, a will-o'-the-wisp procession: first a detachment of village boys each with a lantern or torch, next the returned soldiers winding their bugles, for, German-like, they all had musical instruments, then an excited crowd of brothers and cousins loaded with knapsacks, guns, and military accoutrements of all kinds; each man had something, were it only a tin cup, and proudly they marched in the footsteps of their glorious relatives, bearing the spoils of war. The girls set up a shrill cry of welcome as the procession approached, but the ranks continued unbroken until the open space in front of the Wirthshaus was reached; then, at a signal, the soldiers gave three cheers, the villagers joining in with all their hearts and lungs, but wildly and out of time, like the scattering fire of an awkward squad. The sound had never been heard in Zoar before. The soldiers gave a final "Tiger-r-r!" and then broke ranks, mingling with the excited crowd, exchanging greetings and embraces. All talked at once; some wept, some laughed and through it all, silently stood the three trustees on the dark porch in front of the store, looking down upon their wild flock, their sober faces visible in the glare of the torches and lanterns below. The entire population was present; even the babies were held up on the outskirts of the crowd, stolid and staring.

"Where can Wilhelmina be?" I said again.

"Here, under the window; I saw her long ago," replied one of the women.

Leaning against a piazza-pillar, close under my eyes, stood the little maiden, pale and still. I could not disguise from myself that she looked almost ugly among those florid, laughing girls, for her color was gone, and her eyes so fixed that they looked unnaturally large; her somewhat heavy Egyptian features stood out in the bright light, but her small form was lost among the group of broad, white-kerchiefed shoulders, adorned with breast-knots of gay flowers. And had Wilhelmina no flower? She, so fond of blossoms? I looked again; yes, a little white rose, drooping and pale as herself.

But where was Gustav? The soldiers came and went in the crowd, and all spoke to Mina; but where was the One? I caught the landlord's little son as he passed, and asked the question.

"Gustav? Dat's him," he answered, pointing out a tall, rollicking soldier who seemed to be embracing the whole population in his glee-ful welcome. That very soldier had passed Mina a dozen times, flinging a gay greeting to her each time; but nothing more.

After half an hour of general rejoicing, the crowd dispersed, each household bearing off in triumph the hero that fell to its lot. Then the tiled domiciles, where usually all were asleep an hour after twilight, blazed forth with unaccustomed light from every little window, and within we could see the circles, with flagons of beer and various dainties manufactured in secret during the day, sitting and talking together in a manner which, for Zoar, was a wild revel, since it was nearly eleven o'clock! We were not the only outside spectators of this unwonted gayety; several times we met the three trustees stealing along in the shadow from house to house, like anxious spectres in broad-brimmed hats. No doubt they said to each other, "How, how will this end!"

The merry Gustav had gone off by Mina's side, which gave me some comfort; but when in our rounds we came to the gardener's house and gazed through the open door, the little maiden sat apart, and the sol-dier, in the centre of an admiring circle, was telling stories of the war.

I felt a foreboding of sorrow as I gazed out through the little window before climbing up into my high bed. Lights still twinkled in some of the houses, but a white mist was rising from the river, and the drowsy, long-drawn chant of the summer night invited me to dreamless sleep.

The next morning I could not resist questioning Jacobina, who also had her lover among the soldiers, if all was well.

"Oh yes. They stay—all but two. We's married next mont."

"And the two?"

"Karl and Gustav."

"And Wilhelmina!" I exclaimed.

"Oh, she let him go," answered Jacobina, bringing fresh coffee.

"Poor child! How does she bear it?"

"Oh, so. She cannot help. She say noding."

"But the trustees, will they allow these young men to leave the community?"

"They cannot help," said Jacobina.

"Gustav and Karl write not in the book; they free to go. Wilhelmina marry Jacob; it's joost the same; all r-r-ight," added Jacobina, who prided herself on her English, caught from visitors at the Wirthshaus table.

"Ah! but it is not just the same," I thought as I went up to the garden to find my little maiden. She was not there; the leathery mother said she was out on the hills with the cows.

"So Gustav is going to leave the community," I said in German.

"Yes, better so. He is an idle, wild boy. Now Veelhelminy can marry the baker, a good steady man."

"But Mina does not like him," I suggested.

"Das macht nichts [That doesn't matter]," answered the leathery mother.

Wilhelmina was not in the pasture; I sought for her everywhere, and called her name. The poor child had hidden herself, and whether she heard me or not, she did not respond. All day she kept herself aloof; I almost feared she would never return; but in the late twilight a little figure slipped through the garden-gate and took refuge in the house before I could speak, for I was watching for the child, apparently the only one, though a stranger, to care for her sorrow.

"Can I not see her?" I said to the leathery mother, following to the door.

"Eh, no; she's foolish; she will not speak a word; she has gone off to bed," was the answer.

For three days I did not see Mina, so early did she flee away to the hills, and so late return. I followed her to the pasture once or twice, but she would not show herself, and I could not discover her hiding-place. The fourth day I learned that Gustav and Karl were to leave the village in the afternoon, probably forever. The other soldiers had signed the articles presented by the anxious trustees, and settled down into the old routine, going afield with the rest, although still heroes of the hour; they were all to be married in August. No doubt the hardships of their campaigns among the Tennessee mountains had taught them that the rich valley was a home not to be despised; nevertheless it was evident that the flowers of the flock were those who were about departing, and that in Gustav and Karl the community lost its brightest spirits. Evident to us; but, possibly, the community cared not for bright spirits.

I had made several attempts to speak to Gustav; this morning I at last succeeded. I found him polishing his bugle on the garden bench.

"Why are you going away, Gustav?" I asked. "Zoar is a pleasant little village."

"Too slow for me, miss."

"The life is easy, however; you will find the world a hard place."

"I don't mind work, ma'am but I do like to be free. I feel all cramped up here, with these rules and bells; and, besides, I could n't stand those trustees; they never let a fellow alone."

"And Wilhelmina? If you do go, I hope you will take her with you, or come for her when you have found work."

"Oh no, miss. All that was long ago. It's all over now."

"But you like her, Gustav?"

"Oh, so. She's a good little thing, but too quiet for me."

"But she likes you," I said desperately, for I saw no other way to loosen this Gordian knot.

"Oh no, miss. She got used to it, and has thought of it all these years; that's all. She'll forget about it, and marry the baker."

"But she does not like the baker."

"Why not? He's a good fellow enough. She'll like him in time. It's all the same. I declare it's too bad to see all these girls going on in the same old way, in their ugly gowns and big shoes! Why, ma'am I could n't take Mina outside, even if I wanted to; she's too old to learn new ways, and everybody would laugh at her. She could n't get along a day. Besides," said the young soldier, coloring up to his eyes, "I don't mind telling you that—that there's someone else. Look here, ma'am;" and he put into my hand a card photograph representing a pretty girl, overdressed and adorned with curls and gilt jewelry. "That's Miss Martin," said Gustav with pride; "Miss Emmeline Martin, of Cincinnati. I'm going to marry Miss Martin."

As I held the pretty, flashy picture in my hand, all my castles fell to the ground. My plan for taking Mina home with me, accustoming her gradually to other clothes and ways, teaching her enough of the world to enable her to hold her place without pain, my hope that my husband might find a situation for Gustav in some of the iron-mills near Cleveland, in short, all the idyl I had woven, was destroyed. If it had not been for this red-cheeked Miss Martin in her gilt beads! "Why is it that men will be such fools?" I thought. Up sprung a memory of the curls and ponderous jet necklace I sported at a certain period of my existence, when John—I was silenced, gave Gustav his picture, and walked away without a word.

At noon the villagers, on their way back to work, paused at the Wirthshaus to say good-by; Karl and Gustav were there, and the old woolly horse had already gone to the station with their boxes. Among the others came Christine, Karl's former affianced, heart-whole and smiling, already betrothed to a new lover; but no Wilhelmina. Good wishes and farewells were exchanged, and at last the two soldiers started away, falling into the marching step, and watched with furtive satisfaction by the three trustees, who stood together in the shadow of the smithy, apparently deeply absorbed in a broken-down cask.

It was a lovely afternoon, and I, too, strolled down the station road embowered in shade. The two soldiers were not far in advance. I had passed the flour-mill on the outskirts of the village and was approaching the old quarry, when a sound startled me; out from the rocks in front rushed a little figure, and crying "Gustav, mein Gustav!" fell at the soldier's feet. It was Wilhelmina.

I ran forward and took her from the young man; she lay in my arms as if dead. The poor child was sadly changed; always slender and swaying, she now looked thin and shrunken, her skin had a strange, dark pallor, and her lips were drawn in as if from pain. I could see her eyes through the large-orbed thin lids, and the brown shadows beneath extended down into the cheeks.

"Was ist's [What's wrong]?" said Gustav, looking bewildered. "Is she sick?"

I answered "Yes," but nothing more. I could see that he had no suspicion of the truth, believing as he did that the "good fellow" of a baker would do very well for this "good little thing" who was "too quiet" for him. The memory of Miss Martin sealed my lips. But if it had not been for that pretty, flashy picture, would I not have spoken!

"You must go; you will miss the train," I said, after a few minutes. "I will see to Mina."

But Gustav lingered. Perhaps he was really troubled to see the little sweetheart of his boyhood in such desolate plight; perhaps a touch of the old feeling came back; and perhaps, also, it was nothing of the kind, and, as usual, my romantic imagination was carrying me away. At any rate, whatever it was, he stooped over the fainting girl.

"She looks bad," he said, "very bad. I wish—but she'll get well and marry the baker. Good-by, Mina." And bending his tall form, he kissed her colorless cheek, and then hastened away to join the impatient Karl; a curve in the road soon hid them from view.

Wilhelmina had stirred at his touch; after a moment her large eyes opened slowly; she looked around as if dazed, but all at once memory came back, and she started up with the same cry, "Gustav, mein Gustav!" I drew her head down on my shoulder to stifle the sound; it was better the soldier should not hear it, and its anguish thrilled my own heart, also. She had not the strength to resist me, and in a few minutes I knew that the young men were out of hearing as they strode on towards the station, and out into the wide world.

The forest was solitary, we were beyond the village; all the afternoon I sat under the trees with the stricken girl. Again, as in her joy, her words were few; again, as in her joy, her whole being was involved. Her little rough hands were cold, a film had gathered over her eyes; she did not weep, but moaned to herself, and all her senses seemed blunted. At night-fall I took her home, and the leathery mother received her with a frown; but the child was beyond caring, and crept away, dumbly to her room.

The next morning she was off to the hills again, nor could I find her for several days. Evidently, in spite of my sympathy, I was no more to her than I should have been to a wounded fawn. She was a mixture of the wild, shy creature of the woods and the deep-loving woman of the tropics; in either case I could be but small comfort. When at last I did see her, she was apathetic and dull; her feelings, her senses, and her intelligence seemed to have gone within, as if preying upon her heart. She scarcely listened to my proposal to take her with me; for, in my pity, I had suggested it in spite of its difficulties.

"No," she said mechanically; "I's better here;" and fell into silence again.

A month later, a friend went down to spend a few days in the valley, and upon her return described to us the weddings of the whilom [former] soldiers. "It was really a pretty sight," she said, "the quaint peasant dresses and the flowers. Afterwards, the band went round the village playing their odd tunes, and all had a holiday. There were two civilians married also; I mean two young men who had not been to the war. It seems that two of the soldiers turned their backs upon the community and their allotted brides, and marched away; but the Zoar maidens are not romantic, I fancy, for these two deserted ones were betrothed again and married, all in the short space of four weeks."

"Was not one Wilhelmina, the gardener's daughter, a short, dark girl?" I asked.

"Yes."

"And she married Jacob the baker?"

"Yes."

The next year, weary of the cold lake-winds, we left the icy shore and went down to the valley to meet the coming spring, finding her already there, decked with vines and flowers. A new waitress brought us our coffee.

"How is Wilhelmina?" I asked.

"Eh—Wilhelmina? Oh, she not here now; she gone to the Next Country," answered the girl in a matter-of-fact way. "She die last October, and Jacob he haf anoder wife now."

In the late afternoon I asked a little girl to show me Wilhelmina's grave in the quiet God's Acre on the hill. Innovation was creeping in, even here; the later graves had mounds raised over them, and one had a little head-board with an inscription in ink.

Wilhelmina lay apart, and some one, probably the old gardener, who had loved the little maiden in his silent way, had planted a rose-bush at the head of the mound. I dismissed my guide and sat there alone in the sunset, thinking of many things, but chiefly of this: "Why should this great wealth of love have been allowed to waste itself? Why is it that the greatest power, unquestionably, of this mortal life should so often seem a useless gift?"

No answer came from the sunset clouds, and as twilight sank down on the earth I rose to go. "I fully believe," I said, as though repeating a creed, "that this poor, loving heart, whose earthly body lies under this mound, is happy now in its own loving way. It has not been changed, but the happiness it longed for has come. How, we know not; but the God who made Wilhelmina understands her. He has given unto her not rest, not peace, but an active, living joy."

I walked away through the wild meadow, under whose turf, unmarked by stone or mound, lay the first pioneers of the community, and out into the forest road, untraveled save when the dead passed over it to their last earthly home. The evening was still and breathless, and the shadows lay thick on the grass as I looked back. But I could still distinguish the little mound with the rosebush at its head, and, not without tears, I said, "Farewell, poor Wilhelmina; farewell."

Known primarily as a poet, Edward Rowland Sill, upon his return to Cuyahoga Falls from Berkeley, California, published extensively in the "Contributors Club" of the *Atlantic Monthly,* where the character sketch "Old Morton" appeared in January 1887, a month before Sill's untimely death.

Old Morton

The Middle-Western village produces, or confirms into inveteracy when produced, many a queer type of character. In the same way that isolated valleys in mountainous countries develop and preserve distinct idioms of folk-speech, so do these isolated semi-rustic regions exhibit odd dialectic varieties of human nature. One such queer character, or "odd stick," is remembered in our village as "Old Morton." Bent at a crooked right angle, weather-stained and storm-beaten, like a sort of land species of ancient mariner, gray, unkempt, and his arid face visibly

consoled by perennial founts of tobacco, the old man was wont to hob-
ble through the village street about once a day, usually at mail-time.
For he, too, it was clear, like all the denizens of little towns, and especially those without either correspondence or business, had always
great expectations in connection with the unknown possibilities of each
day's lean but punctual mail-bag. His only employment and means of
support consisted of chance jobs of small joinery in a rickety little shop
on the bank of the river, in the loft of which was his lonely and unseen
lair. There never was a more inoffensive creature; he was very gentle
with small children and all piteous dumb animals; but his bent-over
face had a splenetic gaze down at mother earth,—say, rather, step-
mother pavement,—as he made his way along the street, and his old
blue eyes looked up at you with a sort of protesting hostility, as if, in
the absence of a visible Providence, he took you for a representative of
things in general and accused you of his fate. I was comparatively a
new-comer in the town, and had never exchanged greetings with him;
but one day, as I was hurrying across the stone bridge, he met me, and
stopped me with the paralyzing exclamation, *"Ain't ye glad ye ain't old
Morton!"* I was never more nonplused and put to it for a reply. What I
did respond was, "Who?—*I?*" But whether this counter-interrogative
of mine meant anything or not, I have never known. The particular
nuance of my own inner consciousness that prompted my words had, in
my astonishment, evaporated with them, as I found upon asking myself what under the moon I had meant, while I hurried on my way. *His*
words I understood well enough, and perhaps mine may have been
meant to convey some sudden sense of my small reason for any such
self-gratulation. But it is quite as likely my mental breath was so completely taken away that I made the response in entire idiocy.

I learned afterward that it was a habit of his to address this or a similar question to persons of his acquaintance. His constant idea seemed
to be that, whatever the apparent hardness of any other mortal's lot in
life, it ought to be a sufficient consolation to him to reflect that, after
all, he was not Old Morton.

There was philosophy in the reflection, and I was glad to have im-
bibed it. In fact, what right had I to grumble and sulk about things, so
long as I had not the weak and friendless old man's bent back, and
rheumatism, and shattered nerves, and forlorn abandonment?

Once I was waiting at the provision store, on some family errand of
"harmless necessary," soap, or sugar, or other village bricabrac (such
as it is the pleasant privilege of the literary man of the household, with
his apparent plenitude of leisure, to purvey), when I saw the ancient
philosopher, sitting on a cracker barrel, and gazing at a pair of urchins
whose tow heads barely reached the counter. There was a kind of quiz-
zical and melancholy tenderness in his look. "There's one good thing

about them boys!" he exclaimed with emphasis, as he caught my eye. *"They won't neither one on 'em never be Old Morton!"* And he evidently felt that in pronouncing this decisive judgment he was, as it were, a benignant oracle, decreeing them a blessed fate.

Sarah K. Bolton (1841–1916), a prolific writer of biography, poetry, and fiction, came to Cleveland in 1866 as the bride of Charles E. Bolton, with whom she worked on humanitarian and temperance causes. Her fictional studies of local social and cultural practices are collected in *A Country Idyl and Other Stories* (1898). "The Twilight Hour Society" satirizes not only the illusions of a northeastern Ohio ladies' literary society but also the fatuousness of the Eastern literary establishment.

The Twilight Hour Society

"Heléna, we must send out the invitations this very afternoon for the new literary society. It must be done with great care, too. I wish this to be the most select club of the West."

The speaker was Mrs. Helen Brunswick, who had just returned from Europe. She was a lady of considerable culture and taste, and, what was not an inconvenient addition of wealth. Her husband, a good business man, had died—perhaps opportunely; for, though Mrs. Brunswick was polite to him, she told her bosom friends that "he was not poetical," and, therefore, not a very congenial spirit. His wife was a teacher when he married her, poor, but of very good family, and his money was undoubtedly the chief attraction.

She had one child, whose name, for the sake of elegance, she always called Heléna rather than Helen, and of whom she was very fond; but her one absorbing plan was to make her home a literary centre. She bought, on her return from Europe, an old-fashioned house,—a new one would have seemed vulgar to her aesthetic taste,—and furnished it as nearly as possible like the houses of some celebrated persons which she had seen abroad. She revelled in old tapestries, and bronzes which looked as though they were made in the bronze age.

Heléna sat down, note-book in hand, to make out a list of those who were to be honored members of the new association.

"Shall we invite Fanny Green, mamma?"

"Oh, no, dear! She is only a local poet, getting a few articles into the newspapers here and there. This society will not be established to help struggling newspaper writers or embryo artists. These will make their way somehow if they have talent, but the elegant ladies of Lakeville will not care to associate with such crude aspirants. We must take those from the very highest walks of life, those who enjoy art especially, and can prepare an essay on sculpture or Egyptian lore. The young artists and novelists are usually poor and hard workers, so they would have no time to look up these subjects, which require great research and the leisure that only a lady of wealth has."

"But, mamma, it would so help the rising artists if their pictures could be brought before the society. They would be purchased, probably, for the elegant homes."

"Oh, no! Most elegant ladies want a picture painted by a famous artist, so that when they speak of the work to a friend the talent will be seen at once."

"Don't they know talent when they see it, whether John Smith or Bougereau painted it?"

"Oh, dear, no, Heléna! You must not ask too much of people. I don't care to read a book unless a well-known name is on the title-page. I consider it a waste of time. As soon as a man has made his mark I am glad to read him."

The rising artists and the rising editors and contributors were not invited to membership in the new organization. Thirty-five names were sent out.

"We must not have more than twenty-five in the circle, Heléna, for large societies are never select. If there are but a few, and those very literary, they will praise each other and feel proud of the pleasure of belonging. There's everything in knowing how to handle women. Let them think it is exclusive and there will be a great longing to join; and when they cannot be admitted, from the smallness of the number, the society will become the leading topic of the city. Each member, too, will be all the more interested if she takes her turn in writing an essay, and this would not be possible in a large society."

"Why, mother, half of those whom you have named couldn't write an essay!"

"Well, my child, they have some friend who can help them. Money always buys help, and usually of a very superior kind."

The invitations were sent out, and in due time the elegant ladies arrived. They admired Mrs. Brunswick's rugs, her choice bits of needlework from abroad, and especially her antique bronzes.

The first tribulation of the society was over the adoption of a name. The "Mutual Club" was suggested, but "club" seemed strong-minded to some of the ladies present, and was abandoned. One suggested the "Society for Intellectual Growth," but this seemed to suggest labor, and it would not be best to suggest very much work to such a charming circle. Mrs. Brunswick herself suggested, after many others had spoken, that the "Twilight Hour" would be poetic and refining, and as the members would usually come late in the afternoon, or in the evening if some celebrity were invited, this name would cover all times

and seasons, convey no impression of moral reforms, and frighten no
husbands with the fear that their wives would become unsuited to
pretty gowns by mental wear.

The name was voted a happy thought, and the plan proceeded. A
committee on membership was suggested, only twenty having responded to the invitation, and five more could be admitted. One lady,
the wife of a senator, must be secured at all hazards, and this committee
were to wait upon her at once. Another lady had travelled nearly the
world over, and had several millions in her own right, and must on no
account be omitted. A third was selected for no especial reason except
she had held herself above ordinary society, and the select had come to
regard this as a sign of aristocracy. Real aristocracy is too quiet to at-
tract much attention, but the unreal is very prevalent.

The desired number was made up, and the "Twilight Hour Society,"
as was expected, became the talk of Lakeville. A Gentlemen's Night
was given occasionally, and those only were invited who were supposed to be poetic. There was a leaning toward the ministerial profession, and a few judges and doctors were permitted to enter the select
circle. The time came when it was necessary to invite a celebrity. Mrs.
Wentworth was talking the matter over with Mrs. Brunswick.

"I hear," said the former lady, "that the author of the new book
which has just appeared in Boston, "The Story of a Life," is to be at
Lakeville soon to visit a cousin. The book is selling rapidly. It is a delightful psychological story of a woman's heart, I have heard, and the
men are as eager to read it as the women. Mr. Smithnight, the author,
has become famous suddenly, and all the young ladies are enthusiastic
over him. He is quite young, and very delightful, they say."

"Oh, yes," said Mrs. Brunswick, "anything that comes from Boston is delightful! Society is very deep there. The people are always
making a study of hidden things of the mind, while we at the West
are so very practical over the bread and butter matters of life. Alas! how
far we are drifting from the beautiful and the sublime! We must have
Mr. Smithnight at our next reception, and make it as elegant as possible. How lovely those people are who write books!"

The cousin of Mr. Smithnight, who lived on a side street, and never
would have been thought worthy to step into the Twilight Hour circle,
was visited, and asked if a reception for Mr. Smithnight could possibly
be arranged. The young Plato was glad to be shown off before the admiring gaze of the uncultured West, and readily consented to be present.

"Heléna," said Mrs. Brunswick, as they draped the mantel with
smilax and lilies of the valley, "I have always hoped that you would
marry an author. Perhaps in Mr. Smithnight you will find your ideal."

"I hope he's handsome, mamma, and not too conceited, as so many
literary people are."

"I think you misjudge literary people, dear. They must hold themselves aloof from general society, else they would not be considered so great. You know a writer across the water always seems greater to us than our own authors."

The old-fashioned house of the Brunswicks was lighted, not so gorgeously as to seem loud, and fragrant flowers were in profusion. Very elegant people came in their choicest robes to pay allegiance to the new novelist. Had he been a poet, he must needs have waited till he was fifty for America to find out whether he had genius or no; had he been a scientist, he would not have won his fame till death probably; but having given the public a well-written book which sold, America at once pronounced him a genius. Without doubt there were wheels within wheels which procured its publication. Perhaps he was a cousin to some first-class novelist, or had a governor to recommend his work; for how are publishers to known a thing will be a success? Nearly all the great books, like "Uncle Tom's Cabin" and "Jane Eyre," have been refused for months, and even years.

Mr. Smithnight was present to receive the homage of Lakeville. He had a fine, even commanding, presence: black hair, which lay lightly over his forehead, a stray lock drooping occasionally, which his white hand tossed back; expressive dark eyes; and a bland smile. He was evidently a good student of human nature, for, while he was egotistical,—successful men usually have a good opinion of themselves,—he had the tact to make every lady feel that the intellectual culture of Lakeville was something phenomenal. Mrs. Brunswick thanked him heartily for coming, coming from such a centre of knowledge as Boston, to stimulate the over-practical West. She wanted to enjoy his conversation at another time, when she and dear Heléna could have him all to themselves. As he took his departure he held Heléna's hand somewhat tenderly, and begged the pleasure of frequent visits during his short stay in Lakeville.

"Heléna," said Mrs. Brunswick, after the guests had departed, "I think Mr. Smithnight the most charming celebrity we have ever had. Think how people will speak of it! I know of nothing so delightful as a salon for literary people. How many must envy me the rare pleasure of bringing together these appreciative people and these great people! You know some of our celebrities from other cities have been so dull and stupid, and read such nonunderstandable essays, that our ladies have not known what to say or do. I think some of the manuscripts must have lain in trunks for years. But Mr. Smithnight is so charming, so fresh and entertaining! I think he likes you, Heléna, for I saw him bestowing very admiring glances upon you."

"I don't know. I did n't trouble myself much about him. I liked him, though, well enough."

"Oh, you must be very polite to him, my dear, for literary chances are so rare at the West! Think where such a man would place you."

Mr. Smithnight's stay at Lakeville grew from days into weeks, and finally into months. He was a frequent visitor at Mrs. Brunswick's, and rumor whispered that he was to wed Heléna. Mrs. Brunswick made him the lion of the city. She bought sundry copies of the "Story of a Life," and placed them where they would receive glowing notices by the press, and be read by the most select of Lakeville society. She sent several copies abroad, telling the recipients that it was written by a special friend of Heléna's.

Mr. Smithnight had found no such encouraging aid in Boston. There a few mutual friends helped each other, but the outside world troubled itself little about the strugglers for fame. At last it was publicly announced that Mr. Smithnight and Heléna were engaged. Some common-sense mothers wondered if he had the ability to earn a living, knowing that literature in general is not a paying business. Some wondered whether he was able to spend so much as he seemed to be doing weekly; but marrying a young lady well-to-do might be an effective way of meeting debts.

Mrs. Brunswick would have preferred that the young couple live with her, but Heléna wished a house of her own, which was accordingly purchased. Mr. Smithnight, with his refined taste, helped in the selection of the furniture and the bridal trousseau, and did not hesitate to buy the best.

One afternoon, when the last articles had been purchased, a wild rumor was heard on the street that Mr. Smithnight had been seen driving out of town with a lady who was not Heléna Brunswick; that many bills had been contracted in Mrs. Brunswick's name and left unpaid; and that money had been obtained at the bank fraudulently by the departing celebrity.

Mrs. Brunswick was overwhelmed with the news. Heléna was exceedingly annoyed, but in no wise heart-broken, because for years she had liked a poor young artist of the city, who was not thought high enough to be invited to the Twilight Hour Society.

The literary association finally disbanded. Mrs. Brunswick sold the old-fashioned home and moved to another city, holding no more receptions for celebrities. Heléna married her poor artist, who rose to eminence in his profession.

Charles Waddell Chesnutt (1858–1932) was born in Cleveland. Outside of a grammar school education in Fayetteville, North Carolina, where his family had moved shortly after the Civil War, he was largely self-educated. He taught in a normal school before returning to Cleveland in 1883 to become the first writer to deal with race questions from an African-American point of view. With the publication of *The Wife of His Youth and Other Stories of the Color Line* (1899), Chesnutt was placed in the top rank of American short story writers by critic William Dean Howells. The title story of the collection realistically describes the experience of Chesnutt and his wife, Susan, in the Social Circle, a group of prominent Cleveland African-Americans.

The Wife of His Youth

I

Mr. Ryder was going to give a ball. There were several reasons why this was an opportune time for such an event.

Mr. Ryder might aptly be called the dean of the Blue Veins. The original Blue Veins were a little society of colored persons organized in a certain Northern city shortly after the war. Its purpose was to establish and maintain correct social standards among a people whose social condition presented almost unlimited room for improvement. By accident, combined perhaps with some natural affinity, the society consisted of individuals who were, generally speaking, more white than black. Some envious outsider made the suggestion that no one was eligible for membership who was not white enough to show blue veins. The suggestion was readily adopted by those who were not of the favored few, and since that time the society, though possessing a longer and more pretentious name, had been known far and wide as the "Blue Vein Society," and its members as the "Blue Veins."

The Blue Veins did not allow that any such requirement existed for admission to their circle, but, on the contrary, declared that character and culture were the only things considered; and that if most of their members were light-colored, it was because such persons, as a rule, had had better opportunities to qualify themselves for membership. Opinions differed, too, as to the usefulness of the society. There were those who had been known to assail it violently as a glaring example of the very prejudice from which the colored race had suffered most; and later, when such critics had succeeded in getting on the inside, they had been heard to maintain with zeal and earnestness that the society was a life-boat, an anchor, a bulwark and a shield,—a pillar of cloud by day and of fire by night, to guide their people through the social wilderness. Another alleged prerequisite for Blue Vein membership was that of free birth; and while there was really no such requirement, it is doubtless true that very few of the members would have been unable to meet it if there had been. If there were one or two of the older members who had come up from the South and from slavery, their history presented enough romantic circumstances to rob their servile origin of its grosser aspects.

While there were no such tests of eligibility, it is true that the Blue Veins had their notions on these subjects, and that not all of them were equally liberal in regard to the things they collectively disclaimed. Mr. Ryder was one of the most conservative. Though he had not been among the founders of the society, but had come in some years later, his genius for social leadership was such that he had speedily become its recognized adviser and head, the custodian of its standards, and the preserver of its traditions. He shaped its social policy, was active in providing for its entertainment, and when the interest fell off, as it sometimes did, he fanned the embers until they burst again into a cheerful flame.

There were still other reasons for his popularity. While he was not as white as some of the Blue Veins, his appearance was such as to confer distinction upon them. His features were of a refined type, his hair was almost straight; he was always neatly dressed; his manners were irreproachable, and his morals above suspicion. He had come to Groveland a young man, and obtaining employment in the office of a railroad company as messenger had in time worked himself up to the position of stationery clerk, having charge of the distribution of the office supplies for the whole company. Although the lack of early training had hindered the orderly development of a naturally fine mind, it had not prevented him from doing a great deal of reading or from forming decidedly literary tastes. Poetry was his passion. He could repeat whole pages of the great English poets; and if his pronunciation was sometimes faulty, his eye, his voice, his gestures, would respond to the changing sentiment with a precision that revealed a poetic soul and disarmed criticism. He was economical, and had saved money; he owned and occupied a very comfortable house on a respectable street. His residence was handsomely furnished, containing among other things a good library, especially rich in poetry, a piano, and some choice engravings. He generally shared his house with some young couple, who looked after his wants and were company for him; for Mr. Ryder was a single man. In the early days of his connection with the Blue Veins he had been regarded as quite a catch, and young ladies and their mothers had manœuvred with much ingenuity to capture him. Not, however, until Mrs. Molly Dixon visited Groveland had any woman ever made him wish to change his condition to that of a married man.

Mrs. Dixon had come to Groveland from Washington in the spring, and before the summer was over, she had won Mr. Ryder's heart. She possessed many attractive qualities. She was much younger than he; in fact, he was old enough to have been her father, though no one knew exactly how old he was. She was whiter than he, and better educated. She had moved in the best colored society of the country, at Washington, and had taught in the schools of that city. Such a superior person had been eagerly welcomed to the Blue Vein Society, and had taken a leading part in its activities. Mr. Ryder had at first been attracted by her charms of person, for she was very good looking and not over twenty-five; then by her refined manners and the vivacity of her wit. Her husband had been a government clerk, and at his death had left a considerable life insurance. She was visiting friends in Groveland, and, finding the town and the people to her liking, had prolonged her stay indefinitely. She had not seemed displeased at Mr. Ryder's attentions, but on the contrary had given him every proper encouragement; indeed, a younger and less cautious man would long since have spoken. But he had made up his mind, and had only to determine the time when he would ask her to be his wife. He decided to give a ball in her honor, and at some time during the evening of the ball to offer her his heart and hand. He had no special fears about the outcome, but, with a little touch of romance, he wanted the surroundings to be in harmony with his own feelings when he should have received the answer he expected.

Mr. Ryder resolved that this ball should mark an epoch in the social history of Groveland. He knew, of course,—no one could know better,—the entertainments that had taken place in past years, and what must be done to surpass them. His ball must be worthy of the lady in whose honor it was to be given, and must, by the quality of its guests, set an example for the future. He had observed of late a growing liberality, almost a laxity, in social matters, even among members of his own set, and had several times been forced to meet in a social way persons whose complexions and callings in life were hardly up to the standard which he considered proper for the society to maintain. He had a theory of his own.

"I have no race prejudice," he would say, "but we people of mixed blood are ground between the upper and the nether millstone. Our fate lies between absorption by the white race and extinction in the black. The one does n't want us yet, but may take us in time. The other would welcome us, but it would be for us a backward step. 'With malice towards none, with charity for all,' we must do the best we can for ourselves and those who are to follow us. Self-preservation is the first law of nature."

His ball would serve by its exclusiveness to counteract leveling tendencies, and his marriage with Mrs. Dixon would help to further the upward process of absorption he had been wishing and waiting for.

II

The ball was to take place on Friday night. The house had been put in order, the carpets covered with canvas, the halls and stairs decorated with palms and potted plants; and in the afternoon Mr. Ryder sat on his front porch, which the shade of a vine running up over a wire netting made a cool and pleasant lounging place. He expected to respond to the toast "The Ladies" at the supper, and from a volume of Tennyson—his favorite poet—was fortifying himself with apt quotations. The volume was open at "A Dream of Fair Women." His eyes fell on these lines, and he read them aloud to judge better of their effect:—

> "At length I saw a lady within call,
>   Stiller than chisell'd marble, standing there;
> A daughter of the gods, divinely tall,
>   And most divinely fair."

He marked the verse, and turning the page read the stanza beginning,—

> "O sweet pale Margaret,
>   O rare pale Margaret."

He weighed the passage a moment, and decided that it would not do. Mrs. Dixon was the palest lady he expected at the ball, and she was of a rather ruddy complexion, and of lively disposition and buxom build. So he ran over the leaves until his eye rested on the description of Queen Guinevere:—

> "She seem'd a part of joyous Spring:
>   A gown of grass-green silk she wore,
>   Buckled with golden clasps before;
> A light-green tuft of plumes she bore
>   Closed in a golden ring.
>   .   .   .   .
> "She look'd so lovely, as she sway'd
>   The rein with dainty finger-tips,
> A man had given all other bliss,
> And all his worldly worth for this,
> To waste his whole heart in one kiss
>   Upon her perfect lips."

As Mr. Ryder murmured these words audibly, with an appreciative thrill, he heard the latch of his gate click, and a light footfall sounding on the steps. He turned his head, and saw a woman standing before his door.

She was a little woman, not five feet tall, and proportioned to her height. Although she stood erect, and looked around her with very bright and restless eyes, she seemed quite old; for her face was crossed and recrossed with a hundred wrinkles, and around the edges of her bonnet could be seen protruding here and there a tuft of short grey wool. She wore a blue calico gown of ancient cut, a little red shawl fastened around her shoulders with an old-fashioned brass brooch, and a large bonnet profusely ornamented with faded red and yellow artificial flowers. And she was very black,—so black that her toothless gums, revealed when she opened her mouth to speak, were not red, but

blue. She looked like a bit of the old plantation life, summoned up
from the past by the wave of a magician's wand, as the poet's fancy
had called into being the gracious shapes of which Mr. Ryder had just
been reading.

He rose from his chair and came over to where she stood.

"Good-afternoon, madam," he said.

"Good-evenin' suh," she answered, ducking suddenly with a quaint
curtsy. Her voice was shrill and piping, but softened somewhat by age.
"Is dis yere whar Mistuh Ryduh lib, suh?" she asked, looking around
her doubtfully, and glancing into the open windows, through which
some of the preparations for the evening were visible.

"Yes," he replied, with an air of kindly patronage, unconsciously
flattered by her manner, "I am Mr. Ryder. Did you want to see me?"

"Yas, suh, ef I ain't 'sturbin' of you too much."

"Not at all. Have a seat over here behind the vine, where it is cool.
What can I do for you?"

" 'Scuse me, suh," she continued, when she had sat down on the
edge of a chair, " 'scuse me, suh, I 's lookin' for my husban'. I heerd you
wuz a big man an' had libbed heah a long time, an' I 'lowed you would
n't min' ef I'd come roun' an' ax you ef you 'd ever heerd of a merlatter
man by de name er Sam Taylor 'quirin' roun' in de chu'ches ermongs'
de people fer his wife 'Liza Jane?"

Mr. Ryder seemed to think for a moment.

"There used to be many such cases right after the war," he said, "but
it has been so long that I have forgotten them. There are very few now.
But tell me your story, and it may refresh my memory."

She sat back further in her chair so as to be more comfortable, and
folded her withered hands in her lap.

"My name's 'Liza," she began, " 'Liza Jane. W'en I wuz young I
us'ter b'long ter Marse Bob Smif, down in ole Missoura. I wuz bawn
down dere. W'en I wuz a gal I wuz married ter a man named Jim. But
Jim died, an' after dat I married a merlatter man named Sam Taylor.
Sam wuz freebawn, but his mammy and daddy died, an' de w'ite folks
'prenticed him ter my marster fer ter work fer 'im 'tel he wuz growed
up. Sam worked in de fiel', an' I wuz de cook. One day Ma'y Ann, ole
miss's maid, came rushin' out ter de kitchen, an' says she, ' 'Liza Jane,
ole marse gwine sell yo' Sam down de ribber.'

" 'Go way f'm yere,' says I; 'my husban' 's free!'

" 'Don' make no diff'ence. I heerd old marse tell ole miss he wuz
gwine take yo' Sam 'way wid 'im ter-morrow, fer he needed money,
an' he knowed whar he could git a t'ousan' dollars fer Sam an' no
questions axed.'

"W'en Sam come home f'm de fiel' dat night, I tole him 'bout ole
marse gwine steal 'im, an' Sam run erway. His time wuz mos' up, an'
he swo' dat w'en he wuz twenty-one he would come back an' he'p me

run erway, or else save up de money ter buy my freedom. An' I know he'd 'a' done it, fer he thought a heap er me, Sam did. But w'en he come back he did n' fin' me, fer I wuz n' dere. Ole marse had heerd dat I warned Sam, so he had me whip' an' sol' down de ribber.

"Den de wah broke out, an' w'en it wuz ober de cullud folks wuz scattered. I went back ter de ole home; but Sam wuz n' dere, an' I could n' l'arn nuffin' 'about 'im. But I knowed he 'd be'n dere to look fer me an' had n' foun' me, an' had gone erway ter hunt fer me.

"I 's be'n lookin' fer 'im eber sence," she added simply, as though twenty-five years were but a couple of weeks, "an' I knows he 's be'n lookin' fer me. Fer he sot a heap er sto' by me, Sam did, an' I know he 's be'n huntin' fer me all dese years,—'less'n he 's be'n sick er sump'n, so he could n' work, er out'n his head, so he could n' 'member his promise. I went back down de ribber, fer I 'lowed he'd gone down dere lookin' fer me. I's be'n ter Noo Orleens, an' Atlanty, an' Charleston, an' Richmon'; an' w'en I 'd be'n all ober de Souf I come ter de Norf. Fer I knows I 'll fin' 'im some er dese days," she added softly, "er he 'll fin' me, an' den we 'll bofe be as happy in freedom as we wuz in de ole days befo' de wah." A smile stole over her withered countenance as she paused a moment, and her bright eyes softened into a far-away look.

This was the substance of the old woman's story. She had wandered a little here and there. Mr. Ryder was looking at her curiously when she finished.

"How have you lived all these years?" he asked.

"Cookin', suh. I 's a good cook. Does you know anybody w'at needs a good cook, suh? I 's stoppin' wid a cullud fam'ly roun' de corner yonder 'tel I kin git a place."

"Do you really expect to find your husband? He may be dead long ago."

She shook her head emphatically. "Oh no, he ain't dead. De signs an' de tokens tells me. I dremp three nights runnin' on'y dis las' week dat I foun' him."

"He may have married another woman. Your slave marriage would not have prevented him, for you never lived with him after the war, and without that your marriage does n't count."

"Would n' make no diff'ence wid Sam. He would n' marry no yuther 'ooman 'tel he foun' out 'bout me. I knows it," she added. "Sump'n 's be'n tellin' me all dese years dat I 's gwine fin' Sam 'fo' I dies."

"Perhaps he 's outgrown you, and climbed up in the world where he would n't care to have you find him."

"No, indeed, suh," she replied, "Sam ain' dat kin' er man. He wuz good ter me, Sam wuz, but he wuz n' much good ter nobody e'se, fer he wuz one er de triflin'es' han's on de plantation. I 'spec's ter haf ter suppo't 'im w'en I fin' 'im, fer he nebber would work 'less'n he had ter. But den he wuz free, an' he did n' git no pay fer his work, an' I don' blame 'im much. Mebbe he's done better sence he run erway, but I ain' 'spectin' much."

"You may have passed him on the street a hundred times during the twenty-five years, and not have known him; time works great changes."

She smiled incredulously. "I'd know 'im 'mongs' a hund'ed men. For dey wuz n' no yuther merlatter man like my man Sam, an' I could n' be mistook. I 's toted his picture roun' wid me twenty-five years."

"May I see it?" asked Mr. Ryder. "It might help me to remember whether I have seen the original."

As she drew a small parcel from her bosom he saw that it was fastened to a string that went around her neck. Removing several wrappers, she brought to light an old-fashioned daguerreotype in a black case. He looked long and intently at the portrait. It was faded with time, but the features were still distinct, and it was easy to see what manner of man it had represented.

He closed the case, and with a slow movement handed it back to her.

"I don't know of any man in town who goes by that name," he said, "nor have I heard of any one making such inquiries. But if you will leave me your address, I will give the matter some attention, and if I find out anything I will let you know."

She gave him the number of a house in the neighborhood, and went away, after thanking him warmly.

He wrote the address on the fly-leaf of the volume of Tennyson, and, when she had gone, rose to his feet and stood looking after her curiously. As she walked down the street with mincing step, he saw several persons whom she passed turn and look back at her with a smile of kindly amusement. When she had turned the corner, he went upstairs to his bedroom, and stood for a long time before the mirror of his dressing-case, gazing thoughtfully at the reflection of his own face.

III

At eight o'clock the ballroom was a blaze of light and the guests had begun to assemble; for there was a literary programme and some routine business of the society to be gone through with before the dancing. A black servant in evening dress waited at the door and directed the guests to the dressing-rooms.

The occasion was long memorable among the colored people of the city; not alone for the dress and display, but for the high average of intelligence and culture that distinguished the gathering as a whole. There were a number of school-teachers, several young doctors, three or four lawyers, some professional singers, an editor, a lieutenant in the United States army spending his furlough in the city, and others in various polite callings; these were colored, though most of them would not have attracted even a casual glance because of any marked difference from white people. Most of the ladies were in evening costume, and dress coats and dancing pumps were the rule among the men. A band of string music, stationed in an alcove behind a row of palms, played popular airs while the guests were gathering.

The dancing began at half past nine. At eleven o'clock supper was served. Mr. Ryder had left the ballroom some little time before the intermission, but reappeared at the supper-table. The spread was worthy of the occasion, and the guests did full justice to it. When the coffee had been served, the toastmaster, Mr. Solomon Sadler, rapped for order. He made a brief introductory speech, complimenting host and guests, and then presented in their order the toasts of the evening. They were responded to with a very fair display of after-dinner wit.

"The last toast," said the toast-master, when he reached the end of the list, "is one which must appeal to us all. There is no one of us of the sterner sex who is not at some time dependent upon woman,—in infancy for protection, in manhood for companionship, in old age for care and comforting. Our good host has been trying to live alone, but the fair faces I see around me to-night prove that he too is largely dependent upon the gentler sex for most that makes life worth living,—the society and love of friends,—and rumor is at fault if he does not soon yield entire subjection to one of them. Mr. Ryder will now respond to the toast,—The Ladies."

There was a pensive look in Mr. Ryder's eyes as he took the floor and adjusted his eyeglasses. He began speaking of woman as the gift of Heaven to man, and after some general observations on the relations of the sexes he said: "But perhaps the quality which most distinguishes woman is her fidelity and devotion to those she loves. History is full of examples, but has recorded none more striking than one which only to-day came under my notice."

He then related, simply but effectively, the story told by his visitor of the afternoon. He gave it in the same soft dialect, which came readily to his lips, while the company listened attentively and sympathetically. For the story had awakened a responsive thrill in many hearts. There were some present who had seen, and others who had heard their fathers and grandfathers tell, the wrongs and sufferings of this past generation, and all of them still felt, in their darker moments, the shadow hanging over them. Mr. Ryder went on:—

"Such devotion and confidence are rare even among women. There are many who would have searched a year, some who would have waited five years, a few who might have hoped ten years; but for twenty-five years this woman has retained her affection for and her faith in a man she has not seen or heard of in all that time.

"She came to me to-day in the hope that I might be able to help her find this long-lost husband. And when she was gone I gave my fancy rein, and imagined a case I will put to you.

"Suppose that this husband, soon after his escape, had learned that his wife had been sold away, and that such inquiries as he could make brought no information of her whereabouts. Suppose that he was young, and she much older than he; that he was light, and she was black; that their marriage was a slave marriage, and legally binding only if they chose to make it so after the war. Suppose, too, that he made his way to the North, as some of us have done, and there, where he had larger opportunities, had improved them, and had in the course of all these years grown to be as different from the ignorant boy who ran away from fear of slavery as the day is from night. Suppose, even, that he had qualified himself, by industry, by thrift, and by study, to win the friendship and be considered worthy the society of such people as these I see around me to-night, gracing my board and filling my heart with gladness; for I am old enough to remember the day when such a gathering would not have been possible in this land. Suppose, too, that, as the years went by, this man's memory of the past grew more and more indistinct, until at last it was rarely, except in his dreams, that any image of this bygone period rose before his mind. And then suppose that accident should bring to his knowledge the fact that the wife of his youth, the wife he had left behind him,—not one who had walked by his side and kept pace with him in his upward struggle, but one upon whom advancing years and a laborious life had set their mark,—was alive and seeking him, but that he was absolutely safe from recognition or discovery, unless he chose to reveal himself. My friends, what would the man do? I will presume that he was one who loved honor, and tried to deal justly with all men. I will even carry the case further, and suppose that perhaps he had set his heart upon another, whom he had hoped to call his own. What would he do, or rather what ought he to do, in a such a crisis of a lifetime?

"It seemed to me that he might hesitate, and I imagined that I was an old friend, a near friend, and that he had come to me for advice; and I argued the case with him. I tried to discuss it impartially. After we had looked upon the matter from every point of view, I said to him, in words that we all know:—

> 'This above all: to thine own self be true,
> And it must follow, as the night the day,
> Thou canst not then be false to any man.'

Then, finally, I put the question to him, 'Shall you acknowledge her?'

"And now, ladies and gentlemen, friends and companions, I ask you, what should he have done?"

There was something in Mr. Ryder's voice that stirred the hearts of those who sat around him. It suggested more than mere sympathy with an imaginary situation; it seemed rather in the nature of a personal appeal. It was observed, too, that his look rested more especially upon Mrs. Dixon, with a mingled expression of renunciation and inquiry.

She had listened, with parted lips and streaming eyes. She was the first to speak: "He should have acknowledged her."

"Yes," they all echoed, "he should have acknowledged her."

"My friends and companions," responded Mr. Ryder, "I thank you one and all. It is the answer I expected, for I knew your hearts."

He turned and walked toward the closed door of an adjoining room, while every eye followed him in wondering curiosity. He came back in a moment, leading by the hand his visitor of the afternoon, who stood startled and trembling at the sudden plunge into this scene of brilliant gayety. She was neatly dressed in gray, and wore the white cap of an elderly woman.

"Ladies and gentlemen," he said, "this is the woman, and I am the man, whose story I have told you. Permit me to introduce to you the wife of my youth."

Martha Wolfenstein (1869–1906) was brought from Prussia to America as an infant. She moved to Cleveland in 1878 when her father, Samuel Wolfenstein, became superintendent of the Jewish Orphan Asylum in Cleveland. Besides managing the household after her mother's death in 1885, she began writing short stories based on her father's reminiscences of a childhood in a Central European ghetto. A collection of her short stories, including "Babette," which had previously been published in the *Jewish Review & Observer*, appeared in *A Renegade and Other Tales* (1905), published before her death at age thirty-seven from tuberculosis. The use of the old-fashioned familiar form in the dialogue imitates the cadences of Yiddish.

Babette

At first thought it would appear strange that everyone should know her. She is so modest, is Babette; so small and quiet, but for all that she has attractions for the many.

For those who seek the beautiful, she has the beauty in her snow-white hair, her soft face, and small neat figure; and those who delight in the quaint, love to look at her, as she wanders through the garden, in her ancient dress of gray cashmere, dropping old-fashioned curtseys to every visitor.

But these are not the attractions that make her popular. No, to most people she is a joke. They visit her in hordes, and make conversation after this manner:

"How do you do, Babette? Well, how goes it to-day?"

"Thank you," says Babette, with a gracious curtsey. "It goes very well. When one is young and healthy, need one complain?"

The visitors smile.

"Why don't you get married, Babette? You'll be an old maid first thing you know."

"Oh," says Babette with an odd little simper, "I am young, I have plenty of time."

The visitors grin broadly.

"How about your dowry, Babette? Has it arrived yet?"

A sudden shadow of care flits over her soft face.

"No," says she, sadly. Then she brightens, "But I am expecting it at any moment. Perhaps with the next mail."

And then they roar with laughter.

It is strange to think they laugh. A little spinster of eighty, pensioner of an Old People's Home, fancying herself young and betrothed, and that she has a fortune coming to her—is that amusing? It is not even sad. No, it is beautiful, only beautiful; for Babette was wofully unhappy before she began to fancy this; so unhappy that she prayed she might die.

Then merciful Nature closed the eyes of her weary soul, and now it sleeps, and dreams this fair dream, that she is young, and beloved of a good man, whose wife she is to be.

There is but one dark spot in this fair dream. They are poor, she and her beloved, and they must await the coming of her dowry before they can marry.

But Babette is hopeful and happy. She does not care that the people laugh. She has long stopped wondering why they laugh.

'Tis a world of mystery any way, a world where the young rule and the aged sit aside, and where those who break the commandments most vigorously, rise highest. What is the use of wondering in a world where wagons and cars run alone, and where one speaks into a box on the wall, and, lo!—another who is in the market full three miles away replies? That is, they say he replies. To be sure she, Babette, has never heard him, but the fact remains that when one says, "A pound of butter and a dozen eggs," these articles soon thereafter arrive. She herself has seen the butter and counted the eggs.

So Babette is quite happy. All day she wanders in the garden or sits peacefully over her knitting. Only twice does she become restless. It is at nine in the morning and at three in the afternoon. These are the postman's hours. Then she walks down to the garden-gate and looks wistfully in the direction from which he is coming, for he it is who is going to bring her fortune.

It is ten years since Babette first came to the Old People's Home, and those who know her best, know hardly more than those who met her but yesterday.

She is like a stray leaf of a forgotten book which one might find on the highway. One may read there hints of a simple, homely tale; a searcher might discover the whole. But who in a busy world stoops to pick up a stray leaf; and who in a fighting world cares for a simple, homely tale?

"An old servant, past work, and doting, with not a relative in the world," the people say of her—and that is all they know.

They would probably wonder, they who speak thus, to learn that Babette was once a fair young girl to whom one wrote: "Thy hair ripples golden like a field of ripe grain when the wind plays upon it; and thine eyes are blue as the corn-flowers that grow between."

His name was Luke, he who wrote thus, and far back in the days when Louis Philippe was king, he wandered through fair Alsatia with a knapsack on his back and an easel in his hand. And on a summer's day he came to the borders of the village in the Jews' street of which lived Babette with her parents.

There he saw Babette and loved her, and he told her that he loved her. But she was a pious Jewish maiden, and he was a Christian; so she smiled pensively, and wept a little; but she wandered no more on the borders of the village.

And when a year thereafter her mother said, "Thy cousin Aaron wishes thee to wife," Babette did not say nay. He was a kindly plodding youth, was cousin Aaron, and they had been fond of each other from childhood. So Babette was well content, and prepared her wedding fineries with a happy heart.

Then came the year of the cholera, which with one blow cut down Babette's parents, her two brothers, and her betrothed. Babette was stunned with the frightful blow. When she recovered and looked about her, she found herself alone in the world, homeless and very poor.

Then she bethought herself of a distant kinsman who lived in an eastern province, far away on the Russian borders, and thither she journeyed. Uncle Sigmund, as she called her relative, took her in and made her welcome. At first she pined as if to die with homesickness; but when there are many children in a household and an invalid wife besides, there is much to do, and soon Babette found no time for tears.

Uncle Sigmund made an open bargain with her.

"Do thou but work diligently and faithfully, and I shall keep thee as my own. And every month, God willing, I will give thee a silver dollar. That is, I will put it away for thee, that thou mayest not be a wretched being, a maiden without a dowry."

Babette wept when he spoke of a dowry, but she said nothing and labored faithfully.

Time went by, and what with youth and health and hard work, her cheeks began to bloom again, and she laughed as she had done before. After a few years Uncle Sigmund's invalid wife died, and Babette became sole mistress of the household. At Passover she received a pair of shoes, a bonnet, and linen for her outfit; at New Year, a dress and flannel for a petticoat. But there was the silver dollar laid away each month, and Babette was content. And she baked and brewed and made and mended all day long.

Now, there was a kind-faced tailor who came occasionally to fetch Uncle Sigmund's old coats, out of whose ample breadths he made jackets and trousers for the younger boys.

One Sabbath morning, the tailor walked home with Babette after synagogue, and Babette with her strange French manners gave him her prayer-book to carry. People shook their heads with wonder, and gossips began to whisper that the tailor remains longer at Sigmund Glaser's house over a half-dollar's worth of work, than at another's when he is fitting him a new frock-coat of broadcloth.

Babette was with Uncle Sigmund five years to the day when she came to him hand-in-hand with the kind-faced tailor, saying that they were fond of each other and wished to marry.

Uncle Sigmund had always been counted a gentleman, but now he became suddenly wild with indignation.

"Have I not clothed and fed thee and kept thee as my own?" he cried.

Babette said nothing of how hard she had worked.

"Have I not put a silver dollar by for thee every month?"

"For my dowry," suggested Babette, mildly.

"And now thou wouldst leave my poor children!"

"Thy daughter Emma is already eighteen," said Babette, faintly; but Uncle Sigmund seemed quite deaf.

"Woe is me! Ingratitude! Now that my poor wife is dead she would leave me and my motherless little ones," he cried—and then he wept.

Babette, too, was moved to tears. She kissed his hands, and promised that she would remain with him so long as he needed her, and that she and her betrothed would be patient and wait.

A year passed, and Babette and the kind-faced tailor came again.

"Why dost thou hurry? Thou art still young, Babette, thou hast plenty of time," said Uncle Sigmund.

"And still we would marry," pleaded Babette.

"Now that Emma is betrothed, wait at least till after the wedding."

And after Emma's wedding, it was his rheumatism, and after that the housewifely arts which the younger daughters must learn; and each time there was a new reason, and each time he wept.

The truth of the matter was this, that in the course of years Babette had learned to prepare her uncle's soups to just the right degree of spiciness and to darn his socks without a single knot; and though Uncle Sigmund was not a hard-hearted man as men go, he loved his spicy soups and his easy socks better than he loved Babette, and he trembled lest he lose them.

Time went by, and Babette's songs grew fainter over her work. And when she kneaded bread, she could not help but think how sweet it were, if for her own household she were kneading it; and when she sat through the long winter evenings knitting socks, she could not help but wish yearningly that it were for her kind-faced tailor that she knit them.

After a while the tailor moved to another town. Then he ceased to write. Then came word that he had gone to America; and then that he had taken himself a wife in the New World.

Babette gave her uncle not a word of reproach, for with the years he had grown childish and ill. But the life went quickly out of her hair, the light out of her eyes. Silently she packed into the bottoms of her kist all the household linen she had stitched through the long years; but when she laid among it the pattern of a baby's cap which she had once cut out of a paper, she wept bitterly.

Babette now grew rapidly old. She lay and trembled in the long nights, for the future loomed a dark waste before her. Uncle Sigmund would die, and she would be left alone. His children, whom she had raised, were all married and away. Moreover they were of a strange kind. They ate the forbidden, and broke the Sabbath, and they disliked Babette, because of a secret fear lest their father should remember her too kindly in his will.

Then Babette would think of the silver dollars which lay in the strong-box for her, and how these would sustain her in her old age; and in the dark sea of the future these were to her like friendly harbor lights.

At last, one day Uncle Sigmund went to sleep to wake no more. Then came the children and grandchildren to divide the small inheritance; but Babette stood aside.

When each had received his share, they looked about them, and saw Babette.

"What shall we do with Babette?" they cried and shrugged their shoulders and lifted their eyebrows. "What shall we do with her? She is old."

Then Babette summoned all her pride.

"I will trouble none of you," she said. "Give me but my money and I will go my ways."

"Thy money! What money? There is no will."

"You will find it in the strong-box,—a silver dollar a month—there must be more than five hundred of them. It was to have been my dowry," she added softly.

At this they put up a great laugh. Babette and a dowry! It was most amusing.

"Do thou but fetch a husband," said the eldest, "and as I live, we will provide the dowry."

Babette could only moan and wring her hands. And again she lay and trembled in the long nights. Again the future loomed a dark sea before her, waste and shoreless now, the harbor lights were out.

Then, one long sleepless night, an awful terror possessed her. She was too old to enter into a new service. No one would take her for a servant. What if they should give her over to public charity! Her terror made her bold.

"Five and forty years have I served this house faithfully," she cried, "and now will you cast me off?"

"For heaven's sake, don't be dramatic. Who speaks of casting thee off? The money is not here, but thou wilt be provided for," they cried.

Then followed a family council, where each disclosed some untoward circumstance which prevented him from taking care of her. Babette waited with madly beating heart until the youngest there,—a granddaughter of Uncle Sigmund,—who was married and lived in America, said she would take her with her, since servants were hard to get in the States. And that is how in her old age Babette came to go to the New World.

Then with fainting spirit and work-weary hands she began again her old-time labors: to tend little children, to cook and bake and mend and make. But it was not for long, for after a few years her body grew too weak for work, her eyes could no longer follow the seam, and she began to forget how much yeast goes to a baking.

One day Babette fell ill and would not mend for weeks. They took her to the hospital. When she was better, her mistress came and told her that she had a new servant, and that upon her application Babette was to be admitted to the Old People's Home.

"A pleasant place, Babette," said she, "where they give thee meat and drink without pay, and where thou mayest sit with thy hands in thy lap all day long."

Babette was dazed with her misery. The dreaded thing had come to pass. She was given over to charity. She could but hide her withered face and sob in the bitterness of her woe.

They took her to the Home; and the air that she breathed there was to her as fumes of fire; and the bread that she ate was as gall. For months they thought she would die, and she prayed that she might die. It was then that Nature, more merciful than Man, closed the eyes of Babette's soul, and it fell asleep, and began to dream the fair dream that she was young and beautiful and beloved of a good man whose wife she was to be.

Any fine day you wish, you may see her, sitting peacefully in the garden with her knitting. Only at nine in the morning and at three in the afternoon does she grow restless. These are the postman's hours. Then she walks down to the garden-gate, and looks wistfully in the direction from which he is coming. When he arrives, she curtseys politely.

"Have you anything for me to-day?" says she.

"Not to-day, Babette," says the postman.

"I am expecting a fortune," says Babette.

"I'm glad to hear it," says the postman. "Perhaps it will come to-morrow."

"It surely will."

Then Babette rises on tiptoe, and the postman bends to hear.

"When it arrives," whispers she, with an odd little simper, "I am to be married."

"You don't say so!" cries the postman.

Then they smile and nod at each other, and the postman goes whistling down the street, and Babette goes back to her knitting.

Poetry

The *Trump of Fame* (1812–16), a small, four-page weekly published in Warren, was the first newspaper on the Reserve. It allocated space among its reprinted articles and moralistic editorials for this "classified" lovelorn poetic exchange in a satiric style reminiscent of eighteenth-century wit. The spurned lover appeals to the sympathy of his love (and presumably of Western Reserve readers). The two weeks in which it took Mary to reply to Robert's poem allowed for the whetting of her sly humor.

To Mary

When late beneath thy cottage roof,
Enraptur'd with thy graceful mien,
The happiest hours of life I past,
In social hours that ne'r return.

But why, alas! no more return,
Those "social joys" in mutual love;
Why not return those "happy hours,"
Each others constancy to prove.

How oft beneath the willows shade,
Beside the murmuring rill,
Whose flowery banks and gentle flood,
Has prov'd a mirror to thy mien.

Ah yes, how oft those wandering steps,
Have led in pensive hours to stray,
And R——t gaz'd upon those charms,
Which she in triumph bears away.

Ah! why allow'd no more to view,
The fairest form in beauty's brain;

Say, must thy R****t bid adieu,
Nor gaze upon those charms again?
                              ROBERT.
                    Aurora, [September 2,] 1812

To Robert

Dear Robert 'twas with much surprize
I saw your name with mine in print,
Scarcely could I believe my eyes,
The De'il I thought was surely in't.

Detraction did speak better things
And glad I am so false to find it;
So, as some tuneful poet sings,
Friend Robert, "never seem to mind it;"

For did not "Truth a beam impart,"
So truly piteous is your strain,
That tho' I had withdrawn my heart,
Dear Bob, I give it back again.

Your "willows shade" and "murm'ring rill,"
And "flow'ry banks and gentle flood"
Were very picturesque, yet still
You left out many things as good.

You might have told how once we met
Beneath a thickets bow'ring shade;
How on a mossy bank we sat,
And what fine, tender things you said,

Of love and dove, and bless and press,
And heart and dart, and kiss and bliss;
How ardently we did carress—
Can Robert have forgotten this?—

And how we gaz'd upon the stream,
Whose limped wave reflected bright
The image, and argentine beam
Of the inconstant "queen of night."

But why should I these things rehearse?
Your memory is as good as mine is,
Yet 'twould have vastly help'd your verse—
I'll meet you there again, Bob—Finis.
                              MARY.
                    [September 23, 1812]

Jeremiah Ingalls, Jr., (1797–1858) was an elder of the North Union Shaker Community in Cleveland. He had entered the United Society of Believers in Christ's Second Appearing (the Shakers) with his first son after parting from his wife shortly before the birth of their second son. The invocation of his divinely inspired hymn begins in "spirit language," the Shaker equivalent of "speaking in tongues." Published here for the first time, the handwritten original of the poem is in the Shaker Collection of the Western Reserve Historical Society. The poem expresses Christ's love in maternal imagery familiar to followers of Mother Ann Lee, founder of the United Society.

O ce le ac ne voo na vi na, O ce le ac ne voo na vi
My lovely children I'll not leave thee, But unto you will I draw nigh
I will protect in times of trouble, When sore afflictions roll and roll
And earthly trials like a bubble, Shall flee from thy immortal soul.

With gentle showers I'll ever bless you, And give you Angels food
    to eat
With my pure love I will caress you, And you shall taste my bless-
    ing sweet
While judgments fill the land around you, And earthquakes shake from
    pole to pole
With my protection I'll surround you, So trust with me your needy
    soul.

O my dear children be encouraged, And labor for the heavenly prize
For I will cause your souls to flourish, And to eternal glory rise
There in my pure & heavenly kingdom, You'll chant your holy songs
    of praise
With holy saints you'll take dominion, Shout triumph o'er your trou-
    bled days.

Given by divine inspiration at N[orth] U[nion]

Be so kind as to receive this as a token of love and remembrance from
    your friend and brother in Mother's gospel.

JEREMIAH INGALLS

An enduring Great Lakes ballad, "Red Iron Ore" commemorates the spirit of the nineteenth-century lake trade and a life of excitement, routine, and hard work for those "bold sailors" who carried the cargo that maintained the long boats. It is sung to the tune of the Irish ballad "Derry Down."

Red Iron Ore

Come all ye bold sailors that follow the Lakes,
On an iron ore vessel your living to make,
I shipped in Chicago, bid adieu to the shore,

Bound away to Escanaba for red iron ore.
Chorus: Derry down, down, down, derry down.
Next morning we hove up alongside the *Exile,*
And the *Roberts* made fast to an iron ore pile,
They let down their chutes, and like thunder did roar,
They poured into us that red iron ore.
Some sailors took shovels, while others got spades.
And some took wheelbarrows, each man to his trade,
We looked like red devils; our fingers got sore,
We cursed Escanaba and that damned iron ore.
The tug *Escanaba,* she towed out the *Minch,*
The *Roberts,* she thought, had been left in a pinch,
And as they passed by us, they bid us goodbye,
Saying, "We'll meet you in Cleveland next Fourth of July."
We sailed out alone, through the passage steered we,
Past the Foxes, the Beavers, and Skilagalee,
We soon passed by the *Minch* for to show her the way,
And she never hove in sight till we were off Thunder Bay.
The *Roberts* rolled on across Saginaw Bay,
And over her bow splashed the white spray,
And bound for the rivers, the *Roberts* did go,
Where the tug *Kate Williams* took us in tow.
Down through to Lake Erie, Oh Lord, how it blew,
And all round the Dummy a large fleet hove to.
The night dark and stormy, Old Nick it would scare,
But we hove up next morning and for Cleveland did steer.
Now the *Roberts* is in Cleveland, made fast stem and stern,
And over the bottle we'll spin a good yarn,
But old Captain Shannon had ought to stand treat
For getting to Cleveland ahead of the Fleet.
Now we're down from Escanaba, and my two hands are sore
From pushing a wheelbarrow; I'll do it no more.
I'm sore-backed from shoveling, so hear my loud roar,
Now I'm ashore in Cleveland, I'll shake red iron ore.

Captain Pearl R. Nye (1872–1950) was born in Chillicothe on a family canal boat, typical of the vessels responsible for much of the business of freighting on canals. He was raised and educated by his parents in the story and song of canals and spent his life plying the channels as a boat captain, folk singer, and canal-music historiographer. Cloea Thomas recorded Captain Nye's renditions in 1945 and was a faithful transcriber and editor for many of his songs. A popular song of the time, this tale is about marital infidelity and justice meted out by the wise and "Clever Skipper."

Clever Skipper

There was a clever skipper,
In Akron he did dwell,
Who had a lovely woman,
and a tailor she loved well,
She was always pert to meet him,
So Listen what I say:
she was walking up South Howard Street,
Who but the tailor did she chance for to meet?
Tum a rally tally dally
Tum a rally tally day.

They wined, dined and danced,
It was late by the clock,
When up stepped the Captain
And loudly did he knock;
Tum a rally tally dally
Tum a rally tally day.
They were surprised,
Tailor said, so quiet, meek,
"Now my lovely woman,
And O where shall I creep?"
Tum a rally tally dally
Tum a rally tally day.

In yonder cupboard
My husband has a chest;
Yes, in that cupboard,
A cover, you may hide;
Tum a rally tally dally
Tum a rally tally day.
They hurried, she locked him up,
Coat, boots and hat,
She locked him up
With the balance of his clothes,
Tum a rally tally dally
Tum a rally tally day.

And she ran downstairs
And opened the door,
There stood the skipper
With a couple others more,
Tum a rally tally dally
Tum a rally tally day.

She kindly saluted
And gave to him a kiss.
Says he, "My lovely woman,
What do you mean by this?"
Tum a rally tally dally
Tum a rally tally day.

I didn't come to rob;
Or break you of your rest,
I am going on south
And came for my chest;
Tum a rally tally dally
Tum a rally tally day.
These two canalers
Jolly, brave and strong
They picked up the chest
And wagged it along;
Tum a rally tally dally
Tum a rally tally day.

They hadn't got more
Than the middle of the town,
Till the weight of the tailor,
Made the sweat trickle down,
Tum a rally tally dally
Tum a rally tally day.
They sat the chest down
To take a moment rest
Says one to the other,
"What the devil's in the chest?"
Tum a rally tally dally
Tum a rally tally day.

Neither of the two
The chest could undo,
Till up stepped the skipper
With the balance of the crew.
Tum a rally tally dally
Tum a rally tally day.
He unlocked the chest
In the presence of them all,
And there lay the tailor
Like a hog in a stall,
Tum a rally tally dally
Tum a rally tally day.

Now I have got you,
'Twill be like on sea,
Not leave you here
Making trouble for me,
Tum a rally tally dally
Tum a rally tally day.
They took him on board,
For Portsmouth they did steer,
This is the last
Of the tailor we do hear.
Tum a rally tally dally
Tum a rally tally day.

The Ohio & Erie Canal joined the Cuyahoga River in Cleveland, where canal boats competed with steamers and lake schooners. The canal boatmen could not use mules and horses on the river and resorted to tug boats. The problems and anxieties they experienced are recounted in the song "Down the River," another of the canal songs collected by Captain Pearl R. Nye.

Down the River

1.

I towed into Cleveland about twelve o'clock
And the first man I met was the Collector on the dock,
He looked at me, then at my team—Oh boy, he made he shiver.
Then said "My bully driver, you must go down the river."
Says I, "Now Mr. Biddle, down the river I'll not go
For the saddle mule is balky and the leader he won't tow."
Says he, "The tug will take you, so come now, cut out the sass.
I'll keep your mules here safely, boy, oft turn them out to grass."

2.

The river gets my nerve, and there, there I cannot sleep,
The schooners, barges, tugs are careless and on us they creep;
Then squeeze and crush us, then we sink, our all is lost, that river—
We love our boat, you know we do, and that is why I shiver.
A tug will run wide open, then those waves—what can we do?
And often boats they ruin, sink, oh! the story is not new!
"Fish House," "Whiskey Island," "Slips," yes—and that old river bed,
They make me have the "jimmies" and sometimes wish I were dead.

3.

There's "Grasselies Chemical," yes, and "Acid Works"—
"The Pump"—other places that do not make me shirk,

"The Dog Pond," "Paper Mills" are near, but how I dread that river—
There's nothing safe,—you know it and that is why I shiver.
You know whatever happens there, you will be recompensed,—
But oh! our stuff is precious, yes, can't be bought with dollars—cents,
He said, "Your load is needed, boy, and everything is right,
The craft will all respect you when they see your lights at night."

4.

"Rhodes" and "Biddler's Slip" has lumber waiting now for you,
"Woods and Jinks," "Jim Krangle," "Saginaw Nay," "Bodfords," too.
So don't be scared, you've never died, be brave, why should you
    shiver?
I know all you've said is true, quite lively is the river."
My fears were soon disposed of, I was willing then to go
Anywhere he sent us,—where'er our mules or tug can tow—
I learned to love the rivers, for we oft their course would wend,
We worked in perfect harmony and soon were best of friends.

William Dean Howells engaged poetry to extol and eulogize the martyred John
Brown, a nineteenth-century Calvinist son of Hudson in the Western Reserve who
heard God's call to commit his revolutionary act on behalf of the blacks at Harpers
Ferry. "Old Brown" was Howells's very first publication, a single leaf, in 1859.

Old Brown

I.

Success goes royal crowned through time,
 Down all the loud applauding days,
 Purpled in history's silkenest phrase,
And brave with many a poet's rhyme.

While Unsuccess, his peer and mate,
 Born of the same heroic race,
 Begotten of the same embrace,
Dies at his brother's palace gate.

The insolent laugh, the blighting sneer,
 The pointing hand of vulgar scorn,
 The thorny path, and crown of thorn.
The many-headed's stupid jeer,

Show where he fell. And by-and-by,
 Comes history, in the waning light,
 Her pen-nib worn with lies, to write
The failure into infamy.

Ah, God! but here and there, there stands
    Along the years, a man to see
    Beneath the victor's bravery,
The spots upon his lily hands—

To read the secret will of good,
    (Dead hope, and trodden into earth,)
    That beat the breast of strife for birth,
And died birth-choked, in parent blood.

II.

Old Lion! tangled in the net,
    Baffled and spent, and wounded sore,
    Bound, thou who ne'er knew bonds before:
A captive, but a lion yet.

Death kills not. In a later time,
    Oh, slow, but all-accomplishing,
    Thy shouted name abroad shall ring,
Wherever right makes war sublime.

When in the perfect scheme of God,
    It shall not be a crime for deeds
    To quicken liberating creeds,
And men shall rise where slaves have trod;

Then he, the fearless future man,
    Shall wash the guilt and stain away,
    We place upon thy name to-day—
Thou hero of the noblest plan.

Oh, patience! felon of the hour!
    Over thy ghastly gallows tree
    Shall climb the vine of Liberty,
With ripened fruit and fragrant flower.

Edward Rowland Sill divided his life between northeastern Ohio and California, which he documents and reflects upon in his poems. "The House and the Heart" (1868) is written in a curious, maybe even experimental, three-stress unrhymed form while "Christmas in California" (1872) is in strictly conventional quatrains.

The House and the Heart

Every house has its garret,
Lumbered with rubbish and relics,—
Spinning-wheels leaning in corners,

Chests under spider-webbed rafters,
Brittle and yellow old letters,
Grandfather's things and grandmother's.
There overhead, at the midnight,
Noises of creaking and stepping
Startle the hush of the chambers—
Ghosts on their tiptoes repassing.

Every house with its garden;
Some little plot—a half-acre,
Or a mere strip by the windows,
Flower-beds and narrow box-borders,
Something spicily fragrant,
Something azure and golden.
There the small feet of the sparrow
Star the fresh mould round the roses;
And, in the shadowy moonlight,
Wonderful secrets are whispered.

Every heart with its garret,
Cumbered with relics and rubbish—
Wheels that are silent forever,
Leaves that are faded and broken,
Foolish old wishes and fancies,
Cobwebs of doubt and suspicion—
Useless, unbeautiful, growing
Year by year thicker and faster:
Naught but a fire or a moving
Ever can clear it, or clean it.

Every heart with its garden;
Some little corner kept sacred,
Fragrant and pleasant with blossoms;
There the forget-me-nots cluster,
And pure love-violets, hidden,
Guessed but by sweetness all round them;
Some little strip in the sunshine,
Cheery and warm, for above it
Rest the deep, beautiful heavens,
Blue, and beyond, and forever.

Christmas in California

Can this be Christmas—sweet as May,
    With drowsy sun, and dreamy air,
And new grass pointing out the way
    For flowers to follow, everywhere?

Has time grown sleepy at his post,
    And let the exiled Summer back,
Or is it her regretful ghost,
    Or witchcraft of the almanac?

While wandering breaths of mignonette
    In at the open window come,
I send my thoughts afar, and let
    Them paint your Christmas Day at home.

Glitter of ice, and glint of frost,
    And sparkles in the crusted snow;
And hark! the dancing sleigh-bells, tost
    The faster as they fainter grow.

The creaking footsteps hurry past;
    The quick breath dims the frosty air;
And down the crisp road slipping fast
    Their laughing loads the cutters bear.

Penciled against the cold white sky,
    Above the curling eaves of snow,
The thin blue smoke lifts lingeringly,
    As loath to leave the mirth below.

For at the door a merry din
    Is heard, with stamp of feathery feet,
And chattering girls come storming in,
    To toast them at the roaring grate.

And then from muff and pocket peer,
    And many a warm and scented nook,
Mysterious little bundles queer,
    That, rustling, tempt the curious look.

Now broad upon the southern walls
    The mellowed sun's great smile appears,
And tips the rough-ringed icicles
    With sparks, that grow to glittering tears.

Then, as the darkening day goes by,
    The wind gets gustier without,
And leaden streaks are on the sky,
    And whirls of snow are all about.

Soon firelight shadows, merry crew,
    Along the darkling walls will leap
And clap their hands, as if they knew
    A thousand things too good to keep.

Sweet eyes with home's contentment filled,
 As in the smouldering coals they peer,
Haply some wondering pictures build
 Of how I keep my Christmas here.

Before me, on the wide, warm bay,
 A million azure ripples run;
Round me the sprouting palm-shoots lay
 Their shining lances to the sun.

With glossy leaves that poise or swing,
 The callas their white cups unfold,
And faintest chimes of odor ring
 From silver bells with tongues of gold.

A languor of deliciousness
 Fills all the sea-enchanted clime;
And in the blue heavens meet, and kiss,
 The loitering clouds of summer-time.

This fragrance of the mountain balm
 From spicy Lebanon might be;
Beneath such sunshine's amber calm
 Slumbered the waves of Galilee.

O wondrous gift, in goodness given,
 Each hour anew our eyes to greet,
An earth so fair—so close to Heaven,
 'T was trodden by the Master's feet.

And we—what bring we in return?
 Only these broken lives, and lift
Them up to meet His pitying scorn,
 And some poor child its foolish gift:

As some poor child on Christmas Day
 Its broken toy in love might bring;
You could not break its heart and say
 You cared not for the worthless thing?

Ah, word of trust, His child! That child
 Who brought to earth the life divine,
Tells me the Father's pity mild
 Scorns not even such a gift as mine.

I am His creature, and His air
 I breathe, where'er my feet may stand;
The angels' song rings everywhere,
 And all the earth is Holy Land.

Jessie Hunter Brown Pounds (1861–1921) was born in Hiram and raised in Cleveland. She graduated from Hiram College and married the local pastor. She remained in Hiram and wrote local-color stories, pageants, and over 800 hymns. "Beautiful Isle" (1897), her best-known hymn, was sung at President William McKinley's funeral in 1901.

Beautiful Isle

Somewhere the sun is shining,
　　Somewhere the song-birds dwell;
Hush, then, thy sad repining;
　　God lives, and all is well.

CHORUS
Somewhere, Somewhere,
　　Beautiful Isle of Somewhere!
Land of the true, where we live anew—
　　Beautiful Isle of Somewhere!

Somewhere the days are longer,
　　Somewhere the task is done;
Somewhere the heart is stronger,
　　Somewhere the guerdon won.

Somewhere the load is lifted,
　　Close by an open gate;
Somewhere the clouds are rifted,
　　Somewhere the angels wait.

Edmund Vance Cooke (1864–1932), born in Ontario, Canada, was educated in Cleveland's public schools and became a lifelong resident of the city. A poet and popular lecturer, Cooke celebrated the Lake Erie hero of the War of 1812 in his modern sonnet "Oliver Hazard Perry" from *Rimes To Be Read* (1897).

Oliver Hazard Perry

"We've met the enemy and they are ours;
Two ships, two brigs, one schooner and one sloop."
His words charge down the years—a warlike group,
Grim, gallant, glorious! All the flowers
Matured by summer suns and autumn showers
We use to deck the memory of that group,
Born of the times when banners rise or droop
In the harsh conflict of contending powers.

But look thou, Perry! gallant man and true!
See'st thou that smoke of commerce, not of war?
Rejoice with us that now no battles mar,

And now there is no work for thee to do;
No lookout's eye sights carnage from afar;
No dismal red is mixed with Erie's blue.

Constance Fenimore Woolson, one of the Reserve's earliest and most authentic local colorists, achieved an international reputation based on her novels and short stories. Her sensitivity to regional life is reflected also in poetry, as she draws upon the Great Lakes country for "Lake Erie in September," published in 1872 in *Appleton's Journal* and "Cornfields," published in *Harper's Magazine* also in 1872.

Lake Erie in September

Oh, grey and sullen sky! Oh, grey and sullen beaches!
Oh, grey and sullen billows, coming rolling, rolling in!
Oh, are ye not aweary of chill September dreary,
With days so grey the earth knows not when its grey nights begin?

All through the summer noons, all through the summer twilights,
Came the vessels, snowy-winged, gaily sailing, sailing by;
Your waters then were dancing, your beaches gold were glancing,
While the south wind blew the sunbeams and moonbeams through the
    sky.

At times the east wind came, the east wind off the ocean,
And vessels from Ontario went sweeping, sweeping past—
From prairies blew the west wind, of all the winds the best wind,
And Huron's fleet went scudding down the lake upon its blast.

But now your winds are still, your sluggish waves are sullen,
The cheerless rain, nor fast nor slow, is dropping, dropping down;
The beach below is soggy, the air above is foggy,
And one dark ship, with ragged sail, is lying off the town.

Oh grey and sullen sky! Oh, grey and sullen beaches!
Why lie ye here in lethargy, all glooming, glooming pale?
If not the summer's soft rest, then why not have the tempest?
If ye cannot have the zephyr, then why not have the gale?

And since the summer's gone, grey sky to winter darken,
And shadow all these sullen waves to inky, inky black—
Let these dull forests bristle, as loud the fierce winds whistle,
And sweep that one dark ship, a wreck, adown the foaming track.

Wake up, wake up, O Lake! and lash your sluggish waters
In fury, till your whole expanse is raging, raging mad—
Well may it be wrong-doing if it but be strong-doing!
Give us one thing or the other: strong! whether good or bad.

For the very heart is sad with this monotone of Nature,
The very soul is palsied with this half-drawn, half-drawn breath;
A grey sky is most dreary, a grey life the most weary,
If all our sunny life is gone, then forth! to fight with Death.

Cornfields

In the broad Ohio lowlands, in the sun's white heat,
In the shadowless stillness of the clear August noon,
We feel the full earth's pulses hot and strong beneath our feet,
The ripeness and the richness of their rhythmical beat,
Saying, "Ripen, corn; ripen, corn; green fields, ripen mellow"
Saying, "Ripen, corn; ripen, corn; green ears, ripen yellow,
    For the harvest comes soon."

In the broad Ohio lowlands thick the green ranks grow,
In straight unbroken furrows to the east, to the west,
The tree-tops in the distance are the only hills they know,
So they proudly lift their tasselled heads, whispering low,
Saying, "Rustle, leaves; rustle, leaves, hear the furrows' voices;"
Saying, "Rustle, leaves; rustle, leaves; all the field rejoices,
    For our lot is the best."

They know not of the shadow where the cool mountains stand;
They know not of the brook with the dark rocks at its mouth;
They only know the river and its level banks of sand—
They only know the river moving slow through the land,
Saying, "Float, lilies; float, lilies; August's gold-crowned daughters;"
Saying, "Float, lilies; float, lilies; on my sun-warmed waters
    I bear you toward the South."

They know the mellow richness of the brown fervid earth;
They feel the prisoned dew-drops caught in the misty morn;
They think of the soft rain-clouds, of their early spring-time birth,
And they sing of the harvest in their ripe lusty mirth,
Saying, "Shine, heavens; shine, heavens; pour thy splendour on us;"
Saying "Shine heavens; shine heavens; send down now upon us
    The glory of the corn."

Other Writings
by Nineteenth-Century
Western Reserve Authors

Badger, Joseph
 Hymns and Spiritual Songs, origi-
 nal and selected for the use of
 Christians, 1844
 A Memoir of Rev. Joseph Badger,
 1851
Chesnutt, Charles Waddell
 The Goophered Grapevine, 1887
 The Conjure Woman, 1899
 Frederick Douglass, 1899
 The House behind the Cedars,
 1900
 Baxter's Procrustes, 1904
Cooke, Edmund Vance
 A Patch of Pansies, 1894
 A Morning's Mail, 1907
 Baseballogy, 1912
 Just then Something Happened,
 1914
 Cheerful Children, 1923
 Companionable Poems, 1924
 Nature Trails about Cleveland,
 1931
 Born without a Chance, 1940
Ellis, Edward Sylvester
 Tecumseh, Chief of the Shawa-
 noes: A Tale of the War of
 1812, 1898
Finney, Charles Grandison
 Lectures on Systematic Theology,
 embracing ability (natural,
 moral, and gracious), repentance,
 impenitence, faith and unbelief,
 1847

Lectures on Revivals of Religion,
 1850
Sermons on Important Subjects,
 1851
Memoirs of Rev. Charles G.
 Finney, 1876
Garfield, James Abram
 Oration Delivered by Hon. J. A.
 Garfield at Ravenna, July 4,
 1860, 1860
 College Education: Address De-
 livered before the Literary
 Societies of Hiram College,
 Hiram, Ohio, June 14, 1867,
 1867
 Discovery and Ownership of the
 Northwestern Territory, and the
 Future of the Republic: Its Dan-
 gers and Its Hopes, an Address
 Delivered before the Literary
 Societies of Hudson College,
 1873
 Settlement of the Western Reserve,
 1874
 Life and Character of Almeda
 Booth, 1877
 The Works of James Abram
 Garfield, ed. Hinsdale,
 1882–83
Howells, William Cooper
 Recollections of Life in Ohio from
 1813 to 1840, 1895
Howells, William Dean
 Poems, 1843

My Year in a Log Cabin, 1893
Stories of Ohio, 1897
The Kentons, 1902
The Leatherwood God, 1916
Years of My Youth, 1916
Selected Letters, 1981
Malvin, John
    *North into Freedom: The Autobi-
    ography of John Malvin, Free
    Negro, 1795–1880*, ed. Peskin,
    1966
Pounds, Jesse Hunter Brown
    Norman Macdonald, 1884
    The Young Man from Middlefield,
    1901
    Rachel Sylvestre, 1904
    Memorial Selections, 1921
Rice, Harvey
    Sketches of Western Life, 1888
Riddle, Albert Gallatin
    Bart Ridgeley, 1873
    *Alice Brand: A Romance of the
    Capital*, 1875
    *History of Geauga and Lake
    Counties, Ohio*, 1878
    *The House of Ross, and Other
    Tales*, 1881
    The Hunter of the Shagreen,
    1882
    Hart and His Bear, 1883
    *Castle Gregory: A Story of the
    Western Reserve in Olden
    Times*, 1884
    *Mark Loan: A Tale of the Western
    Reserve Pioneers*, 1884
    *The Young Sugar Makers of the
    West Woods*, 1885

*The Tory's Daughter: A Romance
    of the Northwest, 1812–1813*,
    1888
*Ansel's Cave: A Story of Early
    Life in the Western Reserve*,
    1893
Sill, Edward Rowland
    Poems, 1887
    *The Prose of Edward Rowland
    Sill*, 1900
Stone, Lucy, and Antoinette
Brown
    *Soulmates: The Oberlin Corre-
    spondence of Lucy Stone and
    Antoinette Brown*, ed. Lasser
    and Merrill, 1983
Ward, Artemus (Charles Farrar
Browne)
    *Yankee Drolleries: The Most Cele-
    brated Works of the Best Ameri-
    can Humorists*, 1860
    *The Complete Works of Charles F.
    Browne, Better Known as "Ar-
    temus Ward,"* 1865
Wickham, Gertrude Van Renselaer
    *Memorial to the Pioneer Women of
    the Western Reserve*, 1896
Woolson, Constance Fenimore
    Solomon, 1870
    The Old Stone House, 1873
    *Castle Nowhere: Lake-Country
    Sketches*, 1875
    Black Point, 1879
    *"Always, your attached friend":
    The Unpublished Letters of
    Constance Fenimore Woolson to
    John and Clara Hay*, 1893

PART TWO

The Twentieth Century

Nonfiction Perspectives

MEMOIRS AND REMINISCENCES

Clarence Darrow (1857–1938), one of America's most famous jurists, wrote an autobiographical novel, *Farmington* (1904), about his Reserve birthplace, Kinsman, as well as an autobiography, *The Story of My Life,* from which this childhood reminiscence is taken. Darrow's youth on the Western Reserve could be more accurately labeled a generic "boy's life" than a prelude to his greatness.

My Childhood in Kinsman

Some years before I was born my parents left Meadville and moved back to the little village of Kinsman, about twenty miles away. I have no idea why they made this change, unless because my father's sister lived in Kinsman. All life hangs on a thread, so long as it hangs; a little movement this way or that is all-controlling. So I cannot tell why I was born on the 18th of April in 1857, or why the obscure village of Kinsman was the first place in which I beheld the light of day. When I was born the village must have boasted some four or five hundred inhabitants, and its importance and vitality is evident because it has held its own for seventy-five years or more. If any one wants to see the place he must search for the town, for in spite of the fact that I was born there it has never been put on the map.

But in truth, Kinsman is a quiet, peaceful and picturesque spot. Almost any one living in its vicinity will inform the stranger that it is well worth visiting, if one happens to be near. The landscape is gently rolling, the soil is fertile, beautiful shade trees line the streets, and a lazy stream winds its way into what to us boys was the far-off unknown world. Years ago the deep places of the stream were used for swimming-holes, and the shores were favorite lounging-places for boys dangling their fishing-lines above the shaded waters. There I spent many a day expectantly waiting for a bite. I recall few fishes that ever rewarded my patience; but this never prevented my haunting the famous pools and watching where the line disappeared into the mysterious unfathomed depths.

The dominating building in Kinsman was the Presbyterian Church, which stood on a hill and towered high above all the rest. On Sunday the great bell clanged across the surrounding country calling all the people to come and worship under its sheltering roof. Loudly it tolled at the death of every one who died in the Lord. Its measured tones seemed cold and solemn while the funeral procession was moving up the hillside where the departed was to be forevermore protected under the shadow of the church.

If I had chosen to be born I probably should not have selected Kinsman, Ohio, for that honor; instead, I would have started in a hard and noisy city where the crowds surged back and forth as if they knew where they were going, and why. And yet my mind continuously returns to the old place, although not more than five or six that were once my schoolmates are still outside the churchyard gate. My mind goes back to Kinsman because I lived there in childhood, and to me it was once the centre of the world, and however far I have roamed since then it has never fully lost that place in the storehouse of miscellaneous memories gathered along the path of life.

I have never been able to visualize the early history of my parents. Not only had they no money, but no occupation; and under those conditions they began the accumulation of a family of children which ultimately totalled eight. These were born about two years apart. I was the fifth, but one before me died in infancy; it is evident that my parents knew nothing of birth-control, for they certainly could not afford so many doubtful luxuries. Perhaps my own existence, as fifth in a family, is one reason why I never have been especially enthusiastic about keeping others from being born; whenever I hear people discussing birth-control I always remember that I was the fifth.

All his life my father was a visionary and dreamer. Even when he sorely needed money he would neglect his work to read some book. My mother was more efficient and practical. She was the one who saved the family from dire want. Her industry and intelligence were evident in her household affairs and in my father's small business, too. In spite of this, she kept abreast of the thought of her day. She was an ardent woman's-rights advocate, as they called the advanced woman seventy years ago. Both she and my father were friends of all oppressed people, and every new and humane and despised cause and ism.

Neither of my parents held any orthodox religious views. They were both readers of Jefferson, Voltaire, and Paine; both looked at revealed religion as these masters thought. And still, we children not only went to Sunday school but were encouraged to attend. Almost every Sunday our mother took us to the church, and our pew was too near the minister to permit our slipping out while the service was going on. I wonder why children are taken to church? Or perhaps they are not, nowadays. I can never forget the horror and torture of listening to an endless sermon when I was a child. Of course I never understood a word of it, any more than did the preacher who harangued to his afflicted audiences.

At Sunday school I learned endless verses from the Testaments. I studied the lesson paper as though every word had a meaning and was true. I sang hymns that I remember to this day. Among these was one in which each child loudly shouted "I want to be an angel!—and with the angels stand; a crown upon my forehead, a harp within my hand!" Well do I remember that foolish hymn to this very day. As a boy I sang it often and earnestly, but in spite of my stout and steady insistence that I wanted to wear wings, here I am, at seventy-five, still fighting to stay on earth.

On religious and social questions our family early learned to stand alone. My father was the village infidel, and gradually came to glory in his reputation. Within a radius of five miles were other "infidels" as well, and these men formed a select group of their own. We were not denied association with the church members; the communicants of the smaller churches were our friends. For instance, there was a Catholic society that met at the homes of one of its adherents once in two or three weeks, and between them and our family there grew up a sort of kinship. We were alike strangers in a more or less hostile land.

Although my father was a graduate of a theological seminary when he settled in Kinsman, he could not and would not preach. He must have been puzzled and perplexed at the growing brood that looked so trustingly to the parents for food and clothes. He must have wearily wondered which way to turn to be able to meet the demand. He undertook the manufacture and sale of furniture. His neighbors and the farmers round about were the customers with whom he dealt. Even now when I go back to Kinsman I am shown chairs and bedsteads that he made. He must have done honest work, for it has been more than fifty years since he laid down his tools. Now and then some old native shows me a bed or table or chair said to have been made by me in those distant days, but though I never contradict the statement, but rather encourage it instead, I am quite sure that the claim is more than doubtful.

Besides being a furniture maker, my father was the undertaker of the little town. I did not know it then, but I now suppose that the two pursuits went together in small settlements in those days. I know that the sale of a coffin meant much more to him and his family than any piece of furniture that he could make. My father was as kind and gentle as any one could possibly be, but I always realized his financial needs and even when very young used to wonder in a cynical way whether he felt more pain or pleasure over the death of a neighbor or friend. Any pain he felt must have been for himself, and the pleasure that he could not crowd aside must have come for the large family that looked to him for bread. I remember the coffins piled in one corner of the shop, and I always stayed as far away from them as possible, which I have done ever since. Neither did I ever want to visit the little shop after dark.

All of us boys had a weird idea about darkness, anyhow. The night was peopled with ghosts and the wandering spirits of those who were dead. Along two sides of the graveyard was a substantial fence between that and the road, and we always ran when we passed the white stones after dusk. No doubt early teaching is responsible for these foolish fears. Much of the terror of children would be avoided under sane and proper training, free of all fable and superstition.

My mother died when I was very young, and my remembrance of her is not very clear. It is sixty years since she laid down the hard burden that fate and fortune had placed upon her shoulders. Since that far-off day this loving, kindly, tireless and almost nameless mother has been slowly changed in Nature's laboratory into flowers and weeds and trees and dust. Her gravestone stands inside the white fence in the little country town where I was born, and beside her lies a brother who died in youth. I have been back to the old village and passed the yard where she rests forever, but only once have gone inside the gate since I left my old home so long ago. Somehow it is hard for me to lift the latch or go down the walk or stand at the marble slab which marks the spot where she was laid away. Still I know that in countless ways her work and teaching, her mastering personality, and her infinite kindness and sympathy have done much to shape my life.

My father died only twenty-five years ago. He is not buried in the churchyard at Kinsman. The same process of the reduction of the body to its elements has gone on with him as with my mother. But in her case it has come about through accumulating years; with him it was accomplished more quickly in the fiery furnace of the crematorium and his ashes were given to his children and were wafted to the winds.

Who am I—the man who has lived and retained this special form of personality for so many years? Aside from the strength or weakness of my structure, I am mainly the product of my mother, who helped to shape the wanton instincts of the child, and of the gentle, kindly, loving, human man whose presence was with me for so many years that I could not change, and did not want to change.

Since then a brother and sister, Everett and Mary, have passed into eternal sleep and have gone directly through the fiery furnace and their ashes are strewn upon the sands. I know that it can be but a short time until I shall go the way of all who live; I cannot honestly say that I want to be cremated, but I am sure that I prefer this method of losing my identity to any other I might choose.

The memory pictures of the first fifteen years of life that drift back to me now are a medley of all sorts of things, mainly play and school. Never was there a time when I did not like to go to school. I always welcomed the first day of the term and regretted the last. The school life brought together all the children of the town. These were in the main simple and democratic. The study hours, from nine to four, were broken by two recesses of fifteen minutes each and the "nooning" of one hour which provided an ideal chance to play. It seems to me that one unalloyed joy in life, whether in school or vacation time, was baseball. The noon time gave us a fairly good game each day. The long summer evenings were often utilized as well, but Saturday afternoon furnished the only perfect pleasure we ever knew. Whether we grew proficient in our studies or not, we enjoyed renown in our community for our skill in playing ball. Saturday afternoons permitted us to visit neighboring towns to play match games, and be visited by other teams in return.

I have snatched my share of joys from the grudging hand of Fate as I have jogged along, but never has life held for me anything quite so entrancing as baseball; and this, at least, I learned at district school. When we heard of the professional game in which men cared nothing whatever for patriotism but only for money—games in which rival towns would hire the best players from a natural enemy—we could scarcely believe the tale was true. No Kinsman boy would any more give aid and comfort to a rival town than would a loyal soldier open a gate in the wall to let an enemy march in.

We could not play when the snow was on the ground, but Kinsman had ponds and a river, and when the marvelous stream overran its banks it made fine skating in the winter months. Then there were the high hills; at any rate, they seemed high to me, and the spring was slower in coming than in these degenerate days, it seemed. To aid us in our sports there was a vast amount of snow and ice for the lofty, swift slides downhill, and few experiences have brought keener enjoyment, which easily repaid us for the tedious tug back to the top. I am not at all sure about the lessons that I learned in school, but I do know that we got a great deal of fun between the study hours, and I have always been glad that I took all the play I could as it came along.

But I am quite sure that I learned something, too. I know that I began at the primer and read over and over the McGuffey readers, up to the sixth, while at the district school. I have often wondered if there was such a man as Mr. McGuffey and what he looked like. To me his name suggested side-whiskers which, in Kinsman, meant distinction. I never could understand how he learned so much and how he could have been so good. I am sure that no set of books ever came from any press that was so packed with love and righteousness as were those readers. Their religious and ethical stories seem silly now, but at that time it never occurred to me that those tales were utterly impossible lies which average children should easily have seen through.

McGuffey furnished us many choice and generally poetical instructions on conduct and morals. And the same sort were found in other books, also. I remember one that I used to declaim, but I do not recall the book where it was found; this was an arraignment of the tobacco habit. It is not unlikely that this gem had something to do with the Methodist Church not permitting a man who smokes to be ordained as a preacher. Anyhow, I haven't heard of or seen this choice bit of literature and morals for sixty years, but here it is, as I remember it:

> " 'I'll never chew tobacco;
> No, it is a filthy weed.
> I'll never put it in my mouth,'
> Said little Robert Reed.
>
> Why, there was idle Jerry Jones,
> As dirty as a pig,
> Who smoked when only ten years old,
> And thought it made him big.
>
> He'd puff along the open streets
> As if he had no shame;
> He'd sit beside the tavern door
> And there he'd do the same."

The girls made their hatred of liquor just as clear, although I do not recall their words, but I do know the title of one recitation. The name carried a threat to all of us boys, declaring:

> "The lips that touch liquor
> Shall never touch mine."

From what I see and hear of the present generation I should guess that Doctor McGuffey and his ilk lived in vain.

I am inclined to think that I had the advantage of most of the boys and girls, for, as I have said, my home was well supplied with books, and my father was eager that all of us should learn. He watched our studies with the greatest care and diligently elaborated and supplemented whatever we absorbed in school. No one in town had an education anywhere near so thorough as his education that hard work and rigorous self-denial had afforded him.

I am never certain whether I have accomplished much or little. This depends entirely upon what comparisons I make. Judged with relation to my father, who reared so large a family and gave us all so good an education from the skimpy earnings of a little furniture store in a country town, I feel that my life has been unproductive indeed. How he did it I cannot understand. It must have been due largely to the work and management of my mother, who died before I was old enough to comprehend. But from the little that I remember, and from all that my older brothers and sisters and the neighbors have told me, I feel that it was her ability and devotion that kept us together, that made so little go so far, and did so much to give my father a chance for the study and contemplation that made up the real world in which he lived. In all the practical affairs of our life, my mother's hand and brain were the guiding force. Through my mother's good sense my father was able to give his children a glimpse into the realm of ideas and ideals in which he himself really lived.

But I must linger no longer at the threshold of life, which has such a magic hold on my conscious being.

In due time I finished my studies at the district school, and now grown to feel myself almost a man, was given newer and larger clothes, and more books, along with which came a little larger vision; and I went to the academy on the hill, and timorously entered a new world.

My eldest brother, Everett, who was always the example for the younger children, was then, by what saving and stinting I cannot tell, pursuing his studies at the University of Michigan; and my oldest sister, Mary, was following close behind. I have not the faintest conception how my father and mother were able to accomplish these miracles, working and planning, saving and managing, to put us through.

Any one who desires to write a story of his ideas and philosophy should omit childhood, for this is sacred ground, and when the old man turns back to that fairyland he lingers until any other undertaking seems in vain.

But the first bell in the academy tower has stopped ringing and I must betake myself and my books up the hill.

Jane Edna Hunter (1882–1971), a black South Carolinian trained as a nurse, moved to Cleveland in 1905. She earned a law degree from Marshall Law School as well as honorary degrees from numerous other universities. In 1911 she founded the Working Girls Association, later renamed the Phillis Wheatley Association, a refuge for young black women; she worked indefatigably for the life of Cleveland's African-American community, particularly women. Her memoirs, *A Nickel and a Prayer,* were published in 1940 and contained this account of the rise and fall of a near mythic "Great Mogul of organized vice." More important, "Miss Janey" describes the public outcry against the spread of vice in the African-American community.

Starlight

As a child on Woodburn Plantation I had often been thrown into teeth-chattering, blood-curdling panic by my terror of wildcats. Now, as a guardian of a social enterprise, I found myself facing a much more dreadful monster—commercialized vice. Like Apollyon who bestrode the path of Christian, this creature, spawned by greed and ignorance, was hideous to behold. "Out of its belly came fire and smoke, and its mouth was as the mouth of a lion." The service it imposed upon the wretched of my race was hard, "and its wages were death." It tried to win us by fair promises; it wrestled with us, and had almost pressed to death. But when we fell, we rose. "And although we must continue to wage bitter warfare with it, we know that we shall be more than conquerors through Him that loved us."

The story of American history, and, indeed, of all western history in the nineteenth century, is a record of unprecedented aggrandizement of urban populations. In Cleveland this mushroom growth, as regards its Negro population, achieved in the decade between 1910 and 1920 the phenomenal acceleration of three hundred per cent. Drawn from rural regions and villages by the lure of better wages, the Negroes, like other underprivileged groups, offered a glaring mark for the rapacity of realtors and the dishonesty of politicians. Where once they had been scattered throughout the city, their very numbers now confined them to definite sections, and these "black belts" quickly underwent a degeneration, civic and fiscal, of a type known to virtually all American cities.

Here was a golden opportunity for unscrupulous politicians; and greedily they seized upon it to serve their purposes, playing upon the ignorance of the Negro voter to entrench themselves in office, and then delivering the Negro over to every force of greed and vice which stalked around him. My second insight into this unholy alliance of organized vice and corrupt politics came to me in the course of my professional labors. Dr. A____, from whom I took cases, maintained two practices—one in the downtown section, one for Negroes on the edge of the underworld. It was while attending one of his patients, the madame of a house of prostitution, that I acquired first-hand experience with a resort of this character, and learned the ties which linked its evils with municipal politics. There were two children in this evil den—one a child of two, my patient's daughter; the other her niece, a girl of fourteen who acted as a porter, admitting patrons and collecting the two dollars charged them for their visits.

It was from the latter, Willie Mae, that I learned the set-up and acquired my knowledge of "Starlight," the unsavory creature who thrived upon the tolls which he exacted from this place and hundreds like it. His name, Willie Mae told me, came from the fact that he always wore a large, flashing diamond beneath his black bow tie. He was the "Great Mogul" of organized vice. Suave, impressive, impervious to shame, and gifted with the art of leadership, he was a born political henchman; and many a young colored girl, misled by hopes of an easy, glamorous existence, became the victim of his false promises and found herself, too late, a hopeless prisoner of shame and degradation.

Chance brought me in immediate contact with his first victim, a beautiful mulatto girl named Osie, whom he waylaid as she was on her way home from high school and won over with promises of marriage and a life of luxury. When her parents found her days later, she was living in a house of prostitution at Scovill Avenue and Fourteenth Street, where gambling and liquor offered a good time to libertines of both races, and dissolute white men sought a thrill with loose Negro girls. Osie's task was to keep the patrons drinking; and when business boomed, to seek fresh recruits for the trade. Pending the addition of these recruits, the greed of her husband frequently compelled his helpless victims to entertain as many as forty men in a single night. The time came, however, when this helpless first wife, Osie, was divorced by "Starlight" and abandoned by all her associates. She went from bad to worse; the police, acting under "Starlight's" orders, had denied her even the right to practice the unsavory profession to which he had dragged her; and at length, broken in health, stricken with pneumonia, she crawled back to her mother's home to die there, mourned only by her own mother. I stood at her bedside, when her eyes closed in death, and heard her unhappy mother cry, "Thanks be to God, now my trouble is over." Once more it was borne in upon me that only but for the grace of God this fate might easily enough have been mine, and I felt a renewed determination to help the homeless and imperiled daughter of my people.

"Starlight," meanwhile, waxed wealthier and more powerful each year. New houses of prostitution were opening frequently with procurers hunting Negro girls at our very doorsteps, and the issue had reached a point where it was no longer possible to ignore it.

What to do? Very early in the history of our social work for girls, tours of the dance halls, which I made with Mrs. Mary Rathburn Judd, General Secretary to the Young Women's Christian Association, had opened my eyes to the evil influence which the commercial dance hall was exerting upon the morals of the Negroes. Even then it was apparent that the only answer lay in supplying similar recreation under wholesome influences; and though this step involves the risk of alienating those of our supporters to whom dancing under any auspices was abhorrent, I now determined that the Phillis Wheatley should inaugurate a recreational hall. We rented a barn in the rear of our home for ten dollars a month, put in a new floor, plastered the walls, and announced our first party. Guests came only on invitation; no admission was charged at the parties which were held twice a month. The new addition to the Phillis Wheatley Association proved a huge success. Not only did we use the hall for dances, but we had it fitted up as a gymnasium. A Sunday school in the neighborhood held a bazaar, and from the proceeds bought dumb bells, Indian clubs, and other paraphernalia.

Preventive measures, however, were not enough. We determined to carry the warfare into the enemy's camp and do battle with the political corruption, "Starlight's" chief mainstay, which had made of our neighborhood a region of brawling vice, known throughout the city as the "Roaring Third."

At the moment, the Democratic and Republican parties were engaged in one of their periodical battles over the local railway system; the Democrats declaring for reduced fare, the Republicans aligning themselves with the stockholders of the Street Railway Company for "good service" at the existing fare. Eventually the issue came before the electorate, and fearing the outcome, the Republicans determined to clinch it by organizing the Negro vote in their favor. The task was not difficult. By tradition then the Negro vote was still overwhelmingly Republican, and all that was needed was to ensure that this vote should be delivered in bloc. The respectable Negro vote, the vote largely of the church people, was won by appeals to racial pride. The other, a numerically stronger vote, was in the pocket of "Starlight," placed there by the far-flung ramifications of his evil influence. If you care to investigate this chapter of Cleveland politics, you will discover how completely "Starlight" justified the confidence that was reposed in him by his masters, the politicians, and how intimate can be the relations between a general and public economic issue like that of a street railway franchise and the more private, but basically not less, economic issue of the prevalence of organized vice.

The Republicans won in 1910, and a part of "Starlight's" share in the victory was the privilege of naming a councilman to be elected to that body from our district. Great was the pride of the Negroes in this person, Tim Flagman, a popular young lawyer, who took his seat in the Councilmanic Chamber. Social leaders, especially those of us associated with the Phillis Wheatley, did not join in these plaudits, however, for well we knew what it foreboded; and when Tim was promptly slated for the all-important post of Chairman of the Fire and Police Committee, not the faintest doubt remained to us that evil days were upon us, and that henceforth vice would enjoy a free hand in the city. Our fears were not long in being realized. New dives and brothels opened all around us, all attempt at concealment was abandoned, the headway which the Negro had made toward the state of good citizenship at the time was tumbled gutterward, and faith in Negro leadership was turned to derision.

It was only this result, however, which could open the eyes of the gullible and misguided, and pave the way to a reaction. Now with evidence all around them of how shamefully they had been duped by "Starlight's" promises, the law-abiding citizens set to work to fight his baneful influence before and after municipal elections. Prominent in this movement were the members of St. John's A. M. E. Church, the Antioch Baptist Church, and other members of my group who had been "anti-Starlight" from the outset.

Our war cry was "Down with 'Starlight' and corruption," and we did not lack the campaign material; for scarcely a week went by that I was not summoned to police court to assume responsibility for some girl who had been arrested in a house of prostitution for which this monster was responsible. We had no campaign funds, but we did not lack enthusiasm. As the election drew near and our infectious zeal spread in every direction, our opponents began to feel a little worried. One ward-heeler came to my office and asked what I was doing, what I wanted for my district—in short, where I was standing.

"Go back and tell your boys I'm not standing," I told him, "I'm on my knees."

"Hell, get up then," he blurted out rudely; "you've got the boys worried sick."

This was the welcome news; and in the light of our enthusiasm, defeat now seemed impossible. Alas, for the simplicity of our illusions! Never once had it occurred to us that only the count determines an election, and that many a victory is won, after the polls have closed. The returns were simply incredible! We were barely in the running. It was not until years later that I learned how we had been cheated out of a hard-earned victory.

Politicians think their maneuvers irresistible. I was very much amused after this campaign by the various attempts which were made by "Starlight" and his crowd to tie the Phillis Wheatley to their chariot. "Starlight" went so far as to apply for membership in the Association; and when we respectfully returned the check he sent us for dues, he came back with an offer to furnish a living-room in the house. We informed him that we would not accept the offer, since his actions did not accord with the purposes and spirit of the Phillis Wheatley Association—a rebuff which he received with unruffled suavity.

His next move was covert and more successful. He sent to the Phillis Wheatley Home a light mulatto woman named Dora, who was fairly well educated, has pleasant manners, and dressed like a Paris fashion plate. It was not generally known that Dora was a scout for the "Starlight-Tim" combination. As a free lancer, she sought to recruit new blood for their underworld practices, and became identified with numerous social, religious, and political groups. In this way she interested herself in the work of our Association. It happened that one of the girls living in the Phillis Wheatley was reported as keeping late hours, in violation of dormitory rules. Dora learned of this and came to me under the pretense of friendship for Inez, and requested that I permit her to admonish the girl. Very soon it was discovered that Dora's real purpose was to entice Inez, because of her attractiveness, away from the institution and lure her into the "Starlight-Tim" dives, for this is where I subsequently found Inez. This experience was sufficient to put me on guard against future activities of this woman in the affairs of the Phillis Wheatley Association.

In fact, it was necessary at all times to guard our girls from evil surroundings. I kept a vigilant ear at the switchboard in my office to catch conversations of a doubtful character, and to intercept assignations. No effort we made to restrict tenancy to girls of good character could not exclude the ignorant, the foolish, and the weak, for these had to be protected as well. In the company of a policeman whom I could trust, I would sometimes follow couples to places of assignation, rescue the girl, and assist in the arrest of her would-be seducer.

Two years passed, and once more we were facing an election. This time our candidate was Howard E. Murrell, a successful business man with marked talents for organizing and directing a campaign. The contest proved much more bitter than the first one. Feeling on election day reached the pitch of violence. One of our workers, more daring than prudent, became engaged in controversy with one of "Starlight's" crowd, and had her coat torn from her shoulders. While I had always sought to avoid controversy, I could not stand by and allow one of my followers to be treated in this fashion, and I hurried to her succor.

My arch enemy saw me and stopped me forty paces from our door. "Might as well give up, 'Miss Janey,' " he announced suavely; "you're wasting time and energy. Go home and take it easy, Do now." The quiet insolence of the man made my blood boil. Everything decent and right which my parents had implanted in me and stood for, was affronted by his presence. I shook my finger in his face. "Some day I'll get you, you rascal."

The events of the next few hours, however, were to corroborate "Starlight's" boasting. Hour after hour, I sat in my office waiting for the belated returns from our district. Shortly before midnight, the issue still not known, I heard the crash of drums and the screeching of horns. It was "Starlight" and his forces, two thousand strong, sweeping down the street past the Phillis Wheatley, throwing their search-lights into our windows and shouting their derision. Out of defiance or a desire to show myself a good loser, I threw open the door on Central Avenue and stood there on the threshold. The unruly mob surged up the steps. One burly Negro rushed forward, his fist clenched to strike me. But someone in the crowd roared, "Don't you touch her," and he fell back. The mob rejoined the procession; and as they moved out on Central Avenue, I heard someone say, "Ain't Miss Hunter brave?" It was a pleasing tribute, doubly so in defeat; but the cold fact remained that we were in for two more years of "Starlight" and that our efforts had gone for nothing.

Then, abruptly, one month from the day I faced and denounced him, word of his death flashed through the district. He had contracted pneumonia; and, weakened by over-exertion and exposure during the election, had been unable to fight it. It seemed too good to be true. It was only when I stood watching the funeral procession that bore him to the church for burial that I felt sure that "Enemy No. 1" of Cleveland had at long last been vanquished. What a mockery it seemed—that procession, the masses of flowers, the stately music, the marching societies in gleaming regalia, the religious ceremony—all to honor a man who had destroyed virtue and spread ruin.

With the passing of "Starlight" in 1921, better days dawned for the Third District. Politicians had come to feel a certain respect for my influence, and the Phillis Wheatley Association continued to afford a safe refuge for the unprotected. From this time on I took no further active part in politics, except to keep our followers informed of the calibre of the men on the municipal and county tickets. Since direct campaigning seemed futile, the moral seemed to be that our best hope lay in our work of education and protection; and so we went on supplying recreation and beauty to the young, counsel and correction to the wayward, and a home to the homeless. Sweeping changes in social conditions we felt would have to await a more enlightened and responsible electorate.

But I am sorry to admit that the death of "Starlight" dealt no serious blow to open and protected prostitution. The evil was too deep-rooted for that; the foundations which he laid for an underworld of gambling, prostitution, and vice generally remained to menace unborn generations.

Dance halls multiplied, and their unsavory atmosphere is a growing cause of concern to parents. Under a former city administration, measures were taken to supervise these places. A dance hall inspector was appointed, and the establishments that met certain standards were licensed for operation. This reform, however, has been largely nullified by political pressure exerted by unionized orchestras who dislike the peril to their livelihood presented by effective regulation and consequent reduction of attendance. Slot machines and the policy racket have also operated to lower dance hall standards. Few, indeed, are the commercialized amusements which have escaped exploitation and control by gangsters.

A survey made in 1939, of conditions in my neighborhood, shows that the old evils still flourish in most places of amusement. The dice roll, strong liquor flows; lewd men and wretched women crowd about gambling tables in basements, often wagering as high as forty dollars, to emerge with a dime. They stagger out in the early morning, the men sometimes waiting to catch some innocent girl, as she rushes off to work or hurries home from a night job. Dives, run by Greeks and Italians in my district, flourish beside schools, and are frequented regularly by children of both the senior and junior high schools. At my instigation and with my assistance, a Negro policeman succeeded in having the license of one of these places revoked.

These are the ancient evils. But my last tour of inspection brought me in touch with something more anomalous; vice as a spectacle not for the ignorant or the unfortunate, but for patrons from society's leading families. It is located, this night club of which I am speaking, in the heart of a newly created Negro slum district, and its appointments are elaborate and costly. Here to the tune of St. Louis voodoo blues, half-naked Negro girls dance shameless dances with men in Spanish costumes, while daughters from highly respectable families, attended by escorts, clap their dainty, white hands and shout their approval. The whole atmosphere is one of unrestrained animality, the jungle faintly veneered with civilized trappings.

When one of the entertainers discovered my presence and announced in a loud voice that Miss Jane Hunter was present, the applause which greeted his announcement filled me with the deepest confusion. As unobtrusively as possible, I took my departure, saddened and disgusted.

Decent and self-respecting members of my race, I told myself, are not allowed to live in respectable white neighborhoods; yet a white aristocracy penetrates Negro slums to enjoy, patronize, and encourage the worst that my race has to offer. Inter-racial co-operation built the Phillis Wheatley Association and is carrying on its work; a co-operation of Negroes and whites for worthy purposes; which can gauge the spiritual contribution the Negro has made to American life, since his arrival in America. But in the meeting of black and whites in night clubs of the type I had encountered, there is to be found only cause for regret and head-hanging by both races. On the one side an exhibition of unbridled animality, on the other a blase quest for novel sensations, a vicarious gratification of the dark and violent desires of man's nature, a voluntary return to the jungle.

And behind it all, the hideous god of greed; greedy landlords avowed to reap enhanced returns at the moral cost of the community; racketeers and gangsters frightening the honest but cowardly into the service of evil; and dishonest politicians using public office to undermine the decency and morality of society. Yet at the bottom, the responsibility rests with the citizens of our community. Given what is lacking, unselfishness, imagination, courage, they could easily enough rout the forces of vice which they have supinely allowed to flourish.

It was these virtues that made possible the building of Phillis Wheatley. Out of the prayers and nickels—the interested benevolence of a few Negro working women—has grown a movement which has erected buildings for the welfare of hundreds of homeless women, and radiated the influences of fellowship throughout an entire country. We have proved that white and black can co-operate unselfishlessly for the common social good.

Langston Hughes (1902–67) moved to Cleveland in 1916 and graduated from Central High School. He was a poet and a novelist, and many of his plays were first produced by the Gilpin Players of Karamu House, which had been founded in 1917 as a cultural center for the African-American community. This selection from his autobiography, *The Big Sea* (1945), describes his high school years spent living in a multiethnic Cleveland urban neighborhood.

Central High

I had no sooner graduated from grammar school in Lincoln than we moved from Illinois to Cleveland. My stepfather sent for us. He was working in a steel mill during the war, and making lots of money. But it was hard work, and he never looked the same afterwards. Every day he worked several hours overtime, because they paid well for overtime. But after a while, he couldn't stand the heat of the furnaces, so he got a job as a caretaker of a theater building, and after that as janitor of an apartment house.

Rents were very high for colored people in Cleveland, and the Negro district was extremely crowded, because of the great migration. It was difficult to find a place to live. We always lived, during my high school years, either in an attic or a basement, and paid quite a lot for such inconvenient quarters. White people on the east side of the city were moving out of their frame houses and renting them to Negroes at double and triple the rents they could receive from others. An eight-room house with one bath would be cut up into apartments and five or six families crowded into it, each two-room kitchenette apartment renting for what the whole house had rented for before.

But Negroes were coming in in a great dark tide from the South, and they had to have some place to live. Sheds and garages and store fronts were turned into living quarters. As always, the white neighborhoods resented Negroes moving closer and closer—but when the whites did give way, they gave way at very profitable rentals. So most of the colored people's wages went for rent. The landlords and the banks made it difficult for them to buy houses, so they had to pay the exorbitant rents required. When my step-father quit the steel mill job, my mother went out to work in service to help him meet expenses. She paid a woman four dollars a week to take care of my little brother while she worked as a maid.

I went to Central High School in Cleveland. We had a magazine called the *Belfry Owl*. I wrote poems for the *Belfry Owl*. We had some wise and very good teachers, Miss Roberts and Miss Weimer in English, Miss Chesnutt, who was the daughter of the famous colored writer, Charles W. Chesnutt, and Mr. Hitchcock, who taught geometry with humor, and Mr. Ozanne, who spread the whole world before us in his history classes. Also Clara Dieke, who painted beautiful pictures and who taught us a great deal about many things that are useful to know—about law and order in art and life, and about sticking to a thing until it is done.

Ethel Weimer discovered Carl Sandburg for me. Although I had read of Carl Sandburg before—in an article, I think, in the *Kansas City Star* about how bad free verse was—I didn't really know him until Miss Weimer in second-year English brought him, as well as Amy Lowell, Vachel Lindsay, and Edgar Lee Masters, to us. Then I began to try to write like Carl Sandburg.

Little Negro dialect poems like Paul Lawrence Dunbar's and poems without rhyme like Sandburg's were the first real poems I tried to write. I wrote about love, about the steel mills where my step-father worked, the slums where we lived, and the brown girls from the South, prancing up and down Central Avenue on a spring day.

One of the first of my high school poems went like this:

> Just because I loves you—
> That's de reason why
> My soul is full of color
> Like de wings of a butterfly.
>
> Just because I loves you
> That's de reason why
> My heart's a fluttering aspen leaf
> When you pass by.

I was fourteen then. And another of the poems was this about the mills:

> The mills
> That grind and grind,
> That grind out steel
> And grind away the lives
> Of men—

In the sunset their stacks
Are great black silhouettes
Against the sky.
In the dawn
They belch red fire.
The mills—
Grinding new steel,
Old men.

And about Carl Sandburg, my guiding star, I wrote:

Carl Sandburg's poems
Fall on the white pages of his books
Like blood-clots of song
From the wounds of humanity.
I know a lover of life sings
When Carl Sandburg sings.
I know a lover of all the living
Sings then.

Central was the high school of students of foreign-born parents—
until the Negroes came. It is an old high school with many famous
graduates. It used to be long ago the high school of the aristocrats, until the aristocrats moved farther out. Then poor whites and foreign-
born took over the district. Then during the war, the Negroes came.
Now Central is almost entirely a Negro school in the heart of Cleveland's vast Negro quarter.

When I was there, it was very nearly entirely a foreign-born school,
with a few native white and colored American students mixed in. By
foreign, I mean children of foreign-born parents. Although some of the
students themselves had been born in Poland or Russia, Hungary or
Italy. And most were Catholic or Jewish.

Although we got on very well, whenever class elections would come
up, there was a distinct Jewish-Gentile division among my classmates.
That was perhaps why I held many class and club offices in high school,
because often when there was a religious deadlock, a Negro student
would win the election. They would compromise on a Negro, feeling,
I suppose, that a Negro was neither Jew nor Gentile!

I wore a sweater covered with club pins most of the time. I was on
the track team, and for two seasons, my relay team won the city-wide
championships. I was a lieutenant in the military training corps. Once
or twice I was on the monthly honor roll for scholarship. And when we
were graduated, Class of '20, I edited the Year Book.

My best pal in high school was a Polish boy named Sartur Andrze-
jewski. His parents lived in the steel mill district. His mother cooked
wonderful cabbage in sweetened vinegar. His rosy-cheeked sisters were

named Regina and Sabina. And the whole family had about them a quaint and kindly foreign air, bubbling with hospitality. They were devout Catholics, who lived well and were very jolly.

I had lots of Jewish friends, too, boys named Nathan and Sidney and Herman, and girls named Sonya and Bess and Leah. I went to my first symphony concert with a Jewish girl—for these children of foreign-born parents were more democratic than native white Americans, and less anti-Negro. They lent me *The Gadfly* and *Jean-Christophe* to read, and copies of the *Liberator* and the *Socialist Call*. They were almost all interested in more than basketball and the glee club. They took me to hear Eugene Debs. And when the Russian Revolution broke out, our school almost held a celebration.

Since it was during the war, and Americanism was being stressed, many of our students, including myself, were then called down to the principal's office and questioned about our belief in Americanism. Police went to some of our parents' homes and took all their books away. After that, the principal organized an Americanism Club in our school, and, I reckon, because of the customary split between Jews and Gentiles, I was elected president. But the club didn't last long, because we were never quite clear about what we were supposed to do. Or why. Except that none of us wanted Eugene Debs locked up. But the principal didn't seem to feel that Debs fell within the scope of our club. So the faculty let the club die.

Four years at Central High School taught me many invaluable things. From Miss Dieke, who instructed in painting and lettering and ceramics, I learnt that the only way to get a thing done is to start to do it, then keep on doing it, and finally you'll finish it, even if in the beginning you think you can't do it at all. From Miss Weimer I learnt that there are ways of saying or doing things, which may not be the currently approved ways, yet that can be very true and beautiful ways, that people will come to recognize as such in due time. In 1916, the critics said Carl Sandburg was no good as a poet, and free verse was no good. Nobody says that today—yet 1916 is not a lifetime ago.

From the students I learnt that Europe was not so far away, and that when Lenin took power in Russia, something happened in the slums of Woodlawn Avenue that the teachers couldn't tell us about, and that our principal didn't want us to know. From the students I learnt, too, that lots of painful words can be flung at people that aren't *nigger. Kike* was one; *spick,* and *hunky,* others.

But I soon realized that the kikes and the spicks and the hunkies—scorned though they might be by the pure Americans—all had it on the niggers in one thing. Summer time came and they could get jobs quickly. For even during the war, when help was badly needed, lots of employers would *not* hire Negroes. A colored boy had to search and search for a job.

My first summer vacation from high school, I ran a dumb-waiter at Halle's, a big department store. The dumb-waiter carried stock from the stock room to the various departments of the store. I was continually amazed at trays of perfume that cost fifty dollars a bottle, ladies' lace collars at twenty-five, and useless little gadgets like gold cigarette lighters that were worth more than six months' rent on the house where we lived. Yet some people could afford to buy such things without a thought. And did buy them.

The second summer vacation I went to join my mother in Chicago. Dad and my mother were separated again, and she was working as cook for a lady who owned a millinery shop in the Loop, a very fashionable shop where society leaders came by appointment and hats were designed to order. I became a delivery boy for that shop. It was a terrifically hot summer, and we lived on the crowded Chicago South Side in a house next to the elevated. The thunder of the trains kept us awake at night. We could afford only one small room for my mother, my little brother, and me.

South State Street was in its glory then, a teeming Negro street with crowded theaters, restaurants, and cabarets. And excitement from noon to noon. Midnight was like day. The street was full of workers and gamblers, prostitutes and pimps, church folks and sinners. The tenements on either side were very congested. For neither love nor money could you find a decent place to live. Profiteers, thugs, and gangsters were coming into their own. The first Sunday I was in town, I went out walking alone to see what the city looked like. I wandered too far outside the Negro district, over beyond Wentworth, and was set upon and beaten by a group of white boys, who said they didn't allow niggers in that neighborhood. I came home with both eyes blacked and a swollen jaw. That was the summer before the Chicago riots.

I managed to save a little money, so I went back to high school in Cleveland, leaving my mother in Chicago. I couldn't afford to eat in a restaurant, and the only thing I knew how to cook myself in the kitchen of the house where I roomed was rice, which I boiled to a paste. Rice and hot dogs, rice and hot dogs, every night for dinner. Then I read myself to sleep.

I was reading Schopenhauer and Nietzsche, and Edna Ferber and Dreiser, and de Maupassant in French. I never will forget the thrill of first understanding the French of de Maupassant. The soft snow was falling through one of his stories in the little book we used in school, and that I had worked over so long, before I really felt the snow falling there. Then all of a sudden one night the beauty and the meaning of the words in which he made the snow fall, came to me. I think it was de Maupassant who made me really want to be a writer and write stories about Negroes, so true that people in far-away lands would read them—even after I was dead.

But I did not dare write stories yet, although poems came to me now spontaneously, from somewhere inside. But there were no stories in my mind. I put the poems down quickly on anything I had at hand when they came into my head, and later I copied them in a notebook. But I began to be afraid to show my poems to anybody, because they had become very serious and very much a part of me. And I was afraid some other people might not like them or understand them.

However, I sent some away to a big magazine in New York, where nobody knew me. And the big magazine sent them right back with a printed rejection slip. Then I sent them to one magazine after another—and they always came back promptly. But once Floyd Dell wrote an encouraging word across one of the rejection slips from the *Liberator*.

A native of Niles, a town in the steel-producing Mahoning Valley, Kenneth Patchen (1911–72) worked in the mills before becoming a writer and painter. His collection of short stories *In Quest of Candlelighters* (1939) contains the autobiographical "Bury Them in God," a Joycean collage of youthful memories of the death of a favorite sister and the subsequent religious ceremonies, and the process of trying to write about the incident fifteen years later.

Bury Them in God

My father walks into the kitchen with the alertness of one expecting great events. There is a curious, half-startled sorrow on his blackened face. I follow him into the cellarway and watch in silence while he takes off his mill clothes. The smell of rancid oil and smoke pours from his tired body.

"When did she die?"

I cannot answer. I want to pound him with my fists. You dirty, cheap, sweaty-nosed monster. . . Noreen is dead! Does it make no difference to you? 'When did she die?' as calmly as 'Is supper ready?' I can see him at the head of the table, making thick noises with his lips as he wolfs the best pieces of meat; and Noreen is sitting *in the chair beside him,* her eyes never lifting, eating hesitantly, on edge to anticipate his next roar. The butter! Damnit! why don't you listen when I ask for something! Yes father, I'm sorry. And mother moving like a wornout ghost from one plate to the next. . . Woman! for God's sake sit down and stop fussing over them. If they ain't got sense enough to feed themselves, then let them starve. . . Yes, yes, yes Tom, yes father.

He takes a cake of Lava from the shelf over the sink and soaps his chest and belly. Rivulets of dirt follow the muscle ridges in jerky, tormented descent. His biceps whirl into sudden balls that stretch the skin to breaking. You stinking great ox. My father can beat up your father.

240 pounds of sheer beating-up. Watch this! and he laughs as the steel bar bends like sluggish jelly in his hands.

I look at the clock. It is four in the morning. She has been dead almost three hours.

The sound of weeping and hushed voices comes to us as the parlor door is opened. Before my mother can speak, he asks, "Anyone come yet?"

Uncle George and Aunt Anne, Uncle Jim and his second wife, Mr. and Mrs. Town, Joe, Bessie. . . Carl is at the phone now; it will take a day or so for some of them to get here, Uncle Ed from Michigan, Cousin Will from Pennsylvania, and Sally, and Red Williams, and Big Sam, and . . .

"The priest was with her to the end. He said she died" (and my mother sobs uncontrollably) "so happy. Oh Tom, I can't stand it, I can't stand it."

My father bends over awkwardly to unlace his shoes; their steel plates gleam ominously in the light. He opens his mouth to speak, coughs instead, a dry, sharp, heat-withered cough. For the first time I realize that they do not want me with them.

I put down the *Argosy-All-Story-Weekly*. I place it carefully beside me on my cot-bed. I am frantic with love. Rain beats softly on the window. My body arches, tense, quivering. I have been lying on my stomach reading and waiting for Noreen to come in from her date. She is late tonight. A new fellow, a fellow who plays in the K of C band. I seem to have a third eye, I can see them in the parked car, his mouth close to her ear, just at the point where the fine hair is altogether different from any on me; always I wanted to touch her face, run my lips along the line of her mouth—not kiss her, of course I did that—but in the way I moved to do it, show her that in me she had someone whose worship would keep her pure forever.

And I am terrified, lost, dissolved as though in a nightmare.

I am not curious about the ending of the story I have been reading. *I know how it ends.* I know that the little grim man in the light sedan is going to elude the police only to die from the bite of the tiny spider which is even now inching down over his sleeping face. I move a chair near the bed that I may have an unobstructed view of his agony. The man's heavy breathing causes the spider to swing gently on its web-spit, like a censer in the devil's church. Now the horrible manicles unclench—I scream and the little murderer opens one eye sleepily—it's only a story, he says in mild disapproval. I feel like laughing. I know that I cannot enter a story and tell people what to do. But I can. Of course I can. Father Riley, I say, and Father Riley strides out of the sacristy, rubbing his pink hands together like a small boy making a snow ball. Listen, you big cheese, I'm not going to be a priest when I grow up and you can put that in your pipe and smoke it—if you smoked one. I don't intend to spend all my life standing in front of an altar dressed in skirts like a woman. Then I wonder if it happens to Father Riley. Until tonight I had always thought that it only happened when a man did that to his wife. I hear the car turning in at the drive. I want to rush down and tell Noreen about it. Noreen, I was just lying here on my stomach reading and suddenly something burst inside me—like a beautiful light when you can taste and hear. . . Noreen, I. . . and I wonder if that can happen to her, if it will feel like that, and I want her to feel it, I want to give that to her, I want to remove it from me and give it to her—but something won't let me think it. What happened is for her, the rich, churning joy, but what I have of it now is not as it was then. I begin to scheme. I try to imagine a woman's body, a wife's body. I try to visualize the places which have been hidden from me. I have a new weapon. I am eager to make war. My father's sweat rushes into my blood. I want to go to the church and light all the candles because I have died and because I have been born.

I fall asleep wondering what the priests do . . . why is it a sin? What would they say if a twelve year old boy had a wife?

Buckets of black tea, cake, sandwiches, ice cream. Death is a thing that swells you up, you want to cry over everyone and laugh at everything. Besides, the men have a nip or two. Death brings the chickens home to roost . . . indeed, ta ta, such a lovely young girl, and only seventeen—with her life before her, cluck, cluck. More tea, Mrs. Town? Aunt Anne?

Ave Maria.

My father is in fine spirits. The carburetor on his car has been on the blink for months, but Uncle Ed, never man better with machinery, no sooner arrives than he fixes it. That reminds someone of the time someone's car was stuck out on the road and after they had got a tow-car out—in the middle of the night at that—the damn thing's just plain out of gas! Cousin Will, tell Tom here what you said to that Republican when he offered you a cigar to vote for him . . .

But the chief talk is of Uncle Jim's second wife. She's not a day under forty but boy is she a number wow! Watch out she don't set her cap for you. I hate her. I want to kick her in the belly. Coming into the house where Noreen. . . What's the matter with the boy? looks a bit blue around the gills. Took him hard, eh? Yes, you slimy-faced lizard, it took me hard.

Stephen, my older brother, hangs around the men like a puppy expecting a kick and being caressed. As the day goes on, he expands with their good spirits. Ah, it's good to be a man and listen to men talk.

How is Effie?

Fine. She says it's easier to have twins.

Guess the second one learns to get out from the first.

No, that ain't it—the second shoves the first one out.

And shoves so hard, he falls out himself, I suppose.

Gloria in excelsis deo.

Yeah, Young Fred's going to the dogs pretty fast. Knocked Old Fred down when he told him to stop bringing women to the house.

Old Fred should talk.

He did have some pips in his day, didn't he?

Heard the story bout him?

Which one?

Seems when he'd come into the poolroom all the boys would say, Clap, clap, here comes Freddie.

My mother's face is red from weeping and from standing over the hot stove. The women are shoving things into their mouths and having the time of their lives between bites. I watch a huge piece of berry pie disappear under Aunt Anne's little black mustache.

The fat breasts jiggle with grief and merriment. . .

I get up from my desk and cross to the window. An owl-gray dusk lowers over the city, a brutal darkness which seems to have the proportions of a human being bringing news of war to his waiting fellows. An ambulance lurches down the street, its red headlights advertising the latest delight in civilization's brothel—I am told that before the war of '14, crowds would gather along driveways which led to the accident wards, avid for sexual excitation. Religion and war will give Mr. Nobody an orgasm when all else has failed. O the Elk and the Moose and the Lion—have you ever watched them come out of their convention halls? Isn't it too much to hope that they would have the manly dignity to beat up their wives? I think it is. War is easier. Race hatred is a great pecker-raiser. Think of all the hot beds a war with Germany would make. The average American woman of fifty is a pooped-out hag, and it's small wonder—you can't expect them to live out their lives with these 'over-grown boys' and come through without dry bleeding somewhere. My own people had no such trouble: they were respecters of dirt. They could have brought me along all right . . . but I would still be groping around in the cave . . . maybe not sitting here waiting for war . . . I am standing turns, lucky tonight to get work, the rougher is just coming out of a drunk and I get his place and the sheets come wolfing out of the rolls and I move my tongs to take them knowing that when I get home the kids will just be getting up for school and the wife will be moving around saying Stephen get washed and get to bed I've got a big washing to do today. I stand at the sink and soap my belly. . .

But I am not thinking of these things. I feel a hot breath in my ear and the arms of a huge blonde woman are around me. Her body is wonderfully soft and warm. Your sister is better off now. No pain, no sorrow, no misery. The words pour over me like a puppy's tongue over a bruised hand. My face sinks into her breast. I am wildly happy. Suddenly I know what a woman is. I can believe in God. I can understand what it is about Uncle Jim's wife that sets the men after her. This body is the purest and wisest thing on earth. It is so much stronger than they are. It rises big and sure above their brutal talk. A joyous flower opens in me. . . I press against her in an ecstasy of devotion. I am glad that Noreen is dead. My fingertips touch that innocent death, my mouth sweetens on the importance of the living who contemplate the beautiful workings of death. Everything in me runs in a great torrent through the scent of the funeral wreaths and lodges in this peaceful body which is mine and which no man may ever again have as it is this moment, all my worship kicking and beating and trampling this purity that it may be gouged out of her and put deep in me. You dirty little brat! You ugly little beast! I can feel the impression of her hand on my cheek. Shame and disgust empty me of childhood. The whole damn sweating and tugging world is at my heels now. Her face is coarse, bloated like a bag of snot. I begin to understand why the men make dirt of the word they use to describe what they want of her. That is my word now, and I shall say it as they do.

The priest walked to the railing and lifted his eyes to The Father and his voice to the mourners who sat there waiting peacefully to be told that it was all for the best. He was a lean man with a fat look. His hands caressed the bible as though it were the belly of Mrs. God. From time to time he squeezed a nipple and the divine milk poured out with his words. Never having had a daughter of his own he was eminently qualified to console my parents in the loss of theirs. He ate of their flesh and drank of their blood and had every right to spit it back in their faces. He was a doctor of the soul and his instruments were made of honey and hell-fire. They paid him to tell them what punks they were. His eyes went off in opposite directions and he had to turn his head sideways to look at you—with a Devil and a God to supervise, I suppose being cockeyed was a distinct advantage to him; he had them both well in hand, at any rate. I watched his right eye for awhile.

My father had a way of clacking his false teeth when his attention was held by anything—he bought them at thirty, not because they were needed but because he thought they looked better than his own; he used to leave them lying about the house because they hurt his mouth, and I have never experienced anything more predatorily savage than those teeth snapping out at me from the most unexpected places.

The priest had him clacking. I moved nearer my mother and her shaking body beat gently against me.

Stephen, on her other side, was enjoying the adulation which our position accorded us. A frog could have peed down his neck and he wouldn't have noticed it. One of father's favorite expressions. You could have goosed him with a nun's glove. Another. My father was not a Catholic. The Church was just another thing for mother to fret about. He didn't like the priests because he said they talked and acted like W.C.T.U. women. Why the Pope's nothing but an oily-haired wop. But Father Riley had him clacking. This beautiful young gi–rl cut down in the first flower of her unfolding womanhood. O better, better I say, better that this untainted maiden should leave this valley of sorrow . . . *clack, clack* . . . If it be the will of G–od. . . O happy, happy these my children who follow unsullied the dictates of their Maker . . . if then, O grieving parents, and friends of this poor sorrowing mother, of this grief-burdened father . . . *clack, clack* . . . if then it be His all-beautiful will. . .

Maiden. I am left with that word. I know in a vague fashion what it means. The fact of this thing stands between me and Noreen's death. It robs the event of all meaning. It is as though I walk at night across a long bridge and there is only the shore which faces me and only the brilliantly-lighted city in whose every window I see her face and her eyes pleading with the terrible man who is crossing the room to her. They stand looking at each other while I walk them nearer and just as I am near enough to call—the lights go out, I can't see her now, I want to see her but it is dark around me and the bridge is crumbling into the water. Suddenly I understand what it is. I am jealous of death. She was defenseless, alone, and he took her. He is white, his eyes, hands, arms, hair, white, and his breath is white as he speaks to her . . . mingling then, she too becomes white and I sink down through the water while she rides into the sky with that *white* . . . that cold, flower-scented white bridegroom whose awful lips are sealed on hers forever.

When Father Riley has everybody crying nicely, he quits.

We file out of the church like schoolboys from a whorehouse, ashamed and yet strangely elated. We've got badges marked God all over us.

I sit with my family in the car behind the hearse. We worm through the streets flaunting our dreadful burden in the faces of the curious. We're not as good as a circus but they watch because there are a lot of us and we're all doing the same thing.

My father turns his head to admire a new real-estate development. *Clack, clack.* Great little burg.

I notice that the right rear tire on the hearse is almost flat. I pray that they will have to stop and fix it—all the coops opening and all the chickens hopping out 'O for heaven's sake! A flat tire on the way to the graveyard. . .'—but it doesn't seem to be losing very much air.

My mother's sobs mingle with father's clacking. Stephen is watching the back of the driver's neck as though he expected it to explode. Absently he fingers a pimple.

We swing in at the gate and thread through avenues of graves. Big monuments jostle little ones—class distinction to the end, a desperate last show in implacable stone.

There it is! A hole in the ground, ten by six by four.

They get the ugly box out and after mumbling over it some more they lower it on ropes and throw the dirt in.

The undertaker's helper is already busy pumping air into the tire.

There is a rap on my door and I go to open. Swanson is forty, a poet with two published books and a manuscript which has been kicking around in publishers' offices for several years. He came in clean and hard on the wave of 'proletarian' writing and was left high and dry when it receded. He refuses to spike his guns and as a result they don't go off at all. It hurts him to think that with the phonies revolution was nothing more than a literary fashion—to be thrown out like a dirty sock. He writes anger now. He has bogged down in hating people who are not worthy of notice. He has lost the thread of argument, Villon's, Heine's, Melville's.

While I am making coffee he wanders over to the bookcase and examines the poetry shelf. Who's this guy? He reads off the title, flicks through the pages. . . Listen to this. He reads slowly, drumming out the words. Boy, is that crap. Why're they all so damned constipated? Bet you could clean up with a physic for all these half-ass metaphysicals. Jesus, they just can't get it out. . . You know, I haven't read a decent poem in months. In months? I say. You're lucky. Who the hell is there? he demands, coming over for coffee. I hear so much talk . . . whosis, whatsis, and when I read the stuff—crap.

Maybe you don't hear the right talk, I tell him.

Yeah? He looks eager. You heard something good? I shake my head and we drink the coffee.

What you working on now?

A short story.

It's not that thing you were telling me about? The kid and his sister. . . ?

Yes, the kid and his sister.

What the devil can you do with that? The kid learns to masturbate and it's mixed up with death. . .

And the sister. . .

Did you get in the stuff about the old man?

Some of it. I'm only about half way through.

Look, I've got an idea. The kid finds the old man in the aunt's bed just before they're ready to go off to the funeral. . .

What does that do?

What do you mean, what does that do? Look. . .

Swanson.

Yeah?

Why do you write?

What do you mean, why do I write? It's as good a way to blow time as any. . .

Did you ever think that . . . oh what the hell.

Think what?

Nothing. Let's forget it.

Ok, I'll tell you what I think. I think that you have never written a goddamn thing that amounts to two cents. I think that you go around with the notion that because you happened to be born in a mill town, it puts a little gravy on your ass. I think that you've got the idea that you're a pretty bright little boy. This crappy story about the kid . . . what've you got? You ring in the Catholic church, ok, the Catholic church. You moon about what a prick your old man was . . . so what? And you got the damnedest, sweetest, prettiest damn sister who kicks the bucket and maybe you wanted to sleep with her . . . so what? you did, you didn't, it wouldn't kill her . . . maybe she'd like it . . . all right, you learn what life is, lying on your belly in a bed, so what? Want me to tell you what do with your damned story. . .

What makes you think I wanted her?

I give you that much credit.

You know a funny thing, Swanson?

I can't wait.

It does make a difference . . . being born in a mill town. Get down off that horseshit New York wise-guy stuff. You're not going to kid me with any of that straight-from-the-shoulder junk. . . I'll tell you something. . . I haven't put a damn thing in that story I didn't sweat blood over . . .

Some guys sweat blood over the ball scores. . .

. . . And just what the hell you get out of coming around here and BS-ing about the way I write. . .

I came for coffee.

All right, you've got the coffee.

Bye then, Little Boy Blue.

You should boy blue me . . . sitting on your tail all day in the 42nd Street library and goosing the ghosts of all the old farts. . .

What old farts do you refer to?

Old long-shirt Whitman who never opened his trap but a couple prairies and the Mississippi river jumped out; old stomach-ulcer Hawthorne . . . you know what you do over there . . . mooning over all the birdturd about how tough it is to be an artist in America . . . it's hard to do anything anywhere if you can't do it . . . and what the devil are all your smart critics doing about the boys who are in there now? Van Wyck Brooks, sure, Brooks, or maybe some of the little magazine-critic punks . . . they're so damn busy figuring out why Mark Twain had his ordeal, that fifty better guys could rot under their noses and they wouldn't know it . . . when the smell gets too bad they may move up to Edwin A. Robinson. . .

Keep your pants on, you're disturbing the ants.

And where do you come in . . . spewing your guts out about the working class? That's where your revolution will hit . . . straight down through the whole damn heap of filth where you'll find them, squatting on their rumps and hating every Goddamn thing you stand for . . . if you mean cheap, degraded, rotten pigs, then I'll know you're not talking through your hat about the working class. They'll rise up against their masters. . . Sure, they'll rise up, to build a bigger manure pile than they had the last time.

Please, Mister, kin I join your Party?

Sneer, you jackass . . . go on home and knock out a poem about how when the workers march into the streets it will be May 1st and everything. It's freaky intellectuals like you who take all the guts out of the struggle between the exploiters and the exploited . . . knock all the howling rubbish about 'the workers' out of your head. Jesus, think of all the poison that's been poured into them! Wake them up, for God's sake wake them up! but don't come bleating to me about how fine and noble they are. . .

You sound drunk, little boy.

Look, you bastard, go out in the street and listen to your working class champing at the bit to sink its teeth into the Japanese or German working class . . . and most of the writing skunks are hell-bent to hop on Roosevelt's war wagon . . . 'Save Democracy'—for the bankers. . .

You're all balled up, dicky bird.

I'm not so balled up that I spend my time with a gang of crap-shooting intellectual turncoats.

I suppose I do.

No you don't Swanson and I'm sorry I got sore but why the hell must you pull that stuff about the divine right of the workers to be sonsabitches. Now get out of here. I'm expecting Mary and I don't want your ugly puss around when she comes.

Look, better take my advice about the old man in the aunt's bed. . .

I'll put you in the aunt's bed.

Is she nice?

She's an AI member of the working class.

That's good enough for me.

So long, Swanson.

Bye, blue eyes.

The candles stand like two huge white carrots bleeding through their tops. Black eyelashes make a rigid net over her dead eyes. This is where you are? The whole box of your body empty of all but its cold meat. . . You would be afraid of this thing that lies here without feeling, without reason, without faith, joy or pain. . . If you were to walk into the room now, Noreen, you would scream in terror of all this whiteness that they have put where you were. White, a white *thing* . . . yet the hair is like your hair, silken, beautifully soft. . . There is a new ring on your finger and the stone writhes like a green snake in the light of the candles.

All right, Swanson, I can't go back there. . .

Lost in the far sleep that reaches out for my people on the byways of the world, lost in the thick snore of my father and rotted in the breasts of my mother, withered in the years that have brought to this night, this night as it advances its westering course to my own death; this night, then, Swanson, all of us amassed like squirming maggots in the gut of being alive and waiting for something to snap that we may be dead. Hollow the organ of memory groaning against all the broken stops. Empty the arms we hold out to the parts of ourselves that other people have taken. Haunted the tread of the feet that have wandered off from our bodies. In how many desolate places am I walking now? Is it strange that our pieces writhe through our sleep with every mouth screaming and with every nerve howling against the cavity of our disrupted souls? Is it strange at all, Swanson, that we are selecting the instruments of our own slaughter? Observe, I feel over all the knives in the case, selecting the one with the keenest edge—*you can understand that*—it is foul luck to find yourself equipped fully, the victim, maybe a person you despise, or better, nearly, someone you love, and then discover that instead of effecting a clean, deep wound, your blade only sogs the flesh, tearing rather than cutting. I believe that you will appreciate the dream of all the hurt and the hounded, an opening, even the tiniest, into the fabric of the past—the desire to mutilate the dead—not only those who died in body then, but also those who, being alive now, are *dead in that time;* for, is it not clear, Swanson, that the only survivors of that time, are the dead? We live only across one surface of time. Only the dead have a continuity of life, being predictable for those who continue to advance from that time. We can distinguish their features, because we are not afraid of them. We can remember nothing we fear; we remember only the fear. So it is, Swanson, I can tell you that of that hour and that time, only Noreen lives. All else is fantasy and crawling nightmare. Consider, to have a twelve year old boy trailing from you like a monstrous foetus, shoving into your life, *being you.* No, there is madness, there is the dissolution that gathers the advancing symbolism of living into a tight hysteria that feeds on itself. My God, how we name everything! How we lie sprawled in the filth of our labels! Are we to be only the cemeteries where are buried our million images? Kill the shadow people, kill the brutes who belly after us, their bloody, grasping paws rending and tearing all that we do. Stay in the now, Swanson; give them back all their smooth tricks for making cattle of our people; tell them to rub their noses in it when they start putting the working class on their neat shelf with the rest of their junk. A human being will walk out from under any tit-waving word of theirs. Of course there will be a new world and if you think it will be built on veneration for the sloth and ignorance of those down under now, you are a traitor to that better world. You are a traitor and a low-life, yellow-bellied skunk.

I arrange the knives in the case . . . the quick, good blades that thirst for murder.

I go down into the cellar and find the thing I want, a thick board with a long nail sticking up out of it. *And they said unto him, Thou art mad. But he continued to affirm that it was so. Then said they, It is his angel* craftily I entered the room where they are gathered round the coffin *But he continued knocking: and when they had opened the door, and saw him, they were as beasts caught in a hunter's net* first I swing out at my mother and the nail catches her in the cheek tearing out flesh adrip with blood and milk *and when they were past the first and the second ward, they came unto the iron gate which held them off the city; which opened to them and thunder came and thunder came and thunder came and fire was upon the earth* my father rushes at me and I get him in the temple and he goes down *And the people gave a shout, saying, It is the voice of a god, and not of a man* I manage to reach a few of the others and I lay about me for the sake of the dream that is in my heart for these my people *And he said, How can I, except some man shall guide me?* I am chuckling under my breath and finally I get over to Noreen and bending over I whisper they've all gone now Noreen they won't put their dirty muggs in your face anymore and then I raise the dripping club and hit her just under the eye but no single drop of blood comes *and forthwith the angel departed from him*

It is enough that I love them.

Allowing her dress to slip from her she stands naked before me.
Mary, I want to say, you are all purity and goodness, Mary, Mary . . .
I believe in the god of us. And I turn out the light.

The city noises are hushed now . . . a whistle . . . a foghorn out in
the silent bay . . . a faint call . . .

Mary.

Mmmm. . .

Are you asleep?

Hnnna. . .

That story, Mary—the one I was telling you about. . .

Mm. . .

I know how to end it now.

End what?

The story. . .

Oh, that. . . think about it in the morning.

No, Mary, I may lose it if I wait.

Well, what's the matter with the way you were going to end it?

That was all a lie. I want to tell the truth now. . .

What is the truth?

I didn't shout at my father before the people who had come for the
funeral.

No, what then?

I didn't call him names and beat him with my fists.

Don't get excited . . . I can believe it.

I didn't tell them all what I thought of them. . .

You've said that half a dozen times. . .

The thing happened the night before the funeral. I had gone in to be
alone with her. I wanted to feel what death was. The candles had burned
low and the Christ on the little silver crucifix was jumping up and
down in the wavering light—suddenly I saw that she was breathing. . .

Go on, I'm listening.

My chest drew in in a gob of terror. I expected her lips to part. The
touch of the hand on my shoulder caused me to sway and I felt a strong
arm go round me. Turning, I looked into the face of my father. His jaw
was set in a line of great suffering and tears flowed from his eyes. His
hold grew tighter on my arm and as I stood watching with him I saw
that the candle flame was steady and that her breast was still.

Mary.

Mmmm. . .

Did you hear what I said?

Of course. You went in to be alone with your sister for the last
time. . .

All right, you go back to sleep, I know how to finish it now.

Ah, no . . . it'll keep until morning.

I put my arms around her and stare at the gray patch of window. Her breathing is even, deep and secure. Slowly I get out of bed, cross to the desk and snap the light on. I begin to write: It happened fifteen years ago in Ohio. I was a sensitive lad, inclined to be a goddamned, ratfaced, little sonofabitch. . . *Hail Mary and twelve Our Fathers*. Hail Mamie and Tom and Jim and Swanson and Willie and me and you and Father Riley too. . .

Sara Brooks (b. 1911) moved from Alabama to Cleveland in 1940. She worked as a housekeeper for almost thirty years for the family of Thordis Simonsen, a free-lance writer and photographer, who transcribed and edited Brooks's vernacular autobiographical narrative, *You May Plow Here* (1986). In an original voice, Sara Brooks expresses a feisty view of race as it characterizes her own identity.

Something Better Gonna Come to Me

But my brother wanted me to come up here to Cleveland with him, so I started to try to save up what little money I had cause when I worked in Mobile, I sent a little money home to my kids. But I saved what I could, and when my sister-in-law came down for me, I had only eighteen dollars to my name, and that was maybe a few dollars over enough to come here. If I'm not mistaken it was about a dollar and fifteen cent over. Vivian was small—she was about three—so I didn't have to pay for her on the train, so you see what the price was *then*.

So we came with Rebecca here, but I didn't have nothin to come here with but just that little money. I didn't have *nothin!* And I found this little purse—at night the train was reelin and rockin, and people was sleepin, and somebody done dropped their purse. I said, "Oh boy!" And I grabbed that purse up off the floor. I didn't know who dropped it, and I didn't ask nobody. Went on in the restroom with it—I was gonna see if it had some money in there. I was so glad—I was gonna have some money when I got to Cleveland! I think it was twenty-five cent was in that purse, so whoever it was was just like me—they didn't have nothin either. But, anyway, I'm tellin you, ain't that somethin! I've come a long ways—I've really come a long ways. I say, "Lord, I got a bed to sleep in, and it's mine, and a chair to sit on, and it's mine. I got a stove to cook on, and I got books to read, and I got a radio to play." Sometime I feel like cryin because there were so many days that I didn't have nothin. So I did progress, and I'm very thankful.

I came to Cleveland in nineteen forty, and I didn't know what I was gonna do when I got here. All I knew to do was housework, so when I come here, that was about all I could get, you know. So I did house-work and the way that I'd get these jobs, they'd have these little employment offices—they were colored ladies would have em in their house. They would get these jobs, and you pay them I think fifty cent for sendin you out on a day's work. So I'd get up *early* in the mornin before day and get myself ready, and I would go with peoples in the neighborhood, cause I was surprised when I come into Cleveland, so many people livin in big old apartment houses, and all of em comin down this set of steps and that set of steps. So peoples livin around my brother, they were goin every mornin, and I would walk with different ones. We'd go clear over on Woodland—that was a long ways cause we was livin on Sixty-fifth between Quincy and Central—and we'd be at the employment office forming a line outside in order to find a job. It was snow on the ground, it was cold when you stand out in line in the mornins in order to get in so you can get somethin if they got it.

But I'd get a day and they give you a card with the name on it and the house number on it and the street, the telephone number, that's all. Then I'd go out and get the bus and go. But I didn't even know how to get around in Cleveland. I learned by gettin lost a lotta times because I worked all over, but I didn't have no dread because I had been among people after I left Orchard and went to Mobile. I mean if you was living in a place and you're not around peoples much, you kinda bashful. But I had been among peoples enough not to be that way, so I didn't think nothin about it. All I wanted was a job, and I learnt my way around myself by gettin lost, but I didn't mind askin where Central was or Scovill because I was livin between those two, so I got on either one of those buses and I made it.

But I worked for different peoples, and I wasn't makin much cause when I first came to Cleveland, I made four-fifty, four-fifty for a day's work. And one time I went on this job and this lady fooled me that she was goin pay me four dollars and fifty cent and when the day end up, I got four dollars. So I didn't like the money I made cause I worked hard and got less money than I did work, but why grumble? It wasn't four-fifty for a week's work one time down South.

And some peoples try to kill you, really. One lady tried to work me to death one day. I got home, I couldn't hardly get in the bathtub. Then she called me later on, she said to me, "I wonder how do you feel?" And I says, "I'm okay." She say, "You know my husband said that I had you doin too much work today." She say, "I'm really sorry about that," she say, "but when you come back, you won't have that much to do." I say, "I'm not comin back." I didn't go back, neither. But it tickled me, when I started workin for a lady here she says, "Sara, there's a toilet in the basement." And I said, "Okay," I said, "but I got arthritis," I says, "and I ain't goin downstairs to the toilet." She says, "Oh, well, I don't mean that you just have to go down to use the toilet. I have two up here." But you see, right then you can think she don't want me to use her toilet. That was here in Cleveland four or five years ago, but I still work for her.

And when I worked for Mrs. Dodd, I used to eat in the kitchen on the sideboard and she ate in the little breakfast nook, but I didn't care—it was clean. And when I used to work for Mrs. Grant in Mobile, she would put the food on the table and I would look after it and they all would eat before I did. I never did eat at the table with them, that's for sure! To come to Cleveland, most of the time you ate with them, but I knew I wasn't goin to eat at the table with the Grants cause I hadn't been eatin at the table with no white ones in the South and I knowed I wasn't gonna eat at the table with em, see? Cause Alice Garrett—that was Mr. Garrett's daughter—she would give us some cookies out the door sometime. And I know my father used to tell—it had to be a tale, but he said that one time he was travelin and he got hungry. He was round the well-to-do neighborhood—white peoples—so he thought, "I'll stop here in this place." So he stopped and he asked the lady, would she allow him to come in and eat some of that grass over there? "You can eat a little." So he's out there nibblin grass with his teeth, lookin for her to call him and give him somethin to eat. After awhile she say, "Hey Nigger! Nigger!" He goes runnin. He thought she was gonna hand him somethin. She say, "There's a little higher grass over there." Now you look into it, you would say that she just took that person to be a fool eatin grass, and if he be fool enough to eat the grass, he deserved to eat it, don't you think?

So I know that white peoples would hand stuff out the back door to colored people that work for em, and look like to me they seemed to have thought that they were more superior than you were. But the way I looked at it, a white person might be judgin me, but I'm judgin them, too. If they seem as if they was scornful of a colored person, at the same time that they was scornful of me, I'm the same way about them. What I'm tryin to say, if my place ain't good enough for you—I ain't good enough to sit down and eat with you or I'm not good enough to drink out of a glass you got because I'm black, I don't want to do it because this is the way I feel about me bein black. I'm black, and that's the way God made me, and I can get along just as good bein black as a person can get along bein white, although they may have a better start than I've had because when I was born, I was born poor. And some of the reason why we are poor is because we didn't have an education when we shoulda had one. Cause long time ago in slavery time they didn't want colored people to have no education. You knew that, didn't you? So the colored person didn't learn like the white person learned and so that's the way the white person got ahead of the colored, and with their better start, they are still ahead of me in the way of education or jobs.

So the biggest obstacle in my life was I had to get out on my own not knowing nothing. The reason why I say not knowing nothing, I only was a girl from the country, worked in the field, so I didn't know nothin but that. So I had to learn different in order to make a living. So when I left home, I learnt from gettin out and goin and doin. I wasn't really book-learned, and so I had to take whatever job that I was able to handle, and that was cleanin and scrubbin floors and things like that, which—that was no disgrace cause it was somethin honest, cause I coulda been out there stealin and robbin and running around with men, but I didn't do that. But I couldn't have a good job so I didn't make no money so I couldn't take care of my kids like I wanted to, and I couldn't give *them* a better education either.

But I worked while I was in Cleveland for different ones, and I was treated all right because if I hadn't been, I'd have somethin to tell, but I ain't got too much to tell. But I worked about a year here, and then I decided to go back. I wanted to go back South for awhile just because I had come up on a visit and I had worked, and I had bought me some nice clothes and new shoes and a big hat, and I wanted to go show them off. I had a *big* hat—I never will forget that! Oh! I had a beautiful hat, cause I love hats anyway. So I had been singin in the choir in Mobile, so I had to go show off at the church what I had done got a hold to cause I didn't have anything when I left down there. My brother begged me to stay. He said, "If you stay, I'll rent you a place," you know, for me to stay in because I was with his family. They had three girls, and they only had two bedrooms, so they used their livin room as a bedroom when I stayed there because they had this foldaway bed for the kids. But it was really too crowded for em because I brought Vivian up with me. Edith, my niece, and my sister-in-law Rebecca would look after Vivian when I was workin. My brother didn't want me to pay anything, but I'd always give Rebecca somethin anyway because times were hard for them as well as for me. But I wanted to go back, so I went back to Mobile.

Herbert Gold (b. 1924) was born, raised, and educated in Cleveland before moving to New York, where he attended Columbia University; he lives and writes in San Francisco. His many novels and short stories are known for their witty and pointed analysis of contemporary society. He wrote recently that "somehow I keep writing about Cleveland, no matter how long I'm away." Though much of his fiction is autobiographically linked to Cleveland, his memoir *My Last Two Thousand Years* (1972) is an authentic account of Cleveland's impact on a fledgling novelist.

My first novel was taken by a publisher in New York. We went back to Cleveland to live. In my mad pride—new father, new novelist—I expected to find a statue to my glory in the Public Square, between

Higbee's Department Store and East Ohio Gas, next to the hectic Civil War heroes on their horses. They hadn't finished the casting. While waiting, I found a job managing a hotel on Prospect Avenue. It was the time of Korea, Senator Joe McCarthy, the Eisenhower mumble. I wanted my child to grow up an American. I hoped to discover both what that was and what it could be.

My novel appeared. I received a telegram from a generous editor. My picture was not on the three-cent stamp, nor was my pigeon-encrusted statue to be found in the Public Square. Writing the book in Paris had been magic, but the novel itself was unmagical; it creaked and groaned with flexings and intentions. I was a graduate student trying to crash like an icebreaker in March through the glacial freeze of Lake Erie. I mean *serious*. I mean choked with metaphor and symbol. I mean polluted.

Blessed amnesia put the book itself out of my mind, but I still felt my body caught in the rhythm of mornings with a notebook in a damp room or a steamy cafe, that sculptural exhilaration of the physical act, writing. A bad book, I learned, can be written with the same sweet joy as good ones. I had to learn what everybody knows.

Despite my nostalgia for Paris, where on our last day my wife and I had walked back and forth across the Pont des Arts, unwilling to quit the bridge over the Seine mildly fluttering below, back and forth in the deepening evening, and she said, "We'll never come back again, we'll never come back together," and wept for the end of something, to be home in Cleveland was a liberation. I returned to the scenes of childhood nightmare and found myself a mere married man with one child, then with two children, with a job, with another novel in another notebook (a better one, pray God), a new life in the jazz clubs of Cleveland, Short Vincent Street, smoky Moe's Main Street, peculiar new part-time jobs, editing an entertainment magazine, teaching, nightclerking in a hotel, not sleeping very much. After the programmatic freedom of Paris, stubborn and familiar Cleveland was a new city to me. I felt tall enough to see from Lakewood, where there were no Jews, to the east side, where my relatives lived. I began to suspect the cost of my childhood quarantine.

There were also some nesting artists and writers, that international Bohemia dispersed like the Jews nearly everywhere, and the little roads and paths near Wade Park, near University Circle, around the Murray Hill Italian ghetto and down East Boulevard, were as romantic and poignant as the rue Chevalier-de-la-Barre or the Place de Furstemberg. I haunted interfaith pizzerias or Cedar Avenue soul-food diners, just as I had smacked my Fulbright lips over onion soup at dawn in Les Halles or *foie haché,* chopped liver, in the ancient ghetto of the rue Vieille du Temple, rue des Rosiers. History didn't have to be old to be historical.

Yesterday, when the Hungarians came to the south side and Magyar Village, when my father rode his White Motors truck to Lakewood, was as elusive and sheltering of its meaning as the time, a mere span earlier, when the Roman legions marched with their short swords into Lutèce, Lutetia, where the Parisii dwelled in a village smaller than Sandusky-on-the-Lake. Paris reminded me of my childhood in Lakewood, and now Lakewood gave resonance to my other childhood as a newly married man and skinny father pedaling his bicycle in Paris.

The Cleveland School of painters was renowned beyond Lorain and Sandusky on the west, Erie and Harrisburg in Pennsylvania, particularly for watercolors. An old German bookseller, Richard Laukhoff, once a friend to Hart Crane and Ernest Bloch, stepped out of his shop in the Colonial Arcade to show me the Blue Boar Cafeteria. "Iff zey eat zair, zey can buy books. But no! Zey eat over zair"—pointing to a paneled businessmen's rathskeller where zey were ordering book-depriving steaks and steins of cold beer instead of bargain trays of steamed tuna fish at the Blue Boar. Now I knew why *Birth of a Hero* disappointed my publisher and me. Tuna fish and creamed chicken were too great a sacrifice for the lovers of literature among Thompson Products executives.

Young poets and novelists chuffed and gasped like beached whales in Cleveland, but kept busy starting magazines, teaching, quarreling, finding jobs for their wives, and showing art movies in the parlor of a natural organizer who lived in a federal housing project under the High Level Bridge. We shared the costs of film rentals. We drank wine and played guitars and there were girls who hung around. We who were married held hands with our wives for protection against temptation. It was togetherness time, that curious moment of the early fifties—the cold war, the creeping baldness of tract houses, North Korean stubbornness, manias about subversion and the President forever smiling. I harried a notebook with plans for a wild manifesto, "The Protocols of the Elders of Bohemia," but even this international non-conspiracy, this local branch sticking out of my back pocket, would never provide the sense of community and purpose I required. Writing novels would not do enough. Nor would wife and children. Both did something, but there must be more.

The poems and secret journals did something, but there must be more.

Shaving, I looked in the mirror mornings, and took the measure of alternating dreams of evasion and responsibility, and with dread and longing gazed into the eyes of my daughters, and watched my father burrow furiously into his old age, and quarreled and had secrets from my wife, and there were discoveries of friendship, and there must be more, too.

We had a yard for the babies. My parents visited us twice a week. I wrote advertisements for committees opposed to the execution of the Rosenbergs, orated at meetings against the outrages of Senator McCarthy, had a part-time job teaching, had a full-time job as a night clerk, wrote my book while the drunks and whores seethed in the hotel about me, was visited by the FBI, and now it was time to leave Cleveland again. I sat in a library with a list of fellowships and found something to fit what I thought I could do. The meeting of France and Africa—why not?

It wasn't the FBI that put me in the library, crafting my message to the committee of judges of philosophy, literature, French, and how smart I might yet prove to be. It was my beloved native turf of Cleveland. After two years of it, oh, time to clear out.

Scott Russell Sanders (b. 1945) was born in Tennessee but raised in southern Portage County, part of the time on the grounds of the Ravenna Arsenal, which serves as the central fact and metaphor for this autobiographical essay reprinted from his collection *The Paradise of Bombs* (1987). He has published fourteen books of essays and fiction, many of which reflect his upbringing in the rural Western Reserve and his fascination particularly with the stories related in the *Portage County Atlas* (1874). He is Professor of English at Indiana University.

At Play in the Paradise of Bombs

Twice a man's height and topped by strands of barbed wire, a chain-link fence stretched for miles along the highway leading up to the main gate of the Arsenal. Beside the gate were tanks, hulking dinosaurs of steel, one on each side, their long muzzles slanting down to catch trespassers in a cross-fire. A soldier emerged from the gatehouse, gun on hip, silvered sunglasses blanking his eyes.

My father stopped our car. He leaned out the window and handed the guard some papers which my mother had been nervously clutching.

"With that license plate, I had you pegged for visitors," said the guard. "But I see you've come to stay."

His flat voice ricocheted against the rolled-up windows of the back seat where I huddled beside my sister. I hid my face in the upholstery, to erase the barbed wire and tanks and mirror-eyed soldier, and tried to wind myself into a ball as tight as the fist of fear in my stomach. By and by, our car eased forward into the Arsenal, the paradise of bombs.

This was in April of 1951, in Ohio. We had driven north from Tennessee, where spring had already burst the buds of trees and cracked the flowers open. Up here on the hem of Lake Erie the earth was bleak with snow. I had been told about northern winters, but in the red clay country south of Memphis I had seen only occasional flurries, harmless as confetti, never this smothering quilt of white. My mother had been crying since Kentucky. Sight of the Arsenal's fences and guard shacks looming out of the snow brought her misery to the boil. "It's like a concentration camp," she whispered to my father. I had no idea what she meant. I was not quite six, born two months after the gutting of Hiroshima and Nagasaki. My birth sign was the mushroom cloud. "It looks exactly like those pictures of the German camps," she lamented. Back in Tennessee, the strangers who had bought our farm were clipping bouquets from her garden. Those strangers had inherited everything—the barn and jittery cow, the billy goat fond of cornsilks, the crops of beans and potatoes already planted, the creek bottom cleared of locust trees, the drawling voices of neighbors, the smell of cotton dust.

My father had worked through the Second World War at a munitions plant near his hometown in Mississippi. Now his company, hired by the Pentagon to run this Ohio Arsenal, was moving him north to supervise the production lines where artillery shells and land mines and bombs were loaded with explosives. Later I would hear stories about those loadlines. The concrete floors were so saturated with TNT that any chance spark would set off a quake. The workers used tools of brass to guard against sparks, but every now and again a careless chump would drop a pocket knife or shell casing, and lose a leg. Once a forklift dumped a pallet of barrels and blew out an entire factory wall, along with three munitions loaders.

In 1951 I was too young to realize that what had brought on all this bustle in our lives was the war in Korea; too green to notice which way the political winds were blowing. Asia was absorbing bullets and bombs as quickly as the Arsenal could ship them. At successive news conferences, President Truman meditated aloud on whether or not to spill *the* Bomb—the sip of planetary hemlock—over China. Senator McCarthy was denouncing Reds from every available podium, pinning a single handy label on all the bugbears of the nation. Congress had recently passed bills designed to hamstring unions and slam the doors of America in the faces of immigrants. The Soviet Union had detonated its own atomic weapons, and the search was on for the culprits who had sold our secret. How else but through treachery could such a benighted nation ever have built such a clever bomb? In the very month of our move to the Arsenal, Julius and Ethel Rosenberg were sentenced to death. Too late, J. Robert Oppenheimer was voicing second thoughts about the weapon he had helped build. In an effort to preserve our lead in the race toward oblivion, our scientists were perfecting the hydrogen bomb.

We rolled to our new home in the Arsenal over the impossible snow, between parking lots filled with armored troop carriers, jeeps, strafing helicopters, wheeled howitzers, bulldozers, Sherman tanks, all the brawny machines of war. On the front porch of our Memphis home I had read GI Joe comic books, and so I knew the names and shapes of these death-dealing engines. In the gaudy cartoons the soldiers had seemed like two-legged chunks of pure glory, muttering speeches between bursts on their machine guns, clenching the pins of grenades between their dazzling teeth. Their weapons had seemed like tackle worthy of gods. But as we drove between those parking lots crowded with real tanks, past guard houses manned by actual soldiers, a needle of dread pierced my brain.

Thirty years later the needle is still there, and is festering. I realize now that in moving from a scrape-dirt farm in Tennessee to a munitions factory in Ohio I had leaped overnight from the nineteenth century into the heart of the twentieth. I had landed in a place that concentrates the truth about our condition more potently than any metropolis or suburb. If, one hundred years from now, there are still human beings capable of thinking about the past, and if they turn their sights on our own time, what they will see through the cross hairs of memory will be a place very like the Arsenal, a fenced wilderness devoted to the building and harboring of the instruments of death.

Our house was one of twenty white frame boxes arrayed in a circle about a swatch of lawn. Originally built for the high-ranking military brass, some of these government quarters now also held civilians—the doctors assigned to the base hospital, the engineers who carried slide-rules dangling from their belts, the accountants and supervisors, the managerial honchos. In our children's argot, this hoop of houses became the Circle, the beginning and ending point of all our journeys. Like campers drawn up around a fire, like wagons wound into a fearful ring, the houses faced inward on the Circle, as if to reassure the occupants, for immediately outside that tamed hoop the forest began, a tangled, beast-haunted woods stretching for miles in every direction.

Through our front door I looked out on mowed grass, flower boxes, parked cars, the curves of concrete, the wink of windows. From the back door I saw only trees, bare dark bones thrust up from the snow in that first April, snarled green shadows in all the following summers. Not many nights after we had settled in, I glimpsed a white-tailed deer lurking along the edge of that woods out back, the first of thousands I would see over the years. The Arsenal was a sanctuary for deer, I soon learned, and also for beaver, fox, turkey, geese, every manner of beast smaller than wolves and bears. Protected by that chain-link fence, which kept out hunters and woodcutters as well as spies, the animals had multiplied to very nearly their ancient numbers, and the trees grew thick and old until they died with their roots on. So throughout my childhood I had a choice of where to play—inside the charmed Circle or outside in the wild thickets.

Viewed on a map against Ohio's bulldozed land, the Arsenal was only a tiny patch of green, about thirty square miles; some of it had been pasture as recently as ten years earlier, when the government bought the land. It was broken up by airstrips and bunkers and munitions depots; guards cruised its perimeter and bored through its heart twenty-four hours a day. But to my young eyes it seemed like an unbounded wilderness. The biggest parcel of land for the Arsenal had belonged to a U.S. senator, who—in the selfless tradition of public servants—grew stinking rich from the sale. The rest was purchased from farmers, some of them descendants of the hardbitten New England folks who had settled that corner of Ohio, most of them reluctant to move. One of the old-timers refused to budge from his house until the wrecking crew arrived, and then he slung himself from a noose tied to a rafter in his barn. By the time I came along to investigate, all that remained of his place was the crumbling silo; but I found it easy to imagine him strung up there, roped to his roof-beam, riding his ship as it went down. Every other year or so, the older children would string a scarecrow from a rafter in one of the few surviving barns, and then lead the younger children in for a grisly look. I only fell for the trick once, but the image of that dangling husk is burned into my mind.

Rambling through the Arsenal's twenty-one thousand acres, at first in the safe back seats of our parents' cars, then on bicycles over the gravel roads, and later on foot through the backcountry, we children searched out the ruins of those abandoned farms. Usually the buildings had been torn down and carted away, and all that remained were the cellar holes half-filled with rubble, the skewed limestone foundations, the stubborn flowers. What used to be lawns were grown up in sumac, maple, blackberry. The rare concrete walks and driveways were shattered, sown to ferns. Moss grew in the chiseled names of the dead on headstones in backyard cemeteries. We could spy a house site in the spring by the blaze of jonquils, the blue fountain of lilacs, the forsythia and starry columbine; in the summer by roses; in the fall by the glow of mums and zinnias. Asparagus and rhubarb kept pushing up through the meadows. The blasted orchards kept squeezing out plums and knotty apples and bee-thick pears. From the cellar holes wild grapevines twisted up to ensnarl the shade trees. In the ruins we discovered marbles, bottles, the bone handles of knives, the rusty heads of hammers, and the tips of plows. And we dug up keys by the fistful, keys of brass and black iron, skeleton keys to ghostly doors. We gathered the fruits of other people's planting, staggering home with armfuls of flowers, sprays of pussywillow and bittersweet, baskets of berries, our faces sticky with juice.

Even where the army's poisons had been dumped, nature did not give up. In a remote corner of the Arsenal, on land which had been used as a Boy Scout camp before the war, the ground was so filthy with the discarded makings of bombs that not even guards would go there. But we children went, lured on by the scarlet warning signs. DANGER. RESTRICTED AREA. The skull-and-crossbones aroused in us dreams of pirates. We found the log huts overgrown with vines, the swimming lake a bog of algae and cattails, the stone walls scattered by the heave of frost. The only scrap of metal we discovered was a bell, its clapper rusted solid to the rim. In my bone marrow I carry traces of the poison from that graveyard of bombs, as we all carry a smidgen of radioactivity from every atomic blast. Perhaps at this very moment one of those alien molecules, like a grain of sand in an oyster, is irritating some cell in my body, or in your body, to fashion a pearl of cancer.

Poking about in the ruins of camp and farms, I felt a wrestle of emotions, half sick with loss, half exultant over the return of forest. It was terrifying and at the same time comforting to see how quickly the green wave lapped over the human remains, scouring away the bold marks of occupation. The displaced farmers, gone only a decade, had left scarcely more trace than the ancient Indians who had heaped up burial mounds in this territory. We hunted for Indian treasure, too, digging in every suspicious hillock until our arms ached. We turned up shards of pottery, iridescent shells, fiery bits of flint; but never any bones. The best arrow points and ax-heads we invariably discovered not by looking, but by chance, when jumping over a creek or scratching in the dirt with a bare incurious toe. This was my first lesson in the Zen of seeing, seeing by not-looking.

With or without looking, we constantly stumbled across the more common variety of mound in the Arsenal, the hump-backed bunkers where munitions were stored. Implausibly enough, they were called igloos. There were rows and rows of them, strung out along rail beds like lethal beads. Over the concrete vaults grass had been planted, so that from the air, glimpsed by enemy bombers, they would look like undulating hills. Sheep kept them mowed. The signs surrounding the igloos were larger and more strident than those warning us to keep away from the waste dumps. These we respected, for we feared that even a heavy footfall on the grassy roof of a bunker might set it off. Three or four had blown up over the years, from clumsy handling or the quirk of chemicals. Once a jet trainer crashed into a field of them and skidded far enough to trigger a pair. These numbers multiplied in our minds, until we imagined the igloos popping like corn. No, no, they were set far enough apart to avoid a chain reaction if one should explode, my father assured me. But in my reckoning the munitions bunkers were vaults of annihilation. I stubbornly believed that one day they all would blow, touched off by lightning, maybe, or by an enemy agent. Whenever I stole past those fields of bunkers or whenever they drifted like a flotilla of green humpbacked whales through my dreams, I imagined fire leaping from one to another, the spark flying outward to consume the whole creation. This poison I also carry in my bones, this conviction that we build our lives in mine fields. Long before I learned what new sort of bombs had devoured Hiroshima and Nagasaki, I knew from creeping among those igloos full of old-fashioned explosives that, on any given day, someone else's reckless step might consume us all.

Of course we played constantly at war. How could we avoid it? At the five-and-dime we bought plastic soldiers, their fists molded permanently around machine guns and grenades, their faces frozen into expressions of bravery or bloodlust. They were all men, all except the weaponless nurse who stood with uplifted lantern to inspect the wounded; and those of us who toyed at this mayhem were all boys. In the unused garden plot out back of the Circle, we excavated trenches and foxholes, embedded cannons inside rings of pebbles, heaped dirt into mounds to simulate ammo bunkers. Our miniature tanks left treadmarks in the dust exactly like those cut into the blacktop roads by real tanks. Running miniature trucks, our throats caught the exact groan of the diesel convoys that hauled army reservists past our door every summer weekend. When we grew tired of our Lilliputian battles, we took up weapons in our own hands. Any stick would do for a gun, any rock for a bomb. At the drugstore we bought war comics and on wet afternoons we studied war movies on television to instruct us in the plots for our games. No one ever chose to play the roles of Japs or Nazis or Commies, and so the hateful labels were hung on the smallest or shabbiest kids. For the better part of my first three years in the Arsenal I was a villain, consigned to the Yellow Peril or the Red Plague. Like many of the runts, even wearing the guise of a bad guy I refused to go down, protesting every lethal shot from the good guys. If all the kids eligible to serve as enemies quit the game, the Americans just blasted away at invisible foes, GI's against the universe.

Whenever we cared to we could glance up from our play in the garden battlefield and see the dish of a radar antenna spinning silently beyond the next ridge. We knew it scoured the sky for enemy bombers and, later, missiles. The air was filled with electronic threats. Every mile or so along the roads there were spiky transmitters, like six-foot-tall models of the Empire State Building, to magnify and boom along radio messages between security headquarters and the cruising guards. Imagining dire secrets whispered in code, I keened my ears to catch these broadcasts, as if by one particular resonance of brain cells I might snare the voices inside my skull. What I eventually heard, over a short-wave radio owned by one of the older boys, were guards jawing about lunch, muttering about the weather, about wives or bills or bowling, swearing aimlessly, or counting deer.

Our favorite family outing on the long summer evenings, after supper, after the washing of dishes, was to drive the gravel roads of the Arsenal and count deer. We would surprise them in clearings, a pair or a dozen, grass drooping from their narrow muzzles, jaws working. They would lift their delicate heads and gaze at us with slick dark eyes, some of the bucks hefting intricate antlers, the fresh does thick-uddered, the fawns still dappled. If the herd was large enough to make counting tricky, my father would stop the car. And if we kept very still, the deer, after studying us awhile, would go back to their grazing. But any slight twitch, a throat cleared or the squeak of a window crank, would startle them. First one white tail would jerk up, then another and another, the tawny bodies wheeling, legs flashing, and the deer would vanish like smoke. Some nights we counted over three hundred.

There were so many deer that in bad winters the managers of the Arsenal ordered the dumping of hay on the snow to keep the herds from starving. When my father had charge of this chore, I rode atop the truckload of bales, watching the tire slices trail away behind us in the frozen crust. Still the weak went hungry. Sledding, we would find their withered carcasses beside the gnawed stems of elderberry bushes. A few generations earlier, wolves and mountain lions would have helped out the snow, culling the slow-of-foot. But since the only predators left were two-legged ones, men took on the task of thinning the herds, and naturally they culled out the strongest, the heavy-antlered bucks, the meaty does. Early each winter the game officials would guess how many deer ought to be killed, and would sell that many hunting tags. Most of the licenses went to men who worked on the Arsenal, the carpenters and munitions loaders and firemen. But a quantity would always be reserved for visiting military brass.

They rolled into the Arsenal in chauffeured sedans or swooped down in star-spangled planes, these generals and colonels. Their hunting clothes smelled of moth balls. Their shotguns glistened with oil. Jeeps driven by orderlies delivered them to the brushwood blinds, where they slouched on canvas chairs and slugged whiskey to keep warm, waiting for the deer to run by. The deer always ran obligingly by, because men and boys hired from nearby towns would have been out since dawn beating the bushes, scaring up a herd and driving it down the ravine past the hidden generals, who pumped lead into the torrent of flesh.

Each deer season of my childhood I heard about this hunt. It swelled in my imagination to the scale of myth, outstripped in glory the remote battles of the last war, seemed more grand even than the bloody feuds between frontiersmen and Indians. I itched to go along, cradling my own shotgun, but my father said no, not until the winter after my thirteenth birthday. If I can't carry a gun, I begged, let me watch the hunt with empty hands. And so, the year I turned eleven he let me join the beaters, who would be herding deer for a party of shooters from the Pentagon.

A freezing rain the night before had turned the world to glass. As we fanned out over the brittle snow, our bootsteps sounded like the shattering of windows. We soon found our deer, lurking where they had to be, in the frozen field where hay had been dumped. Casting about them our net of bodies, we left open only the path that led to the ravine where the officers waited. With a clap of hands we set them scurrying, the white tails like an avalanche, black hoofs punching the snow, lank hams kicking skyward. Not long after, we heard the crackle of shotguns. When the shooting was safely over, I hurried up to inspect the kills. The deer lay with legs crumpled beneath their bellies or jutting stiffly out, heads askew, tongues dangling like handles of leather. The wounded ones had stumbled away, trailing behind them ropes of blood; my father and the other seasoned hunters had run after to finish them off. The generals were tramping about in the red snow, noisily claiming their trophies, pinning tags on the ear of each downed beast. The local men gutted the deer. They heaped the steaming entrails on the snow and tied ropes through the tendons of each hind leg and dragged them to the waiting jeeps. I watched it all to the end that once, rubbed my face in it, and never again asked to work as a beater, or to watch the grown men shoot, or to hunt.

With the money I was paid for herding deer, I bought the fixings for rocket fuel. That was the next stage in our playing at war, the launching of miniature missiles. We started by wrapping tinfoil around the heads of kitchen matches, graduated to aluminum pipes crammed with gunpowder, and then to machined tubes that burned zinc or magnesium. On the walls of our bedrooms we tacked photos of real rockets, the V-2 and Viking; the homely Snark, Hound Dog, Bullpup, Honest John, Little John, Mighty Mouse, Davy Crockett; and the beauties with godly names—Atlas, Titan, Jupiter, Juno, Nike-Hercules—the pantheon of power. By then I knew what rode in the nose cones, I knew what sort of bombs had exploded in Japan two months before my birth, I even knew, from reading physics books, how we had snared those fierce bits of sun. But I grasped these awesome facts in the same numb way I grasped the definition of infinity. I carried the knowledge in me like an ungerminated seed.

There was a rumor among the children that atomic bombs were stored in the Arsenal. The adults denied it, as they denied our belief that ghosts of Indians haunted the burial mounds or that shades of strung-up farmers paced in the haylofts of barns, as they dismissed all our bogies. We went searching anyway. Wasting no time among the igloos, which were too obvious, too vulnerable, we searched instead in the boondocks for secret vaults that we felt certain would be surrounded by deadly electronics and would be perfect in their camouflage. Traipsing along railway spurs, following every set of wheeltracks, we eventually came to a fenced compound that satisfied all our suspicions. Through the gridwork of wire and above the earthen ramparts we could see the gray concrete skulls of bunkers. We felt certain that the eggs of annihilation had been laid in those vaults, but none of us dared climb the fence to investigate. It was as if, having sought out the lair of a god, we could not bring ourselves to approach the throne.

In our searches for the Bomb we happened across a good many other spots we were not supposed to see—dumps and man-made deserts, ponds once used for hatching fish and now smothered in oil, machine guns rusting in weeds, clicking signal boxes. But the most alluring discovery of all was the graveyard of bombers. This was a field crammed with the ratty hulks of World War II Flying Fortresses, their crumpled green skins painted with enigmatic numbers and symbols, their wings twisted, propellers shattered, cockpits open to the rain. In one of them we found a pair of mannequins rigged up in flight gear, complete with helmets, wires running from every joint in their artificial bodies. What tests they had been used for in these crashed planes we had no way of guessing; we borrowed their gear and propped them in back to serve as navigators and bombardiers. Most of the instruments had been salvaged, but enough remained for us to climb into the cockpits and fly imaginary bombing runs. Sitting where actual pilots had sat, clutching the butterfly wings of a steering wheel, gazing out through a cracked windshield, we rained fire and fury on the cities of the world. Not even the sight of the deer's guts steaming on the red snow had yet given me an inkling of how real streets would look beneath our storm of bombs. I was drunk on the fancied splendor of riding those metal leviathans, making them dance by a touch of my fingers. At the age when Samuel Clemens sat on the bank of the Mississippi River smitten by the power of steamboats, I watched rockets sputter on their firing stand, I sat in the gutted cockpits of old bombers, hungry to pilot sky ships.

The sky over the Arsenal was sliced by plenty of routine ships, the screaming fighters, droning trainers, groaning transports, percussive helicopters; but what caught the attention of the children were the rare, rumored visitations of flying saucers. To judge by reports in the newspaper and on television, UFOs were sniffing about here and there all over the earth. We studied the night sky hopefully, fearfully, but every promising light we spied turned into a commonplace aircraft. I was beginning to think the aliens had declared the Arsenal off-limits. But then a neighbor woman, who sometimes looked after my sister and me in the afternoons, told us she had ridden more than once in a flying saucer that used to come fetch her in the wee hours from the parking lot behind the Bachelor Officers' Quarters. Mrs. K. was about fifty when we knew her, a stunted woman who gave the impression of being too large for her body, as if at birth she had been wrapped in invisible cords which were beginning to give way; she had a pinched face and watery eyes, a mousy bookkeeper for a husband, and no children. She was fastidious about her house, where the oak floors gleamed with wax, bathrooms glittered like jeweled chambers, and fragile knickknacks balanced on shelves of glass. When my mother dropped us by her place for an afternoon's stay, we crept about in terror of sullying or breaking something. In all her house there was nothing for children to play with except, stashed away in the bottom drawer of her desk, a dogeared pack of cards, a pair of dice, and a miniature roulette wheel. Soon tiring of these toys, my sister and I sat on the waxed floor and wheedled her into talking. At first she would maunder on about the life she had led on military bases around the world, the bridge parties and sewing circles; but eventually her eyes would begin to water and her teeth to chatter and she would launch into the history of her abduction by the aliens.

"They're not at all like devils," she insisted, "but more like angels, with translucent skin that glows almost as if there were lights inside their bodies." And their ship bore no resemblance to saucers, she claimed. It was more like a diamond as large as a house, all the colors of the rainbow streaming through the facets. The angelic creatures stopped her in the parking lot during one of her stargazing walks, spoke gentle English inside her head, took her on board their craft, and put her to sleep. When she awoke she was lying naked, surrounded by a ring of princely aliens, and the landscape visible through the diamond walls of the ship was the vague purple of wisteria blossoms. "They weren't the least bit crude or nasty," she said, the words coming so fast they were jamming together in her throat, "no, no, they examined me like the most polite of doctors, because all they wanted was to save us from destroying ourselves, you see, and in order to do that, first they had to understand our anatomy, and that's why they had chosen me, don't you see, they had singled me out to teach them about our species," she insisted, touching her throat, "and to give me the secret of our salvation, me of all people, you see, *me*."

My sister had the good sense to keep mum about our babysitter's stories, but I was so razzled by hopes of meeting with these aliens and learning their world-saving secrets that I blabbed about the possibility to my mother, who quickly wormed the entire chronicle from me. We never visited Mrs. K. again, but often we would see her vacuuming the lawn in front of her house. "Utterly crazy," my mother declared.

Mrs. K. was not alone in her lunacy. Every year or so one of the career soldiers, having stared too long into the muzzle of his own gun, would go berserk or break down weeping. A guard began shooting deer from his jeep and leaving the carcasses in heaps on the roads. A janitor poured muriatic acid into the swimming pool and then down his own throat. One Christmastime, the lieutenant colonel who played Santa Claus started raving at the annual gift-giving and terrified the expectant children out of their wits. It took five fathers to muscle him down and make him quit heaving presents from his bag of gewgaws. To this day I cannot see Santa's white beard and red suit without flinching. Life on military reservations had also crazed many of the army wives, who turned to drink and drugs. Now and again an ambulance would purr into the Circle and cart one of them away for therapy. When at home, they usually kept hidden, stewing in bedrooms, their children grown and gone or off to school or buried in toys. Outside, with faces cracked like the leather of old purses, loaded up with consoling chemicals, the crazed women teetered carefully down the sidewalk, as if down a tightrope over an abyss.

The Arsenal fed on war and the rumors of war. When the Pentagon's budget was fat, the Arsenal's economy prospered. We could tell how good or bad the times were by reading our fathers' faces, or by counting the pickup trucks in the parking lots. The folks who lived just outside the chain-link fence in trailers and tarpaper shacks did poorly in the slow spells, but did just fine whenever an outbreak of Red Scare swept through Congress. In the lulls between wars, the men used to scan the headlines looking for omens of strife in the way farmers would scan the horizon for promises of rain.

In 1957, when the Arsenal was in the doldrums and parents were bickering across the dinner table, one October afternoon between innings of a softball game somebody read aloud the news about the launching of Sputnik. The mothers clucked their tongues and the fathers groaned; but soon the wise heads among them gloated, for they knew this Russian feat would set the loadlines humming, and it did.

Our model rocketeering took on a new cast. It occurred to us that any launcher capable of parking a satellite in orbit could plant an H-bomb in the Circle. If one of those bitter pills ever landed, we realized from our reading, there would be no Circle, no dallying deer, no forests, no Arsenal. Suddenly there were explosives above our heads as well as beneath our feet. The cracks in the faces of the crazed ladies deepened. Guards no longer joked with us as we passed through the gates to school. We children forgot how to sleep. For hours after darkness we squirmed on our beds, staring skyward. "Why don't you eat?" our mothers scolded. Aged thirteen or fourteen, I stood one day gripping the edge of the marble-topped table in our living room, staring through a glass bell at the spinning golden balls of an anniversary clock, and cried, "I don't ever want to be a soldier, not ever, ever!"

Each weekend in summer the soldiers still played war. They liked to scare up herds of deer with their tanks and pin them against a corner of the fence. Snooping along afterward, we discovered tufts of hair and clots of flesh caught in the barbed wire from the bucks that had leapt over. Once, after a weekend soldier's cigarette had set off a brushfire, we found the charred bodies of a dozen deer jammed against a fence. We filled ourselves with that sight, and knew what it meant. There we lay, every child in the Arsenal, every adult, every soul within reach of the bombs—twisted black lumps trapped against a fence of steel. I have dreamed of those charred deer ever since. During the war in Vietnam, every time I read or heard about napalm, my head filled with visions of those blackened lumps.

To a child, it seemed the only salvation was in running away. Parents and the family roof were no protection from this terror. My notebooks filled with designs for orbiting worlds that we could build from scratch and for rocket ships that would carry us to fresh, unpoisoned planets. But I soon realized that no more than a handful of us could escape to the stars; and there was too much on earth—the blue fountains of lilacs, the red streak of a fox across snow, the faces of friends— that I could never abandon. I took longer and longer walks through the backwoods of the Arsenal, soaking in the green juices; but as I grew older, the forest seemed to shrink, the fences drew in, the munitions bunkers and the desolate chemical dumps seemed to spread like a rash, until I could not walk far in any direction without stumbling into a reminder of our preparations for doom.

Because the foundations of old farms were vanishing beneath the tangle of barriers and saplings, for most of my childhood I had allowed myself to believe that nature would undo whatever mess we made. But the scars from these new chemicals resisted the return of life. The discolored dirt remained bare for years and years. Tank trucks spraying herbicides to save the cost of mowing stripped the roads and meadows of wildflowers. Fish floated belly-up in the scum of ponds. The shells of bird eggs, laced with molecules of our invention, were too flimsy to hold new chicks. The threads of the world were beginning to unravel.

In a single winter a hired trapper cleared out the beavers, which had been snarling the waterways, and the foxes, which had troubled the family dogs. Our own collie, brought as a puppy from Memphis, began to chase deer with a pack of dogs. At night he would slink back home with bloody snout and the smell of venison on his laboring breath. The guards warned us to keep him in, but he broke every rope. Once I saw the pack of them, wolves again, running deer across a field. Our collie was in the lead, gaining on a doe, and as I watched he bounded up and seized her by the ear and dragged her down, and the other dogs clamped on at the belly and throat. I preferred this wild killing to the shooting-gallery slaughter of the hunting season. If our own dogs could revert to wildness, perhaps there was still hope for the earth. But one day the guards shot the whole wolfish pack. Nature, in the largest sense of natural laws, would outlast us; but no particular scrap of it, no dog or pond or two-legged beast was guaranteed to survive.

There was comfort in the tales forever circulating among the children of marvelous deer glimpsed at dusk or dawn, bucks with white legs, a doe with pale fur in the shape of a saddle on her back, and one year, a pair of ghostly albinos. Several of the children had seen the all-white deer. In 1962 I spent most of the summer sunsets looking for them, needing to find them, hungering for these tokens of nature's prodigal energies. By September I had still seen neither hide nor hair of them. That October was the showdown over the placement of Soviet missiles in Cuba; Kennedy and Khrushchev squared off at the opposite ends of a nuclear street, hands hovering near the butts of their guns. For two weeks, while these desperadoes brooded over whether to start the final shooting, I quit going to school and passed all the hours of daylight outdoors, looking for those albino deer. Once, on the edge of a thicket, on the edge of darkness, I thought I glimpsed them, milky spirits, wisps of fog. But I could not be sure. Eventually the leaders of the superpowers lifted their hands a few inches away from their guns; the missiles did not fly. I returned to my studies, but gazed stupidly at every page through a meshwork of fear. In December the existence of the albino deer was proven beyond a doubt, for one afternoon in hunting season an Army doctor and his wife drove into the Circle with the pair of ghostly bodies tied onto the hood of their car.

The following year—the year when John Kennedy was killed and I registered for the draft and the tide of U.S. soldiers began to lap against the shores of Asia—my family moved from the Arsenal. "You'll sleep better now," my mother assured me. "You'll fatten up in no time." During the twelve years of our stay inside the chain-link fences, almost every night at suppertime outdated bombs would be detonated at the ammo dump. The concussion rattled the milkglass and willowware in the corner cupboard, rattled the forks against our plates, the cups against our teeth. It was like the muttering of local gods, a reminder of who ruled our neighborhood. From the moment I understood what those explosions meant, what small sparks they were of the engulfing fire, I lost my appetite. But even outside the Arsenal, a mile or an ocean away, every night at suppertime my fork still stuttered against the plate, my teeth still chattered from the remembered explosions. They still do. Everywhere now there are bunkers beneath the humped green hills; electronic challenges and threats needle through the air we breathe; the last wild beasts fling themselves against our steel boundaries. The fences of the Arsenal have stretched outward until they circle the entire planet. I feel, now, I can never move outside.

Fiction

Sherwood Anderson (1876–1941) began his writing career in Clyde, on the western edge of the Reserve. While Anderson was best known for *Winesburg, Ohio* (1919), many of his short stories use Ohio regional settings as well. This story, from the collection *Horses and Men* (1923), repeats with more complexity the basic pattern established in *Winesburg, Ohio:* a young poet returns to rural Ohio from Cleveland, finds in rural Erie County his real essence, and departs, prepared for the life of the city.

An Ohio Pagan
CHAPTER I

Tom Edwards was a Welshman, born in Northern Ohio, and a descendant of that Thomas Edwards, the Welsh poet, who was called, in his own time and country, Twn O'r Nant—which in our own tongue means "Tom of the dingle or vale."

The first Thomas Edwards was a gigantic figure in the history of the spiritual life of the Welsh. Not only did he write many stirring interludes concerning life, death, earth, fire and water but as a man he was a true brother to the elements and to all the passions of his sturdy and musical race. He sang beautifully but he also played stoutly and beautifully the part of a man. There is a wonderful tale, told in Wales and written into a book by the poet himself, of how he, with a team of horses, once moved a great ship out of the land into the sea, after three hundred Welshmen had failed at the task. Also he taught Welsh woodsmen the secret of the crane and pulley for lifting great logs in the forests, and once he fought to the point of death the bully of the countryside, a man known over a great part of Wales as The Cruel Fighter. Tom Edwards, the descendant of this man was born in Ohio near my own native town of Bidwell. His name was not Edwards, but as his father was dead when he was born, his mother gave him the old poet's name out of pride in having such blood in her veins. Then when the boy was six his mother died also and the man for whom both his

mother and father had worked, a sporting farmer named Harry Whitehead, took the boy into his own house to live. They were gigantic people, the Whiteheads. Harry himself weighed two hundred and seventy
pounds and his wife twenty pounds more. About the time he took
young Tom to live with him the farmer became interested in the racing
of horses, moved off his farms, of which he had three, and came to live
in our town.

In the town of Bidwell there was an old frame building, that had
once been a factory for the making of barrel staves but that had stood
for years vacant, staring with windowless eyes into the streets, and
Harry bought it at a low price and transformed it into a splendid stable
with a board floor and two long rows of box stalls. At a sale of blooded
horses held in the city of Cleveland he bought twenty young colts, all
of the trotting strain, and set up as a trainer of race horses.

Among the colts thus brought to our town was one great black fellow named Bucephalus. Harry got the name from John Telfer, our
town poetry lover. "It was the name of the mighty horse of a mighty
man," Telfer said, and that satisfied Harry.

Young Tom was told off to be the special guardian and caretaker of
Bucephalus, and the black stallion, who had in him the mighty blood
of the Tennessee Patchens, quickly became the pride of the stables. He
was in his nature a great ugly-tempered beast, as given to whims and
notions as an opera star, and from the very first began to make trouble.
Within a year no one but Harry Whitehead himself and the boy Tom
dared to go into his stall. The methods of the two people with the great
horse were entirely different but equally effective. Once big Harry
turned the stallion loose on the floor of the stable, closed all the doors,
and with a cruel long whip in his hand, went in to conquer or be con-
quered. He came out victorious and ever after the horse behaved when
he was about.

The boy's method was different. He loved Bucephalus and the wicked
animal loved him. Tom slept on a cot in the barn and day or night, even
when there were mares about, walked into Bucephalus' box-stall without fear. When the stallion was in a temper he sometimes turned at the
boy's entrance and with a snort sent his iron-shod heels banging against
the sides of the stall, but Tom laughed and putting a simple rope halter
over the horse's head led him forth to be cleaned or hitched to a cart for
his morning's jog on our town's half-mile race track. A sight it was to
see the boy with the blood of Twn O'r Nant in his veins leading by the
nose Bucephalus of the royal blood of the Patchens.

When he was six years old the horse Bucephalus went forth to race
and conquer at the great spring race meeting at Columbus, Ohio.
He won two heats of the trotting free-for-all—the great race of the

meeting—with heavy Harry in the sulky and then faltered. A gelding named "Light o' the Orient" beat him in the next heat. Tom, then a lad of sixteen, was put into the sulky and the two of them, horse and boy, fought out a royal battle with the gelding and a little bay mare, that hadn't been heard from before but that suddenly developed a whirlwind burst of speed.

The big stallion and the slender boy won. From amid a mob of cursing, shouting, whip-slashing men a black horse shot out and a pale boy, leaning far forward, called and murmured to him. "Go on, boy! Go boy! Go boy!" the lad's voice had called over and over all through the race. Bucephalus got a record of 2.06$\frac{1}{4}$ and Tom Edwards became a newspaper hero. His picture was in the Cleveland *Leader* and the Cincinnati *Enquirer,* and when he came back to Bidwell we other boys fairly wept in our envy of him.

Then it was however that Tom Edwards fell down from his high place. There he was, a tall boy, almost of man's stature and, except for a few months during the winters when he lived on the Whitehead farms, and between his sixth and thirteenth years, when he had attended a country school and had learned to read and write and do sums, he was without education. And now, during that very fall of that year of his triumph at Columbus, the Bidwell truant officer, a thin man with white hair, who was also superintendent of the Baptist Sunday School, came one afternoon to the Whitehead stables and told him that if he did not begin going to school both he and his employer would get into serious trouble.

Harry Whitehead was furious and so was Tom. There he was, a great tall slender fellow who had been with race horses to the fairs all over Northern Ohio and Indiana, during that very fall, and who had just come home from the journey during which he had driven the winner in the free-for-all trot at a Grand Circuit meeting and had given Bucephalus a mark of 2.06$\frac{1}{4}$.

Was such a fellow to go sit in a schoolroom, with a silly school book in his hand, reading of the affairs of the men who dealt in butter, eggs, potatoes and apples, and whose unnecessarily complicated business life the children were asked to unravel—was such a fellow to go sit in a room, under the eyes of a woman teacher, and in the company of boys half his age and with none of his wide experience of life?

It was a hard thought and Tom took it hard. The law was all right, Harry Whitehead said, and was intended to keep noaccount kids off the streets but what it had to do with himself Tom couldn't make out. When the truant officer had gone and Tom was left alone in the stable with his employer the man and the boy stood for a long time glumly staring at each other. It was all right to be educated but Tom felt he had book education enough. He could read, write and do sums, and what other book-training did a horseman need? As for books, they were all right for rainy evenings when there were no men sitting by the stable door and talking of horses and races. And also when one went to the races in a strange town and arrived, perhaps on Sunday, and the races did not begin until the following Wednesday—it was all right then to have a book in the chest with the horse blankets. When the weather was fine and the work was all done on a fine fall afternoon, and the other swipes, both niggers and whites, had gone off to town, one could take a book out under a tree and read of life in far away places that were as strange and almost as fascinating as one's own life. Tom had read "Robinson Crusoe," "Uncle Tom's Cabin" and "Tales from the Bible," all of which he had found in the Whitehead house and Jacob Friedman, the school superintendent at Bidwell, who had a fancy for horses, had loaned him other books that he intended reading during the coming winter. They were in his chest—one called "Gulliver's Travels" and the other "Moll Flanders."

And now the law said he must give up being a horseman and go every day to a school and do little foolish sums, he who had already proven himself a man. What other schoolboy knew what he did about life? Had he not seen and spoken to several of the greatest men of this world, men who had driven horses to beat world records, and did they not respect him? When he became a driver of race horses such men as Pop Geers, Walter Cox, John Splan, Murphy and the others would not ask him what books he had read, or how many feet make a rod and how many rods in a mile. In the race at Columbus, where he had won his spurs as a driver, he had already proven that life had given him the kind of education he needed. The driver of the gelding "Light o' the Orient" had tried to bluff him in that third heat and had not succeeded. He was a big man with a black mustache and had lost one eye so that he looked fierce and ugly, and when the two horses were fighting it out, neck and neck, up the back stretch, and when Tom was tooling Bucephalus smoothly and surely to the front, the older man turned in his sulky to glare at him. "You damned little whipper-snapper," he yelled, "I'll knock you out of your sulky if you don't take back."

He had yelled that at Tom and then had struck at the boy with the butt of his whip—not intending actually to hit him perhaps but just missing the boy's head, and Tom had kept his eyes steadily on his own horse, had held him smoothly in his stride and at the upper turn, at just the right moment, had begun to pull out in front.

Later he hadn't even told Harry Whitehead of the incident, and that fact too, he felt vaguely, had something to do with his qualifications as a man.

And now they were going to put him into a school with the kids. He was at work on the stable floor, rubbing the legs of a trim-looking colt, and Bucephalus was in his stall waiting to be taken to a late fall meeting at Indianapolis on the following Monday, when the blow fell. Harry Whitehead walked back and forth swearing at the two men who were loafing in chairs at the stable door. "Do you call that law, eh, robbing a kid of the chance Tom's got?" he asked, shaking a riding whip under their noses. "I never see such a law. What I say is Dod blast such a law."

Tom took the colt back to its place and went into Bucephalus' box-stall. The stallion was in one of his gentle moods and turned to have his nose rubbed, but Tom went and buried his face against the great black neck and for a long time stood thus, trembling. He had thought perhaps Harry would let him drive Bucephalus in all his races another season and now that was all to come to an end and he was to be pitched back into childhood, to be made just a kid in school. "I won't do it," he decided suddenly and a dogged light came into his eyes. His future as a driver of race horses might have to be sacrificed but that didn't matter so much as the humiliation of this other, and he decided he would say nothing to Harry Whitehead or his wife but would make his own move.

"I'll get out of here. Before they get me into that school I'll skip out of town," he told himself as his hand crept up and fondled the soft nose of Bucephalus, the son royal of the Patchens.

Tom left Bidwell during the night, going east on a freight train, and no one there ever saw him again. During that winter he lived in the city of Cleveland, where he got work driving a milk wagon in a district where factory workers lived.

Then spring came again and with it the memory of other springs— of thunder-showers rolling over fields of wheat, just appearing, green and vivid, out of the black ground—of the sweet smell of new plowed fields, and most of all the smell and sound of animals about barns at the Whitehead farms north of Bidwell. How sharply he remembered those days on the farms and the days later when he lived in Bidwell, slept in the stables and went each morning to jog race horses and young colts round and round the half-mile race track at the fair grounds at Bidwell.

That was a life! Round and round the track they went, young colt-hood and young manhood together, not thinking but carrying life very keenly within themselves and feeling tremendously. The colt's legs were to be hardened and their wind made sound and for the boy long hours were to be spent in a kind of dream world, and life lived in the company of something fine, courageous, filled with a terrible, waiting surge of life. At the fair ground, away at the town's edge, tall grass grew in the enclosure inside the track and there were trees from which came the voices of squirrels, chattering and scolding, accompanied by the call of nesting birds and, down below on the ground, by the song of bees visiting early blossoms and of insects hidden away in the grass.

How different the life of the city streets in the springtime! To Tom it was in a way fetid and foul. For months he had been living in a boarding house with some six, and often eight or ten, other young fellows, in narrow rooms above a foul street. The young fellows were unmarried and made good wages, and on the winter evenings and on Sundays they dressed in good clothes and went forth, to return later, half drunk, to sit for long hours boasting and talking loudly in the rooms. Because he was shy, often lonely and sometimes startled and frightened by what he saw and heard in the city, the others would have nothing to do with Tom. They felt a kind of contempt for him, looked upon him as a "rube" and in the late afternoon when his work was done he often went for long walks alone in grim streets of workingmen's houses, breathing the smoke-laden air and listening to the roar and clatter of machinery in great factories. At other times and immediately after the evening meal he went off to his room and to bed, half sick with fear and with some strange nameless dread of the life about him.

And so in the early summer of his seventeenth year Tom left the city and going back into his own Northern Ohio lake country found work with a man named John Bottsford who owned a threshing outfit and worked among the farmers of Erie County, Ohio. The slender boy, who had urged Bucephalus to his greatest victory and had driven him the fastest mile of his career, had become a tall strong fellow with heavy features, brown eyes, and big nerveless hands—but in spite of his apparent heaviness there was something tremendously alive in him. He now drove a team of plodding grey farm horses and it was his job to keep the threshing engine supplied with water and fuel and to haul the threshed grain out of the fields and into farmers' barns.

The thresherman Bottsford was a broad-shouldered, powerful old man of sixty and had, besides Tom, three grown sons in his employ. He had been a farmer, working on rented land, all his life and had saved some money, with which he had bought the threshing outfit, and all day the five men worked like driven slaves and at night slept in the hay in the farmers' barns. It was rainy that season in the lake country and at the beginning of the time of threshing things did not go very well for Bottsford.

The old thresherman was worried. The threshing venture had taken all of his money and he had a dread of going into debt and, as he was a deeply religious man, at night when he thought the others asleep, he crawled out of the hayloft and went down onto the barn floor to pray.

Something happened to Tom and for the first time in his life he began to think about life and its meaning. He was in the country, that he loved, in the yellow sunwashed fields, far from the dreaded noises and

dirt of city life, and here was a man, of his own type, in some deep way
a brother to himself, who was continuously crying out to some power
outside himself, some power that was in the sun, in the clouds, in the
roaring thunder that accompanied the summer rains—that was in all
these things and that at the same time controlled all these things.

The young threshing apprentice was impressed. Throughout the
rainy days, when no work could be done, he wandered about and waited
for night, and then, when they all had gone into the barn loft and the
others prepared to sleep, he stayed awake to think and listen. He thought
of God and of the possibilities of God's part in the affairs of men. The
thresherman's youngest son, a fat jolly fellow, lay beside him and, for
a time after they had crawled into the hay, the two boys whispered and
laughed together. The fat boy's skin was sensitive and the dry broken
ends of grass stalks crept down under his clothes and tickled him. He
giggled and twisted about, wriggling and kicking and Tom looked at
him and laughed also. The thoughts of God went out of his mind.

In the barn all became quiet and when it rained a low drumming
sound went on overhead. Tom could hear the horses and cattle, down
below, moving about. The smells were all delicious smells. The smell
of the cows in particular awoke something heady in him. It was as
though he had been drinking strong wine. Every part of his body
seemed alive. The two older boys, who like their father had serious na-
tures, lay with their feet buried in the hay. They lay very still and a
warm musty smell arose from their clothes, that were full of the sweat
of toil. Presently the bearded old thresherman, who slept off by himself, arose cautiously and walked across the hay in his stockinged feet.
He went down a ladder to the floor below, and Tom listened eagerly.
The fat boy snored but he was quite sure that the older boys were
awake like himself. Every sound from below was magnified. He heard
a horse stamp on the barn floor and a cow rub her horns against a feed
box. The old thresherman prayed fervently, calling on the name of
Jesus to help him out of his difficulty. Tom could not hear all his words
but some of them came to him quite clearly and one group of words
ran like a refrain through the thresherman's prayer. "Gentle Jesus," he
cried, "send the good days. Let the good days come quickly. Look out
over the land. Send us the fair warm days."

Came the warm fair days and Tom wondered. Late every morning,
after the sun had marched far up into the sky and after the machines
were set by a great pile of wheat bundles he drove his tank wagon off
to be filled at some distant creek or at a pond. Sometimes he was compelled to drive two or three miles to the lake. Dust gathered in the
roads and the horses plodded along. He passed through a grove of trees
and went down a lane and into a small valley where there was a spring
and he thought of the old man's words, uttered in the silence and the

darkness of the barns. He made himself a figure of Jesus as a young god walking about over the land. The young god went through the lanes and through the shaded covered places. The feet of the horses came down with a thump in the dust of the road and there was an echoing thump far away in the wood. Tom leaned forward and listened and his cheeks became a little pale. He was no longer the growing man but had become again the fine and sensitive boy who had driven Bucephalus through a mob of angry, determined men to victory. For the first time the blood of the old poet Twn O'r Nant awoke in him.

The water boy for the threshing crew rode the horse Pegasus down through the lanes back of the farm houses in Erie County, Ohio, to the creeks where the threshing tanks must be filled. Beside him on the soft earth in the forest walked the young god Jesus. At the creek, Pegasus, born of the springs of Ocean, stamped on the ground. The plodding farm horses stopped. With a dazed look in his eyes Tom Edwards arose from the wagon seat and prepared his hose and pump for filling the tank. The god Jesus walked away over the land, and with a wave of his hand summoned the smiling days.

A new light came into Tom Edwards' eyes and grace seemed to come also into his heavy maturing body. New impulses came to him. As the threshing crew went about, over the roads and through the villages from farm to farm, women and young girls looked at the young man and smiled. Sometimes as he came from the fields to a farmer's barn, with a load of wheat in bags on his wagon, the daughter of the farmer stepped out of the farm house and stood looking at him. Tom looked at the woman and hunger crept into his heart and, in the evenings while the thresherman and his sons sat on the ground by the barns and talked of their affairs, he walked nervously about. Making a motion to the fat boy, who was not really interested in the talk of his father and brothers, the two younger men went to walk in the nearby fields and on the roads. Sometimes they stumbled along a country road in the dusk of the evening and came into the lighted streets of a town. Under the store-lights young girls walked about. The two boys stood in the shadows by a building and watched and later, as they went homeward in the darkness, the fat boy expressed what they both felt. They passed through a dark place where the road wound through a wood. In silence the frogs croaked, and birds roosting in the trees were disturbed by their presence and fluttered about. The fat boy wore heavy overalls and his fat legs rubbed against each other. The rough cloth made a queer creaking sound. He spoke passionately. "I would like to hold a woman, tight, tight, tight," he said.

One Sunday the thresherman took his entire crew with him to a church. They had been working near a village called Castalia, but did not go into the town but to a small white frame church that stood amid trees and by a stream at the side of a road, a mile north of the village. They went on Tom's water wagon, from which they had lifted the tank and placed boards for seats. The boy drove the horses.

Many teams were tied in the shade under the trees in a little grove near the church, and strange men—farmers and their sons—stood about in little groups and talked of the season's crops. Although it was hot, a breeze played among the leaves of the trees under which they stood, and back of the church and the grove the stream ran over stones and made a persistent soft murmuring noise that arose above the hum of voices.

In the church Tom sat beside the fat boy who stared at the country girls as they came in and who, after the sermon began, went to sleep while Tom listened eagerly to the sermon. The minister, an old man with a beard and a strong sturdy body, looked, he thought not unlike his employer Bottsford the thresherman.

The minister in the country church talked of that time when Mary Magdalene, the woman who had been taken in adultery, was being stoned by the crowd of men who had forgotten their own sins and when, in the tale the minister told, Jesus approached and rescued the woman Tom's heart thumped with excitement. Then later the minister talked of how Jesus was tempted by the devil, as he stood on a high place in the mountain, but the boy did not listen. He leaned forward and looked out through a window across fields and the minister's words came to him but in broken sentences. Tom took what was said concerning the temptation on the mountain to mean that Mary had followed Jesus and had offered her body to him, and that afternoon, when he had returned with the others to the farm where they were to begin threshing on the next morning, he called the fat boy aside and asked his opinion.

The two boys walked across a field of wheat-stubble and sat down on a log in a grove of trees. It had never occurred to Tom that a man could be tempted by a woman. It had always seemed to him that it must be the other way, that women must always be tempted by men. "I thought men always asked," he said, "and now it seems that women sometimes do the asking. That would be a fine thing if it could happen to us. Don't you think so?"

The two boys arose and walked under the trees and dark shadows began to form on the ground underfoot. Tom burst into words and continually asked questions and the fat boy, who had been often to church and for whom the figure of Jesus had lost most of its reality, felt a little embarrassed. He did not think the subject should be thus freely discussed and when Tom's mind kept playing with the notion of Jesus, pursued and tempted by a woman, he grunted his disapproval. "Do you think he really refused?" Tom asked over and over. The fat boy tried to explain. "He had twelve disciples," he said. "It couldn't have happened. They were always about. Well, you see, she wouldn't ever have had no chance. Wherever he went they went with him. They were men he was teaching to preach. One of them later betrayed him to soldiers who killed him."

Tom wondered. "How did that come about? How could a man like that be betrayed?" he asked. "By a kiss," the fat boy replied.

On the evening of the day when Tom Edwards—for the first and last time in his life—went into a church, there was a light shower, the only one that fell upon John Bottsford's threshing crew during the last three months the Welsh boy was with them and the shower in no way interfered with their work. The shower came up suddenly and a few minutes was gone. As it was Sunday and as there was no work the men had all gathered in the barn and were looking out through the open barn doors. Two or three men from the farm house came and sat with them on boxes and barrels on the barn floor and, as is customary with country people, very little was said. The men took knives out of their pockets and finding little sticks among the rubbish on the barn floor began to whittle, while the old thresherman went restlessly about with his hands in his trouser pockets. Tom who sat near the door, where an occasional drop of rain was blown against his cheek, alternately looked from his employer to the open country where the rain played over the fields. One of the farmers remarked that a rainy time had come on and that there would be no good threshing weather for several days and, while the thresherman did not answer, Tom saw his lips move and his grey beard bob up and down. He thought the thresherman was protesting but did not want to protest in words.

As they had gone about the country many rains had passed to the north, south and east of the threshing crew and on some days the clouds hung over them all day, but no rain fell and when they had got to a new place they were told it had rained there three days before. Sometimes when they left a farm Tom stood up on the seat of his water wagon and looked back. He looked across fields to where they had been at work and then looked up into the sky. "The rain may come now. The threshing is done and the wheat is all in the barn. The rain can now do no harm to our labor," he thought.

On the Sunday evening when he sat with the men on the floor of the barn Tom was sure that the shower that had now come would be but a passing affair. He thought his employer must be very close to Jesus, who controlled the affairs of the heavens, and that a long rain would not come because the thresherman did not want it. He fell into a deep reverie and John Bottsford came and stood close beside him. The thresherman put his hand against the door jamb and looked out and Tom could still see the grey beard moving. The man was praying and was so close to himself that his trouser leg touched Tom's hand. Into the boy's mind came the remembrance of how John Bottsford had prayed at night on the barn floor. On that very morning he had prayed. It was just as daylight came and the boy was awakened because, as he crept across the hay to descend the ladder, the old man's foot had touched his hand.

As always Tom had been excited and wanted to hear every word said in the older man's prayers. He lay tense, listening to every sound that came up from below. A faint glow of light came into the hayloft, through a crack in the side of the barn, a rooster crowed and some pigs, housed in a pen near the barn, grunted loudly. They had heard the thresherman moving about and wanted to be fed and their grunting, and the occasional restless movement of a horse or a cow in the stable below, prevented Tom's hearing very distinctly. He, however, made out that his employer was thanking Jesus for the fine weather that had attended them and was protesting that he did not want to be selfish in asking it to continue. "Jesus," he said, "send, if you wish, a little shower on this day when, because of our love for you, we do not work in the fields. Let it be fine tomorrow but today, after we have come back from the house of worship, let a shower freshen the land."

As Tom sat on a box near the door of the barn and saw how aptly the words of his employer had been answered by Jesus he knew that the rain would not last. The man for whom he worked seemed to him so close to the throne of God that he raised the hand, that had been touched by John Bottsford's trouser leg to his lips and secretly kissed it—and when he looked again out over the fields the clouds were being blown away by a wind and the evening sun was coming out. It seemed to him that the young and beautiful god Jesus must be right at hand, within hearing of his voice. "He is," Tom told himself, "standing behind a tree in the orchard." The rain stopped and he went silently out of the barn, towards a small apple orchard that lay beside the farm house, but when he came to a fence and was about to climb over he stopped. "If Jesus is there he will not want me to find him," he thought. As he turned again toward the barn he could see, across a field, a low grass-covered hill. He decided that Jesus was not after all in the orchard. The long slanting rays of the evening sun fell on the crest of the hill and touched with light the grass stalks, heavy with drops of rain and for a moment the hill was crowned as with a crown of jewels. A million tiny drops of water, reflecting the light, made the hilltop sparkle as though set with gems. "Jesus is there," muttered the boy. "He lies on his belly in the grass. He is looking at me over the edge of the hill."

CHAPTER II

John Bottsford went with his threshing crew to work for a large farmer named Barton near the town of Sandusky. The threshing season was drawing near an end and the days remained clear, cool and beautiful. The country into which he now came made a deep impression on Tom's mind and he never forgot the thoughts and experiences that came to him during the last weeks of that summer on the Barton farms.

The traction engine, puffing forth smoke and attracting the excited attention of dogs and children as it rumbled along and pulled the heavy red grain separator, had trailed slowly over miles of road and had come down almost to Lake Erie. Tom, with the fat Bottsford boy sitting beside him on the water wagon, followed the rumbling puffing engine, and when they came to the new place, where they were to stay for several days, he could see, from the wagon seat, the smoke of the factories in the town of Sandusky rising into the clear morning air.

The man for whom John Bottsford was threshing owned three farms, one on an island in the bay, where he lived, and two on the mainland, and the larger of the mainland farms had great stacks of wheat standing in a field near the barns. The farm was in a wide basin of land, very fertile, through which a creek flowed northward into Sandusky Bay and, besides the stacks of wheat in the basin, other stacks had been made in the upland fields beyond the creek, where a country of low hills began. From these latter fields the waters of the bay could be seen glistening in the bright fall sunlight and steamers went from Sandusky to a pleasure resort called Cedar Point. When the wind blew from the north or west and when the threshing machinery had been stopped at the noon hour the men, resting with their backs against a straw-stack, could hear a band playing on one of the steamers.

Fall came on early that year and the leaves on the trees in the forests that grew along the roads that ran down through the low creek bottom lands began to turn yellow and red. In the afternoons when Tom went to the creek for water he walked beside his horses and the dry leaves crackled and snapped underfoot.

As the season had been a prosperous one Bottsford decided that his youngest son should attend school in town during the fall and winter. He had bought himself a machine for cutting firewood and with his two older sons intended to take up that work. "The logs will have to be hauled out of the wood lots to where we set up the saws," he said to Tom. "You can come with us if you wish."

The thresherman began to talk to Tom of the value of learning. "You'd better go to some town yourself this winter. It would be better for you to get into a school," he said sharply. He grew excited and walked up and down beside the water wagon, on the seat of which Tom sat listening and said that God had given men both minds and bodies and it was wicked to let either decay because of neglect. "I have watched you," he said. "You don't talk very much but you do plenty of thinking, I guess. Go into the schools. Find out what the books have to say. You don't have to believe when they say things that are lies."

The Bottsford family lived in a rented house facing a stone road near the town of Bellevue, and the fat boy was to go to that town—a distance of some eighteen miles from where the men were at work— afoot, and on the evening before he set out he and Tom went out of the barns intending to have a last walk and talk together on the roads.

They went along in the dusk of the fall evening, each thinking his own thoughts, and coming to a bridge that led over the creek in the valley sat on the bridge rail. Tom had little to say but his companion wanted to talk about women and, when darkness came on, the embarrassment he felt regarding the subject went quite away and he talked boldly and freely. He said that in the town of Bellevue, where he was to live and attend school during the coming winter, he would be sure to get in with a woman. "I'm not going to be cheated out of that chance," he declared. He explained that as his father would be away from home when he moved into town he would be free to pick his own place to board.

The fat boy's imagination became inflamed and he told Tom his plans. "I won't try to get in with any young girl," he declared shrewdly. "That only gets a fellow in a fix. He might have to marry her. I'll go live in a house with a widow, that's what I'll do. And in the evening the two of us will be there alone. We'll begin to talk and I'll keep touching her with my hands. That will get her excited."

The fat boy jumped to his feet and walked back and forth on the bridge. He was nervous and a little ashamed and wanted to justify what he had said. The thing for which he hungered had he thought become a possibility—an act half achieved. Coming to stand before Tom he put a hand on his shoulder. "I'll go into her room at night," he declared. "I'll not tell her I'm coming, but will creep in when she is asleep. Then I'll get down on my knees by her bed and I'll kiss her, hard, hard. I'll hold her tight, so she can't get away and I'll kiss her mouth till she wants what I want. Then I'll stay in her house all winter. No one will know. Even if she won't have me I'll only have to move, I'm sure to be safe. No one will believe what she says, if she tells on me. I'm not going to be like a boy any more, I'll tell you what—I'm as big as a man and I'm going to do like men do, that's what I am."

The two young men went back to the barn where they were to sleep on the hay. The rich farmer for whom they were now at work had a large house and provided beds for the thresherman and his two older sons but the two younger men slept in the barn loft and on the night before had lain under one blanket. After the talk by the bridge however,

Tom did not feel very comfortable and that stout exponent of manhood, the younger Bottsford, was also embarrassed. In the road the young man, whose name was Paul, walked a little ahead of his companion and when they got to the barn each sought a separate place in the loft. Each wanted to have thoughts into which he did not want the presence of the other to intrude.

For the first time Tom's body burned with eager desire for a female. He lay where he could see out through a crack, in the side of the barn, and at first his thoughts were all about animals. He had brought a horse blanket up from the stable below and crawling under it lay on his side with his eyes close to the crack and thought about the love-making of horses and cattle. Things he had seen in the stables when he worked for Whitehead, the racing man, came back to his mind and a queer animal hunger ran through him so that his legs stiffened. He rolled restlessly about on the hay and for some reason, he did not understand, his lust took the form of anger and he hated the fat boy. He thought he would like to crawl over the hay and pound his companion's face with his fists. Although he had not seen Paul Bottsford's face, when he talked of the widow, he had sensed in him a flavor of triumph. "He thinks he has got the better of me," young Edwards thought.

He rolled again to the crack and stared out into the night. There was a new moon and the fields were dimly outlined and clumps of trees, along the road that led into the town of Sandusky, looked like black clouds that had settled down over the land. For some reason the sight of the land, lying dim and quiet under the moon, took all of his anger away and he began to think not of Paul Bottsford, with hot eager lust in his eyes, creeping into the room of the widow at Bellevue, but of the god Jesus, going up into a mountain with his woman, Mary.

His companion's notion of going into a room where a woman lay sleeping and taking her, as it were unawares, now seemed to him entirely mean and the hot jealous feeling that had turned into anger and hatred went entirely away. He tried to think what the god, who had brought the beautiful days for the threshing, would do with a woman.

Tom's body still burned with desire and his mind wanted to think lascivious thoughts. The moon that had been hidden behind clouds emerged and a wind began to blow. It was still early evening and in the town of Sandusky pleasure seekers were taking the boat to the resort over the bay and the wind brought to Tom's ears the sound of music, blown over the waters of the bay and down the creek basin. In a grove near the barn the wind swayed gently the branches of young trees and black shadows ran here and there on the ground.

The younger Bottsford had gone to sleep in a distant part of the barn loft, and now began to snore loudly. The tenseness went out of Tom's legs and he prepared to sleep but before sleeping he muttered, half timidly, certain words, that were half a prayer, half an appeal to some spirit of the night. "Jesus, bring me a woman," he whispered.

Outside the barn, in the fields, the wind, becoming a little stronger, picked up bits of straw and blew them about among the hard up-standing stubble and there was a low gentle whispering sound as though the gods were answering his appeal.

Tom went to sleep with his arm under his head and with his eye close to the crack that gave him a view of the moonlight fields, and in his dream the cry from within repeated itself over and over. The mysterious god Jesus had heard and answered the needs of his employer John Bottsford and his own need would, he was quite sure, be understood and attended to. "Bring me a woman. I need her. Jesus, bring me a woman," he kept whispering into the night, as consciousness left him and he slipped away into dreams.

After the youngest of the Bottsfords had departed a change took place in the nature of Tom's work. The threshing crew had got now into a country of large farms where the wheat had all been brought in from the fields and stacked near the barns and where there was always plenty of water near at hand. Everything was simplified. The separator was pulled in close by the barn door and the threshed grain was carried directly to the bins from the separator. As it was not a part of Tom's work to feed the bundles of grain into the whirling teeth of the separator—this work being done by John Bottsford's two elder sons—there was little for the crew's teamster to do. Sometimes John Bottsford, who was the engineer, departed, going to make arrangements for the next stop, and was gone for a half day, and at such times Tom, who had picked up some knowledge of the art, ran the engine.

On other days however there was nothing at all for him to do and his mind, unoccupied for long hours, began to play him tricks. In the morning, after his team had been fed and cleaned until the grey coats of the old farm horses shone like racers, he went out of the barn and into an orchard. Filling his pockets with ripe apples he went to a fence and leaned over. In a field young colts played about. As he held the apples and called softly they came timidly forward, stopping in alarm and then running a little forward, until one of them, bolder than the others, ate one of the apples out of his hand.

All through these bright warm clear fall days a restless feeling, it seemed to Tom ran through everything in nature. In the clumps of woodland still standing on the farms flaming red spread itself out along the limbs of trees and there was one grove of young maple trees, near a barn, that was like a troop of girls, young girls who had walked together down a sloping field, to stop in alarm at seeing the men at work in the barnyard. Tom stood looking at the trees. A slight breeze made them sway gently from side to side. Two horses standing among the trees drew near each other. One nipped the other's neck. They rubbed their heads together.

The crew stopped at another large farm and it was to be their last stop for the season. "When we have finished this job we'll go home and get our own fall work done," Bottsford said. Saturday evening came and the thresherman and his sons took the horses and drove away, going to their own home for the Sunday, and leaving Tom alone. "We'll be back early, on Monday morning," the thresherman said as they drove away. Sunday alone among the strange farm people brought a sharp experience to Tom and when it had passed he decided he would not wait for the end of the threshing season but a few days off now—but would quit his job and go into the city and surrender to the schools. He remembered his employer's words, "Find out what the books have to say. You don't have to believe, when they say things that are lies."

As he walked in lanes, across meadows and upon the hillsides of the farm, also on the shores of Sandusky Bay, that Sunday morning Tom thought almost constantly of his friend the fat fellow, young Paul Bottsford, who had gone to spend the fall and winter at Bellevue, and wondered what his life there might be like. He had himself lived in such a town, in Bidwell, but had rarely left Harry Whitehead's stable. What went on in such a town? What happened at night in the houses of the towns? He remembered Paul's plan for getting into a house alone with a widow and how he was to creep into her room at night, holding her tightly in his arms until she wanted what he wanted. "I wonder if he will have the nerve. Gee, I wonder if he will have the nerve," he muttered.

For a long time, ever since Paul had gone away and he had no one with whom he could talk, things had taken on a new aspect in Tom's mind. The rustle of dry leaves underfoot, as he walked in a forest—the playing of shadows over the open face of a field—the murmuring song of insects in the dry grass beside the fences in the lanes—and at night the hushed contented sounds made by the animals in the barns, were no longer so sweet to him. For him no more did the young god Jesus walk beside him, just out of sight behind low hills, or down the dry beds of streams. Something within himself, that had been sleeping was now awakening. When he returned from walking in the fields on the fall evenings and, thinking of Paul Bottsford alone in the house with the widow at Bellevue, half wishing he were in the same position, he felt ashamed in the presence of the gentle old thresherman, and afterward did not lie awake listening to the older man's prayers. The men who had come from nearby farms to help with the threshing laughed and shouted to each other as they pitched the straw into great stacks or carried the filled bags of grain to the bins, and they had wives and daughters who had come with them and who were now at work in the farmhouse kitchen, from which also laughter came. Girls and women kept coming out at the kitchen door into the barnyard, tall awkward girls, plump red-cheeked girls, women with worn thin faces and sagging breasts.

All men and women seemed made for each other.

They all laughed and talked together, understood one another. Only he was alone. He only had no one to whom he could feel warm and close, to whom he could draw close.

On the Sunday when the Bottsfords had all gone away Tom came in from walking all morning in the fields and ate his dinner with many other people in a big farmhouse dining room. In preparation for the threshing days ahead, and the feeding of many people, several women had come to spend the day and to help in preparing food. The farmer's daughter, who was married and lived in Sandusky, came with her husband, and three other women, neighbors, came from farms in the neighborhood. Tom did not look at them but ate his dinner in silence and as soon as he could manage got out of the house and went to the barns. Going into a long shed he sat on the tongue of a wagon, that from long disuse was covered with dust. Swallows flew back and forth among the rafters overhead and, in an upper corner of the shed where they evidently had a nest, wasps buzzed in the semi-darkness.

The daughter of the farmer, who had come from town, came from the house with a babe in her arms. It was nursing time, and she wanted to escape from the crowded house and, without having seen Tom, she sat on a box near the shed door and opened her dress. Embarrassed and at the same time fascinated by the sight of a woman's breasts, seen through cracks of the wagon box, Tom drew his legs up and his head down and remained concealed until the woman had gone back to the house. Then he went again to the fields and did not go back to the house for the evening meal.

As he walked on that Sunday afternoon the grandson of the Welsh poet experienced many new sensations. In a way he came to understand that the things Paul had talked of doing and that had, but a short time before, filled him with disgust were now possible to himself also. In the past when he had thought about women there had always been something healthy and animal-like in his lusts but now they took a new form. The passion that could not find expression through his body went up into his mind and he began to see visions. Women became to him something different than anything else in nature, more desirable than anything else in nature, and at the same time everything in nature became woman. The trees, in the apple orchard by the barn, were like the arms of women. The apples on the trees were round like the breasts of women. They were the breasts of women—and when he had got on to a low hill the contour of the fences that marked the confines of the fields fell into the forms of women's bodies. Even the clouds in the sky did the same thing.

He walked down along a lane to a stream and crossed the stream by a wooden bridge. Then he climbed another hill, the highest place in all that part of the country, and there the fever that possessed him became more active. An odd lassitude crept over him and he lay down in the grass on the hilltop and closed his eyes. For a long time he remained in a hushed, half-sleeping, dreamless state and then opened his eyes again.

Again the forms of women floated before him. To his left the bay was ruffled by a gentle breeze and far over towards the city of Sandusky two sailboats were apparently engaged in a race. The masts of the boats were fully dressed but on the great stretch of water they seemed to stand still. The bay itself, in Tom's eyes, had taken on the form and shape of a woman's head and body and the two sailboats were the woman's eyes looking at him.

The bay was a woman with her head lying where lay the city of Sandusky. Smoke arose from the stacks of steamers docked at the city's wharves and the smoke formed itself into masses of black hair. Through the farm, where he had come to thresh, ran a stream. It swept down past the foot of the hill on which he lay. The stream was the arm of the woman. Her hand was thrust into the land and the lower part of her body was lost—far down to the north, where the bay became a part of Lake Erie—but her other arm could be seen. It was outlined in the further shore of the bay. Her other arm was drawn up and her hand was pressing against her face. Her form was distorted by pain but at the same time the giant woman smiled at the boy on the hill. There was something in the smile that was like the smile that had come unconsciously to the lips of the woman who had nursed her child in the shade.

Turning his face away from the bay Tom looked at the sky. A great white cloud that lay along the southern horizon formed itself into the giant head of a man. Tom watched as the cloud crept slowly across the sky. There was something noble and quieting about the giant's face and his hair, pure white and as thick as wheat in a rich field in June, added to its nobility. Only the face appeared. Below the shoulders there was just a white shapeless mass of clouds.

And then this formless mass began also to change. The face of a giant woman appeared. It pressed upward toward the face of the man. Two arms formed themselves on the man's shoulders and pressed the woman closely. The two faces merged. Something seemed to snap in Tom's brain.

He sat upright and looked neither at the bay nor at the sky. Evening was coming on and soft shadows began to play over the land. Below him lay the farm with its barns and houses and in the field, below the hill on which he was lying, there were two smaller hills that became at once in his eyes the two full breasts of a woman. Two white sheep appeared and stood nibbling the grass on the woman's breasts. They were like babes being suckled. The trees in the orchards near the barns were the woman's hair. An arm of the stream that ran down to the bay, the stream he had crossed on the wooden bridge when he came to the hill, cut across a meadow beyond the two low hills. It widened into a pond and the pond made a mouth for the woman. Her eyes were two black hollows—low spots in a field where hogs had rooted the grass away, looking for roots. Black puddles of water lay in the hollows and they seemed eyes shining invitingly up at him.

This woman also smiled and her smile was now an invitation. Tom got to his feet and hurried away down the hill and going stealthily past the barns and the house got into a road. All night he walked under the stars thinking new thoughts. "I am obsessed with this idea of having a woman. I'd better go to the city and go to school and see if I can make myself fit to have a woman of my own," he thought. "I won't sleep tonight but will wait until tomorrow when Bottsford comes back and then I'll quit and go into the city." He walked, trying to make plans. Even a good man like John Bottsford, had a woman for himself. Could he do that?

The thought was exciting. At the moment it seemed to him that he had only to go into the city, and go to the schools for a time, to become beautiful and to have beautiful women love him. In his half ecstatic state he forgot the winter months he had spent in the city of Cleveland, and forgot also the grim streets, the long rows of dark prison-like factories and the loneliness of his life in the city. For the moment and as he walked in the dusty roads under the moon, he thought of American towns and cities as places for beautifully satisfying adventures, for all such fellows as himself.

J. William Terry (1895–1966) spent his boyhood on the Reserve. He was a reporter for the *Cleveland Plain Dealer* while attending Baldwin-Wallace College and later became a career journalist with the *New York Times* and other prominent newspapers. His novel, *A Restless Breed* (1956), includes the following disclaimer: "While the author has attempted to draw an authentic picture of folk in a Western Reserve county seat, he has not portrayed actual individuals or events." This depiction of Western Reserve belles might otherwise have caused consternation in "New Hartford."

Step-Sisters

The three Jenks girls were New Hartford's only professional streetwalkers. Of course there always were wild young wenches who'd go on the prowl for fun. And from time to time some woman would bring in two or three strumpets and operate a house south of the railroad until one of the ministers heard about it and called on the police, who would then dump the furniture into the yard. But those girls stayed off the street.

The Jenks sisters were commercial, although Cleveland and Youngstown practitioners of the trade would have scoffed at the idea they were professional. Their technique of solicitation, however, succeeded in New Hartford, where the penduluming handbags of urban-trained whores would only have seemed ridiculous. Being local girls probably had much to do with saving the Jenkses from interference by the cops.

Pete Jenks, the girls' father, had a house and barn of sorts on a couple of otherwise useless acres two miles out of town on the road to Hardscrabble. Such money as he had before the girls started paying board came from night scavenging of New Hartford privies. That was a business gradually declining in face of advance in plumbing. Occasionally, when money ran out in the winter, he'd cut up fallen tree trunks and sell the wood for seventy-five cents a cord. Before Pete married her, Fannie washed dishes and swept floors at the Southside Hotel, a cheapjohn hostelry and assignation house.

Floss and Bella, the two elder daughters, were experienced in the grass with the boys ahead of puberty. In their teens they took to walking into town Saturday nights for the dancing over Bloxton's feed store, where they were easy for almost any of the young fellows.

Pete said there was too much helling around nights and the girls cost him too much. It was time they went to work. Through his scavenging connections he got them various jobs as hired girls. They liked being in town where they could meet fellows south of the tracks after supper dishes were done, but they were slovenly and untrained for housework. So they were fired with more speed than they were hired and soon no woman in town would have either of them in her house. Sometimes hardpressed farm women would have them in emergency.

One Saturday night when she was twenty Floss was picked up at the dance by a tobacco drummer in need of entertainment over a barren weekend. Instead of going with her to the river flats or the cemetery grove he took her to bed at the Southside Hotel. When, during a lull in their bawdry, she told him she'd never gone to a hotel with a man before, he said a girl was a fool not to get paid for her fun. He poohpoohed her idea that local fellows wouldn't give money for it. There were lots of men, he told her, who'd rather make it a business deal than go through the monkeyshines of pretending it was love heat. From his flair for salesmanship he gave her detailed tutelage.

Floss tried it on a nondescript tobacco-chewing widower who drove hack for Crow—heeding the drummer's saying older men were the best prospects. The fellow didn't even protest that a dollar was too much when she went with him to the livery hayloft. She made many less successful attempts, but Floss wasn't bashful or finicky. If she could get three men in a week it got her almost as much money as seven days of housework. And housework wasn't fun.

She had to tell Bella what she was doing. Naturally Bella wanted to join in the business. Less bold than her sister, she was afraid to undertake it alone—not afraid of picking up men but afraid of asking them for money. So at first Floss had to take her along and make the financial suggestion.

In time they ventured from south of the tracks up Market Street and then along Bridge Street, where on Saturday afternoons and band concert nights they appeared to most New Hartfordans as just two more country girls come to town. Here there were more desirable men than on the Southside—farm hands and town workers, who lacked the social knack or boldness for getting girls for nothing. And eventually the sisters became skilled in giving the inviting eye to drummers, who made the best customers.

The sisters had no greediness for money. When they were working out, as they called being hired girls, they turned over a good part of what they made toward home upkeep. Now that they were hustling, as they called their whoring, they paid board regularly to Pete—more than they should have. And they bought things for their mother and their kid sister, Lill. They even brought whiskey home for their father. Pete and Fannie were careful not to imperil such windfalls by asking questions about the source. But Pete would brag to cronies that pretty girls like his daughters didn't have to work out. Actually Floss and Bella weren't pretty, not even good looking, just well enough formed not to be repulsive.

Lill, however, was sort of pretty. She wasn't born until five years after Bella's birth and so for a long while was only The Brat to her sisters. When she was coming into her teens they had a period of maternal-like pride in her that gave them notions about keeping her decent. That probably was the nearest they came to admitting any lack of decency in their practices.

When Lill was seventeen Pete began nagging her about working out. What he really meant was that she start going to town with Floss and Bella, something even he couldn't say straight off. When she was younger she'd cried and called her sisters mean when they wouldn't let her go with them. But soon she learned from young neighbors what Floss and Bella were doing. Now, with her father fussing at her to be a hired girl, she pestered them to take her to town. To prove she was no innocent baby, she used all the bawdy words she knew when urging them, and they, who used the same words—most of them spelled with four letters—to excite men, were shocked. They made fun of her to her face, worried about her between themselves and surrendered to her pleading only when she threatened to go to streetwalking alone.

Oldtimers in the trade would hardly have ventured out three together, when one was a neophyte. And at first it almost scotched Floss and Bella's business. South of the tracks three girls abreast filled the sidewalk and obstructed traffic, besides being too spectacular for this district where poor people's sense of failure and sinful people's sense of guilt inclined pedestrians to furtiveness. Three abreast—country wives, farm girls or high school chums—down the center of Bridge or Market Streets' broad sidewalks wasn't unusual. Nevertheless it was so formidable as to discourage approach of fun-seeking males.

It was young Lill who suggested walking singly, one behind the other. This Indian file had a silly look and attracted perilous attention of the citizenry. Finally the three stumbled—more or less literally—on the method of one following two or three paces behind and to the side of another. This, while having the appearance of three in company where two had lagging steps, made each sister individually accessible. Floss, the oldest and tallest, took the lead and Lill, youngest and shortest, was shifted to the rear. Thus they were steps down in three ways, obliquely across the sidewalk, in height and in age.

In addition to Saturdays and Saturday nights, the three took to parading Bridge and Market Streets on various afternoons. Sometimes they'd be out on Sunday evening, even daring, frequently with profit, to drift down the stag line in front of Disciple Church formed by young bucks waiting for girls to come from evening worship.

Catching sight of a prospect along any of the routes, Floss, the veteran, would murmur: "Take him, Bella," or "He's yours, Lill," or "I'll get him," depending usually on the age of the fish to be caught. Then the designated sister would cast a sly wink or, surreptitiously brazen, show four raised fingers with the thumb bent into the palm of the hand. Such invitations failing, there was the hoary device of the dropped handkerchief. Because many of these weren't picked up and returned, the sisters made kerchiefs at home of cheap cotton and went to town well supplied. In time their success was such that they could ignore the cheap fry and concentrate on males who could afford hotel rooms instead of the cemetery grove.

Benefiting by his daughters' liberality, Pete neglected his scavenging and allowed the girls to hitch one of his two nags to a buggy. They had enough walking to do without trudging back and forth to town. If they knew they'd be in town all night they'd stable the nag at Crow's but there were times when it would stay tied until morning at the Court House Park railing.

All the while the three continued to appear plain country females. Many a town hired girl bought more flashy clothes than the Jenks sisters ever dreamed of. And, except for some vulgarian tendencies that they forced Lill to suppress, they had Yankee-like contempt for perfume and face paint.

Even so it wasn't long, of course, before all but the most naive New Hartfordans knew what the Jenks girls were doing. But the doings of three such simple farm wenches could only be amusing, other than to an inadequate wife who heard whispers that her husband had gone to the Southside Hotel with one of the Jenkses.

Probably the three wouldn't have escaped restraint had not the clergy been among the naive—all but Father McGowan.

"I suppose," said Moira, a widow who'd lived much of her life in Brooklyn and wasn't ignorant about human misbehavior, "You know what those Jenks farm girls are doing."

"They serve," said the priest.

"Serve who?"

"Whom," he corrected her, teasing. "They serve the needs of unloved men who lack spiritual-mindedness."

"And you, a priest, call that serving? Why do they allow that kind of girls in town?"

"Why shouldn't they? Is New Hartford better than the Kingdom of God?"

"What a terrible thing to hear from the mouth of a priest."

"Didn't Jesus say such women would enter God's kingdom ahead of carping ecclesiastics? My fear for these Jenkses doesn't concern their places in the heavenly realm but their future on the earth."

The Jenks girls continued their trade unmolested enough years to become an institution in New Hartford. Then early one evening, while Bella and Lill were occupied at the hotel Floss was left customerless. Moving at a good gait along Market Street so as not to appear a loiterer, she spied a man coming from Rufus Drucker's saloon. His clothes spelled farm, his face loneliness. No one being near them, Floss said: "Hello."

The man was Wes Tallman, a childless Rock Corners widower, badly in need of companionship and a woman. But he wouldn't go to the Southside Hotel—was afraid to, because he'd never been to a hotel. When he showed Floss green bills in his wallet, she reluctantly consented to ride with him to his farm.

The farm was thirty acres and had better buildings than most near Rock Corners. Wes was so awkwardly boyish in his hunger for affection that Floss felt a strange kind of warmth for him and stayed next morning to clean the messed-up house, a most surprising thing for her to do. Then she cooked for him and stayed another night. The second day they drove to the Court House, got a license and were married by Squire Thompkins.

Floss had been afraid to tell Bella and Lill what she was going to do. When she found them and told them after she became Mrs. Tallman they were too stunned to raise hell about it.

Forsaken by Floss, Bella and Lill were lost creatures, unable to select their prospects or adjust their ways of solicitation. For the first time New Hartford cops bawled them out and they fell to quarreling, between themselves and with their parents. Then Lill, the sly one, picked up a whiskey drummer from New York City with a big wad of money and an incipient jag. He took her along when he left town. Six months later an errant New Hartford husband chanced upon her in a house in Youngstown's Commerce Street red light district.

Left alone, Bella would wander about south of the railroad like a soul on the bank of the Styx. Appetite was gone out of her flesh. She was fed up with men, with their quick, meaningless lust to be mechanically satisfied and done with. Some days she didn't leave home, until Pete, angry at having lost two of their three sources of income, raised the devil. After that she stayed a few days with Floss at the Tallman farm, and would have stayed longer had not Floss, jealously guarding her husband, chased her away. Back in town Bella went to the hotel with a steady client, who left her without paying, in disgust at her unresponsiveness.

Utterly dejected, she strayed in the early evening north of Court House Square, first along Elm Avenue and then into some of the cross streets at the upper end of town where there were homes of clerks and humble, unmonied folk. She wanted to get away from prowling for men.

On Verney Street she passed a little frame church set tight among the cottages. Its windows were lighted and a good many people were going in. Bella walked on for a block and, impelled by loneliness, turned and went back, just to be near those who were heading into the church.

The Free Methodists were New Hartford's one body of un-Yankeelike emotionally demonstrative religionists. A few country folk and a handful of town artisans together with two or three small businessmen and their families constituted the membership. This year the bishop had sent them the Rev. Freely Talbot, gaunt, sunken-eyed zealot, as pastor. His strange pulpit undulations, alternating between roared warnings of hell fire and gentle talk of the atoning blood of Jesus and pleading like a lover's wooing, had so increased his congregation that, although it was only early fall, he was holding protracted meetings.

Bella Jenks, desperate to be close to non-lustful human beings, passed back and forth in front of the church four times and then found herself among the people going inside. The place was nearly filled but there was an usher who guided her to a pew half way down a side aisle.

Sometimes before she got to going to town Bella had attended the Hardscrabble Baptist Church, in hope of picking up a fellow, so she wasn't much afraid here and knew what to do. A fattish, motherly looking woman, widow of a mail carrier, sat beside her and offered to share a song book.

Bella sat very still through the sermon, as close to the widow as she dared. She paid no attention to what the preacher said, roaring and pleading, but she wondered why men and women in the congregation would cry out "Amen," "Hallelujah" and "Praise the Lord." They hadn't done that at Hardscrabble.

When the minister finished an hour of preaching he announced a hymn. Before singing started he came out from behind the pulpit and stood at the edge of the platform, urging that the unrighteous repent of their evil-doing and come to kneel at the Mercy Seat, where the crimson stains of their sins would be washed whiter than snow in the blood of the Lamb. The congregation sang:

> I've wandered far away from God,
> Now I'm coming home;
> The paths of sin too long I've trod,
> Lord, I'm coming home.

Long arms outstretched, as if in pantomime of God inviting sinners to his embrace, the lanky preacher, his eyes sadly beseeching, kept chanting through the untuneful singing: "Come home. Come home. Come home. He has opened wide His arms of love. Come home. Come home. Come home."

The hymn finished, the people kept singing the chorus. Over and over:

> Coming home, coming home,
> Never more to roam . . .

The preacher still pleaded: "Come home. Come home, home. Come home, sinner, come home."

Bella Jenks' loneliness surged from her heart into her throat and she uttered a choking sob. The mail carrier's widow heard it and reached for the girl with a motherly arm.

"I'll go with you, dear," she whispered, "—to the Mourners' Bench, where Jesus'll comfort you."

Bella, knowing nothing of what it meant, was pliant under the first motherly caress she'd ever felt. Stumbling down the aisle within the widow's arm, she was oblivious to the "Praise God!" and "Hallelujah!" cries throughout the congregation.

"Kneel down, darling, and give your heart to Him," the widow urged. As Bella's knees gave way and she sank against the crude altar rail she burst into violent, nervous sobbing—a sure evidence to Free Methodists of sincere repentance.

Out of their pews the faithful moved forward to form a kneeling mass around the girl. The preacher, coming down from the pulpit to pray with the "seeker," was met at the foot of the pulpit steps by Brother Brewster, who operated a neighborhood grocery store and so had regard for the need of holding public respect.

"She is," he whispered to the preacher, "a common woman of the street."

Whereat Pastor Talbot, who knew that it was sinners and not the righteous who were called to repentance, cried out loudly: "Praise God! A brand has been snatched from the burning!"

After she was "saved" at the free Methodist revival service, Bella went to live in a room at the mail carrier's widow's home and to work at the electric lamp factory. Because she got much less money there than she'd made at the oldest profession and had to buy food and pay rent to the widow, Pete Jenks was forced to resume cleaning privies. The defections of Floss and Lill he could understand and forgive but not that of Bella. "What a slut she turned out to be," he complained to the girls' mother.

The widow, out of her tolerant, motherly heart, was good to Bella. Out of churchly duty the widow instructed her; taught her to pray and go to church, and that she must keep herself unspotted from the world.

Bella liked the Free Methodists and, in time, learned to be one of them. She became a member who could be counted on to be at every service. As the years went by she grew into the pattern of a churchy old maid. She became as fluent in Free Methodist terminology as she'd been in lewd talk in the Southside Hotel. At classmeeting, where mixed metaphor didn't weaken "testimony," she'd tell, with only a dim idea of what she was saying, that she'd been a Jezebel and a Magdalene and Jesus had pulled her from the mirey pit and made her a brand from the burning. She'd ask for prayers that she might grow in saintliness. What progress she made in that direction would depend of course upon one's conception of sainthood.

Floss had flowered into a respectable, energetic farm wife and, to everyone's surprise including her own, mother of a nice daughter. Her rich, yellow butter took prizes at the County Fair. Sometimes she drove into town and brought Bella home with her. But she couldn't keep her there long, for Bella set Wes on edge trying to get him to say grace at the table and take the family to church.

At the lamp factory Bella made enemies of the women and girls by berating them for bad language and complaining to the foreman that they told smutty stories.

As she advanced toward angular, sour-faced middle age, irritating restlessness would possess her. Sometimes after mid-week prayer meeting an unhappy spirit would drive her to go and lurk behind trees or bushes at the fringe of the cemetery grove or the river flats. When a couple came along—man and woman or youth and girl—headed for a secluded place in the grass she'd pounce on them and rail against their sinful purpose, usually succeeding in frightening them away.

Mostly her victims kept still about her, fearing to expose their escapade. But there were young chaps who complained and Police Officer Dungan trailed Bella one night. Having witnessed one of her interventions, he laid hold of her and took her harshly over the coals. When she screamed back that she was doing her Christian duty, he called her a jealous, wornout bat.

Gossiping at Crow's livery barn one day, Alf Elkton said: "It was a hell of a thing that happened to Bella Jenks, when this city has such an over-supply of churchy shrews and had been so damned short of experienced whores."

Dawn Powell (1897–1963) graduated from Lake Erie College in Painesville in 1918. She spent most of her life in Greenwich Village writing plays, novels, and short stories, some with Ohio settings. A laudatory essay by Gore Vidal in 1987 revived interest in her work, which has led to a reissue of several of her novels. *Dance Night* (1930) is a vivid representation of a young woman's growth and maturity as well as a picture of the attraction of Cleveland for young people of northeastern Ohio in the early twentieth century. Elsinore, the heroine of this selection, joins the ranks of usually male Midwestern characters who—like Sherwood Anderson's George Willard, the narrator of *Winesburg, Ohio*—renounce the constraints of home.

Mrs. Pepper cried telling Nettie about how Mrs. Abbott had changed, and Nettie answered that it was very funny for Mrs. Abbott to act that way after the years they'd known each other. They stood in front of Robbins' Jewelry Store discussing it.

"I'd hardly got inside the door, Nettie," said Mrs. Pepper tremulously. "I'd just set my grip down when she came out of the workroom, white as a sheet, and she said to me, 'Mrs. Pepper, you've been coming here a long time, too long, in fact, and I just wanted to tell you that it's going to stop right now. I got no place,' she says, 'for your corsets and trash in my shop, and it'll suit me if you take your stuff somewheres else.' . . . Well, Nettie, you know how I am, tender-hearted, and always a good friend to everyone. I didn't know what in the world to say. I said, what is it, whatever happened? . . . And she said, tightmouthed, the way she is, 'It's my place, Mrs. Pepper, I think I have the right to have or not have people here just as I like.' . . . I said who's been talking behind my back, just tell me their names and I'll make them answer for it."

"What'd she say to that?" Nettie asked, thinking over the slurring remarks she herself had often made about the corsetiere, and feeling rather guilty. "Did she say anyone had talked about you?"

"That's just it," answered Mrs. Pepper. "She looked funny and said, oh, so you know there's talk, do you, but she wouldn't say anything else, so I packed up my few little things and went right across the street to the Bauers, and Mrs. Bauer's letting me have a room upstairs for fittings. But, Nettie, what could anyone have said about me? You know I've always tried to be a lady, I've never done anything a lady wouldn't, you know that, Nettie."

Nettie kept her eyes fixed on a gilt clock in Robbins' window.

"Well, she might have heard about you and Mr. Fischer," she said gently. "After all, you know he is a married man."

Mrs. Pepper's little red mouth made an O of astonishment.

"The very idea! If that isn't like a little town. Just because Mr. Fischer and I both travel from place to place and are old friends, people get to talking! So that's what she heard, you think . . . Nettie, that does make me feel badly! . . . But I'm glad you told me. I never thought people would be so wicked saying things, when I've tried always to be a lady in spite of being alone in the world. Goodness, Mr. Fischer would be so upset to know anyone in Lamptown talked like that!"

Nettie said no more. They started back up the street and Mrs. Pepper forlornly left Nettie at the Bauers' front door. Bauers' rooms were so dark and musty and gloomy. The Bon Ton had seemed gay with girls chattering in and out all the time over hats, telling who was going with who, and laughing . . . But Hermann Bauer never smiled and Hulda Bauer had stopped thinking and settled into a contented jellyfish the day she married Hermann. It was not a jolly place at all for a sun-loving soul, and Mrs. Pepper, lacing a customer into a lavender satin brocade model in her dingy bedroom, dropped a few unexpected tears down the girl's back.

"Mrs. Bauer is good to me, of course," she choked bravely, "and Mr. Bauer is such a fine man that I'd be the last one to complain—but I think dark places like this ought to be torn down, I do, really. It would be a blessing if it burned, it's so gloomy, and when you're in trouble with your dearest friend, too—honey are you sure this doesn't pinch your tummy?"

Nettie tried to find out why Elsinore had taken such a serious step but Elsinore gave her no details. She seemed silent and preoccupied, and all she said was that Mrs. Pepper was a hypocrite and besides the Bon Ton had no place for all those corset boxes and trash. Nettie was glad the extra work was out of the way, she was especially glad because now she was to go with Elsinore, it seemed, on buying expeditions to Cleveland or Columbus. Before, Nettie had kept shop while Elsinore

and Mrs. Pepper went off together, all dressed up for a day in the city.
Elsinore said this time they would close the shop and take an early
train, so Nettie sat up half the night sewing a new frill on her black suit
and washing out white silk gloves. She'd been to Cleveland a few times
but this was most exciting because now she was going as a business
woman, a woman of affairs.

They sat in the chair car going in the next morning. Elsinore, with
dark hollows under her eyes from thinking so desperately of the plan
she had for the day, and Nettie, dressed up and well-pleased with herself, her gloved hands folded over her new gold mesh purse, a blue veil
drooping from her little hat, lace openwork on her black silk stockings.
This was her real sphere, Nettie thought, going to cities and wearing
little veils and white gloves and perfume, being a woman of the world
and she thought it was funny her living in Lamptown when anyone
could tell she was more of a city type . . . She was twenty now and she
certainly was doing more with her life than any other girls her age
were. She was bound she'd be a success, this year she'd join the Eastern
Stars, she thought, and she'd read "Laddie" and "The Little Shepherd
of Kingdom Come"; she'd get baptized, too, join a church, and whenever she met anyone from out of town she'd always correspond with
them so that she'd be getting letters from Cincinnati and Birmingham
and St. Louis all at one time. She'd take dancing lessons, too, only she
didn't see how she'd ever have the nerve to practice in public with all
the younger people. She'd have a hatshop of her own, some day, she'd
call it the Paris Shop, or maybe The Elite, Nettie Farrell, prop.

Nettie glanced guiltily at Elsinore to see if this disloyal thought had
somehow been overheard, but Elsinore was drumming nervously on
the windowsill, watching fields and villages slide past the window.

They went to different stores in the morning buying silks and trim-
mings and they were to meet in the Taylor Arcade for lunch but Nettie
got mixed up the way she always did in Cleveland and waited in the
Colonial Arcade instead. She stood at the entrance watching for
Elsinore till half past one when a dark Jewish man smoking a cigar
spoke to her. Nettie stared him down so haughtily that he rushed con-
tritely into a little cigar store to peer at her over the inner curtains. Nettie, after a minute or two, walked slowly past the cigar store and
somehow dropped her purse so he came out to pick it up. This time
Nettie thanked him very distantly and when he went on asking her if
she was just in town for the day she answered him rather loftily so he
could see she was not an ordinary pickup.

When Elsinore finally decided to look for Nettie in the other Arcade
she saw her through the glass window of a little tea-room at a table
with some stranger. The man was talking and Nettie was sedately
holding a tea-cup, little finger flying. Elsinore went in and Nettie said,

"This is Mr. Schwarz, Mrs. Abbott. He used to travel for the same company Mr. Abbott did, isn't that funny, but now he's in the woolen business and he lives at the Gilsey. We're going to the Hippodrome this afternoon while you're seeing wholesalers."

Elsinore had been wondering how she would get rid of Nettie for the afternoon so she was much more agreeable over tea and cinnamon buns than she usually was with strangers, and Mr. Schwarz, at first wary, began to warm up to the idea of a little party for four. He said he'd call up the hotel and get hold of a friend of his named Wohlman, who also was in woolen, and tonight they'd all go to the Ratskellar and afterwards to a show the Hermits were giving. The idea alarmed Elsinore and she got away as fast as she could.

"Five thirty, then, in the Hollenden lobby," said Nettie gaily, being a woman of the world.

Elsinore took a Woodland Avenue car out to East 55th Street. She didn't dare think of what she was about to do or she might lose courage. She thought of Mrs. Pepper and after three weeks of hating her, even the mental image of the woman was distorted into a fat, lewd beast that deserved annihilation. Elsinore wasn't sorry she'd sent her out of the Bon Ton, she wasn't sorry when Mrs. Pepper's blue eyes welled with tears over this broken friendship; she wished she had it in her to be even crueller; she would like to have hurt her as much as she had been hurt herself. . . .

All these years, then, the town whisper about Fischer and Mrs. Pepper had been well-founded. Elsinore felt as betrayed as if Fischer had really been her own husband, she wanted fiercely to be revenged, not on him, but on the woman. Nor was the desire for revenge a spasmodic thought that died out after the first shock of suspicions proved true; she thought of it night and day ever since the rainy night Mrs. Pepper had gone out with Dode to meet him somewhere; she thought of them on Thursday nights at the Casino watching his heavy mask-like face. . . . She had wondered often about his wife and now she felt somehow identified with her, as if Mrs. Pepper had deliberately wronged them both. What kept her curious indignation at fever pitch was the thought of how long Mrs. Pepper had fooled everyone with her wide innocent blue eyes, her baby face, her dainty lady-like ways, her sweet detachment in mentioning his name. Worse than a vampire, Elsinore grimly decided, worse than the commonest factory girl, because she pretended so much, because she fooled people.

At the other end of the street-car, two girls in white flannel suits giggled over yesterday's moonlight ride on the Steamer Eastland, and the conductor asked them if they were going to the big brewers' picnic next Sunday at Put-in-Bay. Elsinore listened to them intently because she wanted to know things that people around Fischer knew, she wanted to hear and see the same things he did, she could almost be him, she could half-close her eyes and admire women and young girls the way he did. This was what he saw on his way to and from his house, and now that they were close to 55th Street, that must be the church over yonder where he sent his children to Sunday-school, this must be the market where his wife did her trading, this was his stop. . . .

Elsinore's knees were shaky getting off the car. If she could only keep in mind how Mrs. Pepper had fooled her and Mrs. Fischer, she'd be able to go ahead with her plan, but she kept forgetting and having stage-fright over being so near his place and so near to coming face to face with his wife. She asked a street-cleaner where this number was and he pointed out an old house set far back from the street with a sign in the window in black and white—

HARRY FISCHER
Ballroom Dancing

Oh, she'd never have the courage to walk down that pathway with someone probably peeking at her from behind the lace curtains, and perhaps someone following her, too. . . . This frightened her, she looked over her shoulder, now she had a distinct feeling of being followed. If Nettie had taken it into her head to follow her, what would she say?

"I came to arrange private dancing lessons for both of us," she'd tell Nettie if it came to that, and she'd say it was always impossible to get a private word with Fischer about it in Lamptown so she'd just dropped in. . . .

If it was Fischer himself behind her, though, or Mrs. Pepper, or Charles, or someone from Lamptown. . . . Still, there wasn't a chance of any such thing, why should she feel guilty when she was only doing a friendly duty?. . . . She walked quickly up to the grey gingerbread porch. She wondered if he owned this house, if he had a dance-hall in it the way Mrs. Pepper had once said, and it made her ache to think of all the things in his life that she could never guess thinking about him in the Bon Ton. . . . She was on the porch, in a minute she'd turn around and run for her life . . . no, she was ringing the door-bell and her black gloved hand was quite steady. She couldn't run now, even if Fischer himself should confront her, her legs were numb, she doubted if she could even speak. She heard steps inside, the sound of a slap, and a child screeching and then the door opened.

"Well?"

Two tow-headed children on a red scooter stared at her with bold black eyes, their mother tried to push them out of the way of the door, she was a large ash-blonde woman with heavy breasts, and her voice was deep like a singer's with a vaguely Scandinavian accent. His wife. . . . Yes, she was Mrs. Fischer. The lady wanted to know about dancing lessons? Friday and Saturday were his Cleveland days, if she wanted to sign up for the course and leave a five dollar deposit. . . .

"It's not about dancing," Elsinore said, "It's about him that I wanted to see you."

Her voice felt swollen and tight, talking was like trying to scream in your sleep, driving your voice through your shut mouth with all your might and having it come out only a hoarse whisper.

"There's a woman that wants to make trouble for you and I thought someone ought to tell you so you could stop it."

Fischer's wife just stared stupidly at her. The largest towheaded child with a little yelp turned his toy car around and scooted down the hall, its bell going tingalingaling, and the littlest one remembered that his mother had slapped him and resumed his wailing, burying his face in his mother's skirts.

Mrs. Fischer pushed open the screen door.

"Do you want to come inside and tell me what you're talking about, missus?" she said, studying Elsinore from head to foot with a puzzled and not at all friendly eye. "What's this about my husband and who are you, anyway, that's what I want to know?"

Elsinore could feel her face reddening, she must be careful now, or Fischer might guess who had told.

"It doesn't matter who I am," she said hurriedly, "but I thought you ought to know—as one woman to another, understand—that there's someone your husband goes with out of town, there's a woman crazy about him, trying to break up your home."

She'd said it now, but Mrs. Fischer's thick pasty face took on an ugly expression. Her pale blue eyes narrowed, under the heavy colorless brows.

"I suppose you don't want to make trouble, too, hey? I suppose I'm to believe a party coming in out of the blue sky and not saying who she is, just bringing tattle tales to see what harm she can do—"

Elsinore backed away from the door, alarmed at the woman's tone. Mrs. Fischer came out on the porch after her.

"See here, what right have you got, coming to my home making trouble for me? If my husband's doings don't suit you, then you don't need to watch 'em, just mind your own step, that's all. Who are you, coming here with your tattle? Where you from, anyway? Who told you I wanted to hear tales about Harry?"

"I didn't want you to be fooled, that was all," gasped Elsinore, and backed down the porch steps with Mrs. Fischer coming right after her, her hands on her hips. "You had a right to know."

"Well, who said you were the one with a right to tell," Mrs. Fischer asked contemptuously. "I've got enough trouble without strangers trying to cook up more. I'd thank you to clear out, and I'll tell you here and now if anybody's got the right to spy on Harry, it's me, and nobody else, understand? So!"

Elsinore, faint with shame, rushed toward the street. Both children now were crying loudly and the toy car bell dingled raucously in her ears. She knew people were watching her, someone was following her again, that much was certain, she felt their distrustful eyes boring through her back, the footsteps behind her were ominous, but when she dared to look back it was only a mail man and further off two women wheeling go-carts, she could not find those watchful eyes. Foghorns croaked on the lake and made her head buzz, the city noises seemed more than she could bear. She climbed aboard the first street car that came along, it was pure luck that it was going in the right direction. Her face would never stop burning, she was so shamed, yet she was glad in a way because she'd had to do just that thing, she'd simply had to, nothing could have stopped her, and now it was over with, that was all. . . . What would she say to Nettie, she wondered, what could she tell her? . . . She sat next to a big colored woman who asked her where the May Company was, where you got off the Interurban Station, how you got out to Gates Mills? She didn't know, she kept mumbling in reply, and planned what to say to Nettie.

"I went to Halle's for that taffeta, then I walked over to the Square and sat down for a while, then I went to the braid place, then I went into De Klyn's for a sundae and cocoa—no, for a cup of tea, then—then—"

She went into the hotel lobby where she was to meet Nettie. She was dizzy and faint, for she wasn't used to crowds and street cars. Suspicious eyes continued to bore through her, she was certain someone had followed her all day, she was certain someone was reading her guilty thoughts.

It was long after six when Nettie came. Mr. Schwarz, perhaps a little self-conscious, was not with her, but Nettie talked about him a great deal on the way to the depot, because she'd never been out with an older man, a man of the world, before. . . . Elsinore did not breathe easily until she was finally on the train for Lamptown. No one had seen her. No one had followed her. No one knew.

"So then we went down to the Ratskellar," Nettie chattered on excitedly, "and Mr. Schwarz asked me what I'd have since I hated beer so much. So I took a Clover Club cocktail because Mr. Schwarz said that in Cleveland they were absolutely all the go."

Elsinore didn't dare go to the dance on Thursday night, she was afraid to face the dancing teacher for a little while. She closed the shop and sat in the dark watching the Casino windows, seeing couples whirl past and hearing Fischer's big voice boom out the commands. She leaned forward on the wicker settee and wrung her hands each time the music started for a new dance. If there was a circle two-step tonight she might have gotten him for a partner for a minute or two, but now she'd ruined the chances of that. She wouldn't dare go up again, he'd ask what right she had going to his wife. . . . At least Mrs. Pepper hadn't gone to the Casino either, because Nettie had seen her get on the street car going upstate earlier in the day. . . .

The Bauers were in their window peering out at the passing girls, and she reflected bitterly that she might as well be Hulda Bauer now, nothing but a spectator. She saw Grace come out in front of the restaurant and hoo-oo, then the Delaneys' girl, Jen, came running across the street to join her, and they went up the Casino steps together. She saw her own son standing in front of her darkened shop, smoking, waiting for the right moment to go over. When Jen and Grace went up he turned around and stared idly at the dimly outlined hats in the Bon Ton window. Then Elsinore realized that in spite of the darkness, the lights reflected from the street made her faintly visible because Morry frowned and suddenly pressed his face against the pane, staring inside, as if he was seeing a ghost. She stood very still but after all her face probably showed up white and shadowy for Morry shivered and backed away, she saw him toss his cigarette into the gutter and hurry across the street, stopping at the foot of the Casino steps for a puzzled backward glance at the Bon Ton.

There would be next Thursday night and the next and the next. . . . Elsinore grew dizzy thinking of all the torture in store for her, for how could she ever look at Fischer again after her Cleveland visit. . . . His wife must have told him everything and he had told Mrs. Pepper and probably Mrs. Pepper had put two and two together. . . . Elsinore dragged her feet slowly up the stairs to bed, but she wouldn't sleep tonight, she'd lie there listening to the music and the applause, and think. . . . It was no use, she knew that no matter what the risk she'd go next Thursday night. After all, she hadn't told Fischer's wife her name or even that she was from Lamptown, so how could anyone possibly guess?

She drew a rocking chair up to her bedroom window and huddled there in her nightdress.

"Dance Number Three."

Today some factory girls trying on hats had talked about the chance Fischer had to have a studio in Chicago only he'd refused to give up his Cleveland headquarters. It had been a great chance, they said, and he might change his mind, of course. Elsinore thought of dark, silent Thursday nights going on forever, for the rest of her life, and a Lamptown slackening into a dull shuffle with no Fischer to count out the rhythm. . . . Well, there was always a chance for a new millinery store in a big city like Chicago, she could get on there, she could always manage her business, Chicago wouldn't be any harder than Lamptown. Now it seemed a question of the Bon Ton moving to Chicago, and she'd forgotten why.

It must have been a good dance tonight. Everyone sang softly with the orchestra, they blended into one gay humming voice that might be swelling out of the rickety old building itself though no one could believe it to look at the sleep expressionless faces of Hermann and Hulda Bauer in the first floor window.

> "Has anybody here seen Kelly—
> K-e-double l-y-
> Anybody here seen Kelly—"

Elsinore sat in the chair and wished she hadn't been such a coward as to stay away. She'd never stay home again, that was certain.

Walter Havighurst (b. 1901), Professor Emeritus at Miami University, is a prolific writer, in many genres that focus on the region between the Ohio River and the Great Lakes. He wrote *The Upper Mississippi* (1944) in the "Rivers of America" series, *The Long Ships Passing* (1942), *Land of Promise* (1946), regional histories of the Great Lakes, and several historic novels. He has won numerous awards, including the Ohioana Library Association Medal 1946–50. *The Quiet Shore* (1937) opens with this evocative description of the influence of local landscape upon the narrator that conveys "the strength of a native place."

Return

Twilight was the time to get there—all day long the hot fields of Ohio and the sunny Ohio towns, and then at twilight the lake seen through the trees. Dusk lay deep in the wood lot (Grandpa's name still held) but under the waning sky the lake was tranquil with light. It was not water but fluid light on summer evenings, with the sun gone in a smoky splendor over Toledo and the moon growing through the gray haze of Cleveland. Darkness had come to the highway with its swift race of headlamps, a dimness had gathered across the inland fields; but the lake was luminous, shoreless, unearthly. Years ago in the white church at Pride's Crossing the minister had said: *The Peace of God that passes understanding*—that was the water at twilight. That was Lake Erie in the waning day.

It was so in Grandpa's time, when Sandusky was a crossroads and Cleveland was a sprawling town at the canal mouth and Petroleum Nasby wrote a corn-shuck column for the Toledo *Blade*. The lake was the same even then, so slow to give up the day, so tranquil on an August evening. And it was unchanged tonight, with the stacks of Toledo smoking up a dusk somewhere in the west and the false lights of Cedar

Point picking out the roller-coaster beyond the sober, honest flashing of the signal light at Wood End.

Feeling the familiar quiet, Alan dropped his bag beside the leaning trunk of the old apple tree that grew perversely at the edge of land. Why had no one come to meet him? Why was the terrace empty and the place so still? One part of his mind was wondering about the silence, and the other was glad that it was so, that he could walk alone through the wood lot and past the houses and come home first to twilight on that shore. The lake was tranquil. Above the darkening shore the sky looked innocent, untroubled, and the water was as dispassionate and serene as in the days when Grandpa had driven to Sandusky with a load of corn. In other places there were questions and confusion, there was man's sharp strife. There was the tragic immensity of cities and the blind frustration of unnumbered lives, and nobody could think that the world was like this, vast and gentle and compassionate. Already, after thirty hours in America, Alan had seen enough to know the doubts and uncertainties in his land. Bread lines in the cities; P.W.A. projects with the workmen empty-hearted at their toil; men on the roads, not tramps or hobos—they have a different look—but men plodding because there was nothing in the last town and there might be something in the next, anyway the road is better than sitting in wait for nothing; a dog might do that, but a man can't. One day had shown him a good deal. And before that, he had seen it in the American papers in London: doubts, uncertainties, a new shrillness, the future of course— in America there had always been the future—but this was not the familiar future in America, it was half-reluctant and wholly compulsory fore-looking; and in America at last the old hopes were crumbling; freedom, the faith in men, the myth of everyman and his sanctity. The hopes were shadowed and the faith was faltering, and it was hard now in America to dream the old dreams. So he was glad to stand quiet and feel the familiar place about him. It, at least, had not changed. The lake was tranquil with twilight, and around him in the dimness lay the fields of home.

Now he lingered at the end of the hemlock wind-break and there were many things to think of while the surf washed softly on the sands below. The shore dropped off sharply; it was thirty feet to the hard white beach where two sandpipers scurried primly at the water's edge. The modest height gave a suggestive sweep to the lake, and as he stood there Alan Bradley was moved again with youth's vague ardor and unrest: the world for him would always wait out there beyond the water's rim. That had been his earliest dream and his most persistent memory, and he would not outgrow it. Whatever he might seek, whatever purposes or dreams or achievements, in the quiet unshared images of his own heart the lake would always be the way to them. For him the world lay out there. The past was there and the future was there also. So it was not strange that certain hours in London, when life seemed urgent and near and its claims were made upon him, brought a memory of the lake at twilight. This sad pale light of evening, so unclouded and so still, was the first mood of the earth that had moved him. Then he was a boy, troubled and silent and wanting to be alone, his heart pounding painfully and his boy's mind not knowing why. And now at twenty-three, feeling mature as one feels on return to a familiar and missed place, the same mood moved him in the same way.

There were many things to think about this first evening, while the gray skies and the gray cities across the Atlantic faded in his mind and the warm, vibrant, flowing life of mid-America grew familiar. All day there had been a sense of profound home-coming, of manhood returning to the earth that nurtured it, of a mind remembering the life that shaped its growth. And there had been surprise in the spaciousness and order of America. All the way from New York to Ohio he had seen a splendid and a troubled land, and it was hard to say which was true, the men hopeless on the roads or that other country: the soaring new-world cities, the breathless American architecture, the stammering turrets and terraces of stone repeating themselves in New York, Pittsburgh, Cleveland, Detroit, Kansas City, San Francisco, the incredible white shafts and the jeweled towers against the tall American sky; the towns sprawling in the level lands, the warm friendly streets with the elm trees arched above, the shrill curve of a railway track and the train pounding to a stop beneath the swinging spout of a faded water tank; the villages dreaming beside the rivers, the warm sweet summer smell of mud banks, the dusty weeds climbing up at the roadside, the willows twinkling in the hot noon air. And everywhere the strong light, the heat, the strident sound of American voices, the restlessness over this land and the fulfillment too; the pound of motor-driven wheels, the blurred and streaming traffic on Number 20 out of Cleveland, the momentous race along that awful artery of stone.

This, all this was America. This electric life that webbed the continent, it was not gone even though a confusion was in it; perhaps it was the true America still. He had felt it days ago, before land was sighted off Maine and Massachusetts. Something was in that sea-keen air, some new fiber, some significance. All that last evening on shipboard the western horizon had a heroic light.

And now the lake, with daylight lingering there for a last mood of peace. It was America, too. And in a young man's first traveling and return there was this remembrance and discovery. Like all important things of the mind and heart, it would never come a second time, and Alan lingered there while the first white stars came in the evening sky. He coughed quietly and watched a freighter's lights move into the horizon.

This, he reminded himself, was what he had pictured so many times when he was homesick for the hot Ohio sky in August or snow drifting on those sands. It was unchanged: the long and quiet shore and above it the terrace with the clustered houses among the trees and around them the many acres of his grandfather's land. This life remained as he had left it, and so he wondered now at the long bitterness that lay between those houses. He remembered it as from a distance, and it seemed but half real in this fading light. The silent enmity, the sharp prolonged mistrust, could it be unchanged, too? Even as his mind framed the question he knew how pointless it was; this family did not give up old ways so easily. It would remain a proud, defiant hate, the children and grandchildren of Roger Bradley's first wife drawn up against those of his second wife: the Sletter Bradleys against the Murdock Bradleys, farmers against business people, the fields against the city. Their hate would be unchanged, and their pride in each other, too, for in Buffalo Sterling Bradley was known to boast that his brothers were the best farmers in Ohio, and in Pride's Crossing Jonas Bradley bragged that his brothers were the shrewdest business men outside of Wall Street. So it was a curious hate, with a Bradley texture to it, a compound of fear, distrust, and loyalty, and perhaps a common tie that bound them to this place.

There in the dusk were the Bradley houses, set among maples and elms, and in their midst was the big frame Homestead, rambling and of another century, with the long three-sided porch and the four irregular gables. It was strange in America where people drift and are not permanent (*we follow the business wherever it calls*), in America, land of migrations, of restless wandering (one family scattered from Long Island to El Paso; the letters "home" hurrying on the trains all night across the Cascade Mountains and through the echoing canyons of New Mexico and over the Bridges of the Mississippi)—it was strange that one family should be so rooted. Perhaps there were other families like them, American families in Texas, Maine, and Oregon who knew that hold of heritage. For now it seemed to Alan the strength of place that brought the Bradleys back. He knew it was not love for one another, nor loyalty to Grandpa; and he suspected it was something more than hope of inheritance. Perhaps, even in America, it was the strength of a native place.

Chester Himes (1909–84) lived in Cleveland from 1924 to 1941. He graduated in 1926 from East High School and then attended Ohio State University for a year. After his release from prison in 1935, he joined the W.P.A. Ohio Writers' Project, the labor movement, the Communist party, and the *Cleveland Daily News*. Known primarily as a writer of detective novels and expatriate (he died in Spain), Himes wrote studies of social conflict that have become classics of black American protest literature. In this selection, he provides a picture of the seamier side of urban life in Cleveland in 1940.

Marihuana and a Pistol

"Red" Caldwell bought two "weeds" and went to the room where he lived and where he kept his pearl handled blue-steel .38 revolver in the dresser and smoked them. Red was despondent because his girl friend had quit him when he didn't have any more money to spend on her. But at the height of his jag, despondency became solid to the touch and attained weight which rested so heavily upon his head and shoulders that he forgot his girl friend in the feeling of the weight.

As night came on it grew dark in the room; but the darkness was filled with colors of dazzling hue and grotesque pattern in which he abruptly lost his despondency and focused instead on the sudden, brilliant idea of light.

In standing up to turn on the light, his hand grabbed the rough back of the chair. He snatched his hand away, receiving the sensation of a bruise. But the light bulb, which needed twisting, was cool and smooth and velvety and pleasing to the touch so that he lingered awhile to caress it. He did not turn it on because the idea of turning it on was gone, but he returned slowly to the middle of the floor and stood there absorbed in vacancy until the second idea came to him.

He started giggling and then began to laugh and laugh and laugh until his guts retched because it was such a swell idea, so amazingly simple and logical and perfect that it was excruciatingly funny that he had never thought of it before—he would stick up the main offices of the Cleveland Trust Company at Euclid and Ninth with two beer bottles stuck in his pockets.

His mind was not aware that the thought had come from any desire for money to win back his girl friend. In fact it was an absolutely novel idea and the completely detailed execution of it exploded in his mind like a flare, showing with a stark, livid clarity his every action from the moment of his entrance into the bank until he left it with the money from the vault. But in reviewing it, the detailed plan of execution eluded him so that in the next phase it contained a pistol and the Trust Company had turned into a theater.

Perhaps ten minutes more passed in aimless wanderings about the two-by-four room before he came upon a pistol, a pearl handled blue-steel .38. But it didn't mean anything other than a pistol, cold and sinister to the touch, and he was extremely puzzled by the suggestion it presented that he go out into the street. Already he had lost the thought of committing a robbery.

Walking down the street was difficult because his body was so light, and he became angry and annoyed because he could not get his feet down properly. As he passed the confectionery store his hand was tightly gripping the butt of the pistol and he felt its sinister coldness. All of a sudden the idea came back to him complete in every detail—only this time it was a confectionery store. He could remember the idea coming before, but he could not remember it as ever containing anything but the thought of robbing a confectionery store.

He opened the door and went inside, but by that time the idea was gone again and he stood there without knowing what for. The sensation of coldness produced by the gun made him think of his finger on the trigger, and all of a sudden the scope of the fascinating possibilities opened up before him, inspired by the feeling of his finger on the trigger of the pistol. He could shoot a man—or even two, or three, or he could go hunting and kill everybody.

He felt a dread fascination of horror growing on him which attracted him by the very essence of horror. He felt on the brink of a powerful sensation which he kept trying to capture but which kept eluding him. His mind kept returning again and again to his finger on the trigger of the pistol, so that by the time the storekeeper asked him what he wanted, he was frantic and he pulled the trigger five startling times, feeling the pressure on his finger and the kick of the gun and then becoming engulfed with stark, sheer terror at the sounds of the shots.

His hands flew up, dropping the pistol on the floor. The pistol made a clanking sound, attracting his attention, and he looked down at it, recognizing it as a pistol and wondering who would leave a pistol on a store floor.

A pistol on a store floor. It was funny and he began to giggle, thinking, *a pistol on a store floor,* and then he began to laugh, louder and louder and harder, abruptly stopping at sight of the long pink and white sticks of peppermint candy behind the showcase.

They looked huge and desirable and delicious beyond expression and he would have died for one; and then he was eating one, and then two, reveling in the sweetish mint taste like a hog in slop, and then he was eating three, and then four, and then he was gorged and the deliciousness was gone and the taste in his mouth was bitter and brackish and sickening. He spat out what he had in his mouth. He felt like vomiting.

In bending over to vomit he saw the body of an old man lying in a puddle of blood and it so shocked him that he jumped up and ran out of the store and down the street.

He was still running when the police caught him but by that time he did not know what he was running for.

Jo Sinclair (b. 1913), pseudonym of Ruth Seid, was born in New York and grew up in Cleveland, the setting for many of her short stories which were widely published in magazines like the *Saturday Evening Post* and *Colliers,* and her novels, such as *Wasteland* (Harper Prize Novel for 1946) and *The Changelings* (1955). Much of her work is concerned with life in Cleveland's Jewish community and issues of tolerance and bigotry. In this selection, written in 1967, a mother and her son come to understand each other against a backdrop of a world torn by strife.

The Medal

Cleveland was almost as hot as Washington had been, and Mildred felt stifled as she paid the taxi driver. Josh had taken the suitcase; he was on the front porch now, digging in a pocket for his key.

When the taxi pulled away, Mildred walked away slowly. She could not bear the idea of going in; the house was so much Phil's. The screen door closed behind Josh without a sound, and she found that unbearable, too. A boy should let a door slam automatically, she thought almost querulously. How long after death do we have to tiptoe?

She came into the living room, made herself snap up the window shades at once, welcoming the noise. She heard her son's soft steps at the back of the house, and shrank from the thought of the evening stretching ahead.

Where would she continue to get the casual talk? Again, she would have to mask her grieving loneliness, avert her eyes from so many things—a photograph, the piano Phil had loved to play, his big chair.

In the dining room, Mildred rolled up the shades quickly, then went through to the kitchen. The roses on the table were full blown—velvet red, yellow, named Mirandy and Eclipse. Phil had known all his roses by name, as he had planted them or cut them for the house. And she had called their names silently two days ago, as if cutting the two roses for him, just before it was time to leave for the airport.

She permitted herself to relax for an instant, let the sorrow roll over her completely. A woman could not, most of the time. She could not groan, or cry like a lost female animal left alone. The child turned her from bereft wife and hungering lover into the pretense of strong, calm mother. The child was unknowing but rigid censor. Even in her own bedroom, late at night, a woman must not mourn her dead beloved with anything but choked weeping. A boy lay sleeping in the next room, too young to be awakened by such frightening sounds of yearning.

Mildred added water to the vase, mechanically straightened the tablecloth. She thought wearily that she should be proud of Josh, instead of resenting his implacable presence. He had not cried once. It was she who had gone to pieces inside when the telegram had come. Josh had seemed to turn into an expressionless boy, somehow taller, unbelievably quiet.

And that queer look of detachment had stayed with him, through even the flight to Washington—his first plane ride. The quiet boy had walked with her into the White House, a walk which had made her own legs tremble. Mildred remembered the President's kind eyes as he shook hands with her son. "How old are you, Joshua?" he had asked. "Twelve, sir," her son had answered, and the President had said: "I'll bet everyone calls you Josh." The boy: "Yes, sir, they do." The President, very, very gently: "I know how proud you are of your father." And that courteous, stony-quiet voice: "Yes, sir. Thank you." The blue ribbon had gone about Josh's neck. When the President stepped back, the medal had looked too large for the slender, thin-faced boy.

Mildred went back to the living room, to telephone Phil's mother. Dialing, she heard the soft steps in the bedroom. The tiptoe steps of mourning; somehow, Josh kept repeating Phil's death, over and over.

"Hello, Mother," she said into the telephone. "We just got home, dear. Are you feeling any better?"

Amelia Goldmark's deep voice answered with eagerness. They were very fond of each other, the candid old woman and the younger one whose own mother and father were dead.

"It was a fine trip," Mildred said. "He's a little tired, but I do think he enjoyed the plane. And we had time to see a little of Washington."

Carefully, she answered the impatient questions. Her mother-in-law was in her late seventies, and their family doctor had forbidden the trip to Washington. As Mildred described the presentation, her eyes were on the photograph of Phil, which stood on the table near the piano. He was not in uniform, and she was glad. It was Phil in the picture, the man of home and gardening and advertising agency, the tall and boyish husband who studied at the kitchen table and looked up at midnight to say: "That's it for tonight, Mil. How about that corned-beef sandwich?"

"I'm anxious to see the medal," Phil's mother said.

"It's beautiful," Mildred told her. "So simple. We'll tell you all about it tomorrow. Are you sure you feel up to temple?"

As the deep, old voice told of a phone call from the Atlanta cousins, Josh came into the room. He had changed into denims and a short-sleeved shirt. A feeling half resentment and half anguish swept through Mildred as she saw him take from his pocket the case that held the medal, put it down on the table. A little more awe, please, she thought achingly. Not every father wins his son the highest honor his nation can give.

Josh went out to the front porch and sat on the top step, his shoulders hunched. The picture lit up for her again of the way he had stood in the Rose Garden of the White House—so quiet, so poised, like a little stranger she had never seen before.

All through the presentation, Mildred had remembered with a kind of agony Phil's garden, the look of his bare arms and thick, black hair in sunlight as he pruned his roses. The words of the citation had come to her in jerks, a phrase fading, the next one too stark: "Captain Philip David Goldmark . . . veteran of World War II . . . killed . . . his valiant leadership and courageous fighting . . . far beyond the call of duty. . . . "

Amelia Goldmark said reluctantly, "Well, I had better let you rest. Tell Joshua his dog's been good as gold. I suppose you're coming for him later? Those two so hate to be separated."

"I'm not sure, Mother. If Josh isn't too tired."

"Well, we'll be together tomorrow, anyway." The deep laugh had a quaver in it. "Frankly, Bozo's wonderful company. I'd like another day of him."

Mildred went to wash her face and change into a house dress. She unpacked quickly, put on lipstick. Then, still moving briskly, she went out to the porch, leaned against the rail near the hunched figure.

"Darling," she said, "Grandma says Bozo's been a perfect gent of a visitor. Want to drive over and bring him home?"

"Why don't we get him tomorrow, or something?" Josh said.

It was so unlike him that Mildred's stomach lurched. The street was very quiet, deserted looking. Somewhere a screen door slammed, but no one came out into the hot stillness.

"Fine," she said. "I think we'd better have a little supper now. Going to set the table for me?"

Without a word, Josh followed her in. "Just spoons," she said, fighting to retain the casual tone. "We'll have cornflakes and sliced peaches. Plenty of cold milk."

It was a summer dish he loved, but he made no comment. As they sat, Mildred kept her eyes from the vase of roses, began to speak with simulated interest of the fall semester, which would begin in three weeks. She taught mathematics at a junior high school halfway across the city, and on her way each morning she dropped Josh in front of Moreland School. Phil never needed the car because the rapid transit to his downtown office was within walking distance of their suburban home. Had been within walking distance, she amended that thought carefully.

"Are you looking forward to working with the public address system at school?" she asked, making herself smile.

"I guess so," Josh said, not looking up. He was eating listlessly.

"Miss Buchanan told me it's perfect preparation for the speech and drama classes you want later on," she said doggedly, and talked on and on to the silent boy.

Yes, later on, she thought grimly, unable to keep the flooding memory under control. Later on, Phil was to have finished law. One more year of evening classes, of books and briefs spread over the kitchen table. And he had planned to go on making a living at the agency during the long haul of establishing himself as a lawyer. His old joke! "Commercials, PR, legal advice, horticulture lessons? See Goldmark."

When the interminable meal was over, Mildred said brightly. "Run along, darling—there aren't enough dishes for two. Why don't you see if your friends are out in the street. It doesn't seem as hot now."

Josh disappeared at once. The tears came as she washed a few dishes and put a fresh cloth on the table. If only she could be alone for one day—just Mildred, mourning Phil, and no child near enough to stop her wild screams of grief.

She lit a cigarette and sat near the windows, looking out at Phil's lovely yard until she felt under control again. But her feet shuffled with exhaustion when she went to the living room.

It was cool there, dim with the approaching dusk. With a start, she saw that Josh had not gone out. He was sitting in Phil's chair. Quickly, she snapped on the table lamp, then went to the standing lamp behind the piano. The light made the wood shine.

"Feel like practicing?" she said cheerfully.

"Mom, no," Josh said, his voice ragged.

"Would you like me to play something?" she went on with an effort. She had to get normal life back into this house!

"No, thank you." Josh said, and he sounded almost frantic.

His resemblance to his father hurt too much. The face long and thin, the same texture of hair; he had Phil's and Amelia Goldmark's mouth, curved and strongly traced. At the old woman's dinner table, every Sunday, Mildred had never failed to feel a tenderness, a delight sharp as a little ache, at the sight of those three faces marked so indelibly by generation. It had overjoyed her to be close to the three high-strung creatures, so aware of their needs and of her own capacity to minister to them. She had never doubted that capacity for a moment, until today.

Street noises drifted into the room. The live sounds warmed her a little. There was such a spell of death in the house. Phil would have hated it.

Deliberately, she said, "Darling, please don't forget the medal tomorrow. For Grandma to see. Better take it to your dresser now, so you remember it in the morning when we leave for temple."

Protest stiffened his entire body. They had not talked about the medal once, in Washington or on the trip back. They had not talked about Phil, for that matter, Mildred thought quite suddenly.

"Mom, I can't," Josh mumbled.

"Can't what?" Mildred asked, beginning to feel frightened.

"I'm not going to temple," he burst out. "I don't want to. Ever."

She felt sick, a little dizzy, but she said in the calm voice she had created for him: "And afterward, we'll spend the day with Grandma, as usual. She's looking forward to hearing about our trip. She wants to see the medal, hold it for a while. But, of course, you'll take it home again—it belongs to you."

"I don't want the medal," Josh cried. "I want Dad."

His outcry made a slash of pain in Mildred's head. She wanted Phil, too. Wildly, rawly; no substitute would do. But, instinctively, she started toward Josh, to comfort him. To her bewilderment, he jumped up quickly, as if he wanted to run away from her. She stopped at once, looked at him helplessly.

The quiet pose was gone. He looked lost, anguished, as if the telegram had just come.

"Why did he have to die?" Josh demanded.

The bitterness in his voice made Mildred's heart spiral downward. She felt the sudden bleakness of failure: all along, through the happy years of his growing, Phil and she had been so sure that they were preparing a child for life, carefully interpreting the inexplicable in his world along with the facts.

She managed to say, "It isn't for us to answer. The meaning is God's. We both know that."

Josh shook his head. Stunned, she saw his refusal of all the years of unquestioning faith. This was the boy who had listened as raptly to Bible stories as to fairy tales; then, old enough, plunged into Sunday school and Hebrew classes. Only a few weeks ago, he had been studying wholeheartedly for his Bar Mitzvah.

"Josh," she said, her throat dry, "please talk to me."

"Well, don't tell me God," he blurted. "Like the rabbi did. What *reason* is there, Mom? You can't tell me. I know you can't."

He walked away so quickly that he lurched, but he stopped at the screen door and stared out. For the first time since he had been born, Mildred felt her son as a fear instead of an exciting, joyous challenge.

"He was in the big war," Josh said coldly, his back still to her. "That was plenty. Plenty."

Yearning for some kind of right answer, Mildred managed a few lame words: "Some men feel duty strongly. Not—just a one-time thing."

He whirled around, said with a strange, harsh anger, "It wasn't duty! Nobody can kid me. Not the rabbi—not God. Why are you? Don't Mom! He already did his duty. More than a lot of guys. So why did he die? All I want is a reason. A *reason*."

"Josh, don't—please," she begged.

"They—they give you a medal, and—What's such a far-away war got to do with Dad? Or the U.N.? Nobody else on our street volunteered. Nobody in temple. Just Dad. For what?"

His eyes were not a boy's, and Mildred felt the unreal terror of trying to grope toward a strange child.

"I just want a reason," this stranger said to her insistently. "Why'd he go? Why'd he get killed?"

At that last word, which came out slurred with pain, Mildred cried out unthinkingly, from her heart: "Oh, my dearest, I miss him just as much as you do. I love him just as much."

Josh winced. The anger, so false, turned into the honest thing at last—the grief he had been hiding all along. He went slowly back to the couch, sat heavily. As she saw the sprawling body, the hands loose and pitifully awkward, Mildred's world righted itself for the first time since Phil's death.

The shocking knowledge was in her, suddenly, that she had gone away from her son in the weeks since that death. In her own bereavement, she had left him alone. The boy's composure had been a relief to her, not an anxiety.

And there was a deeper shock underlying this one. Josh's questioning of his God, his temple, the lovely pattern of religion his short life had contained with such certainty, brought her the sickening realization of her own uncomforted spirit. In permitting her unabated pain so long, her continuing hunger for Phil's arms and body, hadn't she also questioned a life-long belief?

Mildred came close to Josh, but made no attempt to touch him. He would not want to be held now, babied; that was one of the few things she knew for sure at this moment. Looking down at her son, she saw his father's eyes in a beginning face—his grandmother's eyes. The beautiful, deathless procession of generations wound through her heart; how had she forgotten the faith and hope mankind made of its children by giving them, by forever replenishing its family and its world?

And she thought, with hurt for Josh: A child's inheritance. Did I really think it was a medal? That honor and pride were all he needed, to hold in his hands for riches—father to son?

A feeling of shame came with the awareness of how she had put away Phil's words for herself. She had considered them her own, precious and private possessions left to a woman by her man. And she must have thought, without verbalizing it: Besides, Josh is a child. What could a husband's words mean to him? A lover's words? He doesn't need them. I do.

The shame was something she was not used to, and she had to brace herself to go on with the somber facts: She had seized the words and hidden them for her own comfort, though they belonged as much to Josh. A child needed all of the inheritance. Not just a medal. Not just prayers, either; for look how the old patterns of ritual, of preparation to live as a man under God, could turn meaningless when the heart was unprepared. This boy needed every bit of his inheritance. There must be such a thing as armoring yourself with the broad rituals of mankind—that make the human being, as well as the Jew.

Very suddenly, Mildred could think of Phil's smile without pain, without the loneliness and yearning which had sickened her memories.

"You want a reason, Josh," she said. "Why he went. Knowing he might not come back. He did know that."

Her son stared up at her, his eyes narrowed against the pushing tears.

Mildred nodded, said softly: "Sometimes a reason is just there. Inside a man. What he thinks and feels—believes—like part of his body."

Phil had sat in his room before leaving, and had talked to her. And now, as quietly as Phil had spoken, she talked to their son.

"Your father loved every part of his life," she said. "Worked at it, wanted it every minute. There was no room in him for dying."

The word, dying, no longer hurt, and Mildred knew that she had stopped the senseless fighting of Phil's death. She had to walk for an instant, the thankfulness a feeling of almost explosive physical relief.

When she turned back, leaning back against the piano, she was able to go on: "Your father used to laugh a lot. Remember? And there was something he'd say often—when he felt particularly good. When a favorite rose opened early. When he had potato pancakes for Sunday supper. Simple things. He'd say: 'For a Jew-boy in this world, this year, I'm mighty happy. Mighty satisfied,' And he'd laugh—but it wasn't ever a joke. If he were the type, it would have been a solemn laugh."

Josh's eyes began to absorb her words, and Mildred's memories lost the last vestige of sickness.

"A reason? Oh, Josh," she said tenderly. "Well, let me try to tell you. Before he left for the big one, that first war in his life—my life— he sat in this room and talked. You hadn't been born, but—oh, we used to talk about you a lot."

She smiled. "Your father had you named long before you were born. Well, that night, he said to me: 'You know, I'm crazy about this country, this street, this house. Sometimes, Mil, I think about my grandfather and grandmother—who happened to come here from Germany. Who happened to get to a place called Atlanta, Georgia, first off. Young Jews. Just a little money—enough to buy needles and thread, a few other things for a peddler's kit. No Nazis then, eh? Just the little pogroms, the usual European Jew-hate. Small potatoes—but not to Goldmark the immigrant. So—a young Jew peddled on the roads of Georgia. He had kids. He brought his family up to Ohio for better bread-and-butter. And, Mil, I think of our kid. How maybe Josh'll go to the same school you and I met at. And Mother—think Josh'll love Ann Arbor as much as Mother did? As much as we did? I do.' "

Mildred stopped for a second. Then she took a deep breath, smiled again at the boy listening so intently.

"That's the way we talked that night," she said. "Just a kind of— wondering. I remember he said: 'I think of our pretty house, Mil. And the way I decided I'm going to be a lawyer some day. When it's possible. Because of a word like Nazi in the world. Far away from my house, my city, my darlings. Far as God—near as God. And how that's okay with my world—Phil Goldmark wanting to be a lawyer all of a sudden. Remembering his grandfather's choice—doing a repeat, because that word *choice* is just as good to a grandson, and to *his* son. I tell you, Mil, I'm crazy about this country.' "

Josh's face twisted. "Oh, Mom," he muttered.

"You want a reason," Mildred said. "To hold in your hands instead of a medal? The reason was always the same for Phil Goldmark. The second time he went to a war, we sat here together again. In this room. Now you were in the world, too. We felt you up in your bed, sleeping. The house was full of you, and we talked. Of so many things—people. You, us. A world of countries. The way even Grandma had been born in this country—down in Atlanta—so far from a word like Nazi, that the world was hearing again. Names like Eichmann, Khrushchev, Nasser, places like Havana, Moscow, Tel Aviv, Peiping. And yet things, names and countries, the world—they're never far anymore. Far and near as God. That was your father's way of saying it. A word like Nazi. So far from his son, his wife, his mother—even *her* mother and father. A word like 'choice.' He loved that word." Mildred added, very softly, "He said to me: 'In case it ever comes up, Mil, this Jew-boy is still crazy about this country. This city, this street. The way *choice* hollers in this street. The way this street, this house, is going to go on hollering *choice* loud enough—always.' And he laughed. You know— that laugh of his?"

Josh jumped up and ran toward her. She met him with her own hungry embrace. He was crying. Mildred held him tightly, let him cry, her lips against his hair.

When finally he looked up at her, she saw that Phil had actually given him his reason. Josh's eyes were quite still.

"I kind of forgot about Dad," he said. "Isn't that funny? Just—forgot. The way he talked, the way he was. You know, laughing that way? But no joke—ever. How he meant it, all the way in his eyes, even laughing. Even—dying, I guess he'd mean it all the way. Like what he told you, and—and you just told me. I just kind of forgot."

"I almost did, too," Mildred said in a low voice, and kissed him.

She watched him drag out his handkerchief and mop up. After a while, she said shyly, "Feel like taking a look at the yard before bedtime?"

Josh nodded, took her hand in the old, casual way.

They walked through the house, out the back door. In the yard, a light fragrance seemed to hem them in like delicate boundary lines. When first the house had been bought, Phil had said with a pleased laugh: "Well, I'm going to have a smelly garden, Mil. Always wanted one."

Now, as Mildred and her son walked in the darkness of the yard, they knew the phlox as they passed it, and the scented yellow lilies, the roses Phil had selected so carefully for their perfume. They stopped at the back property line, where the lilacs—long past blossom time—made a tall, thick, hedge of green. They could see the kitchen windows shining with soft light. The light noises of their neighbors came into the yard, muffled, comfortable.

"Isn't it beautiful here?" Mildred said. "Let's plant a tree this fall. Back here, where there's plenty of room for it to grow."

Josh was silent for a moment. Then he said jerkily, "Yeah, let's. Right here, Mom. This city, this street. This—house."

James McConkey (b. 1921), a Lakewood native, is Professor of Literature at Cornell University, and a writer of stories and essays for the *Atlantic, Western Review, Yale Review,* and *The New Yorker.* Northeast Ohio provides the setting for *Crossroads: An Autobiographical Novel* (1968), *The Tree House Confessions* (1980), and several of the stories in *Night Stand* (1965), where this story of the transition from innocence to experience in the southern reaches of the Reserve is to be found.

The Medina Road

Every evening for a week, Michael had been sitting behind the window of his uncle's gas station, watching the valley mist tumble up out of the cut of the brick road that led from Medina. He was spending the summer with his uncle and aunt, operating the station for them from one o'clock until closing time.

Michael was supposed to close the station at eight o'clock. By then most of the traffic from Medina was over, and it would just be wasting electricity to turn the floodlight on. Already he had devised a routine for himself: he first swept the floor and cleaned the washroom, arranged the articles in the window display—the cans of fly spray, Motor Tonic, the flashlights and gas tank covers and windshield wipers; in the back room he made sure that the red light on the battery charger was burning and that the switch on the air compressor was off; and then he brought in the water can and the oil stand and put the locks on the two pumps. When all this was done, he emptied the contents of the cash register into a paper bag, took the revolver from the desk drawer in case somebody tried to hold him up, turned out the lights and locked the door. Usually, though, before he had gone a block he turned back to make sure that the door was really locked and the lights turned off.

On this evening, he was just stepping out the door with the pump locks when he saw the boy walking up through the mist out of the valley, pushing a bicycle. Already night was drawing in; Michael, standing by the pump, saw him only as a shadow until he passed under the faint glow of the corner street light. He was small and thin, and wore a jacket and a pair of blue jeans. A knapsack was strapped to his shoulders, and another bundle dangled over the rear fender of the bicycle. The boy apparently saw the light in the station window, for he walked slowly toward it, holding the bicycle by the saddle and directing the front wheel by tilting the bicycle first this way and then that.

Michael snapped the locks on the pumps and walked back inside to wait, but he couldn't keep from looking out the window. The boy had leaned his bicycle against the pump, and was reaching down for the air hose. Michael went to the door. "No air in the compressor," he said. "Closing up."

The boy said quietly, "Ain't that my luck, though?" He rose and stood without moving, his head slightly cocked as if he were listening to the frogs croaking down in the marsh. A car, its headlights blurred into large interlocking circles, rose up out of the valley and disappeared down the road, its tires humming on the brick. "Lucky son of a bitch," the boy said.

Michael said, "It'll take twenty minutes to get up pressure."

"You won't grow old and die in twenty minutes," the boy said. He spoke slowly, and with a slight drawl; and he kept his eyes straight on Michael's, as if he were expecting a fuss and was ready, though weary, to meet it.

"Maybe not," Michael said, but he remained, still doubtful, in the doorway. It was taking a risk, and Michael wasn't sure what his uncle would say if he closed up late because of a stranger. His uncle and aunt treated him kindly enough, but he really didn't know what went on inside their heads. "You keep the place a lot cleaner than my helper did," his uncle had said, and though the remark was obviously intended as a compliment Michael couldn't tell just how much his uncle meant by it, whether his uncle wanted to show his liking for him and was thinking of him—at least for the summer—as a member of the family, or whether the words were to be taken just on face value.

The boy was watching him patiently. Michael said, "If you got a leak in the tire, it won't do any good to put air in it."

"No," the boy agreed. "I was planning to fix it, too." He fumbled around in the bag on the fender and pulled out a repair kit. "I could fix it while the tank fills up," the boy said. He seemed both shy and determined, and he held out the repair kit in his hand so Michael could have a good look. "I got my own patches and tools," he said.

Embarrassed, Michael turned away. "Well, all right," he mumbled, and walked into the back room to throw the compressor switch. Then he hurried back to make sure that the boy wasn't trying to snitch some merchandise or get his hands into the cash register, That was something you had to be especially careful about in a one-man station. His uncle had told him to be sure to look in the window while he was filling up a car, if anybody went inside to use the lavatory. But the boy was still outside, trying to remove the nut from the rear wheel with a pair of pliers.

Michael found a crescent wrench in the tool chest and took it outside. "Try this," he said, squatting down. Surprised by his voice, the boy jumped; but then he deftly twisted the wrench on the nut, holding the pliers on the one opposite so it wouldn't turn. "You from Medina?" Michael asked.

"Came through there about an hour ago," the boy said.

"Some town," Michael said. He really knew nothing about the place. His uncle had picked him up at the depot at one o'clock in the morning, and he had seen nothing but blackness as they bounced along the streets in the Model A. Since then, while waiting for people to drive in for gas, Michael had often thought of what was in Medina— a movie house, maybe, and a dozen stores around a square, and a bank on the corner with an illuminated clock that chimed the quarter hours. The town he came from was like that. It was the county seat, and there was a two-story courthouse in the square with a faded honor roll out front. Passing the courthouse every day on the way to school, he had reached the point where he could recite, with his eyes closed, most of the names on the roll, from Adams to Wojik. Michael said, "I guess you must have come from a good deal further away than Medina."

"I guess I must," the boy said. He picked up the wheel and carried it into the station. Michael slipped the wrench into his pocket and followed him. "Where's your home?" he asked.

The boy didn't answer. He began pulling the tire loose from the rim, and it made a scratchy sound, like paper ripping, as the shellac broke loose. Though the boy was sweating, he still wore the jacket, and hadn't taken the knapsack from his shoulders. Michael could see the worn streaks in the jacket which the straps from the knapsack had made.

He couldn't understand why the boy should deliberately hold something back. The handle of a long knife was protruding from the end of a leather sheath that was attached to the boy's belt, and Michael looked at it so hard that his staring must have caught the boy's attention, for he reached his hand across to feel the handle. Michael glanced away, toward the desk drawer. The silence was making him nervous. "I don't come from around here, either," he said.

The boy coughed, holding his hand in front of his mouth. He took the tube out of the casing, stretching the rubber to find the puncture; and after he found it, he began scraping the surface around it with a little buffer from his repair kit.

"I come from a place near East Liverpool," Michael said. East Liverpool was where his mother always did the Saturday shopping. It gave him a good feeling to mention the town, but the boy showed no recognition of the name.

"That's right on the river," Michael said.

"What river?" The boy fumbled around in his kit and drew out a tube of cement and a patch.

"The Ohio," Michael said.

The boy looked up with more interest. "I crossed the Ohio at Cincinnati," he said. He stood up, dangling the limp tube over his arm. They were both silent, listening to the throb of the compressor in the back room. Down at the crossing, the bells began to clang, and then a diesel freight rumbled by, picking up speed on the slight grade. Michael could see its lights from the window.

"That's some river, all right," the boy said. In the glow of the overhead bulb, his face looked even thinner than it had outside, almost as if he were ill. There was a smear of grease across his forehead. He was wearing tennis shoes, and the rubber had broken on one of his toes. "I seen one of them river boats there," the boy said. "It had these big wheels on the side, and was painted pure white all over."

"That was the excursion boat. You can see it at East Liverpool once in a while. Usually, it's just tugs and barges you see."

"Ever been on that big white boat?" The boy was rubbing his fingers up and down the smooth rubber tube, his eyes surveying Michael appraisingly.

"I guess I have, all right," Michael said. He didn't know why he had told the lie, and he reddened slightly.

"Don't you *know* for sure?"

"Well, it was either that boat or another just like it," Michael said. "There was one that burned up and sank at Pittsburgh last year."

"It must have been pretty swell, riding that boat," the boy said thoughtfully.

"It was good enough, I guess," Michael murmured. "We only took her as far as Cincinnati. One of the boats goes all the way down to New Orleans." His eyes kept glancing down at the knife handle, but just the same he felt friendlier toward the boy. "Give me the tube,"

Michael said. "I got a better way of fixing it than just cement." He pointed toward the vulcanizer, but the boy didn't give him the tube. The boy said slowly, "There was a fellow at a gas station at a place called Danville that wanted a buck just for selling me a valve core. Said he'd turn me in as a tramp if I didn't give it."

"This won't cost you a penny," Michael said, and reached over and took the tube. If his uncle found out he was using the vulcanizer and the special patches to fix a tube free of charge, he probably wouldn't like it; but Michael whistled to himself as he clamped the tube into the vulcanizer. "If you crossed at Cincinnati," he said, "that means you must of come from Kentucky."

"Tennessee," the boy said. He was a little more at ease now, and rubbed his thumbs under the strap on his shoulder, hunching his back to shift the weight of the knapsack.

"Where you going?"

"Going up north to work with my brother."

"Where's that?"

"A good piece yet," the boy said hesitantly.

"I just wondered, that's all," Michael took the tube from the vulcanizer and examined it before handing it back. "Everybody would like to take a trip like that some day."

The boy nodded. He rubbed the patch and twisted the tube between his fingers. Then he said, "That looks like it ought to hold," and smiled for the first time. Shrugging off his knapsack, he placed it carefully on the desk. "Mind if I sit down?" he asked.

"Do what you like," Michael said.

The boy sat very stiffly on the edge of the chair. He pulled a crushed pack of cigarettes from his pocket, taking one and offering another to Michael. Michael, who had never smoked, put it self-consciously between his lips. The boy lit the cigarettes with a kitchen match from a round metal container stamped with the Boy Scout insignia.

"Most people wouldn't think to bring something like a waterproof match box on a bicycle trip," he said, fingering it carefully.

"You'd need something like that if it rained," Michael said.

"You need it on account of sweat, too." The boy seemed pleased by Michael's approval. "I sat down and figured out everything I'd need. There's a blanket and one of these rubber ponchos on the rear fender of the bike and here—" he dug into the knapsack and drew out a small frying pan and a little coffee pot and three waxed cartons—"is other stuff I need." He kept his hands momentarily on the items before pushing them closer for Michael's inspection. "Along the way, I stop at farmhouses and buy an egg or two, or maybe get a little stuff at a store."

"Where'd you get these?" Michael asked, picking up one of the waxed cartons.

"I had four brothers in the war. One stayed in and got a master sergeant's rating." The boy looked at the box. "They're pretty good," he said. "Hungry?"

Michael replied, "Not much," but the boy looked disappointed. "A little, I guess," Michael said.

The boy ripped open one of the rations, dumping the contents on the table. "There's coffee here," he said, pointing to a package. "These are crackers, and that's a tin of cheese. Cigarettes, too." He surveyed the little pile. "Something like this is a big time-saver on a trip," he said.

"You can see it would be." Michael watched while the boy twisted the key around the tin and then drew the knife from the sheath ("This is one of them combat infantry knives," the boy said, and Michael felt a shock of fear which vanished as quickly as it came, leaving only a faint sense of guilt) and sliced the cheese. Michael took two bottles of orange pop from the cooler by the door and put a dime in the cash register. He handed the boy one of the bottles and sat on the corner of the desk. Both of them crunched down on the cracker sandwiches.

"Pretty good," Michael said. The compressor in the back room wheezed and stopped, and it was silent except for the frogs down in the valley. The boy drank half a bottle of pop, wiped his lips, and listened to the frogs. "We hear those things at home this time of year," he said. "Them, and owls, too."

"You don't find many owls in these parts," Michael said.

"They're about the loneliest thing a man can hear. Home in bed, I used to listen to one that was over in the wood half a mile away." The boy sat back, twining his hands together behind his head. "Here I am talking away like a granddaddy," he said and chuckled. "A fellow don't get many chances to be gabby when he's out on the road. You think you'd meet all sorts of people, but it don't work out like that." He surveyed the room almost wistfully. "Pretty good job you got here," he said. "Wish I could find a job like this somewhere."

"It's good enough," Michael said, and shrugged his shoulders. "Just for the summer. You can bet I won't hold down a job like this all my life."

"What are you going to do?"

"Well, I don't know for sure yet," Michael said.

"A guy can't hang around home forever." The boy wiped the knife against his trouser leg and returned it carefully to its sheath. "I guess maybe I'll never go back if I get a good job."

"You got to get out on your own, all right," Michael agreed. He wanted to tell the boy all about himself, but there was nothing to say except "My father is a salesman," or "I got a year of high school yet," or "I had a dog last year, but he ran off." Michael said: "Things sure seem funny, when you think about them."

"That's how it is, all right," the boy said. He smiled at Michael, and it was as if each of them had known the other for years; and then the boy rose to his feet and said suddenly, "Well, I guess I'd better be going," and began dumping the articles back into the knapsack. "You'll want to close up."

"No hurry," Michael said.

"I got it planned to do fifteen miles yet tonight." The boy stuffed the tube quickly into the tire and mounted it on the rim. Michael helped him fasten the wheel back on the frame.

The boy said, "You see, I've been saving so that I'd have enough money to get there if I stay on schedule, and some left over to pay my way with my brother for a time." He picked up the bicycle, but stopped at the doorway, looking back almost shyly. "I don't know why I didn't want you to know where I was going," he said. "It's near Buffalo, New York. My brother sent a picture postcard of Niagara Falls. That's only ten miles away."

Michael smiled. He watched the boy carry the bicycle out to the air hose and went into the other room to shut off the compressor. Then he came back to open the cash register. After dumping the money into the paper bag, he dropped it into his pocket and took the revolver out of the drawer, examining it to make sure the safety was on. He felt proud of the revolver and peered down at the writing on the barrel to see what make it was, thinking the boy might like to see it.

When he looked up, he saw that the boy had started to re-enter the station to get his knapsack. "Well, so long," the boy said, and gestured a good-bye; but his gaze lowered slowly until he was staring straight at the revolver. Momentarily, his eyes were bewildered, then frightened; and his fingers pressed protectively against his hip pocket. He turned and vanished silently into the dark.

"Wait a minute," Michael said, for the boy had left his knapsack. By the time he reached the door, the boy had already jumped on the bicycle and was peddling furiously away. It was only then that Michael remembered he was holding a revolver in his hand. He dropped it on the desk and ran out to the curb. "Don't be scared," he cried. "That gun doesn't mean anything."

The boy had already passed under the street light, standing up to make the bicycle go faster.

"I'm no damn crook," Michael shouted angrily, and ran under the street light, waving his hands to show he didn't have the gun anymore. But the boy was already merged into the country blackness, and behind Michael the station door was open, the building unattended. He walked slowly back to the station and fumbled through the contents of the knapsack to see if there was some sort of identification, but he could find nothing he hadn't already seen except a smudged highway map with towns marked in red crayon, and a tattered snapshot of an elderly man and woman smiling stiffly straight ahead. They could have been almost anybody.

Michael looked around the room to make sure that everything was still in order, and put the revolver in the same pocket with the paper bag. He turned off the lights and locked the door. Now that he had completed the routine of closing up, he felt undecided about what he should do with the knapsack. Finally he left it on the cement island, between the pumps, in case the boy returned in the night.

Just as he was leaving, Michael thought suddenly that he would never see the boy again. The thought made him feel strange, though he knew it shouldn't. He placed his hand in his pocket, around the revolver butt, and walked quickly toward his uncle's house. He was nearly an hour late, and they would be worrying.

Since the early fifties Herbert Gold has used Cleveland as the setting for many of his best-selling novels and short story collections. *Fathers* (1966) and *Family* (1981) explore his childhood and youth in Cleveland. "Susanna at the Beach," which derives its central metaphor from the biblical Susanna and the Elders, celebrates the triumphal freedom of a heroine on the shores of Lake Erie; it was originally published in the *Atlantic Monthly* in May 1954 and collected in *Love and Like*. Gold received the Sherwood Anderson American Fiction Achievement Award in 1989.

Susanna at the Beach

1

First came the girl. Then one fat man idly floated beside a friend in the water, lolling on his back, spitting, his great trunk rolling in the pleasure of himself. He liked to watch the girl while taking his pleasure.

Finally there were the people on shore. These September loiterers, with thin hocks and thick, with waddling rumps in dark wool or tendoned ones in Hawaiian shorts, with itching faces in devotion to sun or a suave glistening under the equivocation of lotion, all of them squinted and winked and finally moved toward her. They strolled, they turned on their heels, or they merely leaned. They came limping over the hot sand like the good wizards in a story.

The girl over whom the old men watched was diving from the end of a breakwater into the oily, brackish, waste-ridden substance of Lake Erie at Cleveland, Ohio. Her arms, deeply tanned, worked firmly; and heated from within, she scrambled up the rocks in haste after her discipline. She had fled all the billboard schemes of the life of a pretty girl. Lips soft, and half-parted for a grand design rather than a Lucky Strike, hands taking the measure of ambition rather than the bottle of Coca-Cola, she had come to perfect her diving in a worn black cotton bathing suit which was already too small after her summer's growth. They were simple exercises, but she wanted them to be perfect. She had an idea of how they should be.

The old men, shaking off the sand flies which had multiplied among the refuse so late in the season, looked jealously to the thin cloth which held this girl and to the water which sheathed her. The girl measured the angle of her imagination against the remembered sting of an imperfect arc. Clean! she had prayed, but her worried brow was reporting, *No, another flop.* The black cloth gleamed in the wet. The droplets of water peeled down her body like broken beads as she climbed to try it again. The smile at the corners of her mouth was a promise to herself: Well! This time then. Even in the brief instant of her stretching, a crescent-shaped slope at one shoulder flashed dry in the sunlight.

This time she went in straight and slender with the will of perfection.

It was a Tuesday afternoon, and a day of rare Indian summer heat. Still, only the most faithful had returned to the beach: the athletic grandfathers, white-haired and withered, with an eye for the weather; a student with his American history textbook and the glaze of sun in his face meeting the doze of exposure to knowledge; the kids pretending to fish and the dead shad belly-up at the washline of water on the sand; the occasional amorous ones, asking riddles, fondling each other slyly, their pockets a-jingle with desire and streetcar fare; women from the industrial flats nearby, sitting in housedress to recall, complain, worry, and take a sleepy hour's leisure together. Mostly, however, beneath the roar and thump of road construction on the slope above them, almost in the shadow of the Terminal Tower to the east, there were the old men: the salesman sunning himself with neck reaching out and pants rolled above the knee so that by evening he can look "just like Miami Beach, better even"; the fat-thighed wanderer in the straw hat and red woolen trunks with a white canvas belt, his sinewy breasts hanging—he sat in a patch of seaweed to observe the diver and stroke the sand from between his toes; another, the big-bellied swimmer, now paddling and spewing water, shaggily emerged onto the pier in order to get nearer to the girl. His friend accompanied him. Hairy-chested loungers, old-time beaux, their bodies both wasted and swollen, they joined the rest of the men along the breakwater. They watched the girl still diving, still climbing; her deep breathing pressed the erect buds of her adolescence against sleek black cloth, she rocked once on her toes, and then off she sprang.

This girl used herself hard, used her lightness hard; and each man there, turning to her from the beach or the pier, thought it a pity. A

waste—her sufficiency unto herself silenced and saddened them and
made their arms hang tensely forward. Challenged, they turned up the
cards of their own sorts of sufficiencies.

The fat swimmer, swirls of hair on his belly and back, was now
switching himself with a green branch as he talked business with his
friend. They both studied the girl, and their discussion grew lyrical.
They talked business and public affairs. He was saying: "You're John-
cue Smith, let's put it, you want to get married—"

"I know! Got the taxes to pay, the down payments, the terms—"

"Yes, that's what I mean, to get ahead in life. The installments."

"I got the cost of living these days, Freddy."

"You got the government."

"Yes, Freddy, I got the taxes, yes—"

"The essentials of life."

"Yes, yes, all of that, yes"—and they both shook their heads mourn-
fully and let their mouths fall open while the tips of the girl's feet, pro-
pelled by her dive, wriggled above water as she swam.

"Like to bite off a piece of that one, eh Freddy?"

"I saw it first, me, you want to say I didn't?"

A policeman on horseback on the beach looked for purse-snatching,
nuisance-making, or drunkenness. Overhead, a pontooned airplane
swooped low and up. The traffic rushed past the stillness of sun and
beach and water, while, out on the lake, a single leaning sailboat, a visitor from the Clifton Club, kept its distance.

Two women, equipped for conversation with quart bottles of cherry
pop, their dresses pulled over their knees and their stockings rolled
down to their ankles, agreed on questions of mortality, bereavement,
and the pleasures of a city beach. They sat on a log stripped by water
and shaded their eyes first toward the industrial flats from which they
had emerged, then over the lake and into the horizon and beyond. "My
mama she die when she eighty-four," said the tanned younger one.
"Just like baby, like new kid, she need milk to drink."

"Yah," sighed her friend, a fat and weary woman with concentric
rings of flesh about her eyes. "Look that American girlie on the board,
what she think? She hurt herself like that."

"She not able my mother care for herself or nothing."

"I know, dear."

"She dies like so—sssst—after long life. She work hard."

"I *know*, dear."

It ain't right, is it?" She nodded once, decisively, and said, "My father he still strong and smoke big cigar I buy for him. He sleep with
women and give her money and everything. Ain't nice old man like
that. He make eye at every young girl—"

"Bad young girlie," said the plump woman to the sand, the water, and the figure now climbing back onto the rocks.

The tanned one pulled at her dress and said, "That's why, here in this country, many people go off on roof for fall down. My children go away to Detroit and *I* give money to my papa."

"No justice on earth, darling," said the sad plump one.

2

The girl, the fine diver, went off the rocks again, measuring only with a frown the interior demands of her lonely stunt, absent from the beach on the parapets of ambition. She had scraped the cotton suit on a rock. The small split showed an edge of white breast, the first hard growth of the departure from girlhood. Some of the idlers had gathered in silence on the breakwater to watch her. "You want to tell me no, Freddy? I'm telling *you* no," the fat swimmer insisted. But she did not see them; she had nothing to say to them; her regard was absorbed by the patch of black water and the rules of her skill.

Back on the beach, another immature and pretty girl sat with her feet drawn under her on the sands. No one, not even Freddy, the fat swimmer's friend, gave more than a glance to this one, whose tanned plumpness in stylish knee-length shorts promised an eventual stylish willingness while her profile remained strict, suburban, and pure. Her mother, shriveled to creamed skin rather than casual flesh, squatted like the image of her age by her side, but this was not the reason that the free-ranging eyes of the beach passed over the daughter so lightly. The men sensed that she feared to lie on grass because of disease, dirt, and small animals, that she shuddered at the thought of diving into the tricky, steaming, polluted waters, that despite her prettiness she had put herself apart from the play of caprice, open-mouthed with laughter, and the risks of pleasure. "Look at the girl on the pier, the one that's diving again," this cute creature said.

"She's headed for earache, that's for sure," her mother commented with satisfaction. "Maybe she doesn't read the paper and how the water's unsafe. Dangerous for bathing. Full of organisms."

"I'm getting hungry, Mother"—wrinkling her junior-miss nose and hugging herself as her favorite starlet did.

"I *said* we'd stop at the Howard Johnson's."

Meanwhile, the diver scrambled over the rocks, up onto the pier, took three or four mincing, dancing steps, and bent her knees for her renewed essay at a controlled style. Her wide temples glowed pinker and pinker with the blood under her skin and the impact of water. Her innocence—an innocence of lessons—was informed by the heat and by the pressure of her blood which brought her climbing, diving, repeating this gesture again and again past the heaped-up rock. Had she seen them and gone on, it would have spoken for an angry and stubborn pride; but her way was the way of habit, of grace, and of a passionate ignorance, a deep communion with belly-smash on the shore of Lake Erie at Cleveland.

The plump lady from the flats was disturbed. "My doctor say: Playsuit! No stockings! Like that you have no more colds for winter-time. You have upper repertory affection, Doctor Sczymanski say. Neighbor she look at playsuit, close mouth, she say: shame! What can I do, darling?"

"That American girl, *she* have no shame," remarked the tanned woman whose father smoked big cigars. "Everybody is look at her legs"—and they both fell into a musing silence, and looked.

The beach was silent while a skin of complicity tightened like the dry sun about them all. Gradually these visitors to the September sands moved toward the breakwater, each one marvelously hushed because, if they said nothing, it could be presumed to be their habit and their devotion, an abandon to mutism in the heat, a pious thing superior to their daily selves: and thus, if the rip in the girl's suit grew longer, it was not their place to warn her of it. Let each creature hunger for itself alone—Freddy poked his pal to mean this—and thus sent only appetite in the pursuit of others. The veiny old men moved fastest.

Within a few moments the beach was almost deserted except for the couple busily twisting and tickling in their well-worn place. The girl sat up with a jerk, spreading sand in an abrupt movement of her thighs, while her friend grinned, saying, "I'm not connerdicting you." He pulled her down again.

3

The tear in the diver's suit widened; the gash in this black second skin showed, to the fat man, the whiteness of belly, and then, to Freddy's bemusement, the flexing folds of flesh. Just once Freddy saw her fingers feel for the rip, but her body's intelligence calculated on nothing but the demands of perfection, and the thought of care for that clothing which was outside desire did not move further than the impatient, rummaging hand. She did not glance at herself. Turned to her idea, fixed on some inner certainty, she closed the split with her fingers, then forgot it, then let go.

She dived and climbed without liability to the give of cloth or the alteration of her world which Freddy and the big-bellied swimmer brought. She scrambled up dripping, let her eyes roam absently over the tense strollers gathering on the rocks, and dived once more. The pale wetness of her flesh opened to them like a wound under the suit while the girl, if she thought of her body at all, thought only of her skill and of her rehearsals for its sake. She was secure (small splash and ripple) in the exercise of method. She was an expert.

"You trying to tell me no, Freddy?" Behind the fat swimmer and his friend, past the city beach on this September afternoon, the machinery of road construction throbbed and the insect hiss of an afternoon breeze occupied the trees on the slope leading up to the highway past the tables, the shelters, and the park restroom. Because his mouth was dry, the fat man pointed to the girl and whispered, "Lookit." He squeezed the muscles of his friend's arm, thumb and forefinger twanging, and then they both moved forward again. The heat and the effort brought shiny tears to his eyes and a dampness to his forehead. The thickness of his body in swimming trunks, sagging at the middle and the rear, bulging beneath, looked enormous in the sunlight and the intimacy of one leg's motion against the other.

Repetitious, formal, and oblivious, the girl's ambition seemed madness or a mad joke to the watchers. It pleased the fat man; it was a delight to him. He opened his mouth, like a swimmer, and put his tongue sideways to breathe more easily. Freddy—as to him—he could hardly believe it. He wanted to float up an inner tube and go out someplace to think about it.

When she climbed over the rocks once again, the rip widened almost audibly, and still she did not see that her suit was ready to hang in tatters. No one warned her—as we do not warn a madman that he is talking nonsense—but they sighed when she extended her arms for the dive. The fat man sighed, All of them leaned together now, men and women, sharing the girl and sharing each other, waiting for their world's confirmation against the challenge she brought it, an assurance of which they were in need before the return to autumn and the years rapid upon them. A whiteness of breast flashed out, its pink sprouting from the girl's body like a delicate thing nurtured in the dark. But the day was bright and the shadows short. Looking at this tender and abstracted girl, the old Polish woman shivered at her own memories of paleness, of resiliency, of pink colors. The fat man, too, partook of their communion, frowning darkly, the green branch switching at his flanks, his knees slightly bent. He pinched his friend instead of himself. Now, her hair flat on her head and the flush of pleasure high on her cheeks after the repeated slap of her forehead against water, the girl was diving in a diminished rhythm, worn out but blind to risk, finished but unable to stop. The moment when her breast and belly slipped by the surface was the fat man's favorite.

The diver, that object for the vindictive imaginations of old men and old women, seemed to pause to acknowledge their study of her, but saw nothing, saw nothing again, and went on. The fat man's eyelids had dropped. He was moved. As she climbed, dripping and critical, bewitched by mastery of her body, feeling, if the presence of the others had come through to her at all, only a reward of praise earned through the long summer, the fat man released his friend's arm to break the silence at last with a shrill whoop. Then the old Polish woman screamed, "You're nekked, girlie! *Nekked!*"

The fat man, his friend, the salesman, the student, many of them were now yelling their cheers at her. Poised for her dive, she must suddenly have seen them and seen herself in their sight. Her look was one of incredulity. Her eyes turned from herself to their shouting, gaping, heavy-tongued mouths and back to the loose cloth dangling from straps. She did not speak. She turned her face from them. Its stern and peaceful determination hardly altered. Then suddenly the extended arms flashed down; she ran, she did not dive, she jumped and rolled into the oily water. Despite this folding upon herself, their eyes searched out a glimpse of sunlight flesh, white and pink and tender. While the crowd applauded, the student shouted, "She wants to drown herself," and leaped into the water.

"I'll get her! Me too! *Me!*"

The young man reached for her hair and only touched it before she wrenched free. She doubled under, holding herself, and then she was swimming. The crowd was roaring. Four, five, six of the men had pushed to the edge of the breakwater. The girl kicked forward and swam with short, quick, sure strokes, straight out into the lake, while a cluster of young men and old, their smiles strict in pursuit, tumbled down the rocks to be the first to catch her. The fat man, paddling furiously, was ahead of Freddy. The righteousness of a mob's laughter urged them to be swift, but the girl was very strong, very skillful, gifted, and encumbered by nothing but her single thought.

Raymond De Capite (b. 1927) was born and raised in Cleveland and was educated at Western Reserve University. He is a professional journalist and writer and has written two novels portraying Italian immigrants and their American children on Cleveland's old South Side: *The Coming of Fabrizze* (1960) and *The Lost King* (1961), from which this lively and amusing picture of a filial relationship has been selected. *The Lost King* was the basis for Paul Newman and Joanne Woodward's film *Harry and Son* (1984).

Chapter 11

On the way home I stopped at the open market on West Twenty-Fifth Street and Lorain Avenue. I bought hot peppers and plum tomatoes for my father. I bought walnuts and poppy-seed cake. I went across the street to Gray's Drug Store and bought half a gallon of red wine. Candles were on sale and so I bought a golden one as big as a quart bottle.

My father was making coffee when I staggered into the kitchen. I showed him the groceries and the potash. I told him the bad news. He shuffled into the bedroom and closed the door against me.

"The coffee's ready," I said. "Come out and have your breakfast. Don't let a lost job spoil everything. Look what I brought you. It's a poppy-seed cake. And it's still warm."

There was no sound from the bedroom.

"Look what else I brought," I said. "You'll never guess. What a surprise. We'll have a celebration. And wait till you see this candle. What we need in this house is a light of gold. Things have been getting grayer and grayer since Nina left. Why should we live like spiders, Pa? Tell me why. From now on we'll eat and have our discussions by candlelight. Maybe we should dress for dinner. And then after dinner we'll have brandy and cigars. By candlelight. We'll go over the events of the day and make plans for tomorrow. I have this feeling we'll look better to each other by candlelight. We might even become friends, Pa. Tell me one thing. Is there any reason in the world why we should live like spiders?"

He came out and went into the bathroom.

"Now here's your horoscope in the *Plain Dealer,*" I said. "Are you listening? Pay attention. It says: 'Be audacious. Stimulating rays for mental work, developing new ideas, trying new fields. You are in a favorable position for personal, professional and business ventures. You should emphasize your fine imagination, foresight and keen judgment. There's no reason in the world for you to live like a spider.' Well, Pa, how's that sound?"

He was cursing his luck.

Next day I went back on the watermelon wagon and he wouldn't even look at me. He started to do the cooking. No longer could I eat that food. He loaded it with more and more hot pepper. Everything exploded in my mouth. One evening I sat there watching him prepare supper. He fried pork chops with cherry peppers. He put three more of those peppers in the salad. He boiled two potatoes and sliced them in a dish. He put olive oil in a frying pan and dropped in a handful of dried red devil peppers. He fried the peppers black and then poured everything over the potatoes. He sat down and took a deep breath.

"You forgot to set fire to the bread," I said.

Day after day he took terrible punishment. Sweat dripped off him. His mouth hung open and his dark eyes seemed to be melting away. In the middle of the night he would rush to the bathroom where he cursed fate and his scorched bowels. Afterwards he went out to sit on the porch in the dead smoky air. Sometimes he rocked until dawn.

August had come. South wind brought clouds of soot and smoke from the mills. First thing in the morning I wiped all dirt away with a damp cloth. Next morning there would be dirt again as though some witch came in the night to sweep with a black broom over tables and chairs and window sills. All the curtains in the house had gone dark along the edges. It was like living black lace. Nina had promised to come twice a month to wash and iron the curtains. Finally Sophie Nowak offered to do it.

"Please mind your own business," my father told her. "I enjoy the curtains. I look at them and think of my daughter. I don't have much to think about these days. If you wash the curtains I wouldn't think of my daughter at all."

The long slow days of that August seemed to burn hope and delight out of everyone in the neighborhood. It was the worst month of the year. Two and three nights a week there was uproar in the Dew Drop Inn. Men came plunging through the door to fight in the street. Harsh cries went up like ugly birds. Presently the black and white police car came to scatter the crowd. One night the policemen jumped out of their car and someone jumped right in and drove it away.

There were bitter arguments in the coffee house. Seldom did the Greeks fight with their fists. They pounded the tables and insulted each other along with God. Each would listen and wait for the other to finish his speech. It went on to the point of danger and then as if by signal they turned and walked away big with triumph like kings. Most of them worked as painters of structural steel. They were related in various ways and those arguments would start about work or gambling and then shade into old family rivalries and foul play.

It was on one of those hot smoky nights that Rakowski smashed his furniture. He drank himself into a fury and staggered home to smash chairs and lamps and tables. Next morning he burst into tears when he saw the house in ruins. He cried and cried about it. He started to cry about his hatch-tender's job in the steel mill and then he cried because his daughter had run away ten years before with a Russian cabinet-maker. He cried about Poland and America and then because he had so much reason to cry.

A few nights later Florio drank too much wine. At three in the morning he was playing arias from the Italian operas on his phonograph. That music woke everyone in Lincoln Court. Someone called the police. Just before they came we heard this thrilling tenor voice lifted in the night. A sob was torn from the heart of that singer. Now his song was lifted again and given and lost in the giving like the soar of a fountain. Two policemen were pounding on the door.

That tenor was singing himself free of the despair that would soon fill my own heart. I had promised to free myself with a song. It was too late and too soon. For it was on the first day of September that Peggy Haley married Edmund Hatcher.

Three days before the wedding she came over to see me. All she talked about was her Edmund. He was brave and true. He was taking her away from the alley. I listened to her and then I kissed her hard on the mouth. Her body started to come alive. She pushed me away.

"Why did you do that?" I said

"Do what?"

"Push me back like that."

"You shouldn't be kissing me, Paul."

"Why did you kiss me back?"

"I didn't. Besides, it's like a good-by."

"It didn't feel like a good-by."

"Well, it is."

"I just don't understand it," I said. "I really don't."

"Understand what?"

"You never gave me a chance. You were playing with me the whole time. What's wrong with me?"

"You're the one that's playing, Paul. You're playing through life. It was the same in school and everything."

"Was I playing with you? Didn't I tell you I loved you?"

"Are you talking about that night in Lincoln Park?"

"That's right."

"You're acting silly, Paul. Kissing doesn't mean that much."

"I guess it doesn't. But you're the only girl I ever kissed. And you're the only one I ever wanted to kiss."

"Kissing is like dreaming. It's like dreaming about love."

"Is it? When did you know you were dreaming?"

"I'm not sure."

"Did you know it then in the park?"

"Maybe I wasn't too sure right then. I do like you, Paul. I like you an awful lot."

"But you weren't too sure. How about Edmund? What if you wake up some morning after you're married and find out it was all a dream? You were dreaming about love. Like you did with me."

"That won't happen!"

"How do you know? You're talking to an expert on the subject. Ask anybody in Lincoln Court. Ask my father. He thinks I'm dreaming about life and everybody else is living. Maybe he's wrong. Maybe he's dreaming about me."

"Not so loud, Paul."

"And I'm beginning to dream about the neighbors, too. You should hear what they tell me. They stop me on the street. They give me all kinds of advice. They tell me I'm too old to work on a watermelon wagon. They tell me I should wake up. They tell me I'm too old to play the harmonica. I tell them I'm happy and they say no, no, no. Does it sound like I'm dreaming? What kind of life is this? I do my best and everybody thinks it's all wrong!"

"Not so loud. They'll hear you."

"What's the difference if they hear me? They know everything about me."

"I better go."

"Maybe you better. Why did you come over here in the first place? Wait, wait. Don't tell me. Let me guess. You want me to play the harmonica at your reception. Is that it?"

"No!"

"Why then? Do you want to be sure I'm suffering? Take a good look. And then go home. One of these days you won't be able to turn away so easy. You'll have to look things in the face. And I see that look in your eyes, too. Shame on you. Shame on you to be all excited like that just because I feel like I do!"

"I don't feel that way!" she said, bursting into tears. "I came over because my mother said you were at the house one night! Playing the harmonica for me!"

"And you're lying about how you feel!"

"I'm going, Paul!"

"And I'll tell you something else! From now on I'm never going to be in love with anybody! I mean it! Once is too much! This is the last time for me! From now on I'll be looking the other way!"

"Good night, Paul!"

"Good night and good-by!"

On the day of the wedding I was marching from room to room in the house. My father puffed his pipe and watched me. I went into the bathroom and slammed the door against his burning eyes. He called out that it was getting late.

"Late for what?" I said.

"Aren't you going to the wedding?"

"No, I'm not."

"Do you think you can hide from it?"

"What do you want me to do? Go over there and throw rice? Join the celebration? Play the harmonica for them?"

"It's what you promised. You talk a good game."

To spite him I rushed over to St. Augustine's Church. I was late and so I sat in the last pew near the door. The ceremony was ending. Father Murphy was saying those final precious words. A breathless silence followed. Edmund turned to kiss Peggy lightly on the mouth. So shy and innocent was it that my heart ached with sudden pity for them. I slipped out of the church. I went across the street to Lincoln Park.

The church doors opened. People streamed out and formed an aisle. Suddenly Peggy was there. Never had I seen such beauty. The sunlight of morning was caught by the shimmering white swirl of gown and veil. I had to turn away. All the love in my heart meant nothing. My darling Peggy was lost to me forever.

I went home. My father was reading a magazine on the porch. In that moment I resented his loneliness and blamed him for it. I was afraid to talk and so I hurried past him into the kitchen. He followed me. I wanted to cry out. It seemed he was in pursuit of me with loneliness. I went into the bathroom and locked the door.

"Is it over?" he said. "It couldn't happen and wouldn't happen. And now it happened. It's like death a little."

I said nothing.

"I knew you'd end up looking in the window," he said.

He was right again.

That night at the wedding reception I was looking through the window of the Polish National Home. Peggy danced with everyone. She was laughing and laughing. Her cheeks were like roses in the night of her hair. For a while I was hoping she would come to tell me that her heart was secretly broken. I was foolish. Never once did she think that of me.

My final hope was that something would happen to ruin the wedding celebration. The best thing was to shoot myself through the heart and then fall across the doorway. I would die with my eyes open and that look would haunt Peggy the rest of her days. It would be a sensation in the newspapers. They would say I died for love. Afterward they would study my background and say I was unstable. I was thinking about it when trouble started in the hall. The butcher Kroger was serving at the bar and he scolded Rakowski for drinking so much.

"Why don't you stop awhile?" said Kroger.

"Are you paying for it?" said Rakowski.

"Drown yourself then," said Kroger.

A man beside Rakowski was muttering.

"What's that?" said Rakowski.

"Bartender's right," said the man.

"Listen, Greek," said Rakowski, putting his hand on the man.

"I'm no Greek."

"Russian!"

"I'm no Russian."

"What are you?"

"Polish."

"Liar!" said Rakowski.

He hit the man in the face. Kroger reached over to hit Rakowski on the side of the head. Rakowski turned and pulled him right over the bar. A crowd gathered around them. Everyone was pushing. Women were kicking and swinging their purses. Uproar spread through the hall like a wild new dance. The music stopped and started. The accordionist was playing "the Star-Spangled Banner." Someone hit him on the forehead with half a chicken.

Peggy and Edmund were being led through the front door by their families. Peggy was crying. I had moved away.

"They spoil everything," she said. "They just spoil everything."

"Never mind," said her mother. "Never mind them."

"It's all right," said Edmund.

"Your nose is bleeding," said his mother. "Did they hit you?"

"No, Ma, no," he said. "I'm all right."

"It's too much excitement for one day," said his mother. "You be sure to get your rest. Do you hear?"

"Please, Ma, please," he said.

There were kisses and tears. At last Peggy and Edmund were left alone on the sidewalk. They stood there in a helpless way. He took her hand. A piercing scream came from the hall.

"My God," said Peggy. "Let's get away from this place."

"I'll get the car," said Edmund.

He looked around as though lost.

"Well, what are you waiting for?" she said.

He went for the car.

Peggy was wiping her tears away when she saw me.

"Paul," she said blushing. "Where were you?"

"I just came by," I said.

"Why didn't you come in? I was looking for you."

"I had some things to do."

"It's a fine thing," she said.

"What is?"

"You play the harmonica at everybody's wedding and you didn't even play one song for me."

"I played enough songs for you. It was a waste of time. From now on I'll play songs for myself."

"Where's your father?" she said. "We invited him."

"He's home."

"Is he all right? Is he feeling all right?"

"He's having trouble. With his bowels."

"Really, Paul, what's the matter with you?"

"Nothing's the matter with me."

"What a thing to say! And to a bride!"

"What was I supposed to say? He was dreaming of love and a star fell in his lap? My father's having his troubles. Just because you're a bride doesn't change his condition."

Edmund drove up. He got out of the car.

"Where were you, Paul?" he said. "I didn't see you. Why didn't you come in and have something to eat?"

We stood there. They looked abandoned. Once again my heart ached with pity for them.

"Congratulations," I said. "I want to wish you the best of everything. The very best. I mean it."

"Oh, Paul," she said. "You were always so sweet."

Finally she gathered up her white gown and slipped into the car. She scolded Edmund for closing the door before she had the dress safely inside. As they drove off she turned to give me a long look. She wanted to be sure she was leaving a broken heart.

I stood there. My heart felt like a prune. I wanted to lie down and die right on the sidewalk. I looked around. Fire from the steel mills leaped on the sky. The night was choked with smoke and dust. I thought of my father. It was good to know I could go home and have it out with him.

He was drinking wine in the kitchen. I started to slam dishes and cups around. All at once we were in an argument.

"I don't think she was the girl for you," he said.

"I guess not!"

"She's bowlegged, too."

"I know, I know! I wanted a bowlegged girl!"

"Besides, she was too fat for you."

"Too fat for what? I didn't have to carry her through life!"

"Maybe you'll wake up now."

"Wake up to what, Pa?"

"To the way things are!"

"That's why I'm dreaming!"

"By Christ, you act like a baby! Hold still a minute! I'll warm a bottle for you and powder your ass! And then I'll tuck you in and sing you a lullaby!"

We argued and argued. I came close to tears. He blamed me for everything gone wrong. I blamed him. He started to throw his glass at me and then saw there was wine in it. He drained it off. He gave me a scornful look and went into the bedroom.

After a while I made a pot of coffee. I took a cup of it out on the porch. I sat in the rocker and tried to play the harmonica. There was no music in me. I went back into the kitchen to make peace with my father. I invited him to come out and talk things over. I picked up the *Plain Dealer*.

"Listen to this, Pa," I said. "Here's your horoscope in the *Plain Dealer*. Are you listening? It says: 'In romance, personal and domestic affairs, be diplomatic. Some unexpected situations may develop. It's an opportune time for making needed improvements; also for travel and holding conferences.' Did you hear that? Maybe we should light the candle and have a conference. A peace conference."

I told him we should paint the house.

"I'll get that aluminum ladder from Theodore," I said. "He says I can lift it with one finger. We should start before the bad weather sets in. I was thinking we'd paint the house white and the windows black. The windows will match the curtains. And then we'll plaster the cracks in the walls. And how about wine, Pa? We should make some wine. Some strong wine. Some very strong wine to keep us going. Wait then. Maybe we should make whiskey instead. We'll get drunk every day. We won't care what's happening because we won't know."

I told him next year would be full of surprises for us.

"And another thing," I said. "I took your advice, Pa. I ordered a rocking chair with a cushion. We'll rock together. We'll hold hands and rock and make plans for revenge."

There was no sound from the bedroom.

"I might as well tell you the rest of it," I said. "Sam Ross was talking to me. He says he'll have to let me go unless I do better. It was kind of a shock, Pa. And there's something else. Can you stand more bad news? Brace yourself. It's a terrible thing that I lost Peggy. I realize that. But I lost something worse. Are you listening? Two thousand years, Pa. I lost two thousand years of history."

Laughter was like sharp stones in me.

Don Robertson (b. 1929) has won many awards for his fiction, much of it set in his native Cleveland, where he also attended Western Reserve University and served as a reporter on the *Cleveland Plain Dealer*. This selection comes from the first novel of a trilogy: *The Greatest Thing Since Sliced Bread* (1965), *The Sum Total of Now*, and *The Greatest Thing That Almost Happened*. The East Ohio Gas explosion of 1944 is the historic event Robertson used as the setting for this chapter. Leaking liquid natural gas from a huge storage tank ignited on October 20 and caused the most disastrous fire in Cleveland's history. One hundred and thirty people died, 680 were left homeless, and seventy-nine homes and two factories were leveled. The full horror of the catastrophe is mitigated by the point of view of a child—whose wagon, Crimson Streak, is always seen from over his shoulder as NOSMIRC KAERTS.

The neighborhood that adjoined the East Ohio Gas Co.'s storage tanks and liquefication plant was stable, neat, drab and noisy. Slovenians lived there, many Slovenians. And Serbs. And Croats. And Lithuanians. And Czechs. And Ukrainians. and even a few Hungarians and Poles. The Slovenians were the definite majority, however. The neighborhood was famous because of them. The Cleveland mayor, a fellow named Frank J. Lausche, had been born there. And, in this year of 1944, he was the Democratic candidate for governor of Ohio. This made nearly everyone in the neighborhood proud. Everywhere you went, you saw LAUSCHE signs. They were especially prominent along St. Clair Avenue, which was the neighborhood's main artery. It was this St. Clair Avenue that was responsible for a great deal of the noise. It was an official Truck Route. What with the war and all, it trembled and banged night and day with a clamor of immense tractortrailers heading to and from such eastern points as Ashtabula, Conneaut, Erie and Buffalo. These trucks, plus the regular vehicular traffic, plus the street-car line that ran down the middle of St. Clair, made it one of the busiest streets in the city. It certainly had to be one of the loudest. Both sides of St. Clair, extending east from East 55th Street to East 79th Street, were crowded with a vast rickety swarm of small business establishments. Most of them were housed in flimsy frame buildings. The homes in the neighborhood, most of them owneroccupied, were also of frame construction. North of St. Clair, fingering off toward Lake Erie and the plant and the tanks, the streets (East 61st, 62nd, 63rd, 64th and so on) were lined with these frame dwellings. They were neat and un-distinguished, but the people who lived in them had great pride of pos-session. They had lived in them ever since coming to this country, and ownership was important to them. These were not lazy people. The men worked hard (and drank hard too; there were many saloons along St. Clair Avenue, and none of them was hurting for business), and they were big eaters, good Catholics, good Democrats, raised large fami-lies, had homely wives and pretty daughters, kept their wives pregnant and got their daughters married early. Most of the children in this neighborhood attended Wilson Junior High and East High School, and many of the boys were excellent sandlot baseball players. Some of them had even turned professional. (Even Mayor Lausche had once played professional baseball. Thirty years before, he had performed without any particular distinction at third base for Duluth.) But the neighborhood's largest athletic reputation did not come from baseball. It came from the sport of bowling. A good percentage of the nation's really accomplished bowlers, both amateur and professional, came from Cleveland, and many of them lived in this neighborhood along St. Clair Avenue. In this neighborhood, there were two paths to finan-cial success. One, you could open a saloon. Two, you could open a bowling alley. Especially now, what with the war and all and ration-ing. The men of the neighborhood were mostly factory workers, and they were earning more money than they'd ever dreamed of. The big word was Overtime. With all this good money rolling in, naturally the people had to spend it. Even the frugal homeowners in this neigh-borhood. Sure, they saved some of it, but still there was so much left over, and so the people spent a great deal of their time in the saloons and the bowling alleys. For the first time in their lives, these people could afford to be both thrifty and profligate. It was quite a feeling, and they cherished it. After the war, they would have a fine creamy future. So all right, maybe the neighborhood *was* drab. And no one denied that it was noisy. But, the thing was—its residents had nothing to be ashamed of. Most of them owned their own homes. They had been in this country, some of them, forty years or more, and they no longer were strangers (not with their Frank Lausche running for governor!), and they were doing quite well, thank you very much. They were Citizens and Taxpayers, and so what if their names *were* Lausche and Grdina and Grbec and Blabolil and Nagy and Sternad and Redlich and Vasilauskas and Chaloupka and Oravec and Kovacic? They paid their bills; they socked away some of their money; they had a good time with the rest of it; they played baseball; they bowled; their daughters were pretty; they attended mass regularly; they wholeheartedly existed as *Americans,* and hardly anyone was foolish to question this. On this 20th day of October in the year 1944, as the vapor spread out from those tanks there at the end of East 62nd Street on the cliff overlooking Lake Erie, as it trickled along the gutters and into the sewers, as it proceeded slowly and spookily, moving through the neighborhood, making people sniff and frown and idly wonder where the funny smell was coming from, if you'd been walking through this neighborhood, your surroundings would have struck you as being a bit stolid and nondescript, and you certainly would not have been excited. This simply was not the sort of community to get people worked up. It was *there,* and its thereness was about all you could say for it.

"Why didn't you say something when we were back at that lady's house?"
"I didn't have to Go then."
"Can you wait until we get to St. Clair?"
"How far's St. Clair?"
"About a block. As soon as we get there, I'll take you to a gas station or something."
"Okay."

At about 2:30 or so, just as the East-Central football game was beginning, Stanley Chaloupka arrived home from school. Harry Wrobleski stared at the back of Judy Saum's head. Miss Edna Daphne Frost went into her bathroom and washed her face and hands. She was smiling, and her eyes were moist. G. Henderson LeFevre tore open the seal on the bottle of Ancient Age. He dropped two ice cubes into the glass, filled the rest of the glass with whiskey. Casimir Redlich was beginning to worry about Irving Bernstein. Mrs. Imogene Brookes was having trouble with her breath. The passionate optician was on his way home! This could mean only one thing—her telephone call had caused him to get up the nerve to tell his wife. Ah, how about that! Yay! Whoopee! Praise God!

Tiddlelump, they hurried north on Norwood Road toward St. Clair Avenue. Sandra was letting out small pinched sounds. Tiddlelump, they bounced across a street called Glass Avenue, and a block ahead was St. Clair. "Won't be long now," he said.

A squeak came from Sandra.

A piece of rye bread was in one of Stanley Chaloupka's pockets. He took it out, sat down on the front steps of the little frame house at 670 East 63rd Street and began to eat. He chewed slowly. The weather wasn't particularly cold, and it was comfortable just sitting there. He hoped his buddy Morris Bird III had remembered. He didn't want to think how he'd feel if Morris Bird III had forgotten. Oh, but that was stupid. Morris Bird III wasn't the sort to forget something so important. The bread was a little stale, but this was the way Stanley Chaloupka liked it. Chewy bread was the best kind. If people thought he was crazy because he liked stale bread, let them. They didn't know what they were missing. It had been a long time since he'd worried what people thought of him. He would survive. He had survived so far, and he would keep on surviving. He had his Atlantic & Pacific Railroad, and he had the view of the boats and the trains from his bedroom window, and he had great pride in his father's important position at that camp in Georgia, and he'd never deliberately tried to hurt anyone, and so what if people *didn't* understand why he was the way he was. He would stay out of their way. He grinned his big black grin, bestowing it on the houses across the street, on the sky, on all faraway trains and engineers and freighters and captains, on the birds, on the street and the neighborhood and the high swaying old streetcars that lurched up and down St. Clair Avenue, and he felt better than he had felt in months. His buddy was coming. His good dear old friend. The engineer on the Extra runs of the Atlantic & Pacific Railroad. Ah, life was good, and a person had a right to grin. Stanley Chaloupka swallowed the last of his bread, looked up the street toward St. Clair. Morris Bird III would be coming from that direction. A little later, Stanley Chaloupka's mother opened the door behind him. She told him she had fixed some sandwiches for him and Morris Bird III. She asked him did he have any idea how Morris Bird III was coming. No, said Stanley Chaloupka. Well, said Mrs. Chaloupka, it's quite a long trip by bus and streetcar or whatever. Stanley Chaloupka nodded. It's nice to have a friend who's willing to travel such a long distance, said Mrs. Chaloupka. Yes, said Stanley Chaloupka. He thanked his mother for making the sandwiches.

Then he asked her how his grandmother was feeling. Mrs. Eva Szucs suffered from chronic heartburn, and she belched a great deal. This morning she'd been quite sick to her stomach. She's lying down, Mrs. Chaloupka told her son. You and Morris try to be as quiet as you can, all right? Stanley Chaloupka nodded. I'll be quiet, he said. Ah, said his mother, smiling, as if I had to ask *you* to be *quiet*. She went back inside the house. Stanley Chaloupka again turned his gaze up the street toward St. Clair. Something . . . some sort of vague odor . . . made him frown for a moment. But, whatever it was, it went away quickly. He grinned. He grinned widely. He grinned at everything.

St. Clair Avenue! It wouldn't be long now!

Tiddlelump, and Morris Bird III dragged NOSMIRC KAERTS around the corner. This was a right turn, and now they were on St. Clair Avenue. East 63rd Street was just one block ahead. They had almost made it. A turn north on East 63rd Street, a short walk, and they would be at Stanley Chaloupka's home.

But first, though, he had to find someplace where Sandra could Go.

He looked around for a gas station. There was one behind him, but it was about two or three blocks away.

Sandra made an ominous sound.

He looked ahead. The street was lined with narrow wooden buildings. Tiddlelump, he hurried forward, past GRBEC'S VARIETY STORE and a place called FOOD LUNCH BEER and a place called ZARECKS'S 5★ 10★ and 25★ and a place called JOHN'S BARBER SHOP, and then they were in front of a place called OLGA'S HOUSE OF BEAUTY, and he stopped the wagon, turned to Sandra and said: "Go."

She was out of the wagon in about half of a half of a second. She dashed outside inside OLGA'S HOUSE OF BEAUTY, and then Morris Bird III heard a muffled sound of shrieks and laughter. He seated himself on the edge of NOSMIRC KAERTS and began wondering if her Going consisted of #1 or #2. Oh well, it felt good to sit down for a moment. He didn't deny it—he was kind of pooped. It had been kind of that kind of a day.

G. Henderson LeFevre lay on his bed and listened to the sounds of the city and worked on his second drink. His face was warm, but he still saw the face of poor Marva. East High and Central High played through a scoreless first quarter. Judy Saum wondered what she could do to let that stupid Harry Wrobleski know *she* was interested too. Mrs. Brookes went to her closet, dragged out a suitcase and began packing. Tom would be home in about two hours, and she would tell him as soon as he arrived. Irving Bernstein was wearing a new hat. It was a bowler, the first bowler he'd ever owned. He was a thinnish fellow, and the man at the hat store had told him the bowler would make him look more robust. Now, as he drove out St. Clair Avenue toward Casimir Redlich's place, Irving Bernstein kept glancing at himself in the rearview mirror. He didn't quite know whether he liked his new hat. Then he decided he had better like it. It had cost too much for him not to have liked it. Mrs. Barbara Sternad smoked a cigarette and thought about her husband. She sighed. She knew she should have started already with her vacuuming. Ah, but there was time. With Ralph in England, she had nothing *but* time. She patted her hair, adjusted her LONDON kerchief. As she packed, Mrs. Brookes kept looking out the window for sign of G. Henderson LeFevre. He would be coming soon now. He would march next door and tell his wife, and then Imogene Brookes would tell Tom, and then the future would be nothing but marshmallows and chocolate sauce. Casimir Redlich picked up his trumpet and resumed his work with the *Fra Diavolo*. G. Henderson LeFevre grinned at the ceiling and told himself: COURAGE, BOY. SHOW THE WORLD THE STUFF YOU'RE MADE OF. Irving Bernstein parked his car in front of Casimir Redlich's place. He tucked his briefcase under an arm, got out of the car. He adjusted his new hat, cleared his throat, marched up the sidewalk, climbed the porch steps, rang the Redlich doorbell. He had to ring it twice before its sound penetrated the sound of Redlich's trumpet.

Sandra was smiling when she emerged from OLGA'S HOUSE OF BEAUTY. She took her seat in the wagon and said: "Thank you."

"Sure," said Morris Bird III. He stood up, grabbed the wagon handle and started pulling. Tiddlelump.

"A nice lady helped me," said Sandra.

"Great."

"My skirt got all wudged up, and her name was Renee."

"Mm."

"She had the prettiest red hair you ever seen."

"Great. Fine. Big deal."

"They all giggled, and they all were real nice. The ladies in that place, I mean. Some of them had their heads in big Things."

"Mm."

"They giggled real good. They seemed real happy."

"Uh huh," said Morris Bird III.

They passed on old lady who wore a babushka. She smiled at them.

The sun had become quite warm. Morris Bird III unbuckled the chinstrap of his cap. Then they were at the corner of East 63rd Street. They turned, waited for a break in the St. Clair traffic. Then, tiddlelump, they clattered across St. Clair. They headed north on East 63rd.

Up ahead, on the left, was a cluster of gas tanks. Tiddlelump, and all-ofasudden Morris Bird's sensitive smeller detected something peculiar. He blinked. Maybe he was seeing things, but not far in front of him, maybe two or three dozen yards, there was a kind of fog. It was thin and smeary, and it hung close to the gutters. "Huh," he said.

"What?" said Sandra.

"Nothing."

Casimir Redlich wheeled himself to the front door, opened it and said: Irving my friend, I'm afraid your father has dropped dead. Irving Bernstein opened and closed his mouth several times, then asked Casimir Redlich to repeat what he'd just said. Nodding, Casimir Redlich repeated it. Thank you, said Irving Bernstein when Casimir Redlich had finished, thank you very *muhhhhhch*. The last word came out in a sort of wail. Then Irving Bernstein began to keen. He turned and staggered off Casimir Redlich's front porch. His keening was shrill. He lurched to his car and got inside. In sliding into the front seat, he knocked off his hat. It fell to the floor, and he didn't bother with it.

A man in a strange hat came running off a porch. He was crying like a child, only louder. He jumped into an automobile. It leaped away from the curb. He turned around in someone's driveway, only the car's wheels missed the driveway and plowed a furrow in the grass. The tires made shrieky noises. So did the gears. The car backed out into the street, then headed south toward St. Clair.

"What's wrong with him?" said Sandra.

"How should I know?" said Morris Bird III, squinting and sniffing.

Sandra didn't say anything.

The sun really was warm. Morris Bird III took off his cap, handed it back to Sandra. "Here," he said. "Hold this."

Sandra nodded, dropped the cap in her lap with the alarm clock and the jar of Peter Pan Peanut Butter.

Still sniffing, Morris Bird III began checking house numbers. They practically were on top of the fog now, and the smell of it had become stronger, On the left was a 712, then a 694, and then he heard somebody yelling. He squinted ahead.

Stanley Chaloupka was standing on his front porch and waving his arms. "Bird!" he yelled. He was maybe half a block up the street.

"Chaloupka!" hollered Morris Bird III. "Stanley Chaloupka!"

"I smell something funny," said Sandra.

"Never mind that," said Morris Bird III. He began running forward. A few yards more, a few seconds more, and it all would be over. Tiddlelump went the wagon, careening. Sandra shrieked. Morris

Bird III grinned. He ran toward good old Stanley Chaloupka, and he heard birds, and then up jumped a huge hot orange ball, a great big fat whoosh of a

Casimir Redlich knew he had been maybe too abrupt with poor Irving Bernstein, but what would have been gained by beating around the bush? No matter how you sliced such news, it was bound to come as a shock. The way Casimir Redlich saw it, he hadn't really had much of a choice. He wheeled himself into the front room. He was just placing his trumpet to his lips when he was blown through the front of his house. The next thing he knew, he was sitting in the middle of the street. His shirt was on fire, and he was still holding his trumpet. He beat at his shirt and looked around. His house was gone. His mouth was open, and he did believe he was screaming, but he could hear nothing. Up the street, Stanley Chaloupka was enveloped in a smear of flame and incinerated on the spot. So was his mother, who had been standing in the kitchen. His grandmother, Mrs. Eva Szucs, was crushed to death by a roofbeam that fell across her bed and cut her in two. Over in the Hall of Armor of the Museum of Art, a Mrs. Helene K. Dallas was berating a boy named Theodore Karam for allegedly attaching (with the aid of chewing gum) a note saying SEROLOD OSSAVOB SKNITS on the back of the coat worn by a girl named Dolores Bovasso. Not that Mrs. Dallas particularly disagreed with the boy's judgment, but discipline was discipline. At 713 East 62nd Street, Mrs. Barbara Sternad had no sooner plugged in her vacuum cleaner when all the walls of her house turned pink. My Lord, she told herself, I've shortcircuited the house. Then her pink walls fell in. They were followed by orange flame, and she screamed. She shut her eyes, but not before the flames had seared her eyeballs. At Thomas Edison Field, a good two miles away, all the players and spectators looked up. They could feel the heat. Hey, said Harry Wrobleski to his friend Al Panetta, that must be some fire. Al Panetta nodded. Necks were craned. Harry Wrobleski estimated that the fire was about two blocks away, maybe three. Probably somebody's furnace blew up, said Al Panetta. The explosion had come from one of the spherical tanks at the East Ohio Gas Co. liquefication plant. It made a sound that was not so much a boom as a great hollow *whumm,* something like the sound a gas oven gives off when you light it. Only of course this was a much larger *whumm.* It created a yellow and orange balloon of flame that shot both up and out. Its height was about two thousand feet, and it could be seen twenty miles away. Mrs. Imogene Brooks turned on her bedside radio. What she needed was some nice calming music. She had already packed her lingerie and toilet articles. She began folding some blouses. Mrs. Sternad had been blinded. Her dress was on fire. Flaming boards fell on her. Shrieking, she staggered out into her front yard. She fell, rolled on the grass. Her vision was crimson. She beat at the flames with the sides of her arms. All over the neighborhood, houses were exploding. Walls fell away, and people and furniture came flying. Automobile tires blew up. Birds were fried. Some of them hung blackly from utility wires. The air seethed with wisps and puffs of fire. Flames ran along the gutters and down into the sewers, and then manhole covers exploded. G. Henderson LeFevre went to work on his third drink. A moment before, he'd heard a thud, but he'd paid it no mind. The paint on cars and buildings burst into flames from the heat. The roof flew off the liquefication plant, and all the cars in the parking lot were melted. All the people inside the liquefication were either roasted or torn into slivers or both. Windows were broken five miles away, and the heat could be felt within a radius of three miles. On one small street (Lake Court, just west of East 55th Street), eighteen of nineteen houses were flattened within a minute. Grass caught fire. Sidewalks melted and so did streets. Casimir Redlich sat in the middle of East 63rd Street and kept beating at his flaming shirt. DIRTY NAZIS! he shouted. DIRTY RAT NAZIS! An announcer interrupted Mrs. Brookes' nice music to report an explosion had rocked the East Side. Oh, so *that* had been the thump she'd heard a couple of minutes ago. The announcer urged everyone to stay tuned to that station for further details. With Mrs. Dallas holding him by a shoulder so he couldn't get away, Theodore Karam apologized to Dolores Bovasso. And, naturally, Dolores Bovasso had to smirk. All the dishes fell off the shelves in Miss Edna Daphne Frost's diningroom. My stars! she said, running in from the kitchen to find out what on *earth* had happened. Rows of houses, or what was left of them, were burning on both sides of East 61st, 62nd, 63rd and 64th Streets north of St. Clair Avenue. A flying manhole cover knocked down three pedestrians at St. Clair and East 64th. The afternoon papers were right on their final edition deadlines, and the best they could do was run bulletins saying that some sort of mysterious explosion and fire had caused great havoc in the St. Clair-Norwood area. Don't for a moment think that those afternoon paper people weren't disgusted. Why was it that all the good stories seemed to break on the one morning paper's time? Didn't hardly seem fair. Rolling on the grass, making mewing noises, tearing at her dress, Mrs. Sternad finally managed to extinguish the fire in her dress. But she couldn't see anything, and so she didn't know which way to run. G. Henderson LeFevre began hiccoughing. He held his breath. Even though she didn't know which way to run, Mrs. Sternad knew she had to get away from wherever she was. Wailing, she scrambled to her feet and staggered across the street—straight toward a burning house. Casimir Redlich's arms were quite strong. After putting out the fire in his shirt, he started dragging himself south toward

St. Clair. He did not let go of his trumpet. The heat had bent the street-car tracks out of shape on St. Clair. The wisps and puffs of fire flew everywhere. More manhole covers went up. At the liquefication plant, the other tanks still hadn't gone, but they *could* go at any second. Everywhere were fried birds.

Morris Bird III was knocked flat on his back. NOSMIRC KAERTS tipped over, and Sandra fell out. Her coat caught fire. She whooped. Streaks of flame shot over their heads. A shower of glass, all shards and crystals, fell on them. Morris Bird III didn't know whether to try to stand up or what. Some of the glass cut his forehead. He did not particularly feel the cuts. Sandra was kicking and shrieking. Her shoulders were on fire, and so was one of her sleeves. He crawled to where she lay. She beat at him with her fists. "Stop that!" he yelled. He began unbuttoning her coat. The buttons were hot. One of them had just about melted. He hesitated. His head felt hot. He reached up and touched it. His hair was on fire. Quickly he rubbed his hair with a sleeve of his jacket. The fire up there went out. He gently rubbed his head, felt a couple of baldspots. Now Sandra was drooling. He returned to his work with her buttons. The burning places had made her coat stink. Its lower buttons were completely melted. He grunted and tugged, was unable to get the melted buttons undone. Then he thought of his Uncle Alan's evil penknife. He took it from his pocket and opened one of its evil blades. Quickly he cut the coat off Sandra. He pulled it away from her shoulders and threw it out into the street. One of her arms was all pink and blistered. She rubbed it and screamed. The jar of Peter Pan Peanut Butter lay next to her. So did the alarmclock, but its face had been smashed. Morris Bird III's cap, which he'd given her to hold, was nowhere to be seen. A car blew up. Pieces of metal came flying toward them. Morris Bird III rolled over on his stomach and put his hands over his head. Sandra kept yelling. Something struck him on his rear end. He felt something rip, but he didn't feel any pain. He rolled over. Sandra was sitting crosslegged. Her arm wasn't pink anymore; it was red. He sat up, scrootched himself to her. He reached for the jar of Peter Pan Peanut Butter. It was hot, but he managed to hang on to it. He grabbed hold of the top and tried to twist it off. Nothing happened. He grunted, applied more pressure. Still nothing happened. Sandra's legs shot out. She started kicking. She banged her heels against the sidewalk, and no sounds came from her except screams. Morris Bird III struggled with the Peter Pan Peanut Butter jar top. If he ever got it loose, he might be able to help Sandra. A few months ago, he'd burned a hand on a radiator, and his grandmother had rubbed butter on it. The butter had made most of the sting go away. He didn't know whether *peanut* butter had the same effect, but he didn't think he had much to lose if he gave it a try. Unh. Unh. *Unh*. He grunted, bit his tongue. Nothing happened. Then he again remembered the evil penknife. He had dropped it on the sidewalk beside him. He opened another of its evil blades. This blade was shorter, and it had a little scootchy thing at its end for the opening of cans. Grimacing, he applied it to the Peter Pan Peanut Butter jar top. He wondered what had happened to Stanley Chaloupka. Sandra was licking her arm. She still was kicking and screaming, but she also was licking. Then— WHONG!—the top flew off. Morris Bird III used his fingers to scoop out a handful of peanut butter. He smeared it on Sandra's red arm. She blinked at him, kept kicking and screaming. "This'll make it feel better" he hollered. He had no way of knowing if she heard him. He decided maybe it was time he tried to stand up. First he got to his knees. He shook his head like a dog coming out of the water. Then, slowly, he stood up. He looked down at Sandra. She had stopped kicking, and now she was bawling instead of screaming. She was staring at her arm. Then she began licking it again. "Stop that!" hollered Morris Bird III. She looked up at him. Then she nodded. "It feel better?" he asked her, hollering. She nodded. "Good!" hollered Morris Bird III, and then he bent down and righted NOSMIRC KAERTS. One of its rubber tires had split, but otherwise it was in pretty good condition. He wondered what had happened to Stanley Chaloupka. He looked toward Stanley Chaloupka's house, but the house wasn't there anymore. Nothing was there but a pile of burning junk. He looked elsewhere. Lawns were on fire. Telephone poles were on fire. And everywhere were all these dead birds. He looked at Sandra. Well, at least there weren't any dead Birds. Not yet anyway. Out in the street, not much was left of her coat. He looked toward the gas tanks, and for the first time it occurred to him how warm he was. The tanks were surrounded by flames, and the flames rose in immense rhythmic gusts. They made huge hollow sounds: *whumm* and *whumm* and *whumm*. The heat made it hard for him to breathe. Then a great big fat man came running down the middle of the street. Blood was shooting from his nose in a great spray. He staggered, fell, screamed. He got to his feet, pressed his hands to his nose, resumed running. The blood came through his fingers. He ran straight past Morris Bird III and Sandra. He was shrieking something about someone named Mildred. It was impossible to make out his exact words. Morris Bird III looked at the flames and listened to the *whumm* and *whumm* and *whumm,* and then he decided it was time he and Sandra got out of there. He wondered what had happened to Stanley Chaloupka. His face stung. He took off his jacket, threw it in the wagon. He was sweating. He looked toward St. Clair Avenue. The way seemed clear. The street was lined with burning houses, but there still was an open path between them. Morris Bird III squinted. He caught a glimpse of the big fat man who had the bloody nose. The big fat man was almost to St. Clair. Well, if the big fat man could make it, so could Morris Bird III and Sandra. And NOSMIRC KAERTS. There was no question but what they had to take along NOSMIRC KAERTS. Teddy Karam had rented NOSMIRC KAERTS in good faith. They owed it to him. It would be returned. Grimacing again, Morris Bird III bent down and pulled Sandra to her feet. She was staring at the peanut butter on her arm, but most of her bawling had ceased. She still was bawling a *little,* but she was Sandra, and a person had to make allowances. He led Sandra with one hand, pulled NOSMIRC KAERTS with the other. They moved slowly, and Morris Bird III kept an eye out for flying things. Then a burning wire fell across the street. Part of it landed on top of a parked car. The car turned pink. Morris Bird III knocked Sandra down, threw himself on top of her. This was what people in the movies did when there was an enemy air raid, and he figured it was a pretty smart thing to do. The burning wire crackled and snapped. Then the car's tires began exploding. One by one, bang and bang and bang and bang. Then the car itself went up. Morris Bird III pressed his face against his sister's neck. Something scorched the back of his head. His hair was on fire again. "AHH-HHH!" he yelled. He rolled over, rubbed his head back and forth on the sidewalk. The fire went out. He felt his head, and now he had four or five more baldspots. He was crying. Sandra was shaking and gasping. He rubbed the baldspots with peanut butter. He tried to stop crying. He swallowed, fought for air. After a time, he managed to stop crying. The peanut butter didn't feel half bad.

The pain from her seared eyeballs made Mrs. Barbara Sternad weep and scream. She stumbled into a burning automobile, again setting her dress on fire. She fell down and rolled over and over, tearing off most of what was left of her clothes. G. Henderson LeFevre had his fourth drink. His hiccoughs were gone. He was singing to the ceiling, and his belly was warm. Mrs. Sternad's body was covered with blisters and scratches and welts and great blackish burnt places. The only air she could feel was hot air, which of course made her pain worse. Muriel Hatfield came upstairs to Mrs. Brookes' room and asked Mrs. Brookes what she wanted fixed for dinner. I don't care, said Mrs. Brookes. All right, said Muriel, I expect I'll whip up some macaroni and cheese then. Mrs. Sternad tried to crawl on her hands and knees, but her knees were burnt too badly. She had to stand up. It wasn't easy. On her way out of Mrs. Brookes' room, Muriel Hatfield saw the open suitcase. You goin somewhere? she wanted to know. Yes, said Mrs. Brookes. Oh, said Muriel, With that, she left the room. Imogene Brookes shook her head, asked herself what was keeping her passionate optician. Mrs.

Sternad held her arms stiffly in front of herself like a blind woman. She walked straight into a burning wall, pressing her palms against it. She whooped, flapped her palms, did a little dance. One of her shoes flew off. This made her barefoot. (The other shoe had been torn from her foot by the explosion.) Dancing and flapping, she stepped on a burning board. She shrieked, then began hopping. She heard footsteps and shouts. PLEASE! She screamed. PLEASE SOMEBODY STOP AND HELP ME PLEASE PLEASE PLEASE! No one stopped. PLEASE! she screamed. I CAN'T SEE! No one stopped. She fell down. She rubbed her face against what felt like sidewalk. She rubbed with such force that she tore a good deal of skin off her cheeks and forehead and nose. Everything between East 55th and East 67th north of St. Clair was on fire. Mayor Lausche was on his way there in a police car. He had canceled all his campaign appearances. The heat was so intense that no one could get within half a block of the scene of the explosion. Casimir Redlich crawled as best he could. A great big fat man ran past him, and this great big fat man's face was gushing blood, and he was screaming, something about someone named Mildred. It was impossible to make out his exact words. Some of his blood spattered Casimir Redlich. Downtown, in the main office of the East Ohio Gas Co., officials told reporters they didn't have the slightest idea what had happened. They said they would have to keep checking. From East 55th to East 67th, every storewindow along St. Clair was knocked out. Within half an hour of the explosion, thirty of Cleveland's forty firefighting companies were either at the scene or on their way. One fire truck almost ran down Casimir Redlich. He had to roll into the gutter to avoid it. He waved his trumpet at the driver, gave the fellow a piece of his mind. Cleveland Fire Chief James E. Granger arrived and took personal control of operations. More than a hundred buildings had already been destroyed by either the explosion or the fires. No one had any way of knowing if there would be any more explosions. Only one of the tanks had gone up, and there were three others, plus the "holder" tank. NINETYNINE BOTTLES OF BEER ON THE WALL! NINETY-NINE BOTTLES OF BEER! sang G. Henderson LeFevre. IF ONE OF THOSE BOTTLES SHOULD HAPPEN TO FALL, NINETY-EIGHT BOTTLES OF BEER ON THE WALL! Grinning, he kept at the song. NINETYEIGHT BOTTLES OF BEER ON THE WALL! NINETYEIGHT BOTTLES OF BEER! IF ONE OF THOSE BOTTLES SHOULD HAPPEN TO FALL, NINETYSEVEN BOTTLES OF BEER ON THE WALL! At Thomas Edison Field, East High was dominating play, but still hadn't scored. The spectators there still could see the fire. They craned their necks and paid as much attention to it as they did to the game. Sure is some fire, said Al Panetta. You think maybe East High blew up? Harry Wrobleski asked him. Naw, said Al, we're not that lucky. They both laughed. Still, the fire was coming sort of from the direction of East High (north of the field, about a mile away, at East 82nd Street and Decker Avenue), and it didn't hurt to hope. But aw nuts, if you stopped to consider it, the fire wasn't really coming from East High. If you used your head, you could see that. East High was north all right, but it was too far to the east. No, whatever was burning, it wasn't East High. Then everybody stood up. The East High fullback, Jim Roberts, had just burst through the middle of the Central line for thirty yards. Imogene Brookes sat on the edge of her bed and tried to figure out what had happened. Willson Junior High School, at East 55th Street and Luther Avenue, just southwest of the disaster area, was designated by Mayor Lausche as an emergency relief and medical center. One hundred trainees from a local Navy school, including a riot squad, were dispatched to the disaster area. So were some forty MPs and SPs, plus four hundred coastguardsmen, two thousand sailors from various other naval installations, two hundred policemen, thirtyfive doctors, twenty nurses and several dozen Red Cross volunteers. East High scored a touchdown. No one stopped to help Mrs. Sternad. EIGHTYTWO BOTTLES OF BEER ON THE WALL! EIGHTYTWO BOTTLES OF BEER! sang G. Henderson LeFevre. IF ONE OF THOSE BOTTLES WOULD HAPPEN TO FALL, EIGHTYONE WOTTLES OF WEER ON THE BALL! Mrs. Sternad was crawling now, and never mind her burnt hands and knees. She had no idea *where* she was crawling. She couldn't understand why she hadn't passed out. She could taste the blood from the cuts on her face. She crawled across stones and grass and splintered boards. Then her hands and knees gave way. She lay facedown and did not move. She held her breath, made a face, tried to resume crawling. But her hands and knees weren't up to it. She wondered if all her clothes had burned off. She hoped she was decent. She cried. She cried like a small child, keening, gulping her breath. Then a hand touched her on a shoulder. It's okay, someone said. Help me, said Mrs. Sternad. Help me. Please. My eyes, they're so hot, and I can't see anything. Please help me. And then Mrs. Sternad reached forward. She was shaking all over. Please, she said. Please. Please. And the voice said: Okay. It was a very young voice. And then something was being rubbed on her eyes and the other burnt places—on her arms, her shoulders, her legs, her upper chest. The hand that did the rubbing was small and gentle. Thank you, said Mrs. Sternad. Thank you. Thank you. God bless you. And then she sniffed. She was smelling something peculiar. When she realized what it was, she began to laugh. Her mouth became cavernous, and she laughed until her throat was sore. She decided that she had gone out of her mind. No doubt about it. Otherwise she wouldn't have been smelling peanut butter.

Morris Bird III wept. He didn't want to weep. He had wept enough today, and enough was *enough*. But right now what was he supposed to do? This lady, this poor burnt lady: he'd never seen anyone who was such a poor blistered mess. Oh well, at least she was laughing now. Her laughter probably covered the sound of his weeping. Sniffling, he gently applied the peanut butter to her burnt places. He supposed her laughter was a sign that she had gone out of her mind. He supposed pain had that effect sometimes. He wiped at his nose, Her laughter scared him, but at least she wasn't hearing him weep. This was what he had to keep in mind. At least she wasn't hearing him making a big boohoo disgrace of himself. In a situation such as this one, a person had to count his blessings. He hoped he was doing her some good. He was glad he had found her. Maybe, if he helped her, he would be able to make up for his lies to Grandma. And all the other things he owed. This poor burnt lady . . . he hoped God would let him do her some good. She had come crawling through an opening in a fence. For some reason, he had glanced in that direction at just the right time. He and Sandra and NOSMIRC KAERTS had gone perhaps half the distance back down East 63rd Street toward St. Clair Avenue. The fence had been to his right, separating the East 63rd back yards from the back yards on the next street—probably, unless he missed his guess, East 62nd. He'd had no reason to glance in that direction, which meant that maybe God had turned his head that way. That was the way God operated sometimes. At any rate, as soon as Morris Bird III saw her, he went to her. He told Sandra to wait there by NOSMIRC KAERTS, grabbed the jar of Peter Pan Peanut Butter, ran to the place where the burnt lady lay. Most of her clothes had been either burnt off or torn off. A kerchief was tied around her head, It said LONDON, and it had pictures of buildings and churches and such. He rubbed peanut butter on all the burnt places he could find. The kerchief had protected her hair. It was good hair, a fine deep red. Very pretty hair. He had no way of knowing if the rest of her had been pretty. Too much of it was burnt or cut. After he finished applying the peanut butter, he stood over her with his hands on his hips and let her laugh herself out. Finally, and now she was weeping a little, she asked him if she really was smelling peanut butter, he told her yes, and then he told her why. "Oh," she said, and then she began to tremble. He took a deep breath. He wasn't crying anymore. He told her he was willing to try to help her up. He told her they had to get out of there. She nodded, sat up. He bent over her, wrapped his arms around her middle, began to tug. Moaning, she lurched to her feet. But she lost her balance, fell forward, knocked him down, flopped on top of him. The wind was knocked out of him. She smelled like hot meat. He felt as though something was trying to rip open his chest. The burnt lady trembled and screamed. Finally he was able to wriggle out from under her. He swallowed air, and all of it was hot. He wondered what had happened to Stanley Chaloupka. *Whumm* and *whumm* and *whumm* went the great fire over by the gas tanks. He stood up, asked the burnt lady if she wanted to give it another try. She kept trembling and screaming. He repeated the question. Finally she nodded. It wasn't much of a nod, and he was just barely able to make it out. He squatted behind her and lifted her shoulders. When he had her sitting upright, he moved around in front of her and seized her by the wrists. He tugged. Gritting his teeth, he tugged until he felt his insides were about to pop out. The burnt lady was trying to help him. She was trying to use her legs for leverage. "ONE! TWO! THREE!" he hollered, and then allofasudden she was on her feet. He braced himself, caught her when she fell forward. She moaned. He took deep gulping breaths. Then they moved forward. She limped, but she managed to keep her balance. "Just you hang on," he told her. She nodded. They moved slowly. He let her lean just about all her weight on him. They lurched toward Sandra and NOSMIRC KAERTS. He didn't know how much breath he had left to call on. He figured all he could do was hope for the best. His baldspots stung a little, and he did all he could to ignore them. The burnt lady was soft against him. Her moans weren't as loud now as they had been. When they arrived where Sandra was waiting, he had just about run out of breath. Sandra was crying. He told her to Godalmighty shut up. He decided the best thing would be to put the burnt lady in the wagon. He sat her down on the edge of the wagon. She began sliding forward. He leaned against her to keep her from falling off her perch. A fire engine went past. A tremendous stink was coming from all the things that were burning. Gingerly he touched his baldspots. The burnt lady bent double and threw up. Sandra screamed. Morris Bird III slapped the burnt lady on the back. He didn't know whether this did any good, but he didn't think it did any harm. The burnt lady's knees gave way. She slid farther forward, tipping the wagon to one side. He braced her with an arm, pushed her back. The wagon settled back on all four of its wheels. Sandra was still screaming. Again he told her to shut up. He wondered what had happened to Stanley Chaloupka. Then he put his mouth close to the burnt lady's ear and told her that she was sitting on the edge of a wagon. "Look," he said, "we might as well put you in the wagon and give you a ride. So slide back. Just slide back real slow and easy, okay?" The burnt lady nodded. Gently he pushed her. She began to cough and gag. She shoved him away, bent double and threw up again. She threw up until nothing was left. He looked away. Sandra was gasping. Then, when the burnt lady was through, he starting pushing again. This time he got her into the wagon. Her rump slid down inside and her legs flew up. She was sitting sideways, but that would have to do. He didn't want to take the chance of tipping over the wagon by trying to get her turned facing forward. Her head was against her chest, and the top part of her was bent forward almost double. The LONDON kerchief had loosened a little, and some of her hair had fallen over her eyes. Several thick strands were stuck to her face and eyes because of the peanut butter. He braced her, studied her for a moment, then beckoned to Sandra. He told Sandra to walk alongside the wagon and brace the burnt lady. That way, the wagon wouldn't tip over, and the burnt lady wouldn't fall out. Sandra drew back and told him she couldn't do it. He told her she sure *could* do it. He told her she *better* do it. Sandra's eyes were just about white. All right, she told him, she'd try. She came to him. He told her to hold the burnt lady by the shoulder. Sandra nodded, reached out and took hold of the burnt lady's shoulder. "You got her?" said Morris Bird III. Sandra nodded. "Okay," said Morris Bird III, and he released his own grip on the burnt lady. "Now don't let go," he told Sandra. A nod from Sandra, who was biting her tongue. The burnt lady swayed a little, but Sandra managed to keep her from falling out of the wagon. Sandra looked down, saw what the burnt lady had thrown up. Sandra made a face. Morris Bird III told her not to *look* at it for crying out loud. Sandra nodded, looked away. Morris Bird III's baldspots stung worse. The jar of Peter Pan Peanut Butter was in a pants pocket. He pulled it out. It was empty. "AHHHHH NUTS!" he yelled, and he threw it away. Then he spat on his hands, lifted the handle of NOSMIRC KAERTS and started to pull.

Alix Kates Shulman (b. 1932), a native Clevelander, is an essayist, editor, writer of children's books, and novelist. Her *Memoirs of an Ex-Prom Queen* (1972) electrified an entire generation of American men and women who responded to her call for an examination of human relationships. Like Dawn Powell's Elsinore in *Dance Night,* Sasha, the narrator of *Memoirs,* emerges from adolescence in this selection.

Mid-Depression, when I turned five, my family moved to Baybury Heights, Ohio, one of Cleveland's coming brick-and-frame neighborhoods sprinkled with vacant lots and apple trees. My arms were just long enough to reach bottom branches and I quickly took to the trees. But even then, a carefree tomboy roaming free, I longed to be pretty. Every girl did.

"Climbing Sasha," my father called me as I sped through breakfast so I could race to the woods behind our house. Skinny and agile, I scaled the trunks with ease, spending my first summers in the green branches and on the moss beneath. All the kids could manage the apple trees, but only I could scramble straight up to the top of the Spy Tree, a lone slender birch, and see on a clear day all the way downtown to Cleveland's one skyscraper, the Terminal Tower. "Can you see it today?" my brother Ben would call from below. "Is it foggy or clear?" yelled up Susan McCarthy, who lived next door. And they would just have to take my word for it. I took my lunches in the treehouse with the McCarthy kids. After supper, if the boys let me, I played touch football on our quiet street or kick-the-can with everyone in the neighborhood.

Tomboy or not, I spent my indoor time dressing up in my mother's clothes and putting on lipstick and nail polish with the other girls. There was a hummingbird in the hollyhocks behind our house, the most delicate, lovely thing I had ever seen; I wanted to be like her. Even though it hurt when my mother brushed my hair each morning before school, it was worth it to have braids on which to tie pretty matching ribbons. I hoped the ribbons wouldn't get dirty as I climbed Auburn Hill to school past the boys waiting in the vacant lots to pelt us with snow or mud, depending on the season.

Once I started school I learned I would have to choose between hair ribbons and trees, and that if I chose trees I'd have to fight for them. The trees, like the hills, belonged to the boys.

Before and after school, the boys would fan out over the school grounds and take over the ball fields, the apple orchard, the skating pond, the "Mountain" for king-of-the-castle, while we stayed on the concrete playground in the shadow of the school building. There we played girls' games under the teachers' protective eyes. We could jump rope, throw rubber balls for a-meemy-a-clapsy, practice tricks on the bars nestled in the ell of the building, play jacks or blow soap bubbles—all safe, dependable, and sometimes joyous games which the boys disdained because we did them. Best of all, we could trade our playing cards.

When the recess bell rang, while the boys raced past us to the fields, we'd take out our card collections, separating the packs, slipping the rubber bands that divided them onto our wrists, fan out our cards for each other to see, and begin trading; the mate of a pair of kittens for a horse or Pinky; a pair of parrots for a drummer and a ship. Our trading cards were nothing like the boys' silly baseball cards, commercially manufactured for collecting and sold with bubble gum. Our girls' collections were made up of real adult playing cards, one of a kind salvaged from broken packs, which we valued for the charm of the pictures on their backs. Though my collection, being new, was one of the least impressive in the school, I treasured it all the same. I had few sets of four, hardly an unusual pair (though I had a better than ordinary collection of Shirley Temples), but there was at least one card in every category, and like life itself the collection had an open future. No card was so odd as to lack a fixed and perfect place in my endlessly adaptable collection. I loved them all.

And like my cards, I too was adaptable. Though in my summers and on my street I had wandered freely, taking to the woods and the very

tips of the trees, in my first weeks of first grade I learned to stay un-
complainingly in my place on the steps or in the shadow of the school.
I learned masculine and feminine.

"Go on to the Mountain, girls, it's a gorgeous day," Mrs. Hess
would urge as we stood on the steps at recess trading cards. Or, "Why
don't you play some freeze tag? You need the exercise." But we knew
better. We knew that going near the ball fields or behind the backstop
or near the basket hoop or in among the fruit trees or around the
Mountain or near the skating pond were extremely dangerous expeditions, even if we went in a pack—for that was all boys' territory, acknowledged by everyone. Despite Mrs. Hess's prods and assurances,
we knew that at any moment out there a pair or trio or more of boys
might grow bored with their own game and descend on us with their
bag of tricks. If a girl was spotted on their territory the boys felt perfectly free to: give her a pink belly, or lock her in the shed, or not let
her down from a tree, or tie her to the flagpole, or lash at her legs with
reeds, or chase her to the ravine, or look up her dress, or trip her, or
spit mouthfuls of water in her face, or throw mud at her, or "acciden-
tally" knock her down, or hold a hand over her nose and mouth, or
pull her hair, or pummel her with snowballs, or "wash her face" in
snow, or mess her books, or tear her clothes, or scatter her trading
cards, or shout obscene words at her, or throw stones at her, or splash
mud on her dress, or invite her to play on false pretenses, or just hit her
or spit on her or twist her arm behind her back, or not let her drink at
the water fountain.

And it was not only the bullies like Mel Weeks and Bobby Barr who
did such things to us. All the boys did them sooner or later, and some
boy did something to some girl every day. They did it for fun. They
did it to prove themselves. They did it because they hated us. If sometimes a boy got it too, it was only from another boy, never from a girl;
the terror went only one way. And every boy longed, if only secretly,
to be as powerful as the feared and respected bullies.

We knew better than to tell Mrs. Hess. The one time I ran crying to
her with my dress ripped after Bobby Barr had pulled me out of an
apple tree, she hugged and comforted me with a double message: "I
know, dear, those are rough boys. Why don't you play with the girls?"
There was only one thing for a girl to do: stay in the shadow. Prudently
I gave up football, trees, and walking to school unaccompanied for acceptable "girls' things," until, before I was ten, like everyone else I un-
questioningly accepted the boys' hatred of us as "normal." Just as the
Cortney kids wouldn't play with me because I was a Jew, the boys
wouldn't play with me because I was a girl. That was the way things
were. Like our trading cards, we were valued only in our place among
our kind. In fact, from the moment we got kicked out of the trees and
sent into the walk-in doll house back in kindergarten, our movements

and efforts had been so steadily circumscribed, our permissible yearnings so confined, that the only imprint left for us to make was on ourselves. By the third grade, with every other girl in Baybury Heights, I came to realize that there was only one thing worth bothering about: becoming beautiful.

With the U.S. plunge into World War II the gap between the girls and the boys grew to a chasm. While *they* were learning to spot enemy planes, launching the U.S. fleet on the playground, and deploying platoons over the skating pond, *we,* bored breathless by the war, pored over movie magazines, made scrapbooks, joined fan clubs, and planned, should the war last long enough, to become U.S.O. hostesses. Instead of collecting cards (somehow fewer and fewer people had time to play cards and the cards themselves, like other luxuries, were beginning to disappear from circulation) we collected the foil inner wrappers of chewing gum, chocolate bars, and cigarette packs, which themselves all became scarcer and scarcer until they too, like the Cheshire Cat, finally disappeared entirely. We lived instead on the sweets of patriotism, quietly accepting the consolation of the decade: "That's tough."

"What's tough? . . ."

"Life."

"What's life?"

"A magazine."

"Where do you get it?"

"At the drugstore."

"How much does it cost?"

"Ten cents."

"I only have five cents."

"That's tough."

"What's tough? . . . "

My father, an energetic attorney, sat on the Draft Board, making our family eligible for a prestigious B-card, which entitled us to an extra monthly ration of gasoline, and weekly donned his Air Raid Warden's helmet. My glamorous mother rolled her own cigarettes using begged tobacco, served meat substitutes without complaining, and set up a cozy blackout shelter in the basement of our house, decked out with all the comforts of the surface. Once she gave a "blackout party." On the radio, newscasts were as numerous and tiresome as commercials; even my beloved Hit Parade was constantly interrupted with important bulletins and flash announcements of bombings and landings. At school we competed by grade and sex to collect, sort, stack, and reclaim old newspapers, magazines, flattened tin cans, tooth paste tubes, foil balls, rubber tires, rags, old clothes (for the Russians), canned goods, and scrap metal. (The girls seldom won.) Anti-Semitism became temporarily taboo. Life changed in a thousand little ways. But however distracting the regimen of war, the overriding change in my life was the addition to my face of unsightly orthodontal braces in the late spring of 1942, coincident with the Battle of Midway.

Until I donned my metal armor it had always been my mother's comforting word against everyone else's that I was pretty. Though I sat before my three-way mirror studying myself, I couldn't figure out whether to believe my doting mother or the others. I would scrutinize my features, one at a time, then all together, filling in the answers at the end of our common bible, *The Questions Girls Ask,* but I always wound up more confused than when I started.

Does your hair swing loose? Do you tell your date what time you must be home when he picks you up? Do you brush the food particles out of your teeth after every meal? Do you avoid heavy make-up? Do you stand up straight? Do you see to it that your knees are covered when you sit down? Are your cheeks naturally pink? Do you consume enough roughage? Are your ears clean? Do you wear only simple jewelry? Do you protect against body odor? Do you powder your feet? Do you trim your cuticle? Are you a good listener?

It seemed as impossible for me to know how I looked as it was important. Some people said I looked exactly like my mother, the most beautiful woman in the world; others said I resembled my father, who, though very wise, was not particularly comely.

But once the grotesque braces were on, all my doubts disappeared. It became obvious that my mother's word, which she didn't alter to accommodate my new appearance, was pure prejudice. While to her, busily imagining the future, the advent of my braces only made the eventual triumph of my beauty more certain—indeed, it was for the sake of my looks that they had been mounted at all—to me they discredited my mother's optimism.

Sometimes at night, after a particularly harrowing day at school, after receiving some cutting insult or subtle slight, I would cry into my pillow over my plainness. My mother took my insults personally when I told her about them. "What do they know?" she would say, comforting me. "Why, you're the prettiest girl in your class." And when I protested between sobs that no, I was awkward, skinny, and unloved, she would take me in her arms and *promise* me that someday when my braces were removed they would all envy me and be sorry. "You'll see," she would say, stroking my lusterless hair, her eye on some future image of me or some past one of herself. "Just you wait."

I longed to believe her but didn't dare. Before bed each night I would walk to the gable window in my room that seemed to form a perfect shrine and on the first star I saw wish with a passion that lifted me onto my tiptoes to be made beautiful. I performed the rite just so, as though I were being watched. I thought if I wished earnestly enough my life would change and everything I wanted would come true. My grand-mothers, teachers, uncles and aunts, and especially my father, were al-ways encouraging me with their constant homilies: if at first you don't succeed try try again; hard work moves mountains; God helps those who help themselves. Nor was there any lack of precedent: from the seminal Ugly Duckling, a tale which never failed to move me to tears, to Cinderella and Snow White and Pinocchio, there were deep lessons to learn. All those step-daughters and miller's daughters and orphan girls who wound up where I wanted to go likely started out having it even worse than I. I wallowed in fable, searching for guidance. White-bearded Aesop stretched his long bony finger across the centuries to instruct me in prudence, while from Walt Disney's Hollywood studio I learned how to hope. "Some day my prince will come" echoed in my ears even as it stuck in my throat. From my first glimpse of the evening star until the ritual wish was over I would not utter a syllable; but pressing my hands tightly together like a Catholic at prayer to drama-tize my earnestness, I would summon a certain Blue Fairy, blond-haired and blue-eyed and dressed in a slinky blue satin gown, to materialize. "Star bright, star light, first star I see tonight. I wish I may I wish I might, have the wish I wish tonight." I believed she would one day grow before my eyes from the dot size of the star to life size, and landing on my window sill reach out with her sparkling wand, which would glint off my braces and illuminate my darkened room, and touch me lightly, granting my wish. I had actually seen her only once, in Walt Disney's *Pinocchio,* but I believed in my power to summon her. If it wasn't ludicrous for my simpering brother Ben to see himself a general, it couldn't be ludicrous for me to wish for a minor miracle of my own. When I had finished wishing, I would stand in my gable until I could spot five other stars (on a clear night ten), then climb solemnly into bed.

If during those years I wore braces there was ever any sign that I might turn out lovely, no one except my mother noticed it. Certainly not I. Each morning I examined myself anew in the mirror for the fruits of my wishes; each morning I saw only the glum reality of my flaws. Faced with my reflection, I shuddered and looked inward. Those steel bands that encircled my teeth like fetters and spanned my mouth like the Cuyahoga Bridge were far more remarkable, more dazzling, than any other aspect of my countenance; exhibiting obscenely the de-caying remains of the previous day's meal, no matter how thoroughly I had brushed my teeth the night before, they completely monopolized my reflection. The pain they produced in my mouth was nothing to the pain they caused in my heart.

At night I scanned the sky for stars; by day I studied them in the world. Hurrying home from school, I would pore over the movie magazines, cutting out the photos of the stars I loved and pasting them

lovingly in my scrapbooks. Like the boys with their total recall of bat-
ting averages and lineups, I knew by heart the films, studios, ages, husbands, and measurements of every star I loved. I had my favorite
studio, my favorite actress, my favorite singer, my favorite actor; and
my preferences, like those for trading cards in years past, were strong
and inexplicable.

With my classmates I would play guessing games about the stars until dinnertime.

"I'm thinking of a certain movie star whose last initial is B."

"Is it a woman?"

"Yes."

"Is she at Warner Brothers?"

"No."

"Is she famous for her legs?"

"No."

"Is her first initial J?"

"Yes."

"Is it Joan Blondell?"

"No."

"Is it Joan Bennett?"

"No."

"Is it Janet Blair?"

"Yes!"

On weekends, standing in the tub shampooing my hair, in secret I
would pile my frothy curls high on my head before the mirror in the
style of Joan Fontaine or Alice Faye for long magical moments while
the bath water grew cold around my shins. Then rinsing out the soap
at last and rendering my hair limp again for another week, I would return as my poor self to the tepid tub. There was no getting away from
me for very long.

I placed all my faith in the miracle. I wished nightly on my star and
daily on dandelion puffs to be beautiful. I wished on fallen eyelashes, on
milkweed, on meteors, on birthday candles, on pediddles, on wishbones,
on air. Seeking some sign of the coming miracle I told my fortune with
cards and drew prophecies from tea leaves. "Rich man, poor man, beg-
garman, thief, doctor, lawyer, merchant, chief": only a beauty could
land one of the desirables. I examined my palm, my horoscope. I
avoided stepping on cracks. I depetaled daisies. I knocked on wood, set
the knives and forks on the table exactly so, whispered magical sylla-
bles and incantations. I ate gelatin to make my nails hard and munched
carrots to make my hair curl. I crossed my fingers, bit my tongue, held
my breath, and wished steadfastly for the single thing that mattered.

Then suddenly, in August 1945, as the boys of Baybury Heights
reeled in ecstasy over the impact of the A-bomb and the girls of my
class assembled their wardrobes for the coming encounter with junior

high—on the very eve of my entering a new world—the Blue Fairy, that lovely lady, came through. My braces came off, and the world was mine.

Rita Dove (b. 1952), Akron-born graduate of Buchtel High School, moves from the Akron of her Pulitzer Prize-winning poetry to Cleveland for this short story from her collection *Fifth Sunday* (1985). The story juxtaposes the victims of Nazi genocide with a vividly realized castoff of contemporary Cleveland.

Zabriah

Zabriah shows up at the Euclid Arcade, dry though the rain is pouring outside; she waits for someone to notice her and some do, shying away from a woman who looks like a man, a black woman with lint in her nappy hair and one shoe in her hand, a woman built like a pissoir, squat and round and something to be vaguely ashamed of. It's supposed to be summer isn't it, ISN'T IT! she screams, not sure she's spoken at all; no shout reverberates in the muffled roar of the arcade under itself, in the rain, Saturday shoppers going about their purchasing, the vaulted esplanade like the inside of a submarine, the shops ranging in tiers of iron filigree and illumination blooming in the rosettes of art nouveau lampposts; there is room here for every corner of the globe, Brazilian briefcases and Californian soy bean bread, German harmonicas and Swedish napkin rings.

Where Zabriah moves the walls bulge to receive her, the floor rumbles, the air makes room; but what good does it do to circle and circle in ever higher tiers, where does it get you? Zabriah is not tempted by stair case tracery or the membrane, sky-colored, ballooning overhead; she knows where she is going, let someone stop her if they can, all the way down, clack of a heel and thump of a sock, to the other end of the arcade.

They're up to something in there, through that window—hands folded, eyes turned inward, the towering books and a woman in a pale suit at the end of the table, her mouth nibbling at the words printed—Zabriah can't quite see them but she knows they are there—on the papers in her hands. One has to be careful here, one wrong move and you'll find yourself laid out on a marble slab, cold; she opens the door a crack though and what she hears is poison *Black milk* the suited lady is saying *of death we drink you* careful now slip inside *drink you evenings we drink you and drink you* Zabriah bursts upon them, drops her sack of a purse on the floor, holds tight to her shoe though: Is this the Poetry Circle? Yes, they answer, all the pink rabbit eyes blinking, yes we meet every other week, volunteering information, telling this creature anything as long as she leaves them alone; Zabriah feels sorry for them but she has to do this, slamming her shoe on the table. Well I paid my annual dues last December and never heard nothing from you people who's in charge here?

Matt stands slowly, inclines his head kindly to one side; his name is Matt because a button on his shirt says so and another, directly below it, pleads LOVE A JEW TODAY and Matt stands there for awhile, smiling. He is seventy-five years old and poet since his retirement from the post office; he knows every book published in the English language on Fascism and the Holocaust and it is Matt who says We have no leader but you're welcome to stay and listen.

Zabriah sits down, breasts and beads spilling, she folds her arms, pushing up the sleeves of her sweater, the woman in the suit repeats *Black milk of death we* and Zabriah interrupts, Ain't nobody Black around here.

This is a poem, the lady explains. By a German poet, Paul Celan.

Don't remember him, Zabriah says, shaking her head. Is he one of those concentration camp daddies?

No! He was a victim of a concentration camp, and the black milk in this poem symbolizes—

Ain't no Black fang coming down these days, Zabriah mutters, picking up her purse. You speak German?

Yes, I do, the lady replies.

I know German, too, I know German and Russian and I've seen the Warsaw ghetto. Do you want to hear my jew song?

Later. Matt polite, intervening. First Mrs. Moore, then Mrs. Carmichael—

—And if you *really* can speak German, Zabriah continues, eyes boring into the silk bow arranged above the suit as one arm, elbow-deep, digs into the belly of the purse until it finds what it was looking for— then, of course, you know calligraphy. A pause. What—you speak German and don't know calligraphy?

With a heave she pulls out a handful of matchbooks, lines them up all in a row, counts them, scoops them into her arms and stands up. Don't say a word, don't giggle she's coming this way and she's hurting pretty badly, is she lame or is that just the shoe, how she lists to the right, going like a mudslide, don't swallow don't jerk, how young she is, nineteen, maybe twenty. . . .

Everyone gets a pack of matches but they aren't allowed to touch them until she leaves, slamming the door as she goes. The room exhales, the lady finishes *your golden hair Margarete your ashen hair Sulamith* and it's Mrs. Carmichael's turn, in a high quaver reciting *I changed to see a butterfly / Asleep upon the sill;* everyone is bored but what can they do, Mrs. Carmichael is a regular, she comes every time, twice a month, armed with a sheaf of poems written in royal blue ink. *To think that beauty comes so small* she exclaims as Zabriah slips in again, listening patiently for three quatrains before pronouncing: Classical bullshit. And: Love for everyone. And: Let me tell you this ain't the buggy age no more this ain't even the auto-industrial age, this is the jet age. Spaceship twothousandone, put five million on it. Bitch. Got it? Helicopters.

Zabriah strikes a match, lets it drop onto the royal blue poems and Mrs. Carmichael's eyes go wet. Matt jumps to put it out: Who do you think you are, Zabriah asks, the reincarnation of Moses? but Matt doesn't care, he's clapping his hands for attention and stomping his feet and calling out Now it's your turn turn it loose sister! and Zabriah throws off her shawl; she throws back her head and for an instant is beautiful as an ocean liner is beautiful, ablaze and sinking:

> Wa-too-wa-too Lee
> Ho Chi Minh—Ha!

grinding an obscene jelly roll as she punches her fists again and again into the air, making room:

> Deep in the Cherokee valley
> Don't you know my name is Jimmy

she's been to the Warsaw ghetto, she's been to calligraphy school, your ashen hair Sulamith, she sings the same words over and over. Matt starts up a collection, holding out a glass ashtray, come on everyone give a dime a quarter a nickel, Matt himself puts in a dollar bill, sets the tray before Zabriah as she sinks into her seat Sister what a marvellous voice that is, it reminds me of the great gospel singers, Mahalia Jackson . . .

After all that exertion she's not even breathing hard. Who? she asks, quietly.

Mahalia Jackson, he insists, you remember her. . . .

With a sweep of the arm that sends coins and ashtray spinning Zabriah stands up, fixes Matt with a look he's beginning to understand.

I don't remember anyone over the age of twelve, she retorts, pivoting on her one good heel and marching, sallying forth under the voluminous skeleton of the arcade, its airy parabolas, its invisible drums, its iron angels sighing.

Poetry

Edmund Vance Cooke bridges the time period from the nineteenth to the early twentieth century. His collection, *The Uncommon Commoner*, 1913, deals with issues pertinent to Cleveland in those unsettled times. "Tom L. Johnson," written in conventional rhymed verse, is a traditional elegy to a fallen hero. Cooke's query at the beginning of the poem emphasizes the important role he felt Johnson played.

What Jefferson and Lincoln were to the Nation, Johnson was to the City. And as the City looms more and more potential for good or for evil in our central-izing civilization, who shall say that the inspiration of his example shall not yet prove as great as theirs?

Tom L. Johnson

A Man is passing. Hail him, you
Who realize him stanch and strong and true.
He found us dollar-bound and party-blind;
He leaves a City with a Civic Mind,
Choosing her conduct with a conscious care,
Selecting one man here, another there,
And scorning labels. Craft and Graft and Greed
Ran rampant in our halls and few took heed.
The Public Service and the Public Rights
Where bloody bones for wolf and jackal fights.
Now, even the Corporate Monster licks the hand,
Where once he snarled his insolent demand.
Who tamed it? Answer as you will,
But truth is truth, and his the credit still.

A Man is passing. Flout him, you
Who would not understand and never knew.
Tranquil in triumph, in defeat the same,
He never asked your praise, nor shirked your blame,

For he, as Captain of the Common Good,
Has earned the right to be misunderstood.
Behold! he raised his hand against his class;
Aye, he forsook the Few and served the Mass.
Year upon year he bore the battle's brunt;
And so, the hiss, the cackle and the grunt!
He found us striving each his selfish part.
He leaves a City with a Civic Heart,
Which gives the fortune-fallen a new birth,
And reunites him with his Mother Earth;
Which seeks to look beyond the broken law
To find the broken life, and mend its flaw.

A Man is passing. Nay, no demigod,
But a plain man, close to the common sod
Whence springs the grass of our humanity. Strong
Is he, but human; therefore sometimes wrong,
Sometimes impatient of the slower throng,
Sometimes unmindful of the formal thong,
But ever with his feet set toward the height
To plant the banner of the Common Right,
And ever with his eye fixed on the goal,
The Vision of a City with a Soul.

And he is fallen? Aye, but mark him well;
He ever rises further than he fell.
A man is passing? I salute him, then,
In these few words. He served his fellow-men
And he is passing. But he comes again!
. . . .
He comes again! not in that full-fleshed form,
Which revelled in the charge, which rode the storm,
But in that firm-fixed spirit, which was he,
That heritage he left for you and me;
Before no Vested Wrong to bow the knee,
Before no Righteous Fight to shirk, or flee,
Before all else to make men free, free, free!

Sherwood Anderson, better known for his novels and short stories about the mid-West, celebrates in Walt Whitman's cadences the topography of his childhood home in Clyde in this poem from *Mid-American Chants* (1918).

Manhattan

From the place of the cornfields I went into the new places. I went into the city. How men laughed and put their hands into mine.

To a high place overlooking the city I climbed. Men came running
to me. On the stairways there was the endless threshing of num-
berless feet. The faces of women appeared. The soft lips of
women were on my hands and my sinewy arms. Understanding
came in to me.

I am of the West, the long West of the sunsets. I am of the deep
fields where the corn grows. The sweat of apples is in me. I am
the beginning of things and the end of things.

To me there came men whose hands were withered. My soldiers
were small and their eyes were sunken. In them was the pain of
sobs, the great pain that sobs. The sobbing of pain was like the
threshing of feet on the stairways that went up from the city.

In the morning I arose from my bed and was healed. To the cornfields I went laughing and singing. The men who are old have
entered into me. As I stood on the high place above the city they
kissed me. The caress of those who are weary has come into the
cornfields.

Hart Crane (1899–1932) had strong family ties in northeastern Ohio. His youth
spent living in Garrettsville, Warren, and Cleveland, his association with the artistic circles of William Sommer et al., his father's restaurant in Chagrin Falls, and
his brief stint as a reporter for the *Cleveland Plain Dealer* all clearly influenced his
poetry. An impressive monument in the Garrettsville Cemetery—"Harold Hart
Crane: Lost At Sea"—memorializes his death by suicide. "My Grandmother's
Love Letters" lacks the verbal complexity and difficulty often associated with his
poetry, while "Sunday Morning Apples," inspired by a watercolor of Sommer's,
exhibits some of the compressed and cryptic beauty of Crane's mature expression.

My Grandmother's Love Letters

There are no stars to-night
But those of memory.
Yet how much room for memory there is
In the loose girdle of soft rain.

There is even room enough
For the letters of my mother's mother,
Elizabeth,
That have been pressed so long
Into a corner of the roof
That they are brown and soft,
And liable to melt as snow.

Over the greatness of such space
Steps must be gentle.
It is all hung by an invisible white hair.
It trembles as birch limbs webbing the air.

And I ask myself:

"Are your fingers long enough to play
Old keys that are but echoes:
Is the silence strong enough
To carry back the music to its source
And back to you again
As though to her?"

Yet I would lead my grandmother by the hand
Through much of what she would not understand;
And so I stumble. And the rain continues on the roof
With such a sound of gently pitying laughter.

Sunday Morning Apples
TO WILLIAM SOMMER

The leaves will fall again sometime and fill
The fleece of nature with those purposes
That are your rich and faithful strength of line

But now there are challenges to spring
In that ripe nude with head
      reared
Into a realm of swords, her purple shadow
Bursting on the winter of the world
From whiteness that cries defiance to the snow.

A boy runs with a dog before the sun, straddling
Spontaneities that form their independent orbits,
Their own perennials of light
In the valley where you live
      (called Brandywine).

I have seen the apples there that toss you secrets,—
Beloved apples of seasonable madness
That feed your inquiries with aerial wine.
Put them again beside a pitcher with a knife,
And poise them full and ready for explosion—
The apples, Bill, the apples!

Jake Falstaff (1899–1935), pseudonym of Herman Fetzer of Maple Valley, graduated from Akron West High School and was a journalist for the *Akron Times* and later the *Cleveland Press*. His novels authentically describe German-American life in Wayne County. His poems, posthumously collected in *The Bulls of Spring* (1937), record his love for northeastern Ohio. "The Dick Johnson Reel" is a literary ballad; "Valedictory" is an elegant free verse encomium to his home place.

The Dick Johnson Reel

(The old men say their grandfathers heard Dick Johnson sing the chorus of this song in the timberlands of northern Summit County, Ohio.)

Old Dick Johnson, gentleman, adventurer,
Braggart, minstrel, lover of a brawl,
Walked in the timber from Northfield to Hudson.
(Backward, forward and sashay all!)
Old Dick Johnson, joker and wanderer,
Poet, vagabond and beater of the track,
Sang a song of his bravery and prowess:
(Ladies go forward and gents go back!)

CHORUS
Ripsi, rantsi,
Humpsy, dumpsy;
I, Dick Johnson,
Killed Tecumseh!

Old Dick Johnson, fighter of the Indians,
Sang from Boston to the hills of Bath;
Sang the song of his muscle and his musket.
(Swing your partners and leave a path!)
The redskin sleeps where the wheat is growing,
But old Dick Johnson's ghost is free,
And it sings all night from Richfield to Twinsburg:
(All hands 'round with a one-two-three!)

CHORUS
Ripsi, rantsi,
Humpsy, dumpsy;
I, Dick Johnson,
Killed Tecumseh!

Valedictory
(NEW YORK, JUNE 25, 1929)

Forgive me, hearty and amiable city,
If, having beheld your beauty,
I go back to my own places.

If, having seen you as the barbarians saw Semiramis
On the wall of her undefended city,
I do not put down my arms and come,
Beating my breast for madness
And shouting for ecstasy,
To be your servitor.

It is not because I have seen nymphs,
Although I have seen nymphs.

It is not because I have drunk dew,
Though I have been dew-drunken.

It is because I have stood in the evening
At the beginning of a fat valley.
It is because I have opened a barndoor
On an evening in winter.

If I stay, I am too far from the place where I shall lie down
When the time comes to lie down.
I shall lie there a long time
Until I become a part of that fertility.
It will be wise for me to know the clod well
Before I go to sleep upon it;
I am not comfortable in a strange bed.

You are splendid; you are nameless because there is no name great
    enough for you;
You are beautiful with madness as the queen that rode upon the brow
    of an elephant into the fountain courts of Solomon;
But I must go back to my own places;
I must go back to the bitter crows of autumn
And the brooks flowing northward in spring
Bearing ice in their currents.
I must go back to the wind screaming in winter
And the heat flickering in summer.
I must go back to my own places—
To wedding and childbed and patriarchal death.

Langston Hughes's poetry sings with the authentic voice of the African-American writer in the first half of the twentieth century. *The Selected Poems* (1959) were edited by Hughes himself from seven previously published volumes and included poems that had never been published. Hughes viscerally evokes urban life in "Railroad Avenue." He expresses a personal sense of loss in the exploitation of the black experience in "Note on Commercial Theatre."

Railroad Avenue

Dusk dark
On Railroad Avenue.
Lights in the fish joints,
Lights in the pool rooms.
A box-car some train
Has forgotten
In the middle of the
Block.
A player piano,
A victrola.
    942
      Was the number.

A boy
Lounging on a corner.
A passing girl
With purple powdered skin.
    Laughter
    Suddenly
    Like a taut drum.
    Laughter
    Suddenly
    Neither truth nor lie.
    Laughter
Hardening the dusk dark evening.
    Laughter
Shaking the lights in the fish joints,
Rolling white balls in the pool rooms,
And leaving untouched the box-car
Some train has forgotten.

Note on Commercial Theatre

You've taken my blues and gone—
You sing 'em on Broadway
And you sing 'em in Hollywood Bowl,
And you mixed 'em up with symphonies
And you fixed 'em
So they don't sound like me.
Yep, you done taken my blues and gone.

You also took my spirituals and gone.
You put me in *Macbeth* and *Carmen Jones*

And all kinds of *Swing Mikados*
And in everything but what's about me—
But someday somebody'll
Stand up and talk about me,
And write about me—
Black and beautiful—
And sing about me,
And put on plays about me!
I reckon it'll be
Me myself!

Yes, it'll be me.

Kenneth Patchen's poems about the Warren/Youngstown area are gritty reminders
of working-class realities in the industrial valleys of northeastern Ohio. The idiom
of this poem is redolent of natural poetry of Irish immigrants that was recognized
and recorded by Patchen. *Selected Poems* was published in 1957.

May I Ask You a Question, Mr. Youngstown Sheet & Tube?

Mean grimy houses, shades drawn
Against the yellow-brown smoke
That blows in
Every minute of every day. And
Every minute of every night. To bake a cake or have a baby,
With the taste of tar in your mouth. To wash clothes or fix supper,
With the taste of tar in your mouth. Ah, but the grand funerals . . .
Rain hitting down
On the shiny hearses. "And it's a fine man he was, such a comfort
To his old ma.—Struck cold in the flower of his youth." Bedrooms
Gray-dim with the rumor of old sweat and urine. Pot roasts
And boiled spuds; *Ranch Romances* and The Bleeding Heart
Of Our Dear Lord—"Be a good lad . . . run down to Tim's
And get this wee pail filled for your old father now." The kids
Come on like the green leaves in the spring, but I'm not spry
Anymore and the missus do lose the bloom from her soft cheek.
(And of a Saturday night then, in Tim O'Sullivan's Elite Tavern
    itself:
"It is a world of sadness we live in, Micky boy."
"Aye, that it is. And better we drink to that."
"This one more, for home is where I should be now."
"Aye, but where's the home for the soul of a man!"
"It's a frail woman ye act like, my Micky."

"And it be a dumb goose who hasn't a tear to shed this night.")
Rain dripping down from a rusty evespout
Into the gray-fat cinders of the millyard . . .
The dayshift goes on in four minutes.

Alberta Turner (b. 1919) has taught at Cleveland State University and directed its Poetry Center since 1964. She has written several volumes of poetry, and she also writes about poetry and the creative process. This poem is from *Need* (1971).

American Daffodils

Daffodils in America don't scatter
Nor push down through rocks and stumps
To Board a rowboat at the dock.

In America they trim porches,
Walk guests in from the street,
Gesture toward graves.
When the Methodist church in Kipton
Burned, it took bulldozers
To turn daffodils from the altar.
My great aunt planted a row
Around the privy.
Now, come spring,
Each traveler on the Greyhound
Bus from Cleveland to Sandusky
Squats a moment to watch the highway
Wheel past between their stems.

Russell Atkins (b. 1926), a native Clevelander, attended the Cleveland School of Art and the Cleveland Institute of Music. As a young, aspiring poet he received encouragement for his poetry from Langston Hughes. Atkins has been widely published and was co-editor of *Free Lance,* a Cleveland literary magazine founded by him in 1950 and published until 1979. He received an honorary doctorate from Cleveland State University in 1976. Atkins experiments with twentieth-century free verse forms that mirror the fragmentation of sensory imagery.

On The Fine Arts Garden, Cleveland

The Park's beautiful
     really
  something so serious about it
  serene and gloomy
     mildly gloomy

mildly touching, all things

                  softly

and pouring with
mellows the silver fountain

                  silent figures

move reposefully into the living shadows
and then the golden lamps
the while

       slowly filtering—

The poems of James C. Kilgore (1928–88), a faculty member at Cuyahoga Community College from 1966 until his untimely death, have been widely published in poetry magazines. He was a member of the Poetry League of Greater Cleveland and was named "Ohio Poet of the Year 1982" by the Ohio Poetry Day Association. This poem, published in 1971 in his volume *A Time of Black Devotions*, deftly synthesizes three aspects of the poet's experience: his professional academic life, Harlem just outside his hotel, and the more immediate yearning to be back in the Hough neighborhood in Cleveland.

Signs of Ohio, December, 1970
(SCENE: MODERN LANGUAGE ASSOCIATION OF AMERICA)

I merge my words with the words of mind and water and earth,
transmit them to worlds bubbling,
whistling,
blooming in the time tumbling from the past,
cascading into this present,
ebbing toward the future.
Forty floors below this mansional peak,
scholars speak in awe
of the frequency of *greasy* and *greazy;*
I look out toward Harlem,
and my vision is censored by smog
hanging beside the Hudson.
But my mind rides experiential winds:
it breaks through the smutty wall,
swings down to Abyssinia Baptist Church,
listens in on the prayers of Black voices
going up to heaven,
swirls out to 125th Street
to hear the exhortations of young Blacks
calling for the building of a new nation;
it rides on,
across the Allegheny,

swoops down near the burning bosom
of the dying Cuyahoga:
it is a white Christmas in Hough—
yes, it also snows in the ghetto
during the season of premeditated charity.

Away from Hough and the ice-chilled chest
of the burning river,
I seek the planet of a friend;
among her water and wind and earth,
we talk of a bright new world a-coming,
and our lives merge with lives bubbling,
whistling,
blooming in the time
tumbling from the love
coming down into the present
ebbing out toward the future,
suspending time,
then crashing into the waters and winds and earths of ourselves—
and I would be Adam,
go naked in the garden of searing joy:
the noise of communication is great,
and we are deep inside worlds
where no rivers burn,
no air suffocates,
and no earth diminishes:
my mind has flown away from these concrete canyons;
it will not return to the solemn linguistic altar.

Room Service warns me: I must check out soon
I pack up
to merge again my blood
and spirit and flesh with the water
and wind and earth
bubbling and whistling and blooming
beside the burning river
deep inside the wounded life.

Driving at the sun,
watching the desperate rays
surrender
and the half gold
play peekaboo on Blue Mountain,
I pass under a dark dinosaurian body,
speed out into Pennsylvania night,

flip on my lights
for safety,
move the Maverick up the mountains,
down the valleys,
across the black Tuscadora,
searching for signs of Ohio.

Richard Howard (b. 1929), born in Cleveland and educated at Columbia University, won the Pulitzer Prize for Poetry in 1970 for *Untitled Subjects*. He has published many volumes of poetry and is equally famous as one of the English language's foremost translators of French literature. *Fellow Feelings* (1976) includes this five-poem sequence, his tribute to Hart Crane. As a fellow Clevelander, Howard seeks out evidence of Crane's poetic genesis as well as a reconciliation with Crane's tragic death.

Decades
FOR HART CRANE

I   *Crane's Canary Cottage.* I have turned four,
and the tablecloth between my mother and me
(my father opposite, of course) invites
pollution of its pure canary note
by a nest of shiny knives and glasses—"not
for fingering." This is my first meal *out*
and I must behave, on my father's sharp orders
and yours—your father's: it is their bill of fare
we pay for, and who knew how much it cost.

that April evening as we ate? My mother
ate my father, her leftovers mine till now:
I failed like yours—your father—to defend
myself against the opposite sex, my own,
that night the news came, Mother's Day for sure
that April something, nineteen thirty-two,
when Wheelwright said you turned to *Fish Food* (he
turned it to advantage in the very first
of all your elegies, asking final questions:

*what did you see as you fell, what did you hear
as you sank?*). I fed to find the answers, for
that was a sacramental feast. Dear Hart,
our mothers ate our fathers, what do we
eat but each other? All the things we take
into our heads to do! and let strange creatures
make our mouths their home. Our problem is not

to find who remembers our parents—our problem is
to find who remembers ourselves. I love our problem,

it becomes our solution: unbecoming, it dissolves.
I was four, you drowned. Now you remember me.

II   *Laukhuff's Bookstore.* I am fourteen, I live
On the Diet of Words, shoving a ladder around
high shelves while the German ex-organ-maker
smokes with a distant nightmare in his eyes
("You have heard of Essen," he murmurs, "you never
will again": it is nineteen forty-three),
his body on hinges, his elbows hovering wide
over the *Jugendstil* bindings (Werfel, Kraus . . .)
like a not-quite-open penknife. "Hart Crane?

He came here to marry the world . . . You understand?
Maritare mundum: it is the work of magic,
Marandola says it somewhere, to marry the world . . .
And not much time to do it in, he had
to read all the books, to marry, *then* to burn . . .
It is one kind of greatness to grow old—
to be *able* to grow old, like Goethe;
it was Hart's kind to refuse. you understand?"
Laukhuff is asking *me,* laughing through smoke

his postponing, renouncing laugh. No, I don't—
that much I do. I climb down, clutching *The Bridge*
and hand it over. "Will I understand this,
Mr. Laukhuff? Should I buy it?" "Cross it first.
You won't, but there is a certain value, there is
poetic justice in the sense of having missed
the full meaning of things. Sure, buy it. Spend
all you have, your mother will give you more."
The German penknife closes with a click.

Marriage, Hart. The endless war. The words.
Cleveland was our mother-in-lieu. We left.

III   *Les Deux Magots.* I am twenty-four and free,
now, to finger knives and glasses—no cloth
to be stained, nothing but cold zinc dividing
me from your old friend opposite, your coeval
the Fugitive convert who cases the loud cafe
evasively while I lay my cards on the table:
*I tell him of myself, which is as much
as to have asked him pardon*—Shakespeare, no less!—
but he winces at what he hears, and what he sees:

your Montparnasse is dead, my Saint-Germain
dead-set against the capital of gayety
you shared in the Twenties. Gay it is, though,
and so am I, to his disparagement
expressed, dear Hart, in terms of our *decadence*
as the flaming creatures pass. "Such men," he says,
"fare best, as we Southerners say of foxes, when
most opposed—none so spited by their own,
and yet I see how proud these sick cubs grow!"

There is a silence, colder than the zinc
between us. Hopeless. I have lost heart,
as I always do when I rejoin the Fathers,
lost the pride of my "proclivity,"
and the penalty and disgrace of losing is
to become part of your enemy. Have I lost you,
Hart? I need you here, quarrelsome, drunk
on your permanent shore-leave from the opposite sex,
opposing shore, the loss, the losses, the gain . . .

There is always a chance of charity when we are dead.
Only the living cannot be forgiven.

IV   *Sands Street Bar & Grille.* At thirty-four
I am older than your ghost I follow in
under the Bridge that hisses overhead.
Dark enough here to make ghosts of us all,
and only a great layer of ghosts knows how
to be democratic in the dark: no wonder
you gave your hand to Walt, always on edge,
on the beach of embarking, the brink where they fall
into the sea, these castles of our misconduct . . .

Your ghost, anonymous, cruises among ghosts,
our neighborly disgrace. Was it from this
you made your Bridge, reaching up to Walt
and down to me—out of this River, this Harbor,
this Island and these, these sexual shadows, made
an enviable failure, your dread success?
I do not believe in exceptions—if you did it
then it can be done; show me your toys, ghost,
show me your torments out of which you rise,

dripping in your bones, from death to be
a trophy of disaster. What did you learn,
steeped in the great green teacher of the gradual,
when all you knew was sudden, a genius in need

of a little more talent, a poet not by grace
but the violence of good works? I still do not
understand you, but I stand under you here,
marvelling at the shadows where apprenticeship
is not vocation, of course, only voyeurism.

Albatross, siren, you haunt me far from home.
It is dark. Here not seeing is half-believing.

V *Garrettsville.* By forty-four I know
your beginning *lost at land,* your end *at sea:*
sometimes beginnings can be more desperate
than ends, patrimony more than matrimony,
and middle age the worst despair of all.
I do not find you here, or in the bars,
or Laukhuff's, or that yellow restaurant—
not even on the beach you walked with Walt,
hand in hand, you told him: *never to let go.*

But that is where you find me. Take my hand
as you gave yours to him. We suffer from
the same fabled disease, and only the hope
of dying of it keeps a man alive. Keeps!
I press your poems as if they were Wild Flowers
for a sidelong grammar of paternity.
We join the Fathers after all, Hart, rejoin
not to repel or repeal or destroy, but to fuse,
as Walt declared it: wisdom of the shores,

easy to conceive of, hard to come by, to choose
our fathers and to make our history.
What takes us has us, that is what I know.
We lose, being born, all we lose by dying:
all. I have seen the Birthplace—a strange door
closes on a stranger, and I walk away.
Soon the shadows will come out of their corners and spin
a slow web across the wallpaper. Here
is where you met the enemy and were theirs.

Hart, the world you drowned, for is your wife:
a farewell to mortality, not my life.

Robert Wallace (b. 1932) has taught at Case Western Reserve University since 1965. He is well known as the editor of *Light Year,* "an annual of light verse and funny poems" from Bits Press in Cleveland. His poems have appeared in periodicals, and he has had several volumes of his poetry published, including *Views from a Ferris Wheel* (1965), from which this poem has been selected. The traditionally rhymed quatrains contrast two ways of life, old versus modern, accepting both of them in the end.

The Two Roads

The old road runs along by the new
Behind a space of weeds and alders,
But, occasionally forgetful, falters
Up a hill the turnpike arrows through;

Or, bending, wanders unwinding out
Across the summer country's flowing,
As if not sure of where it's going,
At least preferring to go roundabout,

—Being off to find a wood, or hunt
Some crossroads' single clapboard store
Which hides behind its blown screen door
A scented coolness, guarded in front

By one gas-pump; or to thread a town
Too small and distant to be picked
To be a suburb ever, its brick
And burnt-out bank-shell going down

Slowly, filled up with grassy weeds
And treelings leaning out at windows
And at ghostly doors that never close,
Its houses gray with unwieldy needs

In the sun. Then, rising to view
Over a far-off ridge, the old black-
Top comes loyally struggling back
And runs a length beside the new

—Before, ducking under and astray,
It goes off to collect perhaps
A pretty creek that greenly laps
Its grasses, or a field a mile away

Where last month's hooded lightning fell;
A house you might stop at for eggs
Or corn, just to stretch your legs
And pump a cold drink up from the well

Beneath the tall elm-shade, or toss
(Or wish to toss) a stone up, waiting

By the car, to make the phone wires sing
Before going on. Two highways cross,

Recross, the sunny black, the silver,
And, sharing all the country, stride
Rivers on bridges side by side,
And graph the summer's green together.

Grace Butcher (b. 1934), a poet in Chardon, was educated at Hiram College and Kent State University. She combines U.S. championship running with motorcycling and teaching at Kent's Geauga Campus. Her poetry often reflects the variety in her life. She has published widely on sports and literature, as well as producing several volumes of her poems. Like Robert Wallace's poem, "On Motorcycles" (1976) dramatizes the conflict between old and new ways that are so often a part of contemporary life in the Western Reserve.

On Motorcycles Through Amish Country

That late bright afternoon
we rode the boundary line
between winter and spring
along the edge of the equinox,
the sun warm on our backs,
the air cold on our faces.

The other boundary line we rode
was between centuries,
past houses dug by hand
deep into the ground,
not tied to this world
by any wires,
curtained with a curious silence.

We slid through the ancient air
quietly, invisible.
Only the children,
waving and smiling,
could see us
while their fathers carried
heavy pails in and out
of the beautiful barns
and their mothers washed and hung
the simple clothes.

In the cold but fragrant fields
the huge timeless horses

pulled a silver thread
through the dark seams
of the opening earth.

We drifted along the twisting roads,
sun glinting off the strange chrome
of our slow and intricate machines.

Later, back on the highway
we leapt into 80 miles an hour
as if to break through into
our own world again.
But we throttled off in apology
for disturbing the setting sun
as if we were still back
on those slow roads
where the good people
sleep with the darkness,
rise with the light
to don their somber black,
their muted colors.

When we ride through again
years from now,
nothing will have changed.
And we will have
that strange sense
of having returned home
to a place
we do not belong.

Mary Oliver (b. 1935), born in Cleveland and now a resident of Massachusetts, was
Mather Visiting Professor at Case Western Reserve University in 1980 and 1982.
Her many volumes of poetry have received critical acclaim, and she was awarded
the Pulitzer Prize for Poetry in 1983 for *American Primitive*. In ancient ballad form,
the poet pays tribute to her Ohio ancestors in this poem that was originally published in *The River Styx, Ohio and Other Poems* (1972).

Stark Boughs on the Family Tree

Up in the attic row on row,
In dusty frames, with stubborn eyes,
My thin ancestors slowly fade
Under the flat Ohio skies.

And so, I think, they always were.
Like their own portraits, years ago

They paced the blue and windy fields,
Aged in the polished rooms below.

For name by name I find no sign
Of hero in this distant life,
But only men as calm as snow
Who took some faithful girl as wife,

Who labored while the drought, the flood
Crisscrossed the fickle summer air,
Who built great barns and propped their lives
Upon a slow heartbreaking care.

Why do I love them as I do,
Who dared no glory, won no fame?
In a harsh land that lies subdued,
They are the good boughs of my name.

If music sailed their dreams at all,
They were not heroes, and slept on,
As one by one they left the small
Accomplished, till the great was done.

Hale Chatfield (b. 1936) is Poet in Residence at Hiram College and founder of the
Hiram Poetry Review (1967–), which was awarded the Ohioana Award for Editorial
Excellence in 1985. He has published several volumes of poetry, including *Water
Colors* (1979), where the gentle ardor of this erotic poem resonates.

In Ohio: Spring Night

Lying awake beside you
waiting for sleep

I rejoice at the silence
as it pours through our open windows,

find an old joy
in the sound of a train, faint and
terribly far away (I can barely
sort it out among
the noises of my own
body—until it speaks
its distinctive train voice
at some remote crossing);

the many hills almost
imperceptibly throb

with us: you, me, and
the locomotive.

Synchrony blossoms;
its petals are galaxies.

I disassemble us
(an arm across a pillow,
eyelids closed, great wheels,
moonlight on the buds of trees),
am able at last to put us away
in dark, rightful places.

---

d. a. levy (Darryl Allen Levy, 1942–68) was Cleveland's leading beat poet and
counterculture representative in the 1960s. He published his works through the underground press, gathering about him an exciting coterie of young poets. At the
time of his death by suicide, the *Plain Dealer* spoke of levy as "a symbol of the
hippie movement in Cleveland." In this selection from *Cleveland undercovers* (1966),
a litany of Cleveland street names is made exotic by its association with the occult
and surreal.

Cleveland undercovers

I.
SOMETIMES CITY i walk at dawn
past the trucks parked
on the cold mornings edge
of the old viaduct to look at
the sore mouth of the Cuyahoga
eating and eaten by the dawn
and the city   and i
KNOWING
in the east a new sun is rising
and the grass is growing
on the ashes of the city
where once i was born
walking in the dawn
where once in a shopping center
i slipped into my center
and listened to the others sing
and see-saw something of myself
as they sang of the city,
"What can you expect?
when you wake in the morning

and find a republican tugboat
tied to the foot of your bed."
but that was then and
NOW i am, and do not expect
tomorrow or yesterday today.
instead, i write in ecstasy
and when someone stops to say
"Hey, that's not true!"
i yell backwards,
"For who . . . . and fuck rhyme."
i have a city to cover with lines,
with textured words &
the sweaty brick-flesh images of a
drunken tied-up whorehouse cowtown
sprawling & brawling on its back.

As the lakefront rats
race from rock to rock like medieval monks
race from door to door looking for god
i amuse myself,   looking
for Shu & Ptah or the Heb-Sed ceremony
in a crystal toilet bowl gives me visions

i paint them El Greco in my head
and toss a few angels in the sky
playing plastic harps that pluck
the strings of the black lake &
the streets with magical names
challenge me . . . .

if i paint WINDERMERE
on my apartment door like a
Pennsylvania Dutch hex sign
will it keep the angel of death away?

if i etch MAGNOLIA
on the Institute of Music
will the south rise again
as Haitian angels sacrifice chickens
to the music of Hindemith?

if i scratch SCOVILL
on Severance Hall
will George Szell lose his temper
and the cellos pop their strings
in terrified ecstasy?

if i write ERIE
in pastels next to the kitchen sink &
the mushroom stones . . will some decrepit
archeologist climb out of the drain
with flint arrowheads or obsidian fig-
urines wrapped in his fat handkerchief?

if i inscribe MEMPHIS
on the bathroom ikon
will i have a protestant illumination
or excremental visions overwhelm me?

my god eye seems to have
no city to see,
I look into the mind of it
and smile knowing
it is young and becoming one
so it doesn't matter If or Why,
i still have a city to cover with lines.

David Citino (b. 1947), born in Cleveland, is Professor of English at The Ohio State University, Marion Campus, and is founder and editor of the *Cornfield Review*, which often features Ohio poets. He has contributed poems to over 200 magazines. "Cuyahoga Cruise" first appeared in *Western Reserve Studies: A Journal of Regional History and Culture* in 1987. For Citino, the Cuyahoga River is no less the carrier of human experience than is the Mississippi or the Nile.

Cuyahoga Cruise: Riding the Goodtime

Anywhere we feel the human need
to be, there's a river can take us.
Old servants, knees
creaking, the bridges bow and rise
to usher us into the underworld,
land of ancestors. All's new
as the earliest memory.
The boat's throaty horn
resounds from each shore
like a bad dream from both sides
of the brain. In the days
when it seemed the whole world
was working, the river
flowed slowly, thick and volatile
enough to burn its bridges
behind it, sky above ominous

with the bonfires of industry.
Now the water paints
two weedy banks a tepid hue,
trickles thin as cheap wine,
carp mortal as any city
winnowing beneath our feet.
Time's the worst of plagues,
both Moses and Pharoah knew.
Hulett unloaders stand
motionless, grasshoppers
caught in early frost
near mills whose fires
were blown out by winds
prevailing from Brazil and Japan.
The Central Viaduct, the way
for thousands of horses and laborers
to move from old worlds
of Europe's east and west
to the new, stops in mid-air
these days, gray as old photos
in forgotten books. Refineries
float by, busied with no tankers.
The ghost of Rockefeller
haunts depots that lead nowhere,
giving out shiny dimes
to ancient children.
We pass only one ore carrier,
tugless and guided upriver
by bow-thrusters, a self unloader,
its skeleton crew trying
to look lively. Seeing
this nothing, we see all,
river's bends coiling *then*
upon the *now*. Yet here
are spaces made holy
by aching ages of hard labor,
men and women sentenced only
to work, work, work.
In the Flats all things went
up and down, back and forth
to order creation's chaos,
pellets of taconite ore mined
in Minnesota's numbing north,
heartbreaking chunks

of Pennsylvania coal, great lakes
of petroleum, blood and sweat.
In this land the crooked
was made straight,
the unrefined and crude
ground smooth by heroes
who spent hearts, livers, lungs
on life. In the breezes
that play through abandoned rooms
and unoccupied docks,
if we listen as never before
we hear the voices
of our parents, recall what
they stood for, the million acts
of work and love that brought us here
just so we can make this voyage,
the gift of remembering,
our future and our destination.

Rita Dove, professor of English at the University of Virginia, received the Pulitzer
Prize in poetry in 1987 for her collection *Thomas and Beulah,* which honors the life
of her grandparents in Akron, the rubber capital. Here she has preserved her
grandfather's response to one of Akron's most significant and dramatic industries.

The Zeppelin Factory

The zeppelin factory
needed workers, all right—
but, standing in the cage
of the whale's belly, sparks
flying off the joints
and noise thundering,
Thomas wanted to sit
right down and cry.

That spring the third
largest airship was dubbed
the biggest joke
in town, though they all
turned out for the launch.
Wind caught,
"The Akron" floated
out of control,

three men in tow—
one dropped

to safety, one
hung on but the third,
muscles and adrenalin
failing, fell
clawing
six hundred feet.

Thomas at night
in the vacant lot:
    Here I am, intact
    and faint-hearted.

Thomas hiding
his heart with his hat
at the football game, eyeing
the Goodyear blimp overhead:
    Big boy I know
    you're in there.

Other Writings
by Twentieth-Century
Western Reserve Authors

Abbott, Lee
Living after Midnight, 1991
Allis, Marguerite
Now We Are Free, 1952
To Keep Us Free, 1953
The Rising Storm, 1955
Anderson, Sherwood
Winesburg, Ohio, 1919
Triumph of the Egg, 1921
A Story Teller's Story, 1924
Tar: A Midwest Childhood, 1926
Home Town, 1940
Return to Winesburg, 1967
Bourjaily, Vance
Confessions of a Spent Youth, 1960
Bromfield, Louis
The Farm, 1933
Pleasant Valley, 1945
Chase, Joan
During the Reign of the Queen of Persia, 1983
Dahlberg, Edward
Bottom Dogs, 1930
Because I Was Flesh, 1963
Dandridge, Dorothy
Everything and Nothing, 1970
De Capite, Michael
Maria, 1943
No Bright Banner, 1944
Ellis, William D.
The Bounty Lands, 1952

The Cuyahoga. Rivers of America Series, 1967
Falstaff, Jake (Herman Fetzer)
A Centennial History of Akron, 1825–1925, 1925
The Songs and Ballads of Reini Kugel, 1926
The Book of Rabelais, 1928
Reini Kugel, Lover of This Earth, 1929
How Reini Kugel Went to Meet the Spring, 1938
Jacoby's Corners, 1940
The Big Snow: Christmas at Jacoby's Corners, 1941
Come Back to Wayne County, 1942
Midland Humor: A Harvest of Fun and Folklore, 1947
Pippins and Cheese, 1960
To Make You Thirsty: Selections, 1969
Frucht, Abby
Licorice, 1990
Gold, Herbert
Birth of a Hero, 1951
The Prospect Before Us, 1954
Fathers: A Novel in the Form of a Memoir, 1967
Family: A Novel in the Form of a Memoir, 1981
Lovers and Cohorts, 1986
Hargitai, Peter, and Lolette

Kuby, eds.
  *Forum: Ten Poets of the Western
    Reserve*, 1978
Havighurst, Walter
  *The Long Ships Passing:
    The Story of the Great
    Lakes*, 1942
  *Land of Promise: The Story of
    the Northwest Territory*, 1946
  *Life in America: The Mid-
    west*, 1951
  *The Heartland: Ohio, Indiana,
    Illinois*, 1956
  *Wilderness for Sale: The Story
    of the First Western Land
    Rush*, 1956
  *The First Book of Pioneers:
    Northwest Territory*, 1959
  *River to the West: Three Centuries
    of the Ohio*, 1970
  Midwest and Great Plains, 1972
  *Ohio: A Bicentennial His-
    tory*, 1976
  The Great Lakes Reader, 1978
Himes, Chester B.
  Cast the First Stone, 1952
  The Third Generation, 1954
  The Quality of Hurt, 1972
  My Life of Absurdity, 1976
Hopes, David B.
  The Glacier's Daughters, 1981
  *A Sense of the Morning:
    Nature through New
    Eyes*, 1988
Hughes, Langston
  Not Without Laughter, 1930
  The Ways of White Folks, 1947
  Black Misery, 1969
Johnson, Tom L.
  My Story, 1913
Kennedy, Adrienne
  *People Who Led to My
    Plays*, 1987
Lewis, Joanne
  To Market, To Market, 1981
McConkey, James R.
  Cross Roads, 1968

  Tree House Confessions, 1979
  Court of Memory, 1983
  To a Distant Island, 1984
McKenney, Ruth
  Industrial Valley, 1939
Miller, Alicia
  Homebodies, 1988
Miller, Dallas
  Fathers and Dreamers, 1966
Mlakar, Frank
  He, The Father, 1950
Morrison, Toni
  Sula, 1973
  Beloved, 1987
Oliver, Mary
  *No Voyage and Other
    Poems*, 1963
  The Night Traveler, 1978
  Twelve Moons, 1978
  Sleeping in the Forest, 1979
  Dream Work, 1986
Powell, Dawn
  She Walks in Beauty, 1925
  Whither, 1925
  Story of a Country Boy, 1934
Rebeta-Burditt, Joyce
  The Cracker Factory, 1977
Redinger, Ruby
  The Golden Net, 1948
Roberts, Les
  Pepper Pike, 1988
  Full Cleveland, 1989
  Deep Shaker, 1990
Robertson, Don
  The Sum and Total of Now, 1966
  Paradise Falls, 1968
  *The Greatest Thing That Almost
    Happened*, 1970
  Praise the Human Season, 1974
Sanders, Scott R.
  Wilderness Plots, 1983
  Fetching the Dead, 1984
  Bad Man Ballad, 1986
  Secrets of the Universe, 1991
Schumann, Mary
  Bright Star, 1934
  Strife Before Dawn, 1939

Bibliography

The Nineteenth Century

Badger, Joseph. *A Memoir of Reverend Joseph Badger: Containing an Autobiography and Selections from His Private Journal and Correspondence.* Hudson, OH, 1851. 174–75.

Bolton, Sarah Knowles. "The Twilight Hour Society." *A Country Idyl and Other Stories.* New York: Crowell, 1898. 78–89.

Brown, Salmon. "My Father, John Brown." Rpt. in *A John Brown Reader.* Ed. Louis Ruchames. New York: Abelard-Schuman, 1959. 182–89.

Chesnutt, Charles W. "The Wife of His Youth." *The Wife of His Youth and Other Stories of the Color Line.* Cambridge, MA: Riverside, 1899. 1–24.

Clark, Amasa. Papers. Hiram College Archives, Hiram, OH.

Cooke, Edmund Vance. "Oliver Hazard Perry." *Rimes To Be Read.* Chicago: Conkey, 1897. 111.

James A. Garfield–Lucretia Rudolph Garfield Correspondence. Presidential Papers, James A. Garfield Papers, series 3, 1853–81. Library of Congress, Washington, DC.

Foote, Julia A. J. "My Cleveland Home," from *A Brand Plucked from the Fire.* Rpt. in *Sisters of the Spirit.* Ed. William L. Andrews. Bloomington: Indiana UP, 1986. 224–26.

Hay, John. "A Holiday Not in the Calendar." *The Bread-Winners.* 1883. Ridgewood, NJ: Gregg, 1967. 185–96.

Hitchcock, Nabby. Letter to Peter Hitchcock. 11 December 1817. Hitchcock Family Papers, Correspondence, container 2, folder 1, Letters Received. Geauga County Historical Society, Burton, OH.

Hitchcock, Peter. Letter to Nabby Hitchcock. 31 December 1817. Hitchcock Family Papers, Correspondence, container 1, folder 1, Letters Received. Geauga County Historical Society, Burton, OH.

Howells, William Dean. *The Coast of Bohemia.* New York: Harper & Brothers, 1893. 1–9.

——— . "Old Brown." 1859. Rpt. in *Bibliography of American Literature.* Compiled by Jacob Blanck. New Haven: Yale UP, 1963.

Huntington, Hannah. Letter to Samuel Huntington. 25 April 1805. Hannah Huntington Papers, Correspondence, ms. 884, container 1, folder 1. Western Reserve Historical Society, Cleveland, OH.

Huntington, Samuel. Letter to Hannah Huntington. 8 October 1805. Colbert Huntington Greer Collection, Scrapbook. Ashtabula Area Museum and Historical Society, Ashtabula, OH.

Ingalls, Jeremiah. *Compilation of inspired communications and messages given at North Union,* 5 Vols. Shaker Manuscripts, microfilm reel 81. Western Reserve Historical Society, Cleveland, OH.

Joel, Joseph A. "Passover in Camp." Rpt. in *The American Jew in the Civil War.* Ed. Isidore S. Meyer. *Publication of the American Jewish Historical Society* 50, 4 (June 1961): 309–11.

Kohn, Lazarus. "Ethical Testament" letter to Moses and Jetta Alsbacher. 5 May 1839. Ms. vertical file A, Restricted Collection. Western Reserve Historical Society, Cleveland, OH.

Nye, Captain Pearl R. "The Clever Skipper." Rpt. in *Scenes and Songs of the Ohio-Erie Canal.* Ed. Cloea Thomas. Columbus: The Ohio State Archaeological and Historical Society, 1952.

——— . "Down the River." Rpt. in Richard H. Swain, "Captain Pearl R. Nye's Ohio Canal Songs." *Gamut* 10 (Fall 1983): 25.

Pounds, Jessie Brown. "Beautiful Isle." Rpt. In *Jessie Brown Pounds Memorial Selections.* Chicago: Disciples Publication Society, 1921. 52.

"Red Iron Ore." Rpt. in David D. Anderson, "Songs and Sayings of the Lakes." *Midwest Folklore* 12 (1962): 14–15.

Riddle, Albert Gallatin. "The Great Preacher." *The Portrait: A Romance of the Cuyahoga Valley.* Cleveland: Cobb, Andrews, 1874. 129–34.

Sill, Edward Rowland. *The Poetical Works of Edward Rowland Sill.* Cambridge, MA: Riverside, 1917.

——— . "Old Morton." Rpt. in *The Prose of Edward Rowland Sill.* 1900. Freeport, NY: Books for Libraries, 1970. 346–49.

Tourgée, Albion W. *Figs and Thistles: A Romance of the Western Reserve.* New York: Fords, Howard & Hulbert, 1879. 98–106.

Tuttle, Hudson, and Emma Rood Tuttle. "The Legend of Minehonto." *Stories from Beyond the Borderland.* Berlin Heights, OH: Tuttle, 1910. 109–12.

Ward, Artemus [Charles Farrar Browne]. "Oberlin." Rpt. in *Complete Works of Artemus Ward.* New York: Dillingham, 1887. 47–49.

Whittlesey, Elisha. "Execution of O'Mic, June 24th, 1812." Col. Cha[rle]s Whittlesey. *Early History of Cleveland, Ohio.* Cleveland, 1867. 436–42.

Wolfenstein, Martha. "Babette." *A Renegade and Other Tales.* 1905. Freeport, NY: Books for Libraries, 1969. 289–306.

Woolson, Constance Fenimore. "Cornfields." Rpt. in *Constance Fenimore Woolson.* Ed. Clare Benedict. London: Ellis, 1930. 428.

——— . "Lake Erie in September." Rpt. in *Constance Fenimore Woolson.* Ed. Clare Benedict. London: Ellis, 1930. 429.

——— . "Wilhelmina." *Atlantic Monthly* 35 (January 1875): 44–55.

The Twentieth Century

Anderson, Sherwood. "Manhattan." *Mid-American Chants.* New York: Huebsch, 1923. 29.

——— . "An Ohio Pagan." *Horses and Men.* New York: Huebsch, 1923. 315–47.

Atkins, Russell. "On the Fine Arts Garden, Cleveland." *The Poetry of Black America*. Ed. Arnold Adoff. New York: Harper & Row, 1973. 197–98.

Brooks, Sara. "Something Better Gonna Come to Me." *You May Plow Here*. Ed. Thordis Simonsen. New York: Norton, 1986. 195–201.

Butcher, Grace. "On Motorcycles through Amish Country." *Forum: Ten Poets of the Western Reserve*. Eds. Peter Hargitai and Lolette Kuby. Mentor, OH: The Poetry Forum Program, 1978. 37–38.

Chatfield, Hale. "In Ohio: Spring Night." *Water Colors*. Gulfport, FL: Konglomerati, 1979.

Citino, David. "Cuyahoga Cruise: Riding the *Goodtime*." *Western Reserve Studies: A Journal of Regional History and Culture* 2 (1987): 24–25.

Cooke, Edmund Vance. "Tom L. Johnson." *The Uncommon Commoner and Similar Songs of Democracy*. New York: Dodge, 1913. 18–19.

Crane, Hart. *The Collected Poems of Hart Crane*. New York: Liveright, 1933.

Darrow, Clarence. "My Childhood in Kinsman." *The Story of My Life*. New York: Scribner's, 1932. 12–21.

De Capite, Raymond. *A Lost King*. New York: McKay, 1961. 131–44.

Dove, Rita. "Zabriah." *Fifth Sunday*. Lexington: U of Kentucky, 1985. 55–58.

——— . "The Zeppelin Factory." *Thomas and Beulah*. Pittsburgh: Carnegie-Mellon UP, 1986. 24–25.

Falstaff, Jake [Herman Fetzer]. *The Bulls of Spring*. New York: Putnam's, 1937.

Gold, Herbert. *My Last Two Thousand Years*. New York: Random House, 1972. 110–14.

——— . "Susanna at the Beach." *Love & Like*. Cleveland: Meridian, n.d. 47–56.

Havighurst, Walter. "Return." *The Quiet Shore*. New York: Macmillan, 1937. 1–6.

Himes, Chester. "Marihuana and a Pistol." *The Best Short Stories by Negro Writers*. Ed. Langston Hughes. Boston: Little, Brown, 1967. 104–06.

Howard, Richard. "Decades." *Fellow Feelings*. New York: Atheneum, 1976. 1–5.

Hughes, Langston. "Central High." *The Big Sea*. New York: Knopf, 1945. 26–56.

——— . *Selected Poems of Langston Hughes*. New York: Knopf, 1959.

Hunter, Jane Edna. "Starlight." *A Nickel and a Prayer*. Elli Kani, 1940. 120–34.

Kilgore, James. "Signs of Ohio, December, 1970." *A Time of Black Devotion*. Ashland, OH: Ashland Poetry Press, 1971. 40–42.

levy, d. a. *Cleveland Undercovers*. Cleveland: 7 flowers press, 1966.

McConkey, James. "The Medina Road." *Night Stand*. Ithaca, NY: Cornell UP, 1965. 53–64.

Oliver, Mary. "Stark Boughs on the Family Tree." *The River Styx, Ohio and Other Poems*. New York: Harcourt, Brace Jovanovich, 1972. 3.

Patchen, Kenneth. "Bury Them in God." *In Quest of Candlelighters*. New York: New Directions, 1972. 91–107.

——— . "May I Ask You a Question, Mr. Youngstown Sheet & Tube?" *Selected Poems by Kenneth Patchen*. New York: New Directions, 1957. 43–44.

Powell, Dawn. *Dance Night*. New York: Farrar and Rinehart, 1930. 133–47.

Robertson, Don. *The Greatest Thing Since Sliced Bread*. New York: Putnam's, 1965. 196–219.

Sanders, Scott Russell. "At Play in the Paradise of Bombs." *The Paradise of Bombs and Other Essays*. New York: Simon and Schuster, 1988. 1–19.

Shulman, Alix Kates. *Memoirs of an Ex-Prom Queen*. New York: Bantam, 1973. 16–27.

Sinclair, Jo [Ruth Seid]. "The Medal." *Tales of Our People: Great Stories of the Jew in America*. Ed. Jerry D. Lewis. New York: Bernard Geis, 1969. 235–44.

Terry, J. William. "Step Sisters." *A Restless Breed*. Cleveland: New World, 1956. 107–17.

Turner, Alberta. "American Daffodils." *Need*. Ashland, OH: Ashland Poetry Press, n.d. 15.

Wallace, Robert. "The Two Roads." *Views from a Ferris Wheel*. New York: Dutton, 1965. 108–09.

Permissions Acknowledgments

The Alsbacher Document: An Ethical Testament: Letter by Lazarus Kohn to Moses and Jetta Alsbacher, MSS, Vertical File A. Reprinted courtesy of The Western Reserve Historical Society.

Sherwood Anderson: "An Ohio Pagan" from *Horses and Men*. Reprinted by permission of Harold Ober Associates, Inc. Copyright 1923 by B. W. Huebsch, Inc.; copyright renewed © 1950 by Eleanor Copenhaver Anderson.

Russell Atkins: "On the Fine Arts Garden, Cleveland" first appeared in *Experiment* (1947). Reprinted by permission of the author.

Sara Brooks: "Something Better Gonna Come to Me" is reprinted from *You May Plow Here: The Narrative of Sara Brooks,* edited by Thordis Simonsen, by permission of W. W. Norton & Company, Inc. Copyright © 1986 by Thordis Simonsen.

Grace Butcher: "On Motorcycles Through Amish Country" from *Forum: Ten Poets of the Western Reserve*. Copyright © 1978. Reprinted by permission of the author.

Hale Chatfield: "In Ohio: Spring Night" from *Water Colors*. Copyright © 1979. Reprinted by permission of the author.

David Citino: "Cuyahoga Cruise: Riding the *Goodtime*" is reprinted by permission of *Western Reserve Studies: A Journal of Regional History and Culture.* Copyright © 1987.

Amasa and Aurilla Clark: Papers. Reprinted courtesy of the Hiram College Archives.

"Clever Skipper" from *Scenes and Songs of the Ohio-Erie Canal,* collected by Cloea Thomas (1952). Reprinted courtesy of The Ohio Historical Society.

Hart Crane: "My Grandmother's Love Letters" and "Sunday Morning Apples, To William Sommer" are reprinted from *The Collected Poems and Selected Letters and Prose of Hart Crane,* edited by Brom Weber, by permission of Liveright Publishing Corporation. Copyright 1933, © 1958, 1966 by Liveright Publishing Corporation.

Clarence Darrow: Chapter 2, "My Childhood in Kinsman," is reprinted with permission of Charles Scribner's Sons, an imprint of Macmillan Publishing Company, from *The Story of My Life* by Clarence Darrow. Copyright 1932 by Charles Scribner's Sons; copyright renewed © 1960 by Mary D. Simonsen, Jessie D. Lyon, and Blanche D. Chase.

Raymond De Capite: Chapter 11 from *A Lost King*. Copyright © 1961. Reprinted by permission of The David McKay Company.

Rita Dove: "Zabriah" from *Fifth Sunday* (Callaloo Fiction Series, 1985). Reprinted by permission of the author. "The Zeppelin Factory" is reprinted from *Thomas and Beulah* by permission of Carnegie-Mellon University Press. Copyright © 1986 by Rita Dove.

Julia A. J. Foote: "My Cleveland Home" from "A Brand Plucked from the Fire" in *Sisters of the Spirit,* edited by William Andrews. Copyright © 1986. Reprinted by permission of Indiana University Press.

Herbert Gold: Selection from *My Last Two Thousand Years.* Copyright © 1970, 1971, 1972 by Herbert Gold. Reprinted by permission of Random House, Inc. "Susanna at the Beach" first appeared in *Atlantic Monthly* (May 1954). It is reprinted by permission of the author.

Walter Havighurst: "Return" is reprinted with permission of Macmillan Publishing Company from *The Quiet Shore* by Walter Havighurst. Copyright 1937 by The Macmillan Company; copyright renewed © 1965 by Walter Havighurst.

Chester Himes: "Marihuana and a Pistol" was first published in *Esquire Magazine,* 1940. Reprinted by permission of Roslyn Targ Literary Agency, Inc. New York, copyright © 1940, 1968 by Chester Himes.

Richard Howard: "Decades" is reprinted with permission of Atheneum Publishers, an imprint of Macmillan Publishing Company, from *Fellow Feelings* by Richard Howard. Copyright © 1973 by Richard Howard.

Langston Hughes: "Central High" from *The Big Sea* by Langston Hughes. Copyright © 1940 by Langston Hughes. Renewal copyright © 1968 by Arna Bontemps and George Houston Bass. Reprinted by permission of Hill and Wang, a division of Farrar, Straus & Giroux, Inc. "Note on Commercial Theatre," copyright © 1948 by Alfred A. Knopf, Inc., and "Railroad Avenue," copyright 1927 by Alfred A. Knopf, Inc., and renewed © 1955 by Langston Hughes, are reprinted from *Selected Poems of Langston Hughes* by permission of Alfred A. Knopf, Inc.

Hannah Huntington: Papers, Correspondence, MSS, 884, cont. 1, fol. 1. Reprinted courtesy of The Western Reserve Historical Society.

Samuel Huntington: Scrapbook, Colbert Huntington Greer Collection. Reprinted courtesy of The Ashtabula Area Museum and Historical Society.

Jeremiah Ingalls: Shaker Manuscripts in the Library of The Western Reserve Historical Society, Microfilm reel 81. Reprinted courtesy of The Western Reserve Historical Society.

Joseph A. Joel: "Passover in Camp" from *Publication of the American Jewish Historical Society 50,* 4 (June 1961). Reprinted with permission of the Jewish Historical Society, Waltham, MA.

James Kilgore: "Signs of Ohio, December, 1970" from *A Time of Black Devotion.* Copyright © 1971. Reprinted by permission of The Ashland Poetry Press.

James McConkey: "The Medina Road" from *Night Stand: A Book of Stories* (Cornell University Press). Copyright © 1965 by Cornell University. Reprinted by permission of the publisher.

Mary Oliver: "Stark Boughs on the Family Tree," copyright © 1972 by Mary Oliver, from *The River Styx, Ohio, and Other Poems.* Reprinted by permission of Molly Malone Cook Literary Agency.

Kenneth Patchen: "Bury Them in God" from *In Quest of Candlelighters.* Copyright © 1972 by Kenneth Patchen. "May I Ask a Question" from *Collected Poems of Kenneth Patchen.* Copyright © 1943 by Kenneth Patchen. Reprinted by permission of New Directions Publishing Corporation.

Dawn Powell: Excerpt from *Dance Night.* Reprinted by permission of Watkins/Loomis Agency, Inc.

Don Robertson: Excerpt from *The Greatest Thing Since Sliced Bread.* Reprinted by permission of Curtis Brown, Ltd. Copyright © 1965 by Don Robertson.

Scott Russell Sanders: "At Play in the Paradise of Bombs," copyright © 1983 by Scott Russell Sanders, first appeared in *The North American Review* and in *The Paradise of Bombs* (University of Georgia Press, 1987). It is reprinted by permission of the author and the author's agent, Virginia Kidd.

Alix Kates Shulman: Excerpt from *Memoirs of an Ex–Prom Queen*. Copyright © 1969, 1971, 1972 by Alix Kates Shulman. Reprinted by permission of Alfred A. Knopf, Inc.

Jo Sinclair: "The Medal" is reprinted from *Tales of Our People: Great Stories of the Jew in America*, edited by Jerry D. Lewis by permission of the publisher, Bernard Geis Associates. Copyright © 1969 by Jerry D. Lewis.

Alberta Turner: "American Daffodils" from *Need*. Copyright © 1971. Reprinted by permission of The Ashland Poetry Press.

Robert Wallace: "Two Roads" from *Views from a Ferris Wheel*. Copyright © 1965 by Robert Wallace. Reprinted by permission of the author.

Index

Anthology of Western Reserve Literature
was composed in 10½-point Bembo leaded two points
on a Xyvision system with Linotron 202 output
by BookMasters, Inc.;
printed by sheetfed offset on 55-pound
Glatfelter Natural Paperback Offset acid-free stock
that meets the EPA standard of minimum 50% recycled fibers
from de-inked printed waste,
and notch bound with paper covers printed in four
process colors and film laminated
by Thomson-Shore, Inc;
designed by Will Underwood;
and published by
The Kent State University Press
KENT, OHIO 44242